The Best AMERICAN SPORTS WRITING 2001

The Best AMERICAN SPORTS WRITING 2001

Edited and with an Introduction
by Bud Collins

Glenn Stout, *Series Editor*

HOUGHTON MIFFLIN COMPANY

BOSTON • NEW YORK 2001

Visit our Web site: www.houghtonmifflinbooks.com.

ISSN 1056-8034
ISBN 0-618-08625-0
ISBN 0-618-08626-9 (pbk.)

Printed in the United States of America

DOC 10 9 8 7 6 5 4 3 2 1

Contents

Contents

Foreword

WHERE IS SPORT without the words that surround it?

Every day a thousand games are played a million times and pass by. Sweat is shed by the bucket as wins and losses peel off in laughter and cheers. Tears fall every second and disappear.

Words preserve sport, the taste and smell of it. We remember not the simple exercise, but the result and reason why it matters at all, or why it doesn't. With the words as our guide, we follow and learn.

As I read these stories each year, I find myself caring about someone, something, or some sport I know little about and couldn't have imagined ever wanting to know more about. A writer, by way of words alone, has made this happen, something so surprising and delightful that even the familiar sometimes becomes extraordinary, and the exotic moves close at hand. And I read on.

My daughter has grown up with the detritus of this endless project all around her. In our home, piles of newspapers, magazines, and thick manila envelopes fill the places that in other houses are occupied by — oh, I don't know — potted plants, knickknacks, and knockoffs. Over the course of putting together *The Best American Sports Writing 2001,* I've watched her grow from almost four to almost five and begin to read. It has been astonishing to watch letters become words and sentences become stories. And she gets lost in other worlds.

So do I. Still. The experience of creating these books has taken me from smoke-filled rooms in Las Vegas to hospital beds and penitentiaries, from mountain peaks to swamps and ocean wrecks, to locker rooms, playing fields, horse stalls, and a hundred other places. The best part of creation, and, I suspect, reading, is the pleasure that comes from being transported outside ourselves to elsewhere. We become happily lost while finding something lasting in what otherwise — without the words — would remain the unexplored. Most games go unwatched, and athletes remain anonymous. Even the fans' most rabid obsession disregards more than it includes.

Whether or not my team or my sport or your team or your sport appears in this book is, thankfully, immaterial. Final scores do not often matter here. This is not a book of results or an encyclopedia. Neither is it an awards ceremony, a testimonial, or a competition. The collective words of the writers in this book are an invitation, a conversation with those we'll never meet about things we wouldn't otherwise experience. Sports is the most subtle of hooks here, one that by the first sentence begins to be unwrapped by language and made into something we do care about. Here is a place where Parts Otherwise Unknown are made familiar.

I suppose that is because the writers both care and use care to let us know that. When they don't, I can tell and fill landfills with their poor directions. But when they do and whisper in our ear and let us in on the secret, this slim book swells and we find our way. Without the words, I sometimes wonder whether there is such a thing as sports at all.

So where is sport? A part of it is here, in the words that follow. Just listen.

Every season of this process, I read every issue of hundreds of sports and general interest magazines in search of writing that might merit inclusion in *The Best American Sports Writing.* I try not to miss anything, so each year I also contact the sports editors of some three hundred newspapers and request their submissions. Similarly, I ask hundreds of magazine editors to provide complimentary subscriptions and submissions of individual stories.

But none of us is perfect. That is why I encourage writers, readers, and all other interested parties to send me stories they've written or read in the past year that they would like to see reprinted in this volume. No one should feel shy about submitting his or her own material. A good description of the selection process can be found in the December 2000 edition of the Associated Press Sports Editors newsletter.

I forward the best seventy-five stories or so to the guest editor, who makes the final selection. Bud Collins exceeded his reputation as one of the most gracious, cooperative, and enthusiastic people in this business. Even better, he made some great picks.

To be considered for inclusion in *The Best American Sports Writing 2002*, each nonfiction story must have been published in 2001 in either the United States or Canada and must be column-length or longer. Reprints are not eligible. All submissions must be received by February 1, 2002.

All submissions must include the name of the author, the date of publication, and the publication name and address. Photocopies, tear sheets, or clean copies are fine. Reductions to 8½-by-11 are best. Submissions from online publications must be made in hard copy. Owing to the volume of material I receive, no submission can be returned or acknowledged. I also believe it is inappropriate for me to comment on or critique any individual submission. Publications that want to be absolutely certain their contributions are considered are advised to provide a complimentary subscription to the address listed below. Those that already do so should make sure to extend the subscription.

Please send subscriptions or submissions to this exact address:

Glenn Stout
Series Editor
The Best American Sports Writing
PO Box 381
Uxbridge, MA 01569

I may also be contacted by e-mail at BASWeditor@cs.com. No submissions of material will be accepted electronically.

Copies of previous editions of this book can be ordered through most bookstores or online book dealers. An index of stories that have appeared in this series can be found at glennstout.net.

Thanks again go out to the Houghton Mifflin front office, particularly to editors Eamon Dolan and Emily Little, both of whom make this project as enjoyable as possible. I also thank Bud Collins for his exemplary effort, and my wife, Siobhan, and daughter, Saorla, for all the usual reasons and then some. And to all the writers who have kept me company this year, I look forward to continuing our acquaintance in the next edition.

GLENN STOUT

Introduction

WHO WAS Stroganov?

The question didn't flash through my head as it was being dunked in a plate of the beef dish named for him. In my face suddenly — courtesy of a literary critic who doubled as general manager of the Boston Red Sox — and splattered all over it, was enough beef Stroganov to feed a tag team of midget wrestlers.

Ah, the joys of sportswriting.

Still, on most days it beats working for a living. And on many days it is done extremely well across the United States, as the selections in this volume attest. I know some of the writers included, not a majority. But I do believe that their stuff, on view here, would make any writer proud.

Maybe even Stroganov? But who was he?

Only later did I wonder about the namesake of the entrée of my sudden immersion. A nineteenth-century Russian nobleman, Sergei Grigorievich Stroganov, is not to be confused with Nick Strincevich, who pitched fairly nobly (a 48–49 record) for the Pirates during the 1940s. Stroganov's game was archaeological research, which some of us sometimes dabble in. Perhaps to compare cavemen of the Dead Ball Age, like Frank "Home Run" Baker and his American League–leading totals of 11, 10, 12, and 9 dingers between 1911 and 1914, with such descendants as Mark McGwire and Sammy Sosa.

Anyway, my immediate thought, as I wiped away moisturizing embarrassment with a napkin, was astonishment. But not revenge. The man who had just given me a facial in a New York hotel function room was a lot bigger and stronger. He'd batted .292 during a long major-league career — and was drunk. Drink, however, had not dulled the critical faculties welled up within Mike Higgins, overseer of the Red Sox.

"Not Mike's favorite writer, are you?" observed another diner at the large round table, Danny Murtaugh, the Pittsburgh manager. Murtaugh, whom I'd met only minutes before, was kindly trying to take the edge off within a group, as startled as I, partaking of a postgame meal at the 1963 World Series.

Conversation centered on Johnny Podres — until Higgins lurched up to the table. Podres had shut down the Yankees, 4–1, that afternoon, sending the Dodgers halfway through their sweep.

As the heavy-handed critic, satisfied with Stroganov-ing me, staggered off into the maze of tables, Larry Claflin, on my left, laughed, "Obviously Hig's got a beef with you." Larry, a pal and colleague, the baseball writer of the *Boston American,* knew that Higgins didn't care for my chiding him and the Red Sox on their despicable failure to employ black players.

His and the team management's racism was evident as they maintained a vanilla flavor until winning the major-league booby prize: the last team to put a black on the field, Elijah "Pumpsie" Green, in 1959. But "racism" and "despicable" were not words you used in print in connection with my town's golden calves, the Red Sox, in those days. Particularly in the bygone *Boston Herald,* my employer at the time. The business arrangement of the *Herald's* TV and radio stations carrying Sox games put the team pretty much above hard knocks. Prodding and disapproval had to be fairly subtle, but Higgins got the point — and I got the Stroganov.

A small price to pay for the fun of being around games and games-players, and writing about them. And, after all, sportswriters do like to hear from their readers — though not so vividly.

I suppose writers and players have ever conducted an adversarial relationship of sorts: Us and Them. It softens and hardens, waxes and wanes. Both sides have jobs to do, and sometimes try to understand each other while getting the job done.

As you'll see, an athlete may let a writer into his life, as Dale Earnhardt Jr. did Touré in "Kurt Is My Co-Pilot."

Another, Joe DiMaggio, never would, and the writer, Buzz Bissinger, plumbed other sources in "For Love of DiMaggio."

Gene Collier is the star of his "Ex-Sportswriter," saying to hell with the job altogether.

Whatever, we always have each other: Us — as in Us versus Them. Maybe we, the writers, are a duncely confederation of failed jocks, wiseacres, pontificators, and believers in the axiom of a picaresque old boxing impresario, Sam Silverman: "Never louse up a good story with the facts." And maybe it's true, as expressed by Richard Nixon's son-in-law, David Eisenhower, after a stint at the *Washington Post:* "Newspaper reporters aren't as interesting as they think they are."

Nevertheless, for me much of the fun, the part I would miss most, is communing with the brothers and sisters of the scribbling lodge. Are we still ink-stained wretches? Nobody has been armed with a quill pen or even a typewriter for a long time.

The former was most likely used to record one of the earliest quotes in print, dealing with prominent, combative opponents of about three thousand years ago. In the Old Testament's First Book of Samuel (previewing Muhammad Ali against Sonny Liston?), a brash young long-shot called David trash-talked an ogre named Goliath: "I will strike you down and cut off your head!" And, beating the odds, he did just that.

Who among us wouldn't have loved to emulate the style of the crusty English golf writer Leonard Crawley, the *Daily Telegraph*'s expert of not so long ago? Crawley, in tweed plus-fours and Norfolk jacket, his stiff upper lip decorated by a curling, rust-toned Edwardian moustache, showed up at tournaments with his secretary by his side, a man ready to take dictation whenever. He dictated notes as they strolled the course, looked them over, and composed and dictated the story, which his man then phoned to London.

"Isn't that the way to go?" mused the wonderful *Los Angeles Times* columnist Jim Murray, observing Crawley at a U.S. Open. "But I don't quite see myself in the knickers."

But now, in this day of dolt.com and eek-mail, we are software-warped warriors, lap-dancing with infernal machines that can be both divine and diabolical (keep hitting SAVE, stupid!). These indispensable tools of the trade malfunction and/or misplace stories only on deadline. But that can't kill the tribal fun.

Numerous are the computers that have been slapped and kicked, flung and cursed in the service of literature. In fact, I hereby propose to the International Olympic Committee an additional event for the 2004 Games: the computer throw for journalists. It would be reality TV that Everyman could relate to, a crowd of out-of-shape but highly motivated competitors giving their all to redress slights and wounds in the line of duty.

A contender might be one David Israel, who as an operative of the *Chicago Tribune* once pitched a recalcitrant PC an enormous distance from the press box of Dodger Stadium. A tape-measure job, according to witnesses.

If it had landed in a puddle of beef Stroganov, I would have felt bonded to that typing machine. Should I have sent my assailant, Higgins, a dry-cleaning bill, or applied for a restraining order? No. I actually wished him well when he was fired three years later by owner Tom Yawkey, though I hoped that move meant better days for the team and Boston. It did. Yawkey had at last awakened from his own alcoholic haze to see how his bigoted minions had been shortchanging the franchise.

Mine was a drip-dry suit, by the way, which came out of the hotel room sink looking just fine the following day. (Suit? Yes, there was a time when sportswriters, historically as dapper as Ray Bolger's Scarecrow in *The Wizard of Oz*, did arrive at their alleged labors in coats and ties. Tom Fitzgerald, a hockey writer for the *Boston Globe* some time ago, was an exception. Normally a meticulous dresser, he once appeared in the *Montreal Forum* press box in pajamas, explaining that he'd overslept a nap and didn't wish to be late. Today nobody would even notice him.)

Instead of the florists' familiar punch line "Say it with flowers!" Mike Higgins's was "Say it with beef!" His had more punch.

It could have been worse. Genuine punches expressing reader disapproval have been thrown by athletes at scribblers, normally noncombatant types. Verbal assaults are more common.

Irrepressible John Feinstein of the *Washington Post* weathered innumerable assaults from Bobby Knight and produced the best-seller *Season on the Brink*, the first serious look — a definitive one — at the tyrant of the basketball court. In a New York saloon, early one morning, another coach, Pat Riley, was fairly patient as Feinstein explained basketball to him. But Riley had the last word, mercifully breaking up the gathering with "John, you're very young — and very loud."

The diminutive, dynamic *New York Daily News* columnist Mike Lupica happened to be the public object of one of those serial tirades of John McEnroe's. Sort of face-to-face in that Lupica was seated four rows behind the court at Flushing Meadows while McEnroe was at work, enmeshed with Mats Wilander in an arduous five-set semifinal of the U.S. Open.

Despite phenomenal concentration on matters at hand, Mac uncannily seemed to know where everybody he knew was seated in the ballpark, and he picked out Lupica. (He didn't know Kay Graham, publisher of the *Washington Post,* but that hardly stopped him from suggesting, "Sit the f—— down, lady!" the afternoon she dared to walk to her seat before he commenced serving.)

Abruptly pausing to fasten a drop-dead stare on Lupica, Mac then castigated him for something he'd written. Far from being put out, Mike was thrilled, uttering the wishful sentiment of all writers: "Hah, he's reading me."

I suppose it's a badge of honor that the first of the not many words Ted Williams ever spoke to me was the extended ten-letter epithet.

Later, when he returned to Boston as manager of the Washington Senators, Ted addressed me: "Are you still around writing that shit?" — although that time with a twinkle in his deep voice.

Lesley Visser is one of those who can tell you how tough it was "to be out on the frontier," wading through insults and indignities as one of the pioneering female reporters handling the same assignments as men, locker rooms included, and eventually winning acceptance.

"It was a class in humiliation," says she, a CBS-TV luminary who got her baptism of male chauvinism as a reporter for the *Boston Globe.* "Not just the athletes but the supposed grown-ups, the coaches, gave us a rough time. At the 1980 Cotton Bowl game, Bill Yeomans, the Houston coach, march-pushed me out of the locker room, even though it was against the rules, and I was clearly accredited and doing my job. He was yelling, 'I don't give a damn about the ERA — get outttt!'

"I cried, but I got over that."

So did Lisa Olson, scandalously treated by flashers among the New England Patriots after a game in 1990. The publicity, and the unbelievable public antagonism leveled at her for merely pursuing her profession for the *Boston Herald,* drove Olson to flee to an Australian newspaper. Recovering her equilibrium, she returned to do fine work for her present employer, the *New York Daily News.*

Even in the genteel world of golf, at least in Britain, female reporters are still mistreated. Liz Kahn, a distinguished historian of the game who has written for several London dailies, paid her way into tournaments for years. Although on assignment, she was frequently unable to get accreditation, despite belonging to the U.S. Golf Writers Association.

Finally she was granted membership in the British Golf Writers Society, and life improved. Somewhat. "But I had to fight for it" — through dint of an intrepid, crusading personality. "You could say mine was a life on the outside, continually discriminated against. Evicted from clubs and dining rooms to which my male colleagues had full access. It still hurts." Sometimes scribes strike back with other than typing machine. None, however, as spectacularly and literally as my *Boston Globe* compatriot Willie McDonough, never one to pull his punches literarily or otherwise.

"Willie's in the sportswriting pantheon for what he did that Sunday in Foxborough [Massachusetts]. He did what a lot of us would like to do from time to time," grins the *Globe*'s award-gathering columnist Dan Shaughnessy.

Suddenly mad as hell and not going to take it anymore, Willie gave. Big-time. It was 1979 in the dressing room of the New England Patriots, victorious that afternoon. McDonough, interviewing touchdown scorer Harold Jackson, felt a poke in his back. Turning, he faced another literary critic, defensive back Raymond Clayborn.

Possibly to punctuate the poke, Clayborn then jabbed a finger into McDonough's left eye. A mistake that couldn't be edited out. Clayborn should have bumped-and-run. Feeling maligned and threatened, Willie, who suffereth gladly no fingers in any context from anybody, abruptly launched three swiftly brilliant right hands to Clayborn's head. Flattened, on his face, hearing the derisive comments of his teammates, Clayborn realized he'd misread a strong-right offense.

Few of us would endanger our typing fingers like that. But McDonough, probably the best informed of all authorities on pro football, shook out his knuckles and wrote a game story, leaving his bombing of Clayborn — the only cornerback ever beaten by a reporter — for others to chronicle.

Journalists fighting one another may be just as rare. That happened in a Wimbledon interview room when a limey, Nigel Clarke of the *Daily Mail*, and American Charlie Steiner of ESPN began scuffling, rolling on the floor in a grapple, to the astonishment and delight of assembled confreres.

Apparently Steiner objected to something Clarke had written about John McEnroe and took it upon himself to defend his countryman's questionable honor. Because most of our tribe are essentially pacifists, it wasn't Bunker Hill revisited and ended quickly, each combatant realizing his silliness. Fortunately for both, neither possessed a McDonough-esque haymaker.

One of my heroes, Laurie Pignon, a jocular, charming Englishman, also fought — more seriously, against the Germans in World War II. Taken prisoner for almost five years, he was used as a slave laborer in a Polish coal mine. "I made up my mind," he says, "that if I ever got out of there I would never let anything bother me again — the job, the boss, the players."

He returned to continue writing sports for London dailies, and today, a very happy man in his eighties, he freelances. Pignon's philosophy has held up well for him.

Still, this can be a hazardous trade. I was thinking that, and thinking about Laurie, one impenetrable October night in 1982 when I was trying to put up a tent in a raging blizzard somewhere in a Tibetan mountain range as the temperature plummeted below freezing. The Chinese guides were lost. An unforeseen storm had pounced, turning a pleasant trek into a wet, shiveringly bitter trial.

Exceptional sleeping bags and amiable, helpful yak herdsmen pulled our group through. We never did find out where we'd been because the guides, new to their business, had no maps. But it made a pretty good story for *Sports Illustrated*. Anything for a story, of course.

Weather wasn't the problem that balmy summer evening in 1960 when Floyd Patterson won back his heavyweight title from Ingemar Johansson by knocking out the Swede at New York's Polo Grounds. Instead, it was a hot-blooded segment of the crowd running amok. Charging the ring to hail local guy Patterson, they stampeded through the jerry-built press rows, smashing typewriters and any reporters in the way. Al Abrams from the *Pittsburgh Post-Gazette* was in tears, bruised, his typewriter and notes gone. His buddies helped him to piece together a story in longhand that he could dictate to his office.

Luckily I was not in the mob's path. But another Bostonian, Austen "Duke" Lake of the *American,* got trampled, suffering a couple of broken ribs. An ex-college football player and World War I battlefield survivor, Lake, then in his sixties, was a rugged, straightforward character. He didn't own an overcoat and frequently and gruffly shouted a favorite pejorative, "Bafflegab!" at anybody trying to con him, whether a press agent, coach, or athlete.

To the Duke the deadline was sacred, and he had to make it. When his typewriter was knocked off the planking, he hugged it on the ground like a fumble while being stomped. As the crush subsided, he rose, hurting, nevertheless composing his thoughts.

"If I had time I'd show those sons o'bitches a thing or two!" he boiled. He would have, too. However, a slave to the deadline, he found a place to sit and wrote his column in time for the edition.

You wouldn't think covering tennis could be risky, but maybe you didn't know the ferocious champion Richard "Pancho" Gonzalez. Reporters of the pre-computer days, clacking away at typewriters while he played, enraged him, as did courtside photographers with their flashbulbs. Those of that breed considered themselves lucky if he refrained from throttling them. Pancho didn't always refrain.

Reporters were fortunately farther out of reach. But not out of range when he began blasting balls at them with hefty swings to silence those damned typists. Henry McKenna of the *Herald* recalled a night at Boston Garden when he was among those "targeted." Even though the balcony press box was far above the court, Pancho was strafing it mercilessly.

"It was a war zone. Balls were coming at us like shrapnel, and we were ducking as they slammed against the press box," McKenna said. "It was late. The office expected something for the first edition, but all of us said to hell with any deadlines until the matches were finished and Pancho was gone."

A typewriter figured in the 1973 tennis ordeal of Mark Asher of the *Washington Post,* covering the U.S. Indoor Championships at Salisbury, Maryland. Attending to his story while Ilie Nastase and Clark Graebner played Juan Gisbert and Jurgen Fassbender for the doubles title, Mark found himself the uncomfortable center of attention. As Graebner and Nastase forgot about their task, halting play to focus glares on Asher in the building's uppermost tier, customers seated in front of the press row began shushing and screaming at him to be quiet.

Asher, on duty, persisted — "I had a job to do." So thought the patrons, feeling it their obligation to enforce silence. The most adamant among them became a vigilante, determined to gag the *Washington Post.* This enraged fellow confronted Asher and clawed the newsman's offending hands, drawing blood, like an overzealous parent chastising a naughty child. It would take more than that to deaden those dutiful fingers.

More was soon in force. The guy grabbed the typewriter and bolted down the grandstand steps as though sprinting for the end zone — with Asher in "Stop, thief!" pursuit. As the crowd gaped, Asher chased the typewriter-napper the length of the hall and out the door.

"I gave it my best . . . but I couldn't catch the jerk," Asher remembers. Reduced to pencil and longhand, he sighed, "I regret that I had but one Olivetti to give for my paper."

Neither Asher nor anybody else had quite the style of the thoughtful, gentlemanly Allison Danzig, who covered tennis, college football, and Olympic sports peerlessly at the *New York Times* for more than forty years. Seated in the press section of the open-air marquee, a few feet from the Stadium court at Forest Hills, Danzig never bothered players or spectators at the U.S. Championship with his necessary typing.

So skilled and rapid was Al that he could condense his writing into brief bursts within the few seconds between points, maintaining a champion's concentration on the match before him, and the story. He was a whirling dervish on a folding chair. Scrawling his running account of the match with fountain pen, point by point, he made the note, then attacked the typewriter keys fiercely, stopping just before the next ball was served.

He probably could have written a novella during the twenty or thirty seconds it took the players to change ends, in those days a brief interval, not the sit-down stretch of a minute and a half now in force in reverent respect for TV commercials. His copy that he handed, a few graphs at a time, to a Western Union telegrapher for transmission to the *Times* office was as neat and precise as Danzig himself.

A soft-spoken Texan who cooked fiery chili, he had suffered a stern penalty for his love of sports. As a ten-year-old in his home-town, Waco, Al was apprehended sneaking into a minor-league baseball game by the "inconsiderate sheriff. My father," he re-called, "was even less considerate of that sheriff. He gave the man holy hell when he came to get me out."

Though Al was one of the most considerate and generous guys in the newspaper business, one of his Samaritan acts backfired. It was 1935. He and two pals, syndicated columnists Grantland Rice and Henry McLemore, were in Columbus covering the famous Notre Dame football victory over Ohio State, won 18–13 in the last seconds, on a pass from Bill Shakespeare to Wayne Millner.

After completing their stories, they dined together and had a few drinks. A few more than needed by McLemore and the celebrated Rice. They were wobbling as though trampled by Rice's immortal "Four Horsemen."

But the younger Danzig kindly, ably shepherded them into a cab to the railroad station, and then into their berths on the sleeper to New York. Arriving the next day, they were profuse in their thanks to the caretaker. Until . . . McLemore looked at Rice and ex-ploded, "Jee-zus, Granny! Now I remember . . . we drove your car to Columbus."

How Peter Wilson of London's *Daily Mirror* managed to keep his memory intact amazed his comrades of Fleet Street and anybody else who knew him. His column always ran beneath a banner head-line identifying him unpretentiously: "World's Greatest Sports-writer." It should have been accompanied by a subhead: "And World's Greatest Scotch Drinker."

Burly, rumpled, and friendly, an unfailingly courteous fellow with a walrus mustache and upper-class accent, Peter wandered the planet, documenting every big sporting event of interest in Britain, setting records for speedy writing and consumption of Scotch — and remaining journalistically sharp. He was partial to boxing and Olympic track events, feeling, "They are the only pure sports. Man either fights or runs away. The rest are contrived."

"He don't look or sound like a guy that can hold a lot of booze, but look out," was the admiring appraisal of Wilson by boxing pro-moter Sam Silverman, an impressive imbiber himself. "When it comes to Scotch, Peter has flattened more contenders than Joe Louis."

Peter's running mate in touring and tippling was the dashing

Desmond Hackett of the *Express,* an obvious disciple of Beau Brummel, favoring pink cardigans that accompanied well-tailored Saville Row suits. But they parted company on Scotch. "I savor champagne — preferably sipped from the navel of a beautiful woman," was Desmond's heartfelt cry.

That would not seem unseemly to the bon-vivanting notables of Italian sportswriting and TV, Gianni Clerici of *La Gazzetta della Sport* and Rino Tommasi of *La Gazzetta della Sport* and *Il Tempo.* As amusing partners on tennis telecasts, they babble about all sorts of topics that would never make air on U.S. networks: scandals, the sex lives of the players (and themselves), the e-mail that they receive during broadcasts.

How do they get away with it? Clerici, who covers similar ground in his columns, replies, indignantly, "I live in a free country. Don't you?"

For a time, before becoming very widely known nationally in his added role as a TV commentator, Tommasi led a double life. He was himself for *Gazzetta,* his principal paper. However, *Il Tempo* insisted on having its own man at the events that Rino covered. This drove him to adopt a separate identity, bylined as Tommy Salvatore, a combination of his middle name and a twist of his last.

"Who's the better writer — Tommasi or Salvatore?" I once asked Clerici, since I'm unable to read Italian.

"Oh, the ghostly Salvatore. Easily," Gianni answered. "As Tommasi, he takes himself too seriously and is careful and scrupulous about being very boring. Too many statistics and pronouncements. When he's done with *Gazzetta,* he looks at the clock and — oh, Cristo, disastro! — his *Il Tempo* deadline is on top of him. Salvatore takes over and has to get it done fast. He dashes it off, doesn't think about it. He lets down and just has fun, and it comes out much more readable.

"I tell Tommasi he should kill Tommasi and remain Salvatore for the rest of his life. Be better off. Better for the readers. But Rino is too proud of his own name."

It was Salvatore who perished instead. *Il Tempo*'s editor decided he wanted the renowned telecaster in his stable, and so the Rino Tommasi byline appears in both papers.

When that happened, Clerici said, "I think Salvatore's readers should picket *Il Tempo,* demanding his return."

The puckish Clerici remembers a demand for his own departure at a tournament party on the Riviera. Because the invitation pre-scribed "black tie," that is what he wore. Period. Thrown out before he got in, he recalls, "They said, regretfully, that my writing was more interesting than my body."

Though jovial, urbane Brian Dewhurst of the United Press in Australia didn't go that far. He was known fondly and admiringly across the continent as "Daks-dropping Dewhurst." His self-styled performances most often occurred at cocktail parties or receptions where he would be conversing with a prominent personage, prefer-ably female and prim. His mates stayed alert, wondering when "it" would happen.

Brian refused to explain how "it" was done, but at the appropri-ate moment his trousers began to descend, sliding slowly down to crumple at his ankles. Taking no notice of the breeze at his knees, he continued chatting engagingly while the startled lady opposite him gaped, blushed, averted her widening eyes, and retreated be-hind a hasty, "Excuse me, please."

Unfazed by the commotion, he rebelted himself without missing a sip or syllable, explaining that his mother had insisted on his al-ways wearing clean, presentable undershorts.

Mine did the same, and was not timid in scolding me for occa-sionally hanging out somebody else's dirty laundry in a story. Nor did she approve of one of the best quotes an athlete ever dropped on me, unprinted until now. It was a throwaway line from a good-natured Baldwin-Wallace College halfback named George Morris who had led U.S. small colleges in scoring the year I was only ten and growing up in a house on the campus.

Peddling magazines in the neighborhood one day, I recognized Morris, a hero to us kids, and shyly asked my first question to a jock: "Mr. Morris, how did you score all those touchdowns?"

"Kid, it was easy. I just greased my ass and slid on through."

Good advice, wouldn't you say? That and maybe twenty bucks would get you a helping of beef Stroganov.

BUD COLLINS

The Best
AMERICAN
SPORTS
WRITING 2001

WILL BLYTHE

The Marvel

FROM MEN'S JOURNAL

And a child shall lead them to Surfside — B.C.

LIKE LYRIC POETS, mathematicians, and annoying teen singers, New York City point guards often come to greatness early. Sebastian Telfair turned fifteen last summer, and the ninth-grader is already being compared to such previous local prodigies as Kenny Anderson, now of the Boston Celtics, and Stephon Marbury, the star of the New Jersey Nets, who just happens to be Sebastian's second cousin. Bassy, as he is known to nearly everybody, lives on the third floor of Building 3 in the Surfside Gardens projects of Coney Island, the same building in which Marbury grew up. They learned to play basketball on the same court, nicknamed the Garden, which Bassy can see from his bedroom window. The residents of Surfside say that if you can play there, you can play anywhere.

Just as blues scholars once scoured the Mississippi Delta in search of a new Robert Johnson, so now do recruiting buffs comb the nation's summer basketball camps and youth leagues, intent on unearthing the next Michael Jordan. Bassy has been tracked by hoops cognoscenti since he turned ten, when Hoop Scoop, a well-regarded college-basketball-recruiting service, tagged him as the best fifth-grade player in the country, just as it had once designated Marbury. Last season, BasketballPhenoms.com rated Sebastian the top eighth-grader. On another Internet site devoted to high school basketball, an entry on Sebastian concludes with this enthusiastic passage: "He has unlimited potential and has already talked about going straight to the NBA if he is considered to be a top-five pick. Will he be the best point guard to come out of New York City is yet to be seen, but I wouldn't doubt him."

This past July Sebastian burnished a reputation for precociousness with his performance at the celebrated Adidas ABCD Camp at Fairleigh Dickinson University in Teaneck, New Jersey, where he was the youngest player ever to attend, and at 5'10", 135 pounds, certainly one of the skinniest. For a week he more than held his own with a group composed mainly of rising high school seniors, many of whom are currently the most avidly recruited players in the land. His exploits there merely underscore the rather amazing fact that at the age of fifteen, Sebastian Telfair has already been legendary for a third of his life.

One Saturday in the early fall, I drive from my home in Queens down to Coney Island to meet Sebastian. I want to get a sense of what his life as a prodigy has been like. I wonder how a boy anointed year after year as the best basketball player in his age group can hold up under such immense expectations. At a time when some of the NBA's leading players radiate a rude-boy charisma, it's easy to imagine that young Sebastian might easily be the basketball equivalent of a bratty stage child.

It's about four in the afternoon, and Bassy, his father, Otis, whom he calls Daddy, and I are sitting at the family's new dining-room table, which features a glass top mounted on two glass swans. His mother, Erica, is off visiting neighbors. Bassy has just woken up. "I sleep a lot!" he says, laughing, not the least bit sheepish. Physically unimposing, even a little spindly, he comes across as a sweet, even tenderhearted kid. He asks me to be sure to include the names of all his brothers and sisters in the article. They are, for the record: Ethan, six; Octavia, fourteen; Sylvia, eighteen; Sylvester, nineteen; Dion, twenty-two; Jamel, twenty-four; Terica, twenty-four; Dan, twenty-eight; and Helen, twenty-eight. In a back bedroom, Sylvia is sleeping. "She's trying to figure out what job she's gonna get," Otis jokes. "She's got so many appointments."

Six foot two, slender, and fifty-three, Otis wears a blue U.S. Army baseball cap festooned with military pins, including a badge commemorating his combat service in Vietnam. He fought as an LRRP (long-range reconnaissance patrol) in the jungle near Dong Ha, also known as "Rocket City." It was one of the most notoriously feared assignments in that war, partly because it involved setting up ambushes. The problem with that, says Otis, who achieved the rank of sergeant, is that you could just as well *get* caught as catch. On one occasion his unit was pursued through the jungle by the North Vietnamese for fourteen hours. "It seemed like a thousand years," he says. "We would move, stop, fight, and move again. You a nice guy, you ain't making it. You gotta be grouchy-mean to survive. I'll bite your nose off! I'll take your balls!"

About ten years ago, the doctors at Fort Hamilton Veterans Hospital in Brooklyn diagnosed Otis as suffering from post-traumatic stress disorder. He's now on full disability, takes regular medication, and has returned to living with Sebastian's mother after twelve years away. He doesn't say exactly where he's been, but you get the idea that there were some harrowing times. The flashbacks he endured for decades have finally disappeared. "The Veterans Hospital and my wife saved my life," he tells me with great fervor, as Sebastian alternately listens and flips through a magazine. The simple life with wife and kids is a blessing, Otis says.

For the rest of the afternoon, Otis keeps putting food and drink on the table: Coke, pretzels, prunes. Eventually he goes into the kitchen and whips up some sort of ice cream drink that he used to fix for Bassy. From the courtyard below come the sounds of kids playing basketball and baseball. To the north are new two-story apartments where for decades there was nothing but vacant lots of tall grass and rats.

In the late eighties and early nineties, when Bassy was little, the neighborhood reverberated with the noise of gunfire, especially at night, courtesy of the crack trade. "It used to be wild here," Bassy says as he begins to tell the story of his life so far. "It was a war, a no-man's-land. A lot of gunshots, a lot of people being killed."

"My mother had a saying," he says. "'When the sun goes down, you come up.'" Erica was tough, a disciplinarian. Bassy remembers how she used to make him go to the store. "She would call out the window, 'Sebastian!' And all my friends call me Bassy. They'd say, 'Who she calling?' I'd go, like, Oh, man. I'd run to the window, she'd throw the money out, I'd catch it and go to the store."

All the children are devoted to their mother, whom they refer to among themselves as Big E, though they all still call her Mommy. She would tell her boys that there was nothing more important than their brothers. "All of us in the family were real tight," Bassy says. "But we each had a special one, and for me that was my older brother Dan."

As I would discover, there is a bit of tension in the Telfair family these days in the collision between Bassy's half-brother Dan, who has effectively served as Bassy's protector for years, and Otis, who has returned to the family home to reclaim his rightful place. It amounts to a constant but low-level jangle. "I love my father — don't call him my stepfather," Dan would say later, referring to Otis, "but he don't know nothing about basketball."

Dan, on the other hand, knows quite a lot about basketball. At twenty-eight, he works with teens in the neighborhood and hopes to one day become a coach. Bassy started playing ball at the Garden as a five-year-old, under Dan's supervision. Dan made Bassy play with the older kids to show him that there was always going to be somebody better than him. He clearly had a gift for the game, and an appetite as well. When he was nine, someone accused him of having only a right-hand dribble. He immediately began working on his left.

Life was different back in those days, Bassy recalls. "For one thing, I used to be a crybaby," he says with a kind of sage retrospection.

"His mother protected him a lot," Otis says. "'My Bassy, my Bassy . . .'"

Dan will later confirm this. "If Bassy got out of hand, I'd slap him," he says. "And he would go home and tell our mother. And she would slap me."

"And I used to be more emotional on the court," Bassy continues. If a teammate blew a layup after one of his passes, for instance, he would get mad.

"When did you learn to control your temper?" I ask, impressed.

Bassy cracks a smile. "This past summer," he says.

Otis cackles.

Nonetheless there is an uncanny balance to Bassy. He's learning to accept the vagaries of the game, the mistakes and fouls, developing a fatalism born of painful experience. "What happens, happens," he says. "The slapping don't bother me. It used to be" — he sucks in his breath, a kind of whistle — "man, come get me off the court! I was ready to fight sometimes! But I wasn't getting nothing by crying about it, if you know what I mean. And if it was me missing a layup, I wouldn't want someone to get mad."

Despite usually being the youngest player in the game, Bassy evinces no fear of command. Since he was nine or ten and first running with older players, he's possessed the point guard's imperative for leadership. "When I first started playing with the older kids," he says, "they wouldn't listen, so I would just chuck 'em and not give 'em the ball. Now I tell them, if I'm not looking at you, that means you're gonna get the ball, but if I am looking at you, that means you're not gonna get it."

This past summer, when he wasn't off playing in tournaments, Bassy would get up, eat a little cereal or bagels or toast — he hates eggs no matter how they're fixed — and start working out with his half-brother Jamel Thomas, who attended Abraham Lincoln High in Coney Island, went on to Providence College, and last season played for the Portland Trail Blazers. They'd run the beach all the way to the fishing pier, then run the stairs at Surfside, then go to Kaiser Park to work out on the bars. Then they would do push-ups and other exercises. Then they'd go to the Garden and practice shooting. "Jamel told me he wanted me to have a good work ethic," Bassy says. "He don't want me to be lazy." Around noon they would finish, and Bassy would go upstairs, eat something light, and fall out.

In the evening, he would go back out to have fun: ride his bike, talk to his friends. Near the basketball court, they would gather at the benches and, as Bassy says, discuss "boy things. Like how we play against each other. Then we start talking junk." Bassy would bust on John Quintana, the shooting guard three years his senior who will share the backcourt with him this season at Lincoln. "He'll be talking about Iverson," Bassy says, "and I'll be talking about Stephon, and then it come to the point of, 'I could beat you,' and then we get on the court and start playing. That's when we say the worst things: about girlfriends."

"'Your girl wears size 12,'" Otis volunteers.

Bassy says that he cannot mention the kind of things they say. As for girlfriends, Bassy doesn't really have one right now. He plays the field. He's got more important things to take care of these days. "He's busy," Otis says. "There'll be time for a girlfriend."

In fact life is so busy these days that Bassy is feeling just a tad nostalgic for the ease of junior high. It was fun back then, he says. He would come home in the afternoon, skate (he loved skating so much he got a new pair every Christmas), ride his bike (which he messed up jumping it over obstacles — "but I had a lot of help," he says), and of course play some ball. He remembers how sometimes in the old days he and buddies like his best friend Rasheed Walker would put their money together and buy soda and ice and chips and cookies, and get a couple of blankets and a radio and just hang out at the beach, having fun. High school, which he just started this fall, is more professional, he says. Like a job.

As the talk winds down, Bassy stands up and motions for me to follow. He leads me back to his bedroom. "We don't let many people see this," Otis says. "This is his private domain." The room is as neat as a military barracks, dominated by a huge bed with the covers pulled up taut to the headboard. The shelves along one wall are full of trophies. "That's not all of them. I gave some to my relatives," Bassy says. He proudly hands me a sheet with his brother Jamel's stats from his time at Providence.

Otis lingers by the window. "You've got front-row seats at the Garden here," he announces. "Me and my wife'll be in the house sometimes and we hear people cheering, and we say, 'Bassy just did something.'"

But with all these trophies, all this attention, how does Bassy prevent himself from getting a big head? He patiently explains it to me: "Say you're poor and you don't have anything and then you get a lottery. So you get big-headed. But if you grow up with a lot of money, you don't care so much about it. I grew up with attention for basketball, so I don't care that much."

Where does his talent come from? I ask.

He thinks for a moment, scratches his head, then says, "God. And my family."

On Friday night before the high school season gets under way, Bassy takes to the court at the Jumpman Tournament being held at IS8 in Jamaica, Queens, in a dusty neighborhood of churned-up streets and small houses. The PA system is blasting a hip-hop song with lyrics that go like this:

GUY SINGER: Would you lie for me?
GIRL SINGER: No doubt.
GUY SINGER: Would you die for me?
GIRL SINGER: No doubt.

When he sees me arrive, Bassy gives a shy wave, but quickly pulls it back, as if maybe ballplayers don't do that kind of thing, and becomes otherwise absorbed in readying himself for the game.

His IS8 league team, the Bro All Stars, coached by his brother Dan, will be going against the famous Gauchos, a team that features a 7′2″ sophomore named Shagari Alleyne and another promising young point guard, Marlon Smith.

There's something aristocratic about Bassy as he goes about his preparations: the way he slides into the bleachers alone to tie his sneakers, the way he desultorily does his calisthenics, the way he ever-so-slightly keeps his distance from everyone, aware, it seems, that he is always being watched and that perhaps a certain deference is in order.

Before the opening tip, he steers a teammate to the proper spot on the floor. Then he runs down the jump ball and makes a beautiful parabola of a pass from halfcourt to a teammate streaking in for a layup. If he's a blasé noble on the sideline, on the court Bassy's a harried commuter late for his job. He scampers across the court in an anxious frenzy, an alarmed look on his face, his eyebrows perpetually arched upwards, his pupils wide. That's his demeanor. His skills, on the other hand, are luxurious, the product of ten years of constant practice. With his fakes, his crossover, his in-and-out, and his behind-the-back, he can break a guy's ankles, as the saying goes. He dribbles equally well with either hand, the ball seeming to radiate in whichever direction he desires. Not since Kenny Anderson came out of LeFrak City, Queens, in the late eighties has New York basketball seen such a wicked handle.

The real marvel, however, is Bassy's passing. As with the greatest point guards, he actually passes into the future, that spot where a teammate will be a second or two later, in some cases even before the player himself seems to know where he will shortly arrive. It's a kind of quantum basketball, played with an exquisite sense of the entire court and the flow of players. When I earlier asked Bassy about his uncanny passing ability, raising with him my theory about passing forward into time, Bassy chuckled modestly. "I can't really see into the future," he said. But after he makes a laserlike pass through a thicket of players for another assist, the tournament MC, Pete Edwards, confirms what everyone can already feel when he announces to the crowd, as if testifying to something beyond the ken of ordinary mortals: *He can see it.*

Near the end of the first quarter, Bassy has already scored ten points, including a pull-up three from the corner. His anticipated matchup with Marlon Smith, however, is something of a dud. Smith doesn't come off the bench until deep in the quarter, and he owns something of a burgher's game, composed of stolid, middle-class virtues. He's not flashy, he rarely loses the ball, and in a re-strained fashion that Bassy charitably characterizes as "laid-back," he gets the job done. His style is that of a farm boy in the big city.

By contrast, Bassy's game features the constant improvisation of a New York sidewalk scramble. In his most spectacular moment of the evening, he yo-yos the ball between his legs — one of his favor-ite moves — and turns the corner on his defender, heading at top speed toward the left side of the basket. Standing between him and the rim is the 7'2" kid, Alleyne. Skinny and still a little ungainly, the big guy wears goggles that make him look a little like Kareem Ab-dul-Jabbar during Kareem's praying-mantis years. As Bassy barrels toward him, two other defenders leave their men and converge upon the lane. Bassy leaps and corkscrews his body to protect the ball. By God, he looks so small! A child in the world of, well, if not men, then really, really big children. You feel as protective as a mother. You want to call him home from the court and tell him to pick up some bread and milk on the way. For a moment, Bassy, tri-ple-teamed, completely disappears from view, and then his left hand rises up out of the scrum, daintily laying the ball in the bas-ket. And the foul.

Bassy is not the celebratory type, nor does he seem especially sur-prised at the successful outcome of his amazing move, so he just turns and calmly proceeds to the foul line. He clearly (if implicitly) subscribes to the late Alabama coach Bear Bryant's notion of how to behave after scoring a touchdown: Act like you've been there before.

Early in the second quarter, Bassy tries to split a double team and goes down hard when he gets kneed in the thigh. He rolls on the floor, clutching his leg in agony. The gym falls silent. Dan, his baggy pants drooping, hustles out to his little brother's side, then heads to the scorer's table for an ice pack. His dreams of Bassy's "living a little bit better than me" seem, in a moment like this, only as strong as Bassy's physique. "He has the talent for the NBA al-ready," says Pete Edwards, who has watched Marbury and other pros-to-be on this very court. "But he has to get stronger."

Although this time Bassy has suffered only a deep bruise, there's always the possibility that next time might deliver catastrophe. Dan helps him to the bench, where the young legend is soon joined by his little brother, Ethan, who stares quietly at Bassy while the game continues.

Another Friday evening at Surfside. As on most weekends, the Garden is abuzz with activity. Some teenage boys are playing halfcourt, interrupted occasionally by a gang of squealing teenage gals who dart in, steal the ball, and throw it to the other end. On the pathway around the Garden, a little girl on a scooter is being pulled around by a pit bull on a chain. Bassy wheels up on his brother Ethan's scooter. He's wearing a baseball cap turned backward, red-and-black pants, and a diamond earring. Otis, too, has sauntered down to the playground, dressed to the nines in sunglasses, black leather jacket, black pants, black shirt, and a gray broad-brimmed hat.

Sometimes Otis must feel that Bassy is a compensation for some of his suffering, that his son's gifts represent a kind of change in luck, a blessing on the family. Yes, he knows that there is clearly the possibility of riches down the road, but it's more than that. "Stephon, Jamel, Zackie, and Sebastian!" exclaims Otis, incredulous that they should all be in one extended family. Zackie is Zach Marbury, Stephon Marbury's little brother, now a point guard at Rhode Island. "And Bassy may top them!" How strange and marvelous is providence!

On this Friday evening, Otis has tentatively agreed to let Sebastian participate in a commercial being shot for AND 1 sneakers. Bassy's involvement will not jeopardize his amateur standing, because he won't be paid a cent. Around six, the camera crew arrives in a rented van. They've been searching for Sebastian all over Brooklyn. Earlier that morning, they'd waited for a couple of hours by the clock tower in Flatbush hoping that Bassy would show up to accompany another of his youth teams, Brooklyn USA, to a tournament at Rutgers. The All Stars are coached by Thomas Sicignano, better known as Ziggy, who has coached Bassy since he was nine. Ziggy brokered the connection between the Telfairs and the AND 1 people. Dan is a little suspicious about that. "I'd just like to know what Ziggy's getting out of this," he says later that night.

Bassy's participation in the commercial has been a source of considerable disagreement in the family. Bassy himself has always wanted to be on TV ("That's different from magazines and papers," he says). Dan, in his continuing role as Bassy's protector, doesn't think his little brother needs the exposure, and he worries about the possible effect of the ad on his amateur standing. Even Bassy's head coach at Lincoln, Dwayne "Tiny" Morton, is anxious about what the spot might do to his team's chemistry. "How the fuck am I gonna coach a fifteen-year-old with his own commercial?" he asks.

Otis, on the other hand, is eager for Bassy to enjoy the exposure the ad is likely to provide. He feels this balances out the fact that, in his view, "everybody's getting paid but Sebastian and the family." He introduces himself to Rupert Samuel, the director, a young hipster from London with blond-brown hair combed back from his face.

Rupert tells Otis that they're making a thirty-second ad that will celebrate the glories of playing ball for the sheer fun of it, and hope to air on NBC during the last week of the Olympics, when such a spot costs $600,000. For a frenzied week or so, Rupert and crew have been flying around the country in this guerrilla-style campaign, enlisting famous high school and street-ball players to appear on camera, where they rail against the cushy, spoiled life of the Dream Team (a cushy, spoiled life that many of these younger players doubtless dream of enjoying themselves).

The intent, clearly, is to lend AND 1 sneakers a subversive, up-from-the-streets glamour, the same kind of bad-boy aura the company sought for its shoes last season when it aired a striking commercial of Latrell Sprewell having his hair braided to the strains of Jimi Hendrix. Of course Sprewell got paid, and the talent in these new ads is free. So all that Rupert can promise Bassy and his family is the nebulous joy of "exposure." Which he pledges with evangelical fervor. "I don't want you to do anything you're uncomfortable with," Rupert tells Otis, "but he will be seen all over the country."

Otis likes the idea. He strokes his chin, inclines his head toward Rupert. "Let me just clarify the situation," he says, pointing his finger at Rupert. "So this commercial would be on all over the world."

"Okay, I'm a man of my word," Otis says. "Let's do it." He agrees to let Bassy participate as long as the family can see a videotape of the spot before signing a final agreement.

At some point during all of the talk, however, Bassy disappears. "I know what he did," Otis says, irritated with Bassy. "He went and got his older brother Dan. I'm washing my hands of this."

A half-hour passes, then forty-five minutes. Still no Sebastian. "He's running us, and that ain't right," Otis complains to his brother-in-law, Bassy's uncle Poppy. He stares at the ground, on the verge of humiliation. Rupert and the camera crew start packing up. "This kind of thing happens," Rupert says.

Just then some guy sprints out of Building 3 with a message for Otis: "Bassy says tell the cameras to go to 288." That's PS 288, an elementary school a few blocks away where Bassy's Lincoln High team often practices.

Everyone hurries over to the school. Dan and Tiny have arrived as well. There on the front steps is Bassy, decked out in shorts and a jersey, cradling a basketball. Otis confronts him. "You made me look like an asshole, standing there," he says.

"He said it would be better in the gym," Bassy protests, pointing at Rupert.

Uncle Poppy joins in. "Bassy," he says. "I just want to say one thing. That wasn't right."

Then Otis spots Tiny, whom he suspects of having tried, in collusion with Dan, to circumvent the plans for Sebastian's participation in the commercial. "Bassy should never have went to Lincoln," he tells Tiny. "He needs to get away from this environment." What he seems to mean is to get away from any environment in which Otis is not in charge. "Don't say nothing to me," Otis says to Tiny.

"I'm not saying anything," Tiny says, looking affronted.

In the gym, as the crew sets up for the shoot, Bassy sits by himself in the bleachers. Dan has said about him that "he's a good kid who wants to please everybody." I sit down beside Bassy and ask how he feels about the current discord within the family. He is thoughtful, diplomatic. "Everybody got to sit down and talk about it and get on the same page," he says.

When it's time to be filmed, Bassy stands in front of the camera, the basketball resting on his hip. "Hopefully, this will just be the first of many such appearances in front of a camera for you," Rupert tells Bassy.

Bassy nods. He looks completely comfortable standing there. He seems to regard such moments as preordained, the way you get certain subjects in school at a certain time. Like right now in ninth

grade, his teacher assigned him *The Miracle Worker,* about Helen
Keller, a book he is loving. Now it's time to make his first commercial.

"I'll read out the line," Rupert tells Bassy, "and you hit me back
with it straightaway. Kind of annoyed-like, okay? Just get me a little
attitude. Look straight into the lens, because this is where your aggression is going to go. The main thing is, you're kinda angry that
this sort of thing is going on."

Now, anybody who knows Bassy knows that he does not exactly
give off an angry vibe. But Rupert appears to want an angry-young-
brother feel to the spot. "Coach, put me in the game, man," he
prompts.

"Coach, put me in the game, man," Bassy follows. He's earnest,
intense. But he still comes across as sweetly as any mother might
hope.

"I'll walk there," Rupert says.

"I'll walk there," Bassy echoes. He clenches his fist to give the
lines more juice.

"I'll swim there."

"I'll swim there."

"My dream is gold, not green."

"My dream is gold, not green."

"I won't sell as many shoes, but I'll make my jumpers," Rupert
says, drawling a bit. Is it a coincidence that he is sounding "blacker"
than Bassy? He seems to want Sebastian to sound more "street."

"I won't sell as many shoes, but I'll make my jumpers," Bassy answers.

"You won't have to fly me first-class," Rupert says.

"You won't have to fly me first-class." Bassy gives the line the
sweetest reading imaginable, as if he is positively begging not to be
flown first-class.

Rupert stops the proceedings for a moment to huddle with
Bassy. "Say it like you're a little more annoyed," he says.

Bassy nods. From the sidelines Otis shouts, "Put feeling in it!"
He's now shouting every line right after Bassy says it. He wants
Bassy to do it right, but there's something more going on. Otis is
happy! It's as if it's *his* commercial, *his* exposure.

"Put me in the game," Rupert says. "You know I can score."

"Put me in the game," echoes Bassy. "You know I can score."

"Put me in the game," Otis erupts, striding up and down the sideline, waving his arms like a preacher. "You know I can score." Bassy listens to Otis, then goes back to work.

"You didn't tell me about his fucking father," Tiny says to Dan. They're huddled by the door to the gym. Dan shrugs.

Later that night Bassy steps alone onto the Garden. For a moment he has the court to himself. It's as familiar to him as his own bedroom. The air is cool, the camera crew has gone home, and there's still a good portion of Friday evening left to use as he wishes. The little girl on the scooter is still being pulled by her pit bull up and down the sidewalk. A few kids watch as Bassy slashes the ball back and forth between his legs, back and forth, back and forth, a lulling, metronomic motion that is soothing to behold.

He's feeling pretty good. Making a commercial wasn't as exciting as he had expected, but it still gives him a lot of confidence. Now he has a little time for basketball, for the sheer pleasure of doing a thing he loves and does well. He's working on his ball-handling, making a couple of crossover moves. When he's practicing, he relishes thinking about how he's working harder than anybody else, about how he's going to get a leg up on the competition. He doesn't think that much about the future, but when he does, he dreams of how he will dunk by the end of the season. The thrill! He's close — "I look like I dunk now," he says — but he wants the real thing.

Suddenly, from an opening in the fence, Otis is calling. "Bassy," he says. His reverie interrupted, his face impassive, Bassy dribbles over to his father.

Otis is eating a fried apple turnover out of the wrapper. "Here, Bassy," he says, reaching into a bag and holding out a bottle of Clearly Canadian soda. It's cherry, Bassy's favorite flavor. He takes a long swig and hands the bottle back to his father, who sets it down on a planter next to the court. It's an unspoken moment of sweetness, seemingly offered up by Otis to resolve a testy evening. "Thanks," Bassy says.

Then Bassy turns back to the court, and as Otis and the kids watch from the fence he dribbles behind his back, faces the basket, and in the dark begins to shoot.

DOUG MOST

Shot Through the Heart

FROM SPORTS ILLUSTRATED

A basketball tragedy beyond the court — B.C.

A FEW MINUTES shy of 11:00 P.M. on April 23, 1998, Keshon
Moore was driving south on the New Jersey Turnpike, less than an
hour into a twelve-hour trip to North Carolina. His silver Dodge
Caravan was on a stretch of highway that cuts through the central
part of the state. Sandwiched between the refineries and sports arenas to the north and the farms and water towers to the south, the
road is straight, wide, and flat. There are no smokestacks or tall office buildings to provide distractions. The challenge for drivers is
to stay focused; for passengers, to stay awake.

State troopers John Hogan and James Kenna had been patrol-
ling the turnpike for two hours when they spotted the Caravan.
Keshon's heart began to race when he saw the police cruiser come
up on his left, but he relaxed when it roared past. He figured it
was chasing some speeder up ahead. Keshon, twenty-two, hadn't
owned a car for more than a year. He was driving a minivan rented
by his girlfriend's mother. None of his three passengers knew that
Keshon's license had been suspended because of a few unpaid
parking tickets. "I was very leery because of my license," Keshon remembers. "I was doing fifty-five on the dot."

Crunched into the front passenger seat was 6'7" Danny Reyes,
twenty, Keshon's former basketball teammate at Curtis High on
Staten Island in New York City. Behind them slept two friends from
the city playground courts — Rayshawn Brown, twenty, and Jarmaine Grant, twenty-three — both oblivious to the hip-hop tunes
of DJ Clue that were blaring from the van's tape deck.

Suddenly the police cruiser slowed, and the Caravan pulled even with it. The two vehicles rode side by side for half a mile before the cruiser backed off. Keshon, puzzled, drove on carefully, but then the police car slipped in behind him, and its flashing lights came on.

Even on a turnpike where driving seventy-five miles per hour is rarely ticketed, this was not a night for speeding. Traffic was heavy, and a steady rain had left the highway glistening and slick. Keshon had traveled roughly fifty miles in fifty minutes to this rural patch of Mercer County. By the time the cruiser appeared, the Caravan's beige-carpeted floor resembled the floor of a college dorm room, littered with gym bags, cassettes, sneakers, two New York Yankees caps, bottles of Snapple, bags of chips, a Bible, and a copy of John Steinbeck's *The Grapes of Wrath*. Keshon slowed down quickly when he saw the flashing lights in his rearview mirror, and the cruiser almost rammed him from behind. Both cars pulled into the breakdown lane.

The young men in the van had planned to drive all night and arrive before noon in Durham, where coaches at North Carolina Central University were holding an informal tryout for a few dozen players. For the four New Yorkers, it was a last chance. They weren't stars, and they were already in their twenties. Any hope they had of landing a college scholarship and keeping alive their dream of playing professionally, maybe in the CBA or in Europe, rested on this journey. Now the police were interrupting it. Keshon was sure he hadn't been speeding. He wasn't thinking that his race alone might be reason enough for the police to stop him.

It had happened to Hall of Fame second baseman Joe Morgan, who was wrestled to the ground at Los Angeles Airport in 1988 by police who suspected that he was a drug dealer. It had happened to Toronto Raptors guard Dee Brown, stopped at gunpoint outside a Wellesley, Massachusetts, post office in 1990 (when Brown was with the Boston Celtics) by officers who suspected that he had been involved in a crime nearby. It had happened to track coach and former Olympic gold medalist Al Joyner in 1992, when he was stopped and handcuffed for suspicion of driving a stolen vehicle (it turned out to be his wife's, and he was released); he was stopped again two blocks later on suspicion of having committed a felony hit-and-run (he was again released). Racial profiling is one of the most volatile civil rights issues in the United States, and even the most successful African-Americans are not immune to it. Blacks say the police target them for no reason but their skin color. On the roads they call it DWB: Driving While Black.

Tap-tap-tap. State trooper Kenna, then twenty-seven, in his navy shirt with gold shoulder stripes, banged his long black flashlight on the passenger window of the Caravan. Kenna held the flashlight in his left hand; in his right he held a nine-millimeter Glock. "Put your hands up!" he shouted. State trooper Hogan, twenty-eight, who had been driving the police car, stood ten feet behind the van, between it and the cruiser.

Keshon thought he had slipped the van into park as he came to a stop, but he had mistakenly put it in reverse. When he saw Kenna's flashlight and gun and heard the officer order everyone to show hands, Keshon's foot came off the brake. The van lurched backward toward the idling police cruiser — and Hogan.

Both troopers were startled. Kenna stepped sideways to follow the van backward, shouting to Keshon to stop and everyone inside to put up his hands. Hogan jumped to the side to avoid being struck.

The van rolled slowly toward the cruiser, with Kenna on the passenger side and Hogan now on the driver's side. The troopers couldn't see each other, and that made them more anxious. Kenna raised his gun with both hands and pointed it at the window, and Keshon dived from the driver's seat onto the floor behind the passenger seat, where he curled into a fetal position. The van kept rolling.

"Don't shoot, don't shoot!" Danny hollered at Kenna while raising his hands. Rayshawn, who was asleep in the van's middle seat, still fights back tears when he tries to tell what happened next: He woke up to the sound of gunfire.

The trip south had been Keshon's idea. He knew the coaches at North Carolina Central. He made the calls. He collected the seventy-six dollars from each passenger for the minivan rental, gas, and tolls. He decided who would be picked up where and when.

"I was excited," Keshon says. "I was strong. I was hitting the weights. My game was flourishing." He speaks softly, politely, his head down. When your father is a retired U.S. Coast Guard petty officer and your mother is a corrections officer at Riker's Island, a

New York City jail crammed with some of the most violent criminals on the planet, talking back is out of the question.

"My standards were very high," Keshon's father, Rodney Moore, says. "Keshon was always shy, very respectful. He never gave me any problem."

The basketball world is full of Keshon Moores, 5′9″ point guards who refuse to believe they're too short until they wake up one morning with no scholarship, no direction, only a jump shot and a dream. For every Dana Barros, Travis Best, and Damon Stoudamire, thousands of Keshon Moores dot the playgrounds around the country. As a military brat, Keshon bounced from Spain to Arizona to Texas to California and finally, in 1987, to the Coast Guard base on Governor's Island in New York Harbor.

At Curtis High, Keshon's grades were mediocre, his skills solid. "If it wasn't a layup, Keshon didn't take the shot," recalls Tim Gannon, Curtis's basketball coach and assistant principal. "He was very unselfish, the prototypical point guard." He led the team to the 1994 Staten Island championship and finished as the school's all-time assist leader.

Keshon went on to Westchester Community College, in Valhalla, New York, where he hoped to improve his grades as well as his game. After two years there he got a scholarship at North Carolina Central, a Division II school, but he didn't stay long. With two point guards ahead of him, he redshirted and quickly lost interest in school. He returned to New York, moved in with a girlfriend in Manhattan, and worked occasionally as a barber and a security guard. "I was hurt and depressed for a while," Keshon says. "My pops, he was mad at me."

That's an understatement. "I was devastated," Rodney Moore says. "He was treated royally, and he didn't take advantage of his opportunity. Get your bachelor's degree and *then* decide what you want."

Now, in the spring of 1998, Keshon was determined to give North Carolina Central a second try. He would go to summer school and try to walk on with the team. Basketball practice was to start on Saturday, April 25. Keshon planned to enroll as soon as he arrived on campus on Friday.

The first bullet from Kenna's Glock pierced the front passenger window but didn't shatter it, leaving a spiderweb of cracks in the glass. The bullet screamed down past Danny and Keshon, missing them by inches, and lodged near the bottom of the driver's door.

"Don't shoot, don't shoot!" Danny shouted as he put up his hands. Now everyone was alert, diving for cover, curling up for protection.

The Caravan bumped into the police car and started it rolling down a slight grade. The cruiser came to a rest about one hundred feet away.

Kenna cleared the glass from the cracked passenger window with his flashlight. Danny was lying down to shield himself, but Kenna would say it looked as if Danny were trying to reach for something, or even get into the driver's seat, which Keshon had just vacated. Danny, only a few feet from Kenna, begged him not to shoot again.

"The van's not in park!" Danny shouted. "Stop shooting!" But as he leaned toward the driver's seat and reached for the gearshift, two bullets ripped into his right arm.

"Please don't shoot!" he begged. Still reaching for the gearshift, he pulled himself forward by grabbing the steering wheel and turning it. A third bullet hit beneath his left shoulder. A fourth entered his right hip. Blood pooled on the passenger seat in a heap of glass shards.

At Curtis High, many of Keshon's passes wound up in the hands of a skinny, mocha-colored forward one year behind him, a Puerto Rican with Division I skills but a soft side that frustrated his coaches. Danny Reyes had caught the attention of recruiters, who invited him at age eleven to join New York City's elite amateur team, the Gauchos. He was a 1995 honorable mention McDonald's All-American, and of the four young men in the van that April night, he had the best chance of succeeding in basketball.

"He was such a quiet kid, almost to his detriment," says Richard Potter, the assistant coach at Curtis who first saw Danny play in CYO leagues. "He had long arms, he could put it on the floor. I wanted to get him fired up. He could have been an All-American."

But fired up wasn't his nature. The son of a retired policewoman and a retired truck driver, Danny is the youngest of four children in a close Christian family. Once when a brawl erupted in a hallway at Curtis, with seven or eight guys throwing haymakers, Danny was the peacekeeper, pulling bodies away until guards arrived. He still has the Good Samaritan certificate awarded him the next day.

After helping Curtis repeat as champion in 1995, Danny graduated and went with his parents to Puerto Rico for the summer, where he played in the professional Superior Basketball League. "I hoped it was the start of something big," he says. When summer ended, he moved back to New York to live with his sister in Queens.

He had interest from Hartford, Marist, Hofstra, South Carolina State, and Maryland–Baltimore County, but he thought playing at a junior college would be a surer route to a big basketball school. It wasn't. He bounced from Abraham Baldwin Agricultural College in Tifton, Georgia, to New York City Technical College to the Puerto Rico league again in 1996, playing, studying, and waiting for the Division I offer that would never come. A bone bruise to his left knee in 1997 forced him to rest, and suddenly his future was not so promising. "I knew he probably could have been a better player," says Ralph Menar, who coached Danny as a youngster in the Police Athletic League, "but it's not the first time I saw this happen."

Danny was back at New York City Technical College in April 1998, closing in on his associate degree in liberal arts, when he decided to give basketball one more try and accompany Keshon south.

After it bumped the cruiser, the van continued rolling backward, and the shooting continued, too. Not just from Kenna, but now from Hogan as well. Bullets blasted into the rear driver's side of the minivan, where Rayshawn was cowering in the middle seat and Jarmaine in the rear. One bullet struck Jarmaine's right knee, another hit his ribs, and a third entered his right arm. His wounded leg was pinned beneath the middle seat. "I'm hit, I'm hit!" he screamed.

If raw talent had brought Danny to the van that night, hard work and determination had gotten Leroy Jarmaine Grant there. He and his younger brother and two older sisters were raised in a public housing project in the heart of Harlem, at 129th Street and Seventh Avenue. Jarmaine once watched paramedics carry out of the building a five-year-old girl who had been hit by a stray bullet from the street.

Jarmaine played year-round on the court at the St. Nicholas Playground. When his hands got too cold on winter days, he would bolt into the Laundromat across the street, toss a quarter into a dryer, warm his gloves, and run back out to play. "Jarmaine is a basketball fiend," says Pat Mangan, his coach at Rice High, a city basketball power, where Jarmaine led one of the two varsity squads in scoring. "I had to throw him out of the gym."

He graduated in 1993, and when the offers he had hoped for didn't come, he stayed close to home and played at Westchester Community College, where he made a new friend: his roommate, Keshon Moore. Jarmaine became one of the top fifty junior college three-point shooters in the country while earning his two-year degree. He was back in the city in April 1998, living with his mom and thinking about his next move, when Keshon invited him to drive to North Carolina Central.

Rayshawn heard his friends screaming and saw Keshon's legs in the space between the two front seats. He felt the van moving slowly backward and reached to open the sliding door next to him. But just as he grabbed the handle, the van bumped the police cruiser behind it and, as Danny got hold of the steering wheel, veered with its lights out into the dark southbound lanes of the turnpike, directly into the path of a Honda Civic. The collision was fierce. The Honda struck the van, then went left and slammed into the center concrete barrier.

Rayshawn lost his grip on the door handle. He winced in pain as a bullet ripped into his chest from the side, exited and lodged in his right forearm. Danny, jostled by the collision but still frantically reaching for the gearshift, threw the van into drive, causing it to start forward.

The van, now perpendicular to traffic, moved slowly off the highway, across the breakdown lane, and toward an embankment. After all the shooting and shouting, there was silence.

The van was almost at a stop near the ditch beside the highway when one last shot rang out. It was from Hogan's Glock. The bullet passed through the rear-driver's-side window and the back of the driver's seat, taking some fibers of the seat cushion with it as it tore into Danny's lower back while he lay on his side along the two front seats. The bullet missed his spine by an inch.

Basketball had been a hobby for Rayshawn Brown. Of the four players in the van he had the least basketball education but the most classroom dedication. "If you get injured, what do you have left?" Rayshawn says. "Your mind. You have to have your education to fall back on."

His parents separated when he was one, and his mother raised her three children in the Bronx. Basketball was not Rayshawn's first love. Doing flips was. And juggling. And tumbling. He was a natural gymnast, and the circus fascinated him.

He worked hard in school and was interested in architecture and computers. He also began tumbling for the Big Apple Circus, a nonprofit performing group, when he was thirteen. "Rayshawn was probably the most responsible kid I had," says Frank Sellitto, the head instructor at Big Apple Circus. "He had lots of energy."

He earned As and Bs at Jacqueline Kennedy Onassis High School for International Careers. The school had everything Rayshawn wanted except basketball. He had led his junior high basketball team to the eighth-grade city championship. After studying and training with the circus, he practiced on courts near his apartment until midnight. He played his way into tournaments. The circus drills helped him jump higher, cut quicker, and muscle others out of the way. Though only 5'10", he dunked with ease.

He graduated in 1996 and left for Grambling State in Louisiana. But he was never comfortable there. He made high honors studying architecture and played intramural basketball for one semester, then transferred to Alabama A&M. Again unhappy, he lasted only a semester, making dean's list before returning home in the spring of 1997, frustrated but undaunted.

Rayshawn worked part-time at a dry cleaners and played basketball day and night. On a fenced-in court near his apartment building in the fall of 1997, he found himself facing a rare challenge. Covering him was an equally quick and cocky guard who had a mouth that wouldn't stop.

"We were talking smack all game," Keshon Moore recalls with a smile.

"Yeah, I was talking trash," Rayshawn remembers. "He couldn't guard me."

A friendship was born. The next spring Rayshawn was trying to figure out how to afford the tuition at Clemson, where he had just been accepted but had not been offered a scholarship, when Keshon suggested he try for a full ride at North Carolina Central.

The barrage was over. The entire incident had taken barely sixty seconds. The van rested in a thicket of trees. Rayshawn grabbed the door handle

*again and jumped out onto the wet grass. He heard shouts ordering him to
freeze, and he buried his face in the ground.*

*The troopers dragged the three other young men from the Caravan, lay
them face-down in the mud along with Rayshawn, and handcuffed them.
The officers then searched the van for guns, drugs, alcohol, something that
might explain why the young men seemed to have tried to run the troopers
down on the side of the road. They found nothing.*

*Danny, one sneaker on, the other still in the car, was moaning in the
mud, barely conscious and bleeding profusely from his wounds. Paramedics, who arrived about fifteen minutes later, had to cut off his clothes and
work around his handcuffs to treat him. Jarmaine and Rayshawn were also
in agony from their gunshot wounds.*

*Keshon was suffering in a different way, wracked by guilt. He was apolo-
gizing. He saw his friends crying and screaming, and he told the troopers he
simply couldn't get the van into park.*

Eleven shots had been fired, six by Kenna and five by Hogan. Nine
of the bullets had struck flesh. Danny was hit four or five times; it
was hard to tell because he had both exit and entrance wounds.
One bullet wound up in his abdomen. Jarmaine was shot three or
four times, Rayshawn once or twice (his chest and wrist injuries
might have come from the same bullet). Keshon, the smallest and
quickest of the players, somehow avoided the spray of bullets.

Henry Lee, the renowned forensic scientist who testified for the
defense in the O. J. Simpson trial, would re-create the turnpike
shooting several months later as part of a $1 million state investiga-
tion, right down to buying an identical Caravan and wetting the
pavement. Afterward he would say, "It's a miracle that nobody was
killed."

The state police would say that the radar in Hogan and Kenna's
car had clocked the minivan going seventy-four miles per hour.
The problem was, the officers' cruiser, a shiny Ford Crown Victoria
with five hundred miles on it, had no radar. When that became
public, the police said the troopers had determined the van's
speed by following it.

Once both cars were stopped at mile marker 62.8 on the turnpike, Hogan and Kenna made several critical mistakes. They didn't
radio their dispatcher that they were pulling over a vehicle, as they
were required to do. They pulled in straight behind the van, not at

an angle, as police are taught to do, so the front of the cruiser sticks out to protect them from oncoming traffic. And they left their car in neutral, not park, meaning a slight tap could start it rolling.

The young white troopers were scared and confused. It was late and dark. Cars and trucks were speeding by on the wet highway. The van was drifting backward when it should have been still. What's more, several young black men inside seemed to be shifting around a lot. The troopers were not about to wait to see if anyone inside the van had a gun. Kenna would say that he heard Hogan shout, and he thought Hogan's life was in danger. Kenna began shooting.

The troopers would later claim that the van was rolling rapidly, but this was disputed by state investigators, whose forensic tests determined that the van could not have been going more than four miles per hour. That corroborated testimony by the couple in the Honda Civic that crashed into the van. Eric Jusino and his girlfriend, Heather Hendrickson, stepped from their smoking car and walked toward the troopers as the Caravan rolled away. The couple saw the troopers with guns drawn and rushed back toward their car, which by then was engulfed in flames. Jusino's lawyer, Jeff Sponder, says Jusino and Hendrickson didn't witness the shootings, "but they said the van was moving very slowly."

Hogan would tell state investigators that he had dived headfirst to avoid the backward-moving van and had been lying on the ground when he fired his gun. Lee, however, determined after studying bullet trajectories that Hogan had most likely gotten off all five of his shots from a "standing or semi-crouched position."

The troopers also would deny that they had stopped the van after racially profiling Keshon and his friends, but this, too, was called into question by an incident earlier in the evening. Half an hour before they stopped the Caravan, Hogan and Kenna stopped a Temple University law student, Christopher Woodley, for allegedly making an unsafe lane change. Woodley did not have his license, and his vehicle, which had been reported stolen, turned out to belong to his mother. The troopers sent Woodley on his way. Their report on the incident, however, caught the attention of state investigators. The report allegedly listed Woodley as white. He is black. Why would the troopers have lied? The only explanation, officials surmised, was that the troopers had been stopping blacks for no evident reason, looking for drug busts and reporting the drivers as white or as members of other ethnic groups to divert suspicion.

Based partly on testimony from the players in the van, a grand jury indicted Hogan and Kenna on charges of attempted murder, aggravated assault, and filing false police reports. The trial on the first two charges is expected to begin this fall, to be followed by trial on the false-reports charges. The troopers, who have been suspended without pay, have pleaded not guilty to all criminal charges.

The attempted-murder charge, which is highly unusual in cases of this kind, stems from the final shot, fired into Danny's back while the van rolled away. "The issue is, what is the purpose of those shots?" says James J. Gerrow Jr., the assistant prosecutor in Burlington County, New Jersey, who was appointed by Governor Christine Whitman to lead the investigation into the shooting. "Our position is that their purpose was to take the life of Danny Reyes."

The troopers' attorneys angrily dispute that and charge that the state is using Kenna and Hogan as scapegoats for racial profiling. "Essentially they're saying those troopers woke up that morning with the intention of killing some people," says Kenna's lawyer, Jack Arseneault. "That decision to shoot is made instantaneously."

The turnpike incident touched off a political firestorm over racial profiling that would have repercussions well beyond New Jersey. If, as the troopers' allegedly falsified report on Woodley suggests, Hogan and Kenna were profiling black motorists, surely other Jersey troopers were, too. Their boss, State Police Superintendent Carl Williams, seemed to confirm this in comments published by the *Newark Star-Ledger* on February 28, 1999. "Today with this drug problem," Williams said, "it is most likely a minority group that's involved." Whitman fired Williams later that day.

The turnpike victims hired some of the most prominent lawyers in the country — including Johnnie Cochran, who twenty years earlier had himself been stopped and rousted by police while he was a rising assistant district attorney in Los Angeles — and filed civil lawsuits against Hogan and Kenna, the state of New Jersey, and the Turnpike Authority. (The troopers have pleaded not guilty in the civil suit as well.) "This is the poster-boy case for racial profiling," says Peter Neufeld, who represents Danny and Jarmaine and is, like Cochran and Lee, a veteran of the Simpson defense. "Four young men with no criminal records, some parents in law enforcement, on their way to try out for a basketball team, no drugs or guns in their car, only a Bible and a John Steinbeck novel. [The police are] looking for drugs and guns. [They] get a Bible and Steinbeck."

Whitman ordered an investigation into racial profiling in New Jersey, and sure enough, statistics revealed that nearly three in every four motorists stopped on the turnpike were members of minorities. The yearlong probe ended with a report that said racial profiling is "real, not imagined." As far as anyone knew, it was the first time that a state government had acknowledged that profiling occurs. "It was definitely a turning point on the issue," says John Crew, coordinator of the NAACP's national campaign against racial profiling. "These are people who had denied it for a long time."

Five states have since passed laws outlawing racial profiling. Partly as a result of the turnpike shooting and its aftermath, video cameras have been installed in New Jersey State Police cruisers to record all traffic stops. (Last month the New Jersey attorney general's office also announced new police guidelines on deadly force, allowing officers to fire on moving vehicles only if the officers are in "imminent danger" and/or fear "serious bodily injury.") The U.S. House of Representatives passed a bill this year to require the government to monitor race data on police searches across the country. Racial profiling even became a presidential campaign issue, heatedly discussed by Al Gore and Bill Bradley in their Apollo Theater debate in Harlem last February.

Tell the four young men who were in the van that they are lucky to be alive, and they shrug. They know it's true, but it's hard to feel lucky when, in your mid-twenties, a simple free throw hurts your wrist, walking for too long makes your knee ache, or steel plates in your arm remind you that you'll never play ball again. All they want, they say, is to play — if not in college, if not professionally, then at least at 129th Street or in Central Park or at 63rd Street, wherever there's a rim and a game.

It's two years after the shooting, a sticky hot Sunday in April.

Jarmaine Grant, in baggy gray sweats, stands beside the court in Harlem where he honed his jumper. He walks with a limp. He will need to have his kneecap replaced. The bullet lodged in his right arm makes him grimace even when he shoots free throws.

Two friends of Jarmaine's walk down the sidewalk toward him, their hightops slung over their shoulders. Jarmaine gives them each a chest bump. They know his game, the way he used to streak down the court and rain jumpers from everywhere. He watches the friends disappear around the corner for a pickup game and shakes his head. Without basketball, he's lost.

"I miss breathing hard," he says later, sitting on a bench outside the Colonel Charles Young Playground on West 145th Street. Teenagers throw trick passes on the court, but Jarmaine keeps his back to them. It's easier not to watch. "You can lose every game, but just knowing you're out there playing, . . ." he says. "Basketball kept me on the right path."

No one came closer to dying that night on the turnpike than Danny Reyes. Physical therapy has helped him, and he has a job as an editorial assistant at *Essence* magazine, but his sister, Ana Thoericht, says he'll never be the same. "He knows he can't play professional basketball," she says, "and that hurts him deep inside."

Danny's right arm was shattered by bullets, but it was saved from amputation by metal plates and a skin graft from his right thigh, which has left the arm grotesquely discolored and scarred. It took Danny months to regain enough strength to hold a paper cup. As if the physical pain weren't enough, his insurance company added insult by refusing to pay his medical bills on grounds that he had been injured "while committing a felony, or seeking to avoid lawful apprehension or arrest." The payments finally began after Danny's lawyers threatened to sue the company.

On a court in Central Park the game is rough; passes clang off the fences, and there are more air balls than swishes. Teammates yell at each other for dribbling too much and giving up offensive rebounds. A shot goes up from the foul line, and the shortest player on the court rises above all the bodies to try to stuff the rebound. Rayshawn Brown, with his right wrist — the one that suffered severe nerve damage from a gunshot — bandaged to prevent it from bending too far, leaps high, extends his left hand, and slams the ball against the back rim, missing the dunk but drawing *oohs* from the spectators.

He's had to learn how to shoot and write with his left hand while rehabilitating his right. He can't spread the fingers on his right hand wide or bend the wrist to follow through on his jump shots. Twice a week he goes for physical therapy.

For months after the shooting Rayshawn would venture outside only with his mother. Seeing a cop stung. "He's not as carefree as he used to be," his mother says. "He's not as trusting of anybody." But he is playing again, on scholarship at Bloomfield (New Jersey) College, a Division II school about thirty minutes west of Manhattan. For Rayshawn, the dream is still alive.

"My goal is the CBA or USBL," he says, sitting on a bench near his dormitory on another steamy afternoon. He's studying Internet technologies. "You can't let obstacles stand in your way," he says, "or you'll never fulfill your dream."

Keshon Moore could play basketball if he wanted to. He wasn't wounded in the shooting, but his passion for the game is gone. He lives in West New York, New Jersey, with his fiancée, Mimi Pimentel, who gave birth to a girl named Mykaela last month. Until recently Keshon worked in a liquor store in Irvington, New Jersey. He's helping Mimi at home now and looking for a new job, struggling to find direction. He talks about coaching but has no plans for it. He talks about getting his degree but hasn't enrolled anywhere. "It's important to me," he says about finishing his education. "I almost died trying to get it."

"He's so terribly guilt-ridden that he wasn't shot," says Keshon's attorney, Linda Kenney. "He feels that since the police officers were trying to kill him, he should have taken all the bullets for everybody."

He feels responsible for starting the trip and for ending it. "I brought them together," Keshon says. "I was the driver. It was rented for me. I was controlling the vehicle. I told the police it was a mistake. They said, 'You tried to run us over.'"

As for the troopers, they await trial on the criminal charges, to be followed by trial of the civil suits. Kenna, who is married with a two-year-old son at home, is the son of a state police captain. Raised in an Irish-Catholic family, he studied graphic design in college and had no intention of following in his father's footsteps. But for the sake of job stability, he did. His lawyer says that regardless of the outcome of the trials, Kenna is through with police work.

Not Hogan. The son of a warehouse worker and homemaker

who raised five children, he played football and basketball in high school and graduated with the single purpose of becoming a New Jersey state trooper. He succeeded in 1993, the year before Kenna. Hogan will not discuss the shooting, but asked if he's sorry for what happened, he swallows and seems to fight back tears. "This is about my reputation, my life," he says. "It's not about being a trooper anymore." Then he pauses and admits he can't imagine life without his badge. "Law enforcement is the one direction I knew I wanted to go."

His victims wanted only to go further as basketball players, and with the exception of Rayshawn, they struggle with the loss of this purpose. Gannon, who coached Danny Reyes at Curtis High, keeps a deflated ball on his desk to remind his players of life after basketball. "We try to tell them to not let [playing hoops] be the high point of their lives," he says. Too often, he acknowledges, it is.

Reflecting on the shooting, Jarmaine Grant says, "I try to live my life as if it never happened, but then I see my friends playing ball, and I know I can't play, and it hits me. We went on this trip with high hopes and high dreams. You go to sleep in paradise and wake up in hell."

BUCKY McMAHON

Everest at the Bottom of the Sea

FROM ESQUIRE

Take a plunge? No thanks — B.C.

Arrival

YOU TOSS in your seaman's bunk and dream the oldest, oddest beachcomber's dream: Something has siphoned away all the waters of the seas, and you're taking a cold, damp hike down into the world's empty pool. Beer cans, busted pipes, concrete blocks, grocery carts, a Cadillac on its back, all four tires missing — every object casts a long, stark shadow on the puddled sand. With the Manhattan skyline and the Statue of Liberty behind you, you trek due east into the sunrise, following the toxic trough of the Hudson River's outflow — known to divers in these parts as "the Mudhole" — until you arrive, some miles out, at "Wreck Valley."

You see whole fishing fleets asleep on their sides and about a million lobsters crawling around like giant cockroaches, waving confounded antennae in the thin air. Yeah, what a dump of history you see, a real Coney Island of catastrophes. The greatest human migration in the history of the world passed through here, first in a trickle of dauntless hard-asses, and then in that famous flood of huddled masses, Western man's main manifest destiny arcing across the northern ocean. The whole story is written in the ruins: in worm-ridden middens, mere stinking piles of mud; in tall ships chewed to fish-bone skeletons; five-hundred-foot steel-plated cruisers plunked down onto their guns; the battered cigar tubes of German U-boats; and sleek yachts scuttled alongside sunken tubs as humble as old boots.

You can't stop to poke around or fill your pockets with souvenirs. You're on a journey to the continent's edge, where perhaps the missing water still pours into the Atlantic abyss with the tremendous roar of a thousand Niagaras. Something waits there that might explain, and that must justify, your presence in this absence, this scooped-out plain where no living soul belongs. And you know, with a sudden chill, that only your belief in the dream, the focus of your mind and your will on the possibility of the impossible, holds back the annihilating weight of the water.

You wake up in the dark and for a moment don't know where you are, until you hear the thrum of the diesel and feel the beam roll. Then you realize that what awakened you was the abrupt decrease of noise, the engine throttling down, and the boat and the bunk you lie in subsiding into the swell, and you remember that you are on the open sea, drawing near to the wreck of the *Andrea Doria*. You feel the boat lean into a turn, cruise a little ways, and then turn again, and you surmise that up in the pilothouse, Captain Dan Crowell has begun to "mow the lawn," steering the sixty-foot exploration vessel the *Seeker* back and forth, taking her through a series of slow passes, sniffing for the *Doria*.

Crowell, whom you met last night when you hauled your gear aboard, is a big, rugged-looking guy, about 6′2″ in boat shoes, with sandy brown hair and a brush mustache. Only his large, slightly hooded eyes put a different spin on his otherwise gruff appearance; when he blinks into the green light of the sonar screen, he resembles a thoughtful sentinel owl. Another light glows in the wheelhouse: a personal computer, integral to the kind of technical diving Crowell loves.

The *Seeker*'s crew of five divvies up hour-and-a-half watches for the ten-hour trip from Montauk, Long Island, but Crowell will have been up all night in a state of tense vigilance. A veteran of fifty *Doria* trips, Crowell considers the hundred-mile cruise — both coming and going — to be the most dangerous part of the charter, beset by imminent peril of fog and storm and heavy shipping traffic. It's not for nothing that mariners call this patch of ocean where the *Andrea Doria* collided with another ocean liner the "Times Square of the Atlantic."

You feel the *Seeker*'s engine back down with a growl and can guess what Crowell is seeing now on the forward-looking sonar screen: a spattering of pixels, like the magnetic shavings on one of those draw-the-beard slates, coalescing into partial snapshots of the seven-hundred-foot liner. What the sonar renders is but a pallid gray portrait of the outsized hulk, which, if it stood up on its stern on the bottom, 250 feet below, would tower nearly fifty stories above the *Seeker,* dripping and roaring like Godzilla. Most likely you're directly above her now, a proximity you feel in the pit of your stomach. As much as the physical wreck itself, it's the *Doria* legend you feel leaking upward through the *Seeker*'s hull like some kind of radiation.

"The Mount Everest of scuba diving," people call the wreck, in another useful catchphrase. Its badass rep is unique in the sport. Tell a fellow diver you've done the Great Barrier Reef or the Red Sea, they think you've got money. Tell 'em you've done the *Doria,* they know you've got balls. Remote enough to expose you to maritime horrors — the *Seeker* took a twenty-five-foot wave over its bow on a return trip last summer — the *Doria*'s proximity to the New York and New Jersey coasts has been a constant provocation for two generations. The epitome, in its day, of transatlantic style and a luxurious symbol of Italy's post–World War II recovery, the *Andrea Doria* has remained mostly intact and is still full of treasure: jewelry, art, an experimental automobile, bottles of wine — plus mementos of a bygone age, like brass shuffleboard numbers and silver and china place settings, not so much priceless in themselves but much coveted for the challenge of retrieving them.

But tempting as it is to the average wreck diver, nobody approaches the *Doria* casually. The minimum depth of a *Doria* dive is 180 feet, to the port-side hull, well below the 130-foot limit of recreational diving. Several years of dedicated deep diving is considered a sane apprenticeship for those who make the attempt — that, plus a single-minded focus that subsumes social lives and drains bank accounts. Ten thousand dollars is about the minimum ante for the gear and the training and the dives you need to get under your belt. And that just gets you to the hull and hopefully back. For those who wish to penetrate the crumbling, mazelike interior, the most important quality is confidence bordering on hubris: trust in a lucid assessment of your own limitations and belief in your decision-making abilities, despite the knowledge that divers of equal if not superior skill have possessed those same beliefs and still perished.

Propped up on your elbows, you look out the salon windows and see the running lights of another boat maneuvering above the *Doria*. It's the *Wahoo,* owned by Steve Bielenda and a legend in its own right for its 1992 salvage of the seven-hundred-pound ceramic Gambone Panels, one of the *Doria*'s lost art masterpieces. Between Bielenda, a sixty-four-year-old native of Brooklyn, and Crowell, a transplanted southern Californian who's twenty years younger and has gradually assumed the lion's share of the *Doria* charter business, you have the old King of the Deep and the heir apparent. And there's no love lost between the generations.

"If these guys spent as much time getting proficient as they do avoiding things, they'd actually be pretty good" is Crowell's back-handed compliment to the whole "Yo, Vinny!" attitude of the New York–New Jersey old school of gorilla divers. Bielenda, for his part, has been more pointed in his comments on the tragedies of the 1998 and 1999 summer charter seasons, in which five divers died on the *Doria*, all from aboard the *Seeker.* "If it takes five deaths to make you the number-one *Doria* boat," Bielenda says, "then I'm happy being number two." He also takes exception to the *Seeker*'s volume of business — ten charters in one eight-week season. "There aren't enough truly qualified divers in the world to fill that many trips," Bielenda says.

To which Crowell's best response might be his piratical growl, *"Arrgh!"* which sums up his exasperation with the fractious politics of diving in the Northeast. He says he's rejected divers who've turned right around and booked a charter on the *Wahoo*. But, hell, that's none of his business. His business is making the *Seeker*'s criteria for screening divers the most coherent in the business, which Crowell believes he has. Everyone diving the *Doria* from the *Seeker* has to be Tri-mix certified, a kind of doctoral degree of dive training that implies you know a good deal about physiology, decompression, and the effects of helium and oxygen and nitrogen on those first two. That, or be enrolled in a Tri-mix course and be accompanied by an instructor, since, logically, where else are you gonna learn to dive a deep wreck except on a deep wreck?

As for the fatalities of the last two summer seasons — "five deaths in thirteen months" is the phrase that has been hammered into his mind — Crowell has been forthcoming with reporters looking for a smoking gun onboard the *Seeker* and with fellow divers concerned about mistakes they might avoid. "If you look at the fatalities individually, you'll see that they were coincidental more than anything else," Crowell has concluded. In a good season, during the fair-weather months from June to late August, the *Seeker* will put about two hundred divers on the *Doria.*

Nobody is more familiar with the cruel Darwinian exercise of hauling a body home from the *Doria* than Crowell himself, who has wept and cursed and finally moved on to the kind of gallows humor you need to cope. He'll tell you about his dismay at finding himself on a first-name basis with the paramedics that met the *Seeker* in Montauk after each of the five fatalities — how they tried to heft one body still in full gear, until Crowell reached down and un-hooked the chest harness, lightening the load by a couple hundred pounds. Another they tried to fit into a body bag with the fins still on his feet.

But beyond their sobering effect on those who've made the aw-ful ten-hour trip home with the dead, the accidents have not been spectacularly instructive. Christopher Murley, forty-four, from Cin-cinnati, had an outright medical accident, a heart attack on the surface. Vince Napoliello, a thirty-one-year-old bond salesman from Baltimore and a friend of Crowell's, "just a good, solid diver," was a physiological tragedy waiting to happen; his autopsy revealed a 90 percent obstructed coronary artery. Charlie McGurr? Another heart attack. And Richard Roost? A mature, skilled diver plain shit-out-of-luck, whose only mistake seems to have been a failure to re-main conscious at depth, which is never guaranteed. Only the death of Craig Sicola, a New Jersey house builder, might fit the crit-icism leveled at the *Seeker* in Internet chat rooms and God knows where else — that a supercompetitive atmosphere, and a sort of taunting elitism projected by the *Seeker*'s captain and his regular crew, fueled the fatalities of the last two seasons.

Did Sicola, soloing on his second trip, overreach his abilities? Maybe so, but exploring the wreck, and yourself in the process, is the point of the trip.

"You might be paying your money and buying your ticket just like at Disney World, but everybody also knows this is a real expedition," says Crowell. "You've got roaring currents, low visibility, often horrible weather, and you're ten hours from help. We're pushing the limits out here."

All this you know because, like most of the guys on the charter, you're sort of a *Doria* buff. . . . Well, maybe a bit of a nut. You wouldn't be out here if you weren't. A lot of the back story you know by heart. How on the night of July 25, 1956, the *Andrea Doria* (after the sixteenth-century Genoese admiral), 29,083 tons of *la dolce vita,* festively inbound for New York Harbor, steamed out of an opaque fogbank at a near top speed of twenty-three knots and beheld the smaller, outbound Swedish liner *Stockholm* making straight for her. The ships had tracked each other on radar but lined up head-on at the last minute. The *Stockholm*'s bow, reinforced for ice-breaking in the North Sea, plunged thirty feet into the *Doria*'s starboard side, ripping open a six-story gash. One *Doria* passenger, Linda Morgan, who became known as the miracle girl, flew from her bed in her nightgown and landed on the forward deck of the *Stockholm,* where she survived. Her sister, asleep in the bunk below, was crushed instantly. In all, fifty-one people died.

Eleven hours after the collision, the *Andrea Doria* went down under a froth of debris, settling onto the bottom on her wounded starboard side in 250 feet of cold, absinthe-green seawater. The very next day, Peter Gimbel, the department-store heir (he hated like hell to be called that) and underwater filmmaker, and his partner, Joseph Fox, made the first scuba dive to the wreck, using primitive double-hosed regulators. The wreck they visited was then considerably shallower (the boat has since collapsed somewhat internally and hunkered down into the pit the current is gouging) and uncannily pristine; curtains billowed through portholes, packed suitcases knocked around in tipped-over staterooms, and shoes floated in ether. That haunted-house view obsessed Gimbel, who returned, most famously, for a monthlong siege in 1981. Employing a diving bell and saturation-diving techniques, Gimbel and crew blowtorched through the first-class loading-area doors, creating "Gimbel's Hole," a garage-door-sized aperture amidships, still the preferred entry into the wreck, and eventually raised the Bank of Rome safe. When Gimbel finished editing his film, *The Mystery of the Andrea Doria,* in an event worthy of Geraldo, the safe was opened on live TV. Stacks of waterlogged cash were revealed, though much less than the hoped-for millions.

In retrospect, the "mystery" and the safe seem to have been invented after the fact to justify the diving. Gimbel was seeking something else. He had lost his twin brother to illness some years before, an experience that completely changed his life and made of him an explorer. He got lost in jungles, filmed great white sharks from the water. And it was while tethered by an umbilicus to a decosphere the divers called Mother, hacking through shattered walls and hauling out slimed stanchions in wretchedly constrained space and inches of visibility, always cold, that Gimbel believed he encountered and narrowly escaped a "malevolent spirit," a spirit he came to believe inhabited the *Doria*.

But while Gimbel sought absolute mysteries in a strongbox, salvagers picked up other prizes — the *Andrea Doria*'s complement of fine art, such as the Renaissance-style, life-sized bronze statue of Admiral Doria, which divers hacksawed off at the ankles. The wreckage of the first-class gift shop has yielded trinkets of a craftsmanship that no longer exists today — like Steve Bielenda's favorite *Doria* artifact, a silver tea fob in the form of a locomotive with its leather thong still intact. A handful of Northeastern deep divers who knew one another on a first-name basis (when they were on speaking terms, that is) spread the word that it was actually fun to go down in the dark. And by degrees, diving the *Doria* and its two-hundred-foot-plus interior depths segued from a business risk to a risky adventure sport. In the late eighties and early nineties, there was a technical-diving boom, marked by a proliferation of training agencies and a steady refinement of gear. Tanks got bigger, and mixed gases replaced regular compressed air as a "safer" means of diving at extreme depths.

Every winter, the North Atlantic storms give the wreck a rough shake, and new prizes tumble out, just waiting for the summer charters. The *Seeker* has been booked for up to three years in advance, its popularity founded on its reputation for bringing back artifacts. The most sought-after treasure is the seemingly inexhaustible china from the elaborate table settings for 1,706 passengers and crew. First-class china, with its distinctive maroon-and-gold bands, has the most juju, in the thoroughly codified scheme of things. It's a strange fetish, certainly, for guys who wouldn't ordi-

narily give a shit about the quality of a teacup and saucer. Bielenda
and Crowell and their cronies have so much of the stuff that their
homes look as if they were decorated by maiden aunts.

Yet you wouldn't mind a plate of your own and all that it would
stand for. You can see it in your mind's eye — your plate and the
getting of it — just as you saw it last night on the cruise out, when
someone popped one of Crowell's underwater videos into the
VCR. The thirty-minute film, professionally done from opening
theme to credits, ended beautifully with the *Seeker*'s divers fresh
from their triumphs, still blushing in their dry suits like lobsters
parboiled in adrenaline, holding up Doria china while Vivaldi
plays. A vicarious victory whose emotions were overshadowed,
you're sorry to say, by the scenes inside the *Doria,* and specifically
by the shots of *Doria* china, gleaming bone-white in the black mud
on the bottom of some busted metal closet who knew how far in or
down how many blind passageways. Crowell had tracked it down
with his camera and put a beam on it: fine Genoa china, stamped
ITALIA, with a little blue crown. The merit badge of big-boy diving,
the artifact that says it best: I fuckin' did it — I dove da *Doria!* Your
hand reaches out . . .

The cabin door opens and someone comes into the salon, just
in time to cool your china fever. It's Crowell's partner Jenn Samulski, who keeps the divers' records and cooks three squares a day.
Samulski, an attractive blond from Staten Island who has been
down to the *Doria* herself, starts the coffee brewing, and eyes pop
open, legs swing out over the sides of the bunks, and the boat wakes
up to sunrise on the open sea, light glinting off the steely surface
and the metal rows of about sixty scuba tanks weighing down the
stern.

On a twelve-diver charter, personalities range from obnoxiously
extroverted to fanatically secretive — every type of type A, each
man a monster of his own methodology. But talk is easy when you
have something humongous in common, and stories are the coin
of the lifestyle. You know so-and-so? someone says around a mouth-
ful of muffin. Wasn't he on that dive back in '95? And at once,
you're swept away by a narrative, this one taking you to the wreck of
the *Lusitania,* where an American, or a Brit maybe — somebody's
acquaintance, somebody's friend — is diving with an Irish team.

He gets entangled, this diver does, in his own exploration line, on the hull down at 280 feet. His line is just pooling all around him and he's thrashing, panicking, thinking — as everybody always does in a panic — that he has to get to the surface, like *right now.* So he inflates his buoyancy compensator to the max, and now he's like a balloon tied to all that tangled line, which the lift of the b.c. is pulling taut. He's got his knife out, and he's hacking away at the line. One of the Irish divers sees what's happening and swims over and grabs the guy around the legs just as the last line is cut. They both go rocketing for the surface, this diver and his pumped-up b.c. and the Irishman holding on to him by the knees. At 160 feet, the Irishman figures, Sorry, mate, I ain't dying with you, and has to let him go. So the diver flies up to the top and bursts internally from the violent change of depth and the pressurized gas, which makes a ruin of him.

Yeah, he should never have been diving with a line, someone points out, and a Florida cave diver and a guy from Jersey rehash the old debate — using a line for exploration, the cave diver's practice, versus progressive penetration, visual memorization of the wreck and the ways out.

Meanwhile, a couple of the *Seeker*'s crew members have already been down to the wreck to set the hook. The rubber chase boat goes over the bow, emergency oxygen hoses are lowered off the port-side rail, and Crowell tosses out a leftover pancake to check the current. It slaps the dead-calm surface, spreading ripples, portals widening as it drifts aft. Because the *Doria* lies close to the downfall zone, where dense cold water pours over the continental shelf and down into the Atlantic Trench, the tidal currents can be horrendously strong. Sometimes a boat anchored to the *Doria* will carve a wake as if it were under way, making five knots and getting nowhere. An Olympic swimmer in a Speedo couldn't keep up with that treadmill, much less a diver in heavy gear. And sometimes the current is so strong, it'll snap a three-quarter-inch anchor line like rotten twine. But on this sunny July morning, already bright and heating up fast, Crowell blinks beneath the bill of his cap at the bobbing pancake and calculates the current at just a couple of knots — not too bad at all, if you're ready for it.

Crowell grins at the divers now crowded around him at the stern. "Pool's open," he says.

The Dive

You can never get used to the weight. When you wrestle your arms into the harness of a set of doubles, two 120-cubic-foot-capacity steel tanks yoked together on metal plates, you feel like an ant, one of those leaf-cutter types compelled to heft a preposterous load. What you've put on is essentially a wearable submarine with its crushed neoprene dry-suit shell and its steel external lungs and glass-enclosed command center. Including a pony-sized emergency bottle bungee-strapped between the steel doubles and two decompression tanks clipped to your waist, you carry five tanks of gas and five regulators. You can barely touch your mittened hands together in front of you around all the survival gear, the lift bags, lights, reels, hoses, and instrument consoles. And yet, for all its awkwardness on deck, a deep-diving rig is an amazing piece of technology, and if you don't love it at least a little you had better never put it on. It's one thing you suppose you all have in common on this charter — stockbrokers, construction workers, high school teachers, cops — you're all Buck Rogers flying a personal ship through inner space.

The immediate downside is that you're slightly nauseated from reading your gauges in a four-foot swell, and inside your dry suit, in expedition-weight socks and polypropylene long johns, you're sweating bullets. The way the mind works, you're thinking, To hell with this bobbing world of sunshine and gravity — you can't wait to get wet and weightless. You strain up from the gearing platform hefting nearly two hundred pounds and duckwalk a couple of steps to the rail, your fins smacking the deck and treading on the fins of your buddies who are still gearing up.

Some of the experienced *Doria* divers from Crowell's crew grasp sawed-off garden rakes with duct-taped handles, tools they'll use to reach through rubble and haul in china from a known cache. Crowell gestures among them, offering directions through the *Doria*'s interior maze. Your goal is just to touch the hull, peer into Gimbel's Hole. An orientation dive. You balance on the rail like old Humpty-Dumpty and crane your neck to see if all's clear on the indigo surface. Scuba lesson number one: Most accidents occur on the surface. There was a diver last summer, a seasoned tech diver, painstaking by reputation, on his way to a wreck off the North Carolina coast. Checked out his gear en route — gas on, take a breath, good, gas off — strapped it on at the site, went over the side, and sank like a dirt dart. His buddies spent all morning looking for him everywhere except right under their boat, where he lay, drowned. He had never turned back on his breathing gas.

And there was a diver on the *Seeker* who went over the side and then lay sprawled on his back in the water, screaming, "Help! Help!" The fuck was the matter with the guy? Turns out he'd never been in a dry suit before and couldn't turn himself over. Crowell wheeled on the guy's instructor. "You brought him out here to make his first dry-suit dive on the *Doria?* Are ya *crazy?*" Then the instructor took an underwater scooter down with him, and he had to be rescued with the chase boat. *Arrgh!* Crowell laments that there are divers going from Open Water, the basic scuba course, to Trimix in just fifty dives; they're book-smart and experience-starved. And there are bad instructors and mad instructors, egomaniacal, gurulike instructors.

"You will dive only with me," Crowell says, parodying the Svengalis. "Or else it's a thousand bucks for the cape with the clouds and the stars on it. Five hundred more and I'll throw in the wand."

"Just because you're certified don't make you qualified" is Steve Bielenda's motto, and it's the one thing the two captains can agree on.

You take a couple of breaths from each of your regs. Click your lights on and off. You press the inflator button and puff a little more gas into your buoyancy compensator, the flotation wings that surround your double 120s, and experience a tightening and a swelling up such as the Incredible Hulk must feel just before his buttons burst. Ready as you'll ever be, you plug your primary reg into your mouth and tip the world over . . . and hit the water with a concussive smack. At once, as you pop back up to the surface, before the bubbles cease seething between you and the image of the *Seeker*'s white wooden hull, rocking half in and half out of the water, you're in conflict with the current. You grab the floating granny line and it goes taut and the current dumps buckets of water between your arms and starts to rooster-tail around your tanks. This is two knots? You're breathing hard by the time you haul yourself hand over hand to the anchor line, and that's not good. Breath control is as important to deep divers as it is to yogis. At two hundred feet, just getting really excited could knock you out like a blow from a ball-peen hammer. As in kill you dead. So you float a moment at the surface, sighting down the parabola of the anchor line to the point where it vanishes into a brownish-blue gloom. Then you reach up to your inflator hose and press the other button, the one that splutters out gas from the b.c., and feel the big steel 120s reassert their mass, and calmly, feet first, letting the anchor line slide through your mitts, you start to sink.

For the thin air of Everest, which causes exhaustion universally and pulmonary and cerebral events (mountain sickness) seemingly randomly, consider the "thick" air you must breathe at 180 feet, the minimum depth of a dive to the *Doria*. Since water weighs sixty-four pounds per cubic foot (and is eight hundred times as dense as air), every foot of depth adds significantly to the weight of the water column above you. You feel this weight as pressure in your ears and sinuses almost as soon as you submerge. Water pressure doesn't affect the gas locked in your noncompressible tanks, of course, until you breathe it. Then, breath by breath, thanks to the genius of the scuba regulator — Jacques Cousteau's great invention — the gas becomes ambient to the weight of the water pressing on your lungs. That's why breathing out of steel 120s pumped to a pressure of 7,000 pounds per square inch isn't like drinking out of a fire hose, and also why you can kick around a shallow reef at twenty feet for an hour and a half, while at a hundred feet you'd suck the same tank dry in twenty minutes; you're inhaling many times more molecules per breath.

Unfortunately, it's not all the same to your body how many molecules of this gas or the other you suck into it. On the summit of Everest, too few molecules of oxygen makes you lightheaded, stupid, and eventually dead. On the decks of the *Doria*, too many molecules of oxygen can cause a kind of electrical fire in your central nervous system. You lose consciousness, thrash about galvanically, and inevitably spit out your regulator and drown. A depth of 216 feet is generally accepted as the point at which the oxygen in compressed air (which is 21 percent oxygen, 79 percent nitrogen) becomes toxic and will sooner or later (according to factors as infinitely variable as individual bodies) kill you. As for nitrogen, it has two dirty tricks it can play at high doses. It gets you high — just like the nitrous oxide that idiot adolescents huff and the dentist dispenses to distract you from a root canal — starting at about 130 feet for most people. "I am personally quite receptive to nitrogen rapture," Cousteau writes in *The Silent World.* "I like it and fear it like doom."

The fearsome thing is that, like any drunk, you're subject to mood swings, from happy to sad to hysterical and panicky when you confront the dumb thing you've just done, like getting lost inside a sunken ocean liner. The other bad thing nitrogen does is deny you permission to return immediately to the surface, every panicking person's solution to the trouble he's in. It's the excess molecules of nitrogen lurking in your body in the form of tiny bubbles that force you to creep back up to the surface at precise intervals determined by time and depth. On a typical *Doria* dive, you'll spend twenty-five minutes at around 200 feet and decompress for sixty-five minutes at several stopping points, beginning at 110 feet. While you are hanging on to the anchor line, you're off-gassing nitrogen at a rate the body can tolerate. Violate deco and you are subject to symptoms ranging from a slight rash to severe pain to quadriplegia and death. The body copes poorly with big bubbles of nitrogen trying to fizz out through your capillaries and bulling through your spinal column, traumatizing nerves.

Enter Tri-mix, which simply replaces some of the oxygen and nitrogen in the air with helium, giving you a life-sustaining gas with fewer molecules of those troublesome components of air. With Tri-mix, you can go deeper and stay longer and feel less narced. Still, even breathing Tri-mix at depth can be a high-wire act, owing to a third and final bad agent: carbon dioxide. The natural by-product of respiration also triggers the body's automatic desire to replenish oxygen. When you hyperventilate — take rapid, shallow breaths — you deprive yourself of CO_2 and fool the body into believing it doesn't need new oxygen. Breath-hold divers will hyperventilate before going down as a way to gain an extra minute or two of painless O_2 deprivation. But at depth (for reasons poorly understood), hypercapnia, the retention of CO_2 molecules, has the same "fool the brain" effect. It's a tasteless, odorless, warningless fast track to unconsciousness. One moment you are huffing and puffing against the current, and the next you are swimming in the stream of eternity.

Richard Roost, a forty-six-year-old scuba instructor from Ann Arbor, Michigan, one of the five *Doria* fatalities of the last two seasons, was highly skilled and physically fit. His body was recovered from the *Doria*'s first-class lounge, a large room full of shattered furniture deep in the wreck. It's a scary place, by all accounts, but Roost seemed to be floating in a state of perfect repose. Though he had sucked all the gas from his tanks, there was no sign that he had panicked. Crowell suspects that he simply "took a nap," a likely victim of hypercapnia.

So it is that you strive to sink with utter calm, dumping a bit of gas into your dry suit as you feel it begin to vacuum-seal itself to you, bumping a little gas into the b.c. to slow your rate of descent, seeking neutrality, not just in buoyancy but in spirit as well. Soon you've sunk to that zone where you can see neither surface nor bottom. It's an entrancing, mystical place — pure inner space. Things appear out of nowhere — huge, quick things that aren't there, blocks of blankness, hallucinations of blindness. Drifting, drifting . . . reminds you of something Steve Bielenda told you: "The hard part is making your brain believe this is happening. But, hey, you know what? It really is happening!" You focus on the current-borne minutiae — sea snow, whale food, egg-drop soup — which whizzes by outside the glass of your mask like a sepia-colored silent movie of some poor sod sinking through a blizzard.

Your depth gauge reads 160 feet, and you hit the thermocline, the ocean's deep icebox layer. The water temp plunges to 45 degrees and immediately numbs your cheeks and lips. Your dry suit is compressed paper-thin; you don't know how long you can take the cold, and then something makes you forget about it completely: the *Doria,* the great dome of her hull falling away into obscurity, and the desolate rails vanishing in both directions, and a lifeboat davit waving a shred of trawler net like a hankie, and the toppled towers of her superstructure. And it's all true what they've said: You feel humbled and awed. You feel how thin your own audacity is before the gargantuan works of man. You land fins-first onto the steel plates, kicking up two little clouds of silt. Man on the moon.

You've studied the deck plans of the Grande Dame of the Sea — her intricacy and complexity and order rendered in fine architectural lines. But the *Doria* looks nothing like that now. Her great smokestack has tumbled down into the dark debris field on the seafloor. Her raked-back aluminum forecastle decks have melted like a Dali clock in the corrosive seawater. Her steel hull has begun to buckle under its own weight and the immense weight of water, pinching in and splintering the teak decking of the promenade, where you kick along, weaving in and out of shattered windows. Everything is moving: bands of water, now cloudy, now clear, through which a blue shark twists in and out of view; sea bass darting out to snatch at globs of matter stirred up by your fins. They swallow and spit and glower. Everywhere you shine your light inside, you see black dead ends and washed-out walls and waving white anemones like giant dandelions bowing in a breeze.

You rise up a few feet to take stock of your location and see that on her outer edges she is Queen of Snags, a harlot tarted up with torn nets, bristling with fishermen's monofilament and the anchor lines of dive boats that have had to cut and run from sudden storms. She's been grappled more times than Moby Dick, two generations of obsessed Ahabs finding in her sheer outrageous bulk the sinews of an inscrutable malice, a dragon to tilt against. In your solitude you sense the bleak bitch of something unspeakably larger still, something that shrinks the *Doria* down to the size of Steve Bielenda's toy-train tea fob: a hurricane of time blowing through the universe, devouring all things whole.

On the aft deck of the *Wahoo*, Steve Bielenda, a fireplug of a man, still sinewy in his early sixties, is kicked back in his metal folding-chair throne. He wears his white hair in a mullet cut and sports a gold earring. He was wild as a kid, by his own account, a wiseguy, wouldn't listen to nobody. The product of vocational schools, he learned auto mechanics and made a success of his own repair shop before he caught the scuba bug. Then he would go out with fishermen for a chance to dive — there weren't any dive boats then — and offered his services as a salvage diver, no job too small or too big. When he sold his shop and bought the *Wahoo*, it was the best and the biggest boat in the business. Now, as the morning heats up, he's watching the bubbles rise and growling out *Doria* stories in his Brooklyn accent.

"When you say Mount Everest to somebody," he says, "you're sayin' something. Same with da *Doria*. It was the pinnacle wreck. It was something just to go there."

And go there he did — more than a hundred times. The first time in '81, with a serious *Doria* fanatic, Bill Campbell, who had commissioned a bronze plaque to commemorate the twenty-fifth anniversary of the sinking; and often with maritime scholar and salvager John Moyer, who won salvage rights to the *Doria* in federal court and hired the *Wahoo* in '92 to put a "tag" on the wreck — a tube of PVC pipe, sealed watertight, holding the legal papers. Tanks were much smaller then, dinky steel 72s and aluminum 80s, compared with the now-state-of-the-art 120-cubic-foot-capacity tanks. "You got air, you got time," is how Bielenda puts it. And time was what they didn't have down at 180 feet on the hull. It was loot and scoot. Guys were just guessing at their decompression times, since the U.S. Navy Dive Tables expected that nobody would be stupid or desperate enough to make repetitive dives below 190 feet with scuba gear. "Extrapolating the tables" was what they called it; it was more like pick a lucky number and hope for the best. But Bielenda's quick to point out that in the first twenty-five years of diving the *Doria*, nobody died. Back then the players were all local amphibians, born and bred to cold-water diving and watermen to the nth degree. Swimming, water polo, skin diving, then scuba, then deep scuba — you learned to crawl before you walked in those days.

A thousand things you had to learn first. "You drive through a tollbooth at five miles an hour — no problem, right? Try it at fifty miles an hour. That hole gets real small! That's divin' da *Doria*. To dive da *Doria* it's gotta be like writin' a song," the captain says, and he hops up from his chair and breaks into an odd little dance, shimmying his 212 pounds in a surprisingly nimble groove, tapping himself here, here, here — places a diver in trouble might find succor in his gear.

"And you oughta wear yer mask strap under yer hood," he tells a diver who's gearing up. "There was this gal one time . . ." and Bielenda launches into the story about how he saved Sally Wahrmann's life with that lesson.

She was down in Gimbel's Hole, just inside it and heading for the gift shop, when this great big guy — John Ornsby was his name, one of the early *Doria* fatalities — comes flying down into the hole after her and just clobbers her. "He rips her mask off and goes roaring away in a panic," Bielenda says. "But see, she has her mask under her hood like I taught her, so she doesn't lose it. It's still right there around her neck."

The blow knocked Wahrmann nearly to the bottom of the wreck, where an obstruction finally stopped her fall seven sideways stories down. But she never panicked, and with her mask back on and cleared, she could find her way out toward the tiny speck of green light that was Gimbel's Hole, the way back to the world. "She climbs up onto the boat and gives me a big kiss. 'Steve,' she says, 'you just saved my life.'"

As for Ornsby, a Florida breath-hold diver of some renown, his banzai descent into Gimbel's Hole was never explained, but he was found dead not far from the entrance, all tangled up in cables as if a giant spider had been at him. It took four divers with cable cutters two dives each to cut the body free. Bielenda has been lost inside of wrecks and has found his way out by a hairbreadth. He and the *Wahoo* have been chased by hurricanes. One time he had divers down on the *Doria* when a blow came up. He was letting out anchor line as fast as he could, and the divers, who were into decompression, they were scrambling up the line hand over hand to hold their depth. The swells rose up to fifteen feet, and Bielenda could see the divers in the swells hanging on to the anchor line, ten feet underwater but looking down into the *Wahoo!* A *Doria* sleigh ride — that's the kind of memories the *Doria*'s given him. Strange sights indeed. He knows he's getting too old for the rigors of depth, but he's not ready to let go of the *Doria* yet, not while they still have their hooks in each other.

Up in the pilothouse of the *Seeker,* Dan Crowell is fitting his video camera into its watertight case, getting ready to go down and shoot some footage inside the wreck. He tries to make at least one dive every charter trip, and he never dives without his camera anymore if he can help it.

The more you learn about Crowell, the more impressed you are. He's a voracious autodidact who sucks up expertise like a sponge. He has worked as a commercial artist, a professional builder, a commercial diver, and a technical scuba instructor, as well as a charter captain. His passion now is shooting underwater video, making images of shipwrecks at extreme depths. His footage of the *Britannic* was shot at a whopping depth of 400 feet. When Crowell made his first *Doria* dive in 1990, a depth of 200 feet was still Mach I, a real psychological and physical barrier. He remembers kneeling in the silt inside Gimbel's Hole at 210 feet and scooping up china plates while he hummed the theme from *Indiana Jones*, "and time was that great big boulder coming at you."

In '91, Crowell didn't even own a computer, but that all changed with the advent of affordable software that allowed divers to enter any combination of gases and get back a theoretically safe deco schedule for any depth. "In a matter of months, we went from rubbing sticks together to flicking a Bic," Crowell says. It was the aggressive use of computers — and the willingness to push the limits — that separated the *Seeker* from the competition. When Bill Nagle, the boat's previous captain, died of his excesses in '93, Crowell came up with the cash to buy the *Seeker*. He'd made the money in the harsh world of hard-hat diving.

Picture Crowell in his impermeable commercial diver's suit, with its hose-fed air supply and screw-down lid, slowly submerging in black, freezing water at some hellish industrial waterfront wasteland. The metaphorical ball cock is stuck and somebody's gotta go down and unstick it. Hacksaw it, blast it, use a lift bag and chains — the fuck cares how he does it? Imagine him slogging through thigh-deep toxic sludge hefting a wrench the size of a dinosaur bone. His eyes are closed — can't see a damned thing down there anyway — and he's humming a tune to himself, working purely by touch, in three-fingered neoprene mitts. Think of him blind as a mole and you'll see why he loves the camera's eye so much, and you'll believe him when he says he's never been scared on the *Andrea Doria*.

"Well, maybe once," Crowell admits. "I was diving on air and I was pretty narced, and I knew it. I started looking around and realized I had no idea where I was." He was deep inside the blacked-out maze of the wreck's interior, where every breath dislodges blinding swirls of glittering rust and silt. "But it just lasted a few seconds. When you're in those places, you're seeing things in postage-stamp-sized pieces. You need to pull back and look at the bigger picture — which is about eight and a half by eleven inches." Crowell found his way out, reconstructing his dive, as it were, page by page.

You've always thought that the way water blurs vision is an apt symbol of a greater blurring, that of the mind in the world. Being matter, we are buried in matter — we are buried alive. This is an idea you first encountered intuitively in the stories of Edgar Allan Poe. Madman! Don't you see? cries Usher, before his eponymous house crashes down on top of him. And the nameless penitent in "The Pit and the Pendulum" first creeps blindly around the abyss, and then confronts the razor's edge of time. He might well be looking into Gimbel's Hole and at the digital readout on his console; he is literature's first extreme deep diver, immersed in existential fear of the impossible present moment. But the diver's mask is also a miraculous extra inch of perspective; it puts you at a certain remove from reality, even as you strike a Mephistophelian bargain with physics and the physical world.

You're twelve minutes into your planned twenty-five-minute bottom time when the current suddenly kicks up. It's as if God has thrown the switch — *ka-chung!* — on a conveyor belt miles wide and fathoms thick. You see loose sheets of metal on the hull sucking in and blowing out, just fluttering, as if the whole wreck were breathing. If you let go, you would be whisked away into open sea, a mote in a maelstrom. The current carries with it a brown band of bad visibility, extra cold, direly menacing. Something has begun to clang against the hull, tolling like a bell. Perhaps, topside, it has begun to blow. Keep your shit together. Control your breath. Don't fuck up. And don't dream that things might be otherwise, or it'll be the last dream you know. Otherwise? Shit . . . this is it. Do something. Act. Now! You're going to have to fight your way back to the anchor line, fight to hold on for the whole sixty-five minutes of your deco. And then fight to get back into the boat, with the steel ladder rising and plunging like a cudgel. What was moments ago a piece of cake has changed in a heartbeat to a life-or-death situation.

Then you see Dan Crowell, arrowing down into Gimbel's Hole with his video camera glued to his eyes. You watch the camera light dwindle down to 200 feet, 210, then he turns right and disappears inside the wreck. Do you follow him, knowing that it is precisely that — foolish emulation — that kills divers here? Consider the case of Craig Sicola, a talented, aggressive diver. On his charter in the summer of '98, he saw the crew of the *Seeker* bring up china, lots of it. He wanted china himself, and if he'd waited, he would've gotten it the easy way. Crowell offered to run a line to a known cache — no problem, china for everybody. But it wouldn't have been the

same. Maybe what he wanted had less to do with plates than with
status, status within an elite. He must've felt he'd worked his way up
to the top of his sport only tơ see the pinnacle recede again. So he
studied the Doria plans posted in the *Seeker*'s cabin and deduced
where china ought to be — his china — and jumped in alone to
get it. He came so close to pulling it off, too.

Dropping down into Gimbel's Hole, he found himself in the
first-class foyer, where well-dressed passengers once made small
talk and smoked as they waited to be called to dinner. He finessed
the narrow passageway that led to the first-class dining room, a
huge, curving space that spans the width of the *Doria*. He kicked
his way across that room, playing his light off lumber piles of shattered tables. Down another corridor leading farther back toward
the stern, he encountered a jumble of busted walls, which may
have been a kitchen — and he found his china. He loaded up his
goody bag, stirring up storms of silt as the plates came loose from
the muck. He checked his time and gas supply — hurry now, hurry
— and began his journey back. Only he must have missed the passage as he recrossed the dining room. Easy to do: Gain or lose a few
feet in depth and you hit blank wall. He would've sucked in a great
gulp of gas then — you do that when you're lost; your heart goes
wild. Maybe the exit is inches away at the edge of vision, or maybe
you've got yourself all turned around and have killed yourself, with
ten minutes to think about it.

Sicola managed to find his way out, but by then he must've been
running late on his deco schedule. With no time to return to the
anchor line, he unclipped his emergency ascent reel and tied a line
off to the wreck. Which was when he made mistake number two.
He either became entangled in the line, still too deep to stop, and
had to cut himself free, or else the line broke as he ascended. Either way, he rocketed to the surface too fast and died of an embo-
lism. Mercifully, though, right up to the last second, Sicola must
have believed he was taking correct and decisive action to save himself. Which, in fact, is exactly what he was doing.

But with a margin of error so slender, you have to wonder:
Where the hell does someone like Crowell get the sack to make
fifty turns inside that maze? How can he swim through curtains of
dangling cables, twisting through blown-out walls, choosing stair-
ways that are now passages, and taking passages that are now like el-

evator shafts, one after another, as relentlessly as one of the blue
sharks that school about the wreck? By progressive penetration, he
has gone only as far at a time as his memory has permitted. Only
now he holds in his mind a model of the ship — and he can rotate
that model in his mind and orient himself toward up, down, out.
He's been all the way through the *Doria* and out the other side,
through the gash that sank her, and brought back the images. This
is what it looks like; this is what you see.

But how does it feel? What's it like to know you are in a story that
you will either retell a hundred times or never tell? You decide to
drop down into the black hole. No, you don't decide; you just do it.
Why? You just do. A little ways, to explore the wreck and your courage, what you came down here to do. What is it like? Nothing under your fins now for eighty feet but the mass and complexity of
the machine on all sides — what was once luminous and magical
changed to dreary chaos. Drifting down past the cables that killed
John Ornsby, rusty steel lianas where a wall has collapsed. Dropping too fast now, you pump air into your b.c., kick up and bash
your tanks into a pipe, swing one arm and hit a cable, rust particles
raining down. You've never felt your attention so assaulted: It is
everything at once, from all directions, and from inside, too. You
grab the cable and hang, catching your breath — bubble and hiss,
bubble and hiss. Your light, a beam of dancing motes, plays down a
battered passageway, where metal steps on the left-hand wall lead
to a vertical landing, then disappear behind a low, sponge-en-
crusted wall that was once a ceiling. That's the way inside the *Doria*.

There is something familiar about that tunnel, something the
body knows. All your travels, your daily commutes, the Brownian
motion of your comings and goings in the world, straining after
desires, reaching for your beloved — they've all just been an approach to this one hard turn. You can feel it, the spine arching to
make the corner, a bow that shoots the arrow of time. In the final
terror, with your gauges ticking and your gas running low, as dead
end leads to dead end and the last corridor stretches out beyond
time, does the mind impose its own order, seizing the confusion of
busted pipes and jagged edges and forcing them into a logical grid,
which you can then follow down to the bottom of the wreck and
out — in a gust of light and love — through the wound in her side?
Where you find yourself standing up to your waist in water, in the

pit the current has gouged to be the grave of the *Andrea Doria*. Sea-gulls screech in the air as you take off your gear piece by piece and, much lightened, begin to walk back to New York across the sandy plane. And it comes as no surprise at all to look up and behold the *Seeker* flying above you, sailing on clouds. On the stern deck, the divers are celebrating, like rubber-suited angels, breaking out beers and cigars, and holding up plates to be redeemed by the sun.

CHARLES P. PIERCE

The Blessed Fisherman
of Prosper, Texas

FROM ESQUIRE

The angler of many angles — B.C.

AND SO IT CAME to pass that the land was redeemed.

And the land was called Prosper, and it was north of Dallas, and it was a place of desert and scrub weed and tall, thirsting flowers that did wave in the breathless air. And there was sin in the land. Jezebels and Delilahs all, they did come to Prosper to set up shop, for Prosper was unincorporated, and north of Dallas, and beyond the law. And the sinful did come to Prosper and did spill their seed in the various and lubricious chalices who did wink and wave and tempt the weak from the front porches and parlors.

But then there came upon the place the godly, the righteous, and the upper management, looking for homes from which they could journey back into the city with joy in their hearts, and with a minimum of fuss and bother, except on the weekends, when traffic was hellish. And the good land did come to be valued by them (at $50,000 an acre), and the sin was squeezed out of the place, and a town beloved by its people did grow in Prosper, and prosper they did. And so it came to pass that the land was redeemed, and a pilgrim did come here to build a great house by a fishpond:

"Two seconds," says Deion Sanders. "I give that fat one out there two seconds."

A little ways out from the shore, a big old F-16 of a grasshopper is floundering, trying to swim back to shore. There is a stirring in the water beneath him, then a swift flash of bass and the grasshopper is gone. We are walking his property, and Sanders is flushing out great clouds of grasshoppers toward the water. Some of them fall in and get eaten, thereby fattening the bass that Sanders plans to catch as soon as his house is finished, the great pile of a place that is rising even now at the top of the slope that begins at the far bank of the fishing hole. Scripture, of course, tells us that grasshoppers are plenty good eating; John the Baptist liked his with honey. The pond comes alive with hungry fish.

"You want to describe me?" Sanders asks. "Call me a fisherman. I'll always fish."

Since 1989, when he came out of Florida State as a rookie cornerback, a neophyte center fielder, and a full-blown celebrity, Deion Sanders has produced as eccentric a body of work as that produced by any athlete. Having signed this season to play for the Washington Redskins, Sanders is now on his fourth stop in the NFL, which means he has played for exactly as many professional football teams as he has professional baseball teams. He is the only man ever to play in the Super Bowl and in the World Series. He's the first two-way starter in the NFL since 1962. As he grew older, he left baseball behind, and he transformed himself into one of the great defensive backs in the history of the league, but he has remained a full-blown celebrity.

He conspired in creating his own image. He admits freely that he deliberately fabricated "Prime Time," his gold-encrusted *nom d'argent*, which had its official public debut in a *Sports Illustrated* profile that was practically written in blackface, to help himself get rich. His entire career has been an exercise in trying to control the personality that he created. If it weren't for Prime Time, maybe he wouldn't have been associated willy-nilly with the *I, Claudius* atmosphere surrounding the Dallas Cowboys, when, in fact, the worst trouble with the law that Deion Sanders had ever had was a glorified traffic wrangle with a stadium security guard in Cincinnati and a trespassing bust that occurred when Sanders was discovered on private land where he'd gone to . . . fish.

If not for Prime Time, then, maybe the divorce wouldn't have been so ugly, and maybe he wouldn't have been there in Cincinnati contemplating, he says, putting an end to all of it. And maybe it was Prime Time who drove Deion Sanders to Jesus and drove him then to a new life with a new wife and a new baby and a new team and a new house here in Prosper. Anything's possible. Life's strange, and that's what's kept Scripture interesting all these years.

"They never give athletes credit for knowing who they are," he says. "As an athlete, you're in business. And I knew how to market my business. The Lord intended me to be different. He intended everyone to be different. I never tried to emulate anyone, ever. I was the first Deion Sanders, and I'll be the last Deion Sanders.

"I created something that could command me millions of dollars, and it served its purpose. But I was playing a game, and people took it seriously." He took it so seriously, if you believe him now, that he needed to be rescued in one of the oldest ways of all.

He says he's Saved — capital-S Saved — from when he used to chase around and dance the hootchy-kootchy. In fact, he says they're both saved, Deion *and* Prime Time. Saved from the world. Saved from each other. Saved for a good woman and a baby and for his other two children, too. Saved now for the Redskins, for whom he'll lock up the best receivers in the league the way he did for the Falcons, Forty-Niners, and Cowboys. (Daniel Snyder, the Redskins' owner, has hurled money at veterans like Sanders and Bruce Smith in order to buy himself an instant Super Bowl.) Saved, says Deion, to go to Washington and play for the endless dollars of a profligate child.

This might be an act. Might just be the Prime Time shuck again, the gold covered up now in choir robes. (Sanders's spiritual guide, the charismatic preacher T. D. Jakes, is not long on vows of poverty.) But watch him walk his land, stirring up the grasshoppers, admiring the fish, and there is a peace, an ease, a kind of steady grace that might be theological and might not be.

"I'm blessed," says Deion Sanders. "God's blessed me well."

The steady hammering drifts down the hill through the heat of the afternoon, and isn't that the damnedest thing, too? The gospel turned on its head — a bunch of carpenters come out into the desert to work for a fisherman.

All right, so it got in the way. A $30,000 golf cart will do that to a fellow's image, especially when the golf cart has tinted windows, an ice machine, and a mist dispenser, and especially since the fellow who owns it doesn't play golf. If Deion Sanders got defined as a heedless spendthrift, it's only because he moved through most of his life a walking cloudburst of wealth, flashing gold and diamonds, his professional antecedents not Emlen Tunnell or Night Train Lane but Little Richard and the Reverend Ike.

"Just being a cornerback wasn't enough," he explains. "Being a cornerback wasn't looked on as being a *showstopper.* And you've got to understand, I sat in my dorm room at Florida State and created that whole thing in my imagination. I just created a persona with the nickname, but you had to back it up with substance, and I think that once the media got hold of [the fact] that it was all a game for me, they got upset and tried to take things too far.

"I mean, you don't think Eddie Murphy's *Eddie Murphy* at home. Do you think Jim Carrey acts like a darn fool all day? I don't think John Wayne sat around the house with a gun all day, and I don't think he shot the mailman when he came through the door."

He is a bigger man than he appears on television, all sinewy angles and not inconspicuous strength, a sprinter gone bigger. But the first thing that registers about Deion Sanders — besides the fact that at thirty-three he is still youthful and handsome — is that he is disconcertingly slow to speak. He is not bubbly or bright or glib. An interview is a conversation conducted in paragraphs. But by creating Prime Time and, more important, by *selling* Prime Time as effectively as he did, Sanders placed at the heart of his career an intractable personal dissonance.

He played the same way. That was the odd thing about it. The gold came off and the diamonds went into the locker, but the bandanna came on and Deion Sanders lit up the football field with his talent. People who saw only the high-stepping final yards of a touchdown return missed the controlled intelligence that got him there. "If you watch him," says Dave Campo, the former Cowboys defensive coordinator to whom Jerry Jones has handed the head-coaching job this season, "you will see this guy do things that nobody else can do. Nobody."

It is quite possible that Sanders is the best pass defender who has ever played the game. As fast as he is down the field, he is even faster at those five- and ten-yard sprints needed to close on the ball. His matchups with the Forty-Niners' Jerry Rice were breathless, electric things, the finest man-to-man confrontations the NFL had seen since Sam Huff rang hats with Jim Brown back in the dim times before Chris Berman. He is smart and he is canny. He will bait quarterbacks by laying off receivers just enough, then close the

distance like a swooping hawk. And if he doesn't hit hard enough
to suit the NFL's broken-nose lobby, he is still one of a very few players who can change a game all by himself. That he is also a brilliant
and enthusiastic returner of punts means that all doubts regarding
his courage are rendered moot because, if Sanders is reluctant to
hit, he is clearly willing to *be* hit on what is arguably the most dangerous play in the game.

And yet — and there always is an "and yet" to this guy — as tight
a rein as Sanders claims to have had on the Prime Time persona, it
became his public definition. Baseball, for example, never got it,
largely because baseball is the institutional equivalent of your Aunt
Gertrude, who collects both balls of string *and* Winslow Homers in
her attic because she never quite mastered the difference between
that which is classical and that which is simply old.

"One thing about baseball is that the guys who have played a
few years get to thinking they're the authority on this and that,"
Sanders explains. "They're quick to throw their years in your face.
Football isn't like that, because I don't care if you play ten, twelve
years, a rookie will come in and knock your head off and you're going to respect him, you know? That's why I didn't relate to that part
of baseball."

Baseball did not welcome Deion Sanders, whom it saw as a
speedy dilettante who did not respect Our Game the way that Our
Game respects itself. Baseball did not welcome Prime Time, whom
it saw as a space alien. Sanders didn't help himself, either. He got
into an on-field wrangle with Carlton Fisk, which is rather like arguing socialism with the heads on Mount Rushmore. Once, after
broadcaster Tim McCarver upbraided Sanders for playing a football game and a baseball game on the same day, Sanders responded
by dumping a bucket of ice water on McCarver's head. As promising a player as he was — in 1992, as an Atlanta Brave, Sanders hit
.533 in his only World Series — baseball was not a context within
which the subtle interplay between Deion and Prime Time would
ever work.

In fact, by 1996 it had become clear that Sanders was losing control of the balancing act that had been his entire public life. He
was a solid citizen by the standards of the Cowboys — which were
hardly rigid — but his life was coming apart. His marriage dis-
solved swiftly and in rancid fashion. (Once, in court, when asked
whether he'd committed adultery, Sanders replied, "Are you stat-

ing before the marriage of 1996 or after?" — which is pretty clearly not getting the point.) While he insists that it was the public that would not let his Prime Time persona go and that it was that ol' devil media that kept the public hungry, Sanders was clearly dependent upon it himself. If it was a fabrication, then it had become real — a doppelgänger that Sanders was not secure enough to shake.

Today, he says the pressure was enough to make him contemplate suicide — most seriously three years ago in Cincinnati. That he did not follow through with it, he says, is because he heard the Word. And maybe he has. Of course, maybe he's a heretic, too. Nobody — not even Carlton Fisk — ever called him that.

"If there's a heaven, there's got to be a hell, too," he says. "Think on that."

God, you've got to love sportswriting when it draws you into third-century theological disputes. Hey, Saint Athanasius, you da man!

Anyway, long about A.D. 200, a doctrine arose that held that the members of the Trinity were not three distinct personalities but only successive modes through which one God manifested himself. It became known as modalism and, later, Sabellianism, after Sabellius, an ancient Christian theologian who adopted the controversial doctrine as his own. Needless to say, this notion ran so contrary to the essential trinitarianism of Christianity — three persons *in* one God, and not one God acting through three successive agents — that all hell, you should pardon the expression, broke loose.

The Sabellians were given the gate from the early Christian church. The doctrine, however, was a stubborn one, persisting so durably into modern Pentecostalism that in 1916 it caused a split that divided the church into two distinct sects. It is now called the Oneness Doctrine, and it is the main problem that many modern Pentecostals say they have with Bishop T. D. Jakes, who, Deion says, brought him to the Word and the Word to him. Call him a modalist. Call him a Sabellian. Call him a heretic. Deion doesn't care.

"He's the only man I've ever called Daddy," says Sanders, who never really knew his biological father.

Since coming to Dallas from West Virginia in 1996, Jakes has built an empire out of his Potter's House church. His television show is one of the hottest on the television-preacher circuit, and his books sell in the millions. He drives a Mercedes and lives in a $1.7

million lakefront home next door to H. L. Hunt, and he is so wired
into the world of Texas celebrity that he is likely to become the Billy
Graham in a possible Bush Restoration. (Governor Dubya regularly uses Jakes in his outreach to minority communities.) Unlike
many of his more judgmental colleagues, Jakes has involved himself conspicuously in ministering to battered women and gay people. There is nothing of the Christian bluenose to him. He is very
much a man of this particular sinful world. Consider, for example,
his views on the theology of satin sheets, taken from his book *The
Lady, Her Love, and Her Lord:*

> You see, ladies, satin might be pretty, but it destroys all semblance of
> balance and leaves you grabbing for the bedpost and groping for hand-
> fuls of mattress just to turn around in the sack, much less try an acro-
> batic feat of passion.

And, well, amen.

Sanders came to Jakes with his first wife, Carolyn, as they tried to
rescue their marriage. Jakes was the perfect person to minister to
Sanders. From the start, Jakes saw the effort that Sanders was making to reconcile the person he was with the person he'd created. "I
found him to be, though outwardly a flamboyant person, inwardly
very sincere," Jakes says. "I was able to separate the character he
plays on the field and who he really is.

"One thing I've not found him to be is somebody who says things
he didn't mean. When he wasn't into it, he wasn't into it, and
everybody knew it. I have 50 percent of my church like that, and it's
wonderful, because they've learned not to be religiously fraudu-
lent."

It was Jakes who baptized Sanders in 1997 and Jakes who of-
ficiated when he and his new wife, Pilar Biggers, were married in
the Bahamas two years later. Somewhere in there, for whatever reason, Deion made his peace with his own creation and, possibly, with
everyone else's, too. After all, the Father's house has many rooms,
and there are some nice ones down here, too, but you still have to
live with yourself somewhere. If that's heresy, he's making the most
of it.

The Potter's House church is coming loose from the earth. The
Wednesday-night Bible study is shaking the place. A camera on a
crane swoops above the whole congregation like the Divine Eye as

Deion Sanders comes bouncing down the aisle toward where I'm sitting. "Thanks," he says, the gleam of righteous transport in his eye. "Thanks for coming."

It is a huge and theatrical place, rows of pews rising in arcs and layers away from the pulpit. Two huge screens hang from the ceiling; a video of the service will be projected on them, as will whatever Bible verses Bishop Jakes chooses this night for his lesson. Deion flows easily into the enthusiastic congregation, one of many and nobody in particular. The band — pushed by an organ and a gorgeous bass guitar — reaches a long and sustained peak before the introductory prayers. There is a moment of soft and palpable anticipation before Bishop Jakes rises to speak — a gathering of the drama. Deion, who has been swaying to the music, goes still and silent. Worship falls on the place all at once.

Jakes dives into the Gospel of John, and he's talking about how Jesus and the disciples went outside the camp to pray. "They said, 'We don't need your controversies and your factions and your de-nom-in-*na*-tions,'" he thunders. "And they went . . . *outside the camp.*"

"Preach, Daddy," says Deion. He's an enthusiastic celebrant, underlining his Scripture heavily and, when truly moved, waving his left arm in a huge flapping motion. They make the altar call, and a battalion of well-dressed deacons appears, each with a box of Kleenex in his hands, and people come down from all corners of the huge tabernacle. As the service winds up, we all join hands for the benediction, an old woman to my left, me, and Deion, and something feels as though it's cutting the side of my hand, and I look down, and I realize that it's the diamonds on his watch. At the end, he catches me in a sudden embrace.

"Welcome to my world," he says.

And it is a whisper.

STEPHEN RODRICK

Can Riddick Bowe
Answer the Bell?

FROM THE NEW YORK TIMES MAGAZINE

A championship lost and a lost soul — B.C.

RIDDICK (BIG DADDY) BOWE is pacing, as if he's warming up before a title fight. A few purposeful steps to the left, then an abrupt
turn as if he has reached the ropes. He is not, however, in a twenty-
foot ring at Caesars Palace. Nor is his left hand sheathed in a ten-
ounce glove, ready to inflict damage. No, the left hand of the former heavyweight champion of the world is wrapped in a red sweat
rag. It's sweltering inside his twelve-car garage, and Bowe, now
weighing nearly three hundred pounds, daubs perspiration from
his brow and stares thoughtfully at his machines: two Mercedeses, a
Rolls-Royce Seraph, a BMW 750, a Harley, a Bentley, a vintage 1970
Caddy, a customized Ford Suburban, and, Bowe's first car, a 1990
Jeep Cherokee. After a minute, Bowe's small brown eyes widen. He
turns to me and flashes the clownish grin — now made even more
impish by the addition of braces — that delighted and confounded
boxing fans just a few years ago.

"How about if I trade in the Rolls and the BMW?" he asks. His
speech is raspy and slurred, eerily reminiscent of a fortyish Muhammad Ali, just at the onset of his Parkinson's. "I never drive the
BMW. That's smart, right?"

I shrug, trying to convey neutrality. Bowe tosses me the key to the
BMW. "Let's roll."

Bowe rounds up his fiancée, Terri Blakney, and five-year-old
daughter, Diamond, the youngest of his five children, all by his

former wife, Judy. They pile into the Seraph, and we're off to the dealership, where a new Rolls Corniche convertible, retailing at $363,000, awaits him.

Bowe, it turns out, bought that same Rolls two days before when the dealer slyly told him that Rock Newman, Bowe's now estranged manager, coveted it. But the next day, Bowe, believing that he'd been played, returned the car, vowing never to do business again with the dealer. Now he has changed his mind again. "It's a birthday present," reasons Bowe, who would turn thirty-three later in the week.

Such behavior might simply be chalked up to the fickleness of the idle rich had Riddick Lamont Bowe not recently been declared brain-damaged in federal court. After Bowe pleaded guilty to abducting his estranged wife and their children from her North Carolina home in 1998, he could have been put away for more than two years. But based on the testimony of two doctors, last spring a federal judge sentenced Bowe to just thirty days in prison, as well as six months of house arrest.

House arrest doesn't seem to preclude field trips to the Rolls dealer, though. Or, much to my dismay, reaching speeds of up to 105 miles an hour on Washington's Beltway. Bowe, in his Rolls, bobs and weaves through heavy traffic. Not knowing the location of the dealership, I try to keep up in the BMW, passing cars in the breakdown lane. Motorists swerve out of our path. Some recognize the former champ and wave.

After half an hour, we arrive at EuroMotorcars in Bethesda. Matthew Smith, a slight blond man in glasses and tie, greets Bowe warmly. He expertly removes the tags from the cars Bowe is trading in and ushers him inside to fill out paperwork. Smith gives Bowe $175,000 for the Seraph and $70,000 for the BMW; more than $100,000 less than Bowe paid for the two cars a few months earlier. Things go smoothly until the phone rings. It's the used-car lot across the street. There's damage to the BMW from where Bowe's nephew hit a mailbox. Although it has been repaired, Smith now wants to give Bowe only $66,000.

"No way, bro — you give me 70 or put the tags back on the cars and we're out of here," Bowe says. He folds his arms across his chest and stares down his opponent. Smith caves. He'll give Big Daddy 70 for the Beemer.

Bowe struts out into the sunlight, and with his massive hands, he stretches open his eyelids so I can see his pupils. "Now who they saying brain-damaged?" he whispers triumphantly.

The roll of recent heavyweight champs and contenders could be mistaken for a most-wanted list — Mike Tyson, Michael Dokes, Trevor Berbick, to name a few. Riddick Bowe was supposed to be different: too smart, too talented, too endearing to fall like the others. But Bowe, who is younger than the current champ, Lennox Lewis, hasn't fought competitively for years and probably never will again. His days are passed inside a two-story suburban house, with a small pond out back that holds Japanese fighting fish named Tyson, Evander, and Lennox. The shrubbery spells out "Big Daddy," and there's an enormous rec house complete with video arcade and a regulation-size boxing ring. The walls are a shrine with framed relics from the glory days: championship belts, his 1988 Olympic silver medal, and 1997 New York tabloid clippings extolling him for retiring with his brains intact.

Bowe proudly gives me the grand tour, then invites me back the next day with just one request. "Bring videos," he implores. "That's how I pass the time. Comedies, dramas; I watch anything. But don't bring scary. I don't like scary."

Bowe's home holds plenty of places to watch them. There are big screens in the basement, living room, and master suite. Next to one of his VCRs, I find some of his old fight tapes. I ask him if we might watch his final bout, against Andrew Golota. Bowe firmly shakes his head: "We don't watch that one. Ever."

Why would he? Who wants to relive the moment his life enters a long, irrevocable spiral?

Like Mike Tyson, Riddick Bowe survived the Brownsville neighborhood in Brooklyn. Unlike Tyson, he was never a thug. He was the twelfth of thirteen children, and early profiles made much of the fact that Bowe would walk his mom, Dorothy, to and from her night-shift factory job. As a teenager, he racked up three straight Golden Gloves championships, then scored a silver in the 1988 Olympics. In 1992, Bowe fought Evander Holyfield in an epic title bout that included one of the single best heavyweight rounds ever (the tenth). Bowe won on a unanimous decision.

"He was 6'5"; he could box; he could fight inside; he could do anything," recalls his veteran handler Eddie Futch. "He could have been one of the all-time greats."

Bowe also possessed a charisma not seen in the heavyweight ranks since Ali. Sitting on his stool right before his tenth-round war with Holyfield, Bowe flashed a wide-eyed goofball smile for the camera. "People just identified with him," says Seth Abraham, who as president of Time Warner Sports signed Bowe to a $100 million contract with HBO. "He was huggable and appealed to nonboxing fans like an Ali or a Ray Leonard."

After the Holyfield conquest, the new champ took a trip around the world, meeting with Nelson Mandela and Pope John Paul II and visiting starving children in Somalia. His manager, Rock Newman, wanted to turn Bowe into a global celebrity like Ali, but it was the beginning of the end. Never fond of training, Bowe had a hard time getting back into shape after the trip. He kept a refrigerator in his bedroom, and his weight swelled to near three hundred pounds. For his 1993 rematch with Holyfield, Bowe showed up grotesquely out of shape and lost a close decision.

Then he began acting strange. At the weigh-in for a 1994 fight with Larry Donald, he punched his opponent in the face for no apparent reason. After an impressive knockout of Holyfield in their 1995 rubber match, he emerged bloated for a July 1996 Madison Square Garden battle with Andrew Golota, a product of Warsaw's mean streets, escaping with a victory only when Golota was disqualified for repeated low blows. After the fight, Bowe's crew incited a riot by attacking Golota. Futch quit, declaring Bowe a lost cause.

In the fight's aftermath, Bowe continued to behave unpredictably. "He began selling off all his boxing possessions," recalls his former wife, Judy. "Boots, trunks, belts, everything. Things he had promised his kids. People were just marching in and out of the house leaving with all of Bowe's stuff. I think he was in trouble then, but I and everybody else were in denial."

Bowe became obsessed with joining the Marine Corps, and when he entered the ring for a December rematch with Golota, his trunks had sergeant stripes on them. The fight was disastrous, nine rounds of butchery. Golota gruesomely snapped Bowe's head back and forth, but the ex-champion wouldn't quit. At ringside, HBO's

Jim Lampley raved about "a courageous performance by Bowe, who seems not to have any of his faculties." Incredibly, at the end of the ninth round, Golota was disqualified again for low blows. It didn't matter; he had already hit Bowe 408 times, an amount of punishment unheard of at the heavyweight level.

In a postfight interview with HBO, Bowe's speech was nearly incomprehensible. Two months later, he joined the Marine Corps Reserve. He lasted eleven days. Shortly after, Bowe announced his retirement from the ring. He was twenty-nine.

Bowe sits on the floor in the family room as Terri combs out the kinks in his hair. In the VCR is a highlight tape of Ali, Frazier, Foreman, Norton, and Holmes. When vintage Ali pops on the screen, Bowe's face lights up. As the Greatest taunts Frazier, Bowe perfectly mouths the words: "Joe gonna come out smoking, and I ain't going be joking, I'll be picking and poking. Pouring water on his smoking. I might shock and amaze you, I'll destroy Joe Frazier."

The phone rings. Bowe answers: "World's finest, Big Daddy, here. Be brief." He listens a few minutes, grunts, then hangs up. "Guy wants to invest my money," he says. "All day I get these calls." One of the few fighters who seems financially set for life, Bowe doesn't understand the less frugal in his profession. "You make $1 million, you tell me you can't live on the 6 percent — $60,000?" Bowe says. "I once had this brother ask me why I was training so hard. He said, 'You just gonna be back in the ghetto with us.' I'm so afraid of losing my money and seeing him back in the ghetto. It ain't gonna happen."

He turns his attention back to the screen, where the former champions are chatting around a table. Except for Foreman, they're all hard to understand. "It's funny: listen to those guys, they're all punchy," Bowe observes. "And they did it to each other, punching each other. Ain't it something?"

For someone with a diagnosis of brain damage, Bowe has a lucid grasp on the realities of his former profession. "You realize you're taking a chance," Bowe says. "You may not come out as you went in. You may slur. You may not remember things. That's part of the risk."

His evaluation of his own career is also dead-on. "Once I won the title and took care of my family, I didn't care as much," says Bowe, who bought homes for nearly all of his siblings. "That's why I re-spect Ali and Holmes so much: they did it for a long time."

He then asks a question. "I don't talk that bad, do I?" I tell him his voice is thicker and raspier than when he was champ. Bowe pauses. "But that could be caused by a lot of things, right?"

It is only when the conversation turns away from prizefighting that Bowe gets fuzzy. Later in the afternoon, after we watched *Rio Bravo*, Bowe suddenly stood up. "Let me ask you a question. How would I go about getting into Spelman College?" I tell him he'd probably have to go to a community college first. "What about the Naval Academy?" I tell him he's too old. He laughs: "Is that right? You don't think they would make an exception for Bowe?"

At Riddick Bowe's sentencing hearing, Dr. Richard Restak, a clini-cal professor of neurology at George Washington University, was asked to describe the havoc boxing had wreaked on his brain. "You have what we call cerebral reserve where it's almost like any other kind of reserve, financial reserve or whatever," testified Restak. "You write a certain check, all the money is gone. Same thing here. You take a certain number of punches, particularly if they're in close proximity, then you can have a dramatic falloff in a person's ability to cope."

Bowe's coping skills were at issue because of his attempt, in Feb-ruary 1998, to reunite with his family. He and Judy had dated since the age of fourteen, and while their relationship was always turbu-lent, it disintegrated when Bowe's boxing career did. Judy finally left after Riddick knocked her unconscious in April 1997. "That was the first time he had ever knocked me out," recalls Judy Bowe. "I remember my youngest boy, Julius, telling the other kids when they came home that 'Daddy killed Mommy.' They had stopped no-ticing and stopped crying. They were getting used to it way too much."

Judy moved herself and the kids to Cornelius, North Carolina, outside Charlotte. Bowe tried everything to win Judy back. He hung a huge portrait of her minister in his house and sent her a Mercedes truck. When nothing worked, he and his brother Aaron Wright drove to Cornelius on February 25, 1998, prowling the streets until 6:50 A.M., when Bowe spotted his three oldest chil-dren at the bus stop. He ushered them into the Lincoln Navigator and headed to their mom's home. There, Bowe ordered Judy, still in her pajamas, and the couple's two smallest children into the car. On the drive north, Bowe opened a bag filled with duct tape, a buck knife, and pepper spray and announced, "I came prepared."

In South Hill, Virginia, Judy asked Riddick to stop at a McDonald's so that she could get food for their crying kids. In the bathroom, she used her cell phone to call a friend, who notified the police. Judy also called Rock Newman, who promised to check Bowe in for psychiatric testing if she would not have him arrested. The police soon pulled over the Navigator. Judy and the kids were transported home while a limo took Riddick to the hospital.

Federal authorities in North Carolina brought charges against Bowe (though not against his brother). In June 1998, Bowe pleaded guilty to interstate domestic violence and faced eighteen to twenty-four months in prison. Before sentencing, Bowe's lawyers, including Johnnie Cochran, cobbled together a dream team of doctors. They determined that Bowe suffered from frontal lobe syndrome, a form of brain damage that impairs rational thought and impulse control. In court documents, Bowe's IQ was listed at 79, a score bordering on retardation. At the hearing, doctors testified that while Bowe did not have problems with simple everyday tasks, his ability to make wise choices was severely hampered.

Meanwhile, the former champ was plotting a comeback, skipping rope, and hitting the heavy bag. Thell Torrence, Bowe's trainer for the second Golota fight, was flown in for an evaluation. "He looked real good," Torrence said.

Bowe's backers were Jeffrey Jackson, partner in a Washington securities firm that counts Bowe as an investor, and Cecile Barker, a Washington-area software entrepreneur. On January 3, less than two months before his sentencing hearing, Barker sent a letter to HBO announcing, "Riddick Bowe has decided to end his retirement and return to the ring."

Judge Graham Mullen quashed those plans. While he reduced Bowe's sentence to thirty days, he also banned him from the ring for four years.

Bowe seems genuinely contrite about his crime. "I made a mistake," he claims. "I just wanted to be with my babies." About his brain damage, he insists, "That's something lawyers concocted."

Of a postprobation return to the ring, Bowe seems certain. "You know, I'll only be thirty-six," he muses. "Four years fly by fast." He sluggishly shadowboxes in front of the television. "I mean, I've never done anything else. What else am I gonna do? Get a job?"

On a rainy Thursday, Bowe plays Mr. Mom. As part of his divorce settlement with Judy, Bowe gets his kids for the summer, holidays, and one weekend a month. He joyfully bounces his daughter Diamond on his knee while supervising the older children's chores. When fourteen-year-old Riddick Jr. does a halfhearted job of mopping the kitchen floor, Bowe sternly asks, "Junior, why you play me like that?" before giving him a hug.

Riddick has decided to marry Terri, and later in the day, he asks me to come with them as they sign the prenuptial agreement. As we drive in his Ford Suburban, complete with a video screen for every seat, Bowe asks if I know anybody in the media who could cover the wedding. "I want everybody to know Big Daddy's doing O.K."

Bowe's wedding is just like the old days. Former members of the entourage whisper into cell phones. Range Rovers and Mercedeses clog his driveway. Adding to the drama, Judy Bowe, there to pick up the kids, is outside, leaning against a van. When Bowe emerges, resplendent in double-breasted black suit and matching alligator shoes, he puts Terri into a waiting limo and saunters over to Judy. For nearly half an hour, as everyone waits and watches, they chat and smile.

As the motorcade heads toward the courthouse, Judy calls me on my cell phone. "Bowe said he'd marry me again if I'd sign a prenup," claims Judy. "He told me he's just getting married because he's bored." (When I tell Bowe this later, he smiles and shakes his head: "Bro, I didn't say that. I was just trying to keep the peace.")

The proceedings are held in a basement before two dozen friends and family. When someone asks Bowe if he's nervous, he answers, "Nah, bro, this is my second rodeo." Everyone laughs.

The reception is at Morton's steakhouse in downtown Washington. After the sirloin and shrimp, Jeffrey Jackson, Bowe's would-be promoter, offers a Champagne toast. "Here's to the once and future heavyweight champion of the world." The room goes wild. Riddick Bowe stands up. "You guarantee me $10 million after taxes and you got it," he promises in a voice hard to understand. He throws a couple of lethargic jabs. "What else I got to do?"

BUZZ BISSINGER

For Love of DiMaggio

FROM VANITY FAIR

A god and his worshipers — B.C.

THE DEATHWATCH OF Joe DiMaggio was ending now, all that had come with it in those sad final months — the lying and subterfuge, the decisions concerning who could say good-bye and who could not, the infighting over him that had led to screaming and even a threatened lawsuit — dwindling down to a final whisper just past the stroke of midnight.

Phil Rizzuto, the beloved New York Yankee announcer for so many years and former teammate, had been cut off. Not even the president of the United States had a prayer.

Following the operation that had removed a cancerous tumor from DiMaggio's lung, Bill Clinton wanted to wish him well after he learned that the baseball legend had been hospitalized. The overture was declined on the basis that he was too sick to talk, and perhaps that was the only reason for the rejection. But it was also true that DiMaggio found something unforgivable about Clinton that he had no intention of forgiving, just as, during various periods of his life, he had found unforgivable things about Frank Sinatra, and President Kennedy, and his sister Marie, and friends who were no longer friends.

He detested the president for everything from Whitewater to his affair with Monica, and that, too, may have been a motive for turning down that phone call. In fact, DiMaggio took special relish in snubbing the president, and in days of full health he loved to tell the story of that magical night at Camden Yards in Baltimore in September 1995 when he and Clinton were there to witness

Cal Ripken as he broke Lou Gehrig's streak of 2,130 consecutive games. An aide approached DiMaggio and asked if it would be O.K. for the president to shake his hand.

DiMaggio looked at the aide and told him no.

He had shaken Clinton's hand once already, before he became president, and as far as he was concerned, once was enough. When the aide asked if DiMaggio might like to sit with the president for a little bit, DiMaggio said no to that, too.

This story, and a dozen others like it that defined Joe DiMaggio, not the American Knight version or the Yankee Clipper version, had become incandescent in the living room of his home, which had been converted into an intensive-care unit once he had left Memorial Regional Hospital in Hollywood, Florida, in January of 1999. On one of the walls, like a pep-rally banner, was a sign that said, JOE DIMAGGIO HIGHWAY, in honor of New York City's plan to rename the West Side Highway after him. Another sign read, OPENING DAY APRIL 9TH, to give DiMaggio, who had recently turned eighty-four, the goal of living through another opening day for the Yankees. To the extent possible, everything was done to make him comfortable in that converted room with its trays and wheelchair and bed, to supply him with the things that gave him comfort: freshly prepared pasta with bits of lobster; haircuts from his favorite barber, Angelo Sapio; a shave and manicure on an almost daily basis; a steady stock of the old Westerns that he loved so much.

There were few visitors to his home, which lay within the gated community of Harbor Islands in Hollywood, Florida. His granddaughters, Kathie and Paula, came to see him along with their husbands. Joe Nachio, his oldest friend, of some sixty years — whose home in Panama DiMaggio had sought refuge in after the tumultuous divorce from Marilyn Monroe in 1954 — was often there. Dom DiMaggio, himself a former major-league ballplayer, was a frequent visitor as well, although Joe, before he became ill, apparently made little effort to acknowledge his presence when they were at an event together.

Wasn't that your brother?

So what.

Another person was there as well, more than anyone else, in fact. He wasn't a relative, and his entrance into the DiMaggio inner circle had come relatively late, when the former Yankee great was already in his late sixties.

His name was Morris Engelberg, and he was a praying mantis of a man, reflecting his long-gone days as a basketball player in the old Eastern League. He spoke rapidly, in a blitzkrieg mumble straight out of Borough Park in Brooklyn, the words all mashed together. He had a manner that many in the ever-shifting rings of the DiMaggio inner circle didn't like, a facial expression always on the precipice of discovering something rotten. They found him pompous and arrogant. They disliked him perhaps out of plain jealousy over his having staked a claim on DiMaggio, or maybe because they genuinely believed that he had inserted himself into DiMaggio's life to such an extent that DiMaggio had become totally dependent on him, couldn't seem to make a move without first consulting him, even lived across the street from him within the Harbor Islands community.

Engelberg knew he was hated by a long chain of those who had once been intimates of DiMaggio's, but he didn't care. "As long as he loved me, I didn't give a shit," he said. He also knew there was little they could do. In his capacity as DiMaggio's estate lawyer and adviser and de facto agent, Engelberg had helped to make the former baseball player wildly rich in the last decade of his life, rich into the tens of millions.

As a result of that, Engelberg had the power of an intense friendship with DiMaggio that no one could touch. "I don't like the son of a bitch," a friend of DiMaggio's said of Engelberg. "But I admired that relationship. He was certainly good for Joe." Engelberg also had the legal powers that DiMaggio had entrusted him with — the legal power to make medical decisions on behalf of DiMaggio, the legal power he would have as the trustee of DiMaggio's estate, the legal power to determine the use of DiMaggio's name once he was no longer alive.

For more than a decade, Engelberg played every psychological role imaginable to him beyond simply that of financial guru — surrogate son, surrogate wife, surrogate slave. "You know what's so sick about this? I enjoyed it," admitted Engelberg. "The great DiMaggio took me into his life.

"People thought I was running his life, which I did. But he ran my life. He owned me. It was a master-slave. But I loved every minute with him." And given his insertion into DiMaggio's life in virtually every way imaginable, he also knew something else.

"He couldn't live without me. If he hated me, he'd have to stay with me."

During the sixteen years he was with DiMaggio, Engelberg remained silent. But now, in response to the eagerly awaited biography of Joe DiMaggio by Richard Ben Cramer, which is scheduled for publication this October by Simon & Schuster, Engelberg has decided to break his silence. Cramer, a Pulitzer Prize winner and the author of the acclaimed *What It Takes,* about the 1988 presidential race, spent roughly five years on his DiMaggio opus, *Joe DiMaggio: The Hero's Life.* But the book is absent two crucial voices. One is that of DiMaggio himself, who refused to cooperate with Cramer, referring to him as "Benny Boy." The other belongs to Engelberg, who also refused to cooperate with the author.

In a series of lengthy interviews with *Vanity Fair,* Engelberg spoke in remarkable detail for the first time about the private Joe DiMaggio that he alone was able to see after spending thousands of hours in his company. Over the years, as their lives became ever more intertwined, Joe DiMaggio said hundreds of intimate things to Engelberg, things about President Clinton, things about Mickey Mantle, things about the Kennedys, things about Frank Sinatra, things about Marilyn Monroe, things that went deep below the public image that had been as carefully cultivated as a cemetery plot.

In twentieth-century American culture, there was no one like Joe DiMaggio, the elements of his life fitting together into an irresistible package of rags-to-riches glory. His father, Giuseppe, was a fisherman from the small island of Isola Della Femmine near Sicily. In 1898 Giuseppe set out for the new country, and he and his wife, Rosalie, eventually settled in the town of Martinez, northeast of San Francisco. There were nine children in the family, four girls and five boys. All the boys carried the middle name of Paul, and Joseph Paul DiMaggio, born on November 25, 1914, was the second youngest. He came of age in the grip of the Depression. Money for the family was tight, and he quit high school to provide a wage. He worked at a plant that made orange juice, but he hated it, so he quit. He found work on the docks, and he worked at a cannery for a while, and then he loaded trucks. It seemed inevitable that he would follow his father into the waters of San Francisco Bay. Until he discovered baseball, and baseball discovered him.

In 1935 he played for a minor-league team, the San Francisco Seals of the Pacific Coast League, and had a .398 batting average, with 48 doubles and 34 home runs. A year later he traveled by car cross-country to join the mighty New York Yankees. In the company of such legends as Lou Gehrig and Tony Lazzeri, he was humble and barely spoke a word. But his numbers on the field spoke for him, a rookie in the House of Ruth who in 1936 hit .323, with 206 hits, 44 doubles, 29 home runs, and 125 RBIs. The following year he led the American League in home runs with 46 while hitting .346 and driving in 167. In 1939 he led the league in hitting with a mark of .381 and did the same a year later, when he hit .352. In 1941, the year of his epic 56-game hitting streak, he led the league in RBIs with 125 and was also the league MVP. His career took a three-year hiatus when he served in the army in World War II. Then he returned to the game with barely a misstep. In 1947 he was the American League MVP for a third time, and a year later he led the league in RBIs with 155.

No one in sports ever had more grace. No one looked better in a uniform, his fitting him as if it were a Savile Row suit. Virtually no one had been more successful in those Yankee pinstripes — nine world championships in thirteen seasons with a career batting average of .325. There were other players, such as Ted Williams, who hit for higher average. There were other players, such as Jimmie Foxx, who hit more home runs. But there was only one DiMaggio, the "great DiMaggio," as Ernest Hemingway called him in *The Old Man and the Sea.*

He was everything that a professional athlete should be, and he had everything that a professional athlete could want — fame, adulation, canonization by millions who would never forget him for those immaculate acts on a baseball diamond. They saw him as a man of exceptional dignity, and in public he *was* a man of exceptional dignity, virtually flawless in his decency and self-effacement.

But beneath that public posture roiled other qualities, anger and distrust, self-imposed isolation and idiosyncratic behavior, dark moods and bitter memories, hatreds that were more defined than likes.

*

Engelberg, now sixty years old, is a wealthy tax and estate lawyer in Florida with offices in Palm Beach and Hollywood and a list of clients that has included the former spouses of John Paul Getty and Revlon founder Charles Revson. They were demanding clients, and Engelberg's hourly fee of between $300 and $400 gave them a right to be demanding. He served them well. But he served no one the way he served Joe DiMaggio, who wasn't even a paying client of Engelberg's, because Engelberg never charged him a cent.

Because of DiMaggio, Engelberg stepped inside a world that he could never have possibly imagined — the Lotos Club in New York, where DiMaggio was honored with a black-tie dinner; the box of owner George Steinbrenner at Yankee Stadium; a championship boxing bout in Atlantic City where he and the Yankee Clipper were the guests of Donald Trump. But much of his time was spent in a booth at the Deli Den, one of DiMaggio's favorite places in Hollywood, Florida. There, over egg-white omelettes and diluted decaf, the two men shared hour after hour talking about baseball, and politics, and how DiMaggio's great-grandchildren were doing in school. Some of the stories were magnificent and some were mundane, and even DiMaggio himself asked Engelberg, "Do you ever get bored of me?" But Engelberg never did.

"I honestly haven't seen two men closer," says Engelberg's daughter, Laurie Milgrim. "When they were together, I always felt that Morris was looking after Joe," says DiMaggio's granddaughter Kathie Stein. "They had a true friendship. [He was] a very true friend, my grandfather's best friend."

The familiar traits of class and grace emerge in the DiMaggio that was revealed to Engelberg. So does humility. Engelberg saw a man so determined to never publicly flaunt that once, upon his arrival at Yankee Stadium in a limousine, DiMaggio cringed on the floor so the fans who had gathered would not see him. But Engelberg also saw DiMaggio's pessimism and brutal stubbornness and an empty simplicity defined by a refrigerator containing nothing but restaurant doggie bags and by a five-thousand-unit supply of paper plates because DiMaggio couldn't be bothered with real ones. In Engelberg's words, DiMaggio was the "king of replacement." He could never forgive a perceived slight, yet he came to the wedding of Engelberg's daughter without a gift, as if his mere presence were gift enough. A vain and fastidious man, he would take ten minutes to knot and reknot his tie.

Engelberg came to realize that, far from his image as a perpetual recluse, Joe DiMaggio loved being Joe DiMaggio as long as he could control all the tentacles of information and interaction — who sat where, who said what, who wore what. He loved the loyal entourage that he could control at his whim, putting members in or out as if he were flicking a cigarette ash, placing them on "probation," as he called it, or in more extreme cases outright "suspension." He loved getting things for free, whether it was an apartment with hundreds of thousands of dollars in furnishings, or packs of cookies from the American Airlines lounge, where he always crammed his pockets. After growing up so poor, selling papers on the street corner as a kid, he hated to spend money: His clothing collected the white powder of mildew because he refused to turn on the air-conditioning even though he wasn't paying for it; his idea of washing the white Mercedes that had been given to him by the Yankees was to drive it around in a heavy rainstorm for five minutes.

He loved his place in Yankee history, his mood brightening during that Old Timers' Day in 1995, when he got more applause from the fans than Mickey Mantle, even though Mantle, dying of cancer at the time, was so sick he could only appear on the scoreboard screen in a videotaped message to the fans. DiMaggio had a big smile on his face after that, Engelberg remembered. Sitting in George Steinbrenner's private box at the stadium, he was talkative and happy and cut into his hot dogs in his patented style, using a fork and knife to eat them and throwing away the buns.

But there is also genuine poignancy in the DiMaggio Engelberg knew. He saw a man who spent his final years striving for something that he seemed so intent for so long on never having: a life in which he no longer automatically treated the values of family and security and stability as disposable items.

It was Engelberg who promptly traded in his black Mercedes for a white one after DiMaggio mentioned to him one day that he preferred the color white; it was Engelberg who negotiated the card-show deals and the bat deals and the poster deals and the ball deals that made DiMaggio a multimillionaire; it was Engelberg who scoured new restaurants for him beforehand to make sure there were no pictures of Marilyn Monroe in the bathroom; it was Engelberg who went to the store at six in the morning for him to buy the bagels he liked; it was Engelberg who drove an hour and a half one Saturday night to change the channel on DiMaggio's television set so the cable would work again.

"It was obsessive to the point where it probably hurt his family," said Allan Lerner, a Fort Lauderdale lawyer and friend of Engelberg's for the past decade. "Morris gave up his normal life to be with this man. He literally dedicated sixteen years of his life to one person, sixteen years of his life to one person who was not his family."

It was also Engelberg who was there virtually every day of those final five months as DiMaggio lay dying, acting as guardian and gatekeeper and conduit of false information. And it was Engelberg who was there when he died just past that stroke of midnight on March 8, 1999, holding his hand, hearing the last words he ever said, words that were as shocking as they were soft, as unforgettable as they were gentle.

In the public eye, DiMaggio spent his entire life avoiding controversy and unseemly spats. But in the aftermath of his death, Engelberg has done just the opposite. As the zealous legal protector of DiMaggio's name, Engelberg has made himself a detested presence, engaging in petty and ugly disputes with New York State and the cities of Hollywood, Florida, and San Francisco, among others. "Why are you so nasty?" New York governor George Pataki asked Engelberg after the governor's overture to rename the Major Deegan Expressway in honor of DiMaggio was castigated by Engelberg in a letter as a crass political act in "extremely poor taste," given that a plan was already in place to rename the West Side Highway after the baseball great.

In the case of San Francisco, the city's desire to give the DiMaggio name to a playground in the North Beach neighborhood where DiMaggio and his brothers had played as kids was also furiously condemned by Engelberg. In a letter to County Supervisor Gavin Newsom, Engelberg called the idea "totally reprehensible. . . . It is obvious you are using Mr. DiMaggio to bring attention to yourself for the upcoming November 2000 election." Engelberg also said the renaming of the concrete park was not a sufficient honor, and reiterated his preference for several alternative sites that had been suggested in a list supplied by Newsom, such as the city's airport or the San Francisco/Oakland Bay Bridge.

The city went ahead with the renaming despite Engelberg's objections, promising to put roughly $4.4 million into the project. Engelberg in turn responded with the filing of a lawsuit in federal court challenging the city's actions. The suit was thrown out almost as soon as it was filed, on the grounds that a federal court in Florida had no jurisdiction to decide matters taking place a continent away, in California.

Engelberg appealed the ruling, arguing that San Francisco's renaming of a public facility after DiMaggio without the permission of the estate would create a dangerous precedent, allowing anyone to use the DiMaggio name for his own self-interest. But Engelberg had no similar qualms when he attempted at an auction last April at Christie's East to sell dozens of signed items that he said DiMaggio had given him over the years.

The two men first met in 1983 through a mutual acquaintance. A breakfast meeting was set for 8:00 A.M. at the Boca Teca Hotel in Boca Raton, and Engelberg, then almost forty-three years old, awoke that morning at four. He left the house at 5:15, which meant he would arrive more than two hours early, since the ride to the hotel took a maximum of twenty-five minutes. It was back in the days when the portable phone was an oxymoron, but Engelberg carried one anyway. It weighed several pounds and required an aerial, and he instructed his wife and children to be available in case his car broke down.

Engelberg's father had died while his mother was still pregnant with him. He had tried to find a substitute for that loss, and at grade school in Brooklyn in the 1940s, when the teacher went around the room asking kids about their fathers and what they did, Engelberg told the class his father was Joe DiMaggio. He memorized his batting statistics. He wore his hair in a DiMaggio pompadour. He craved him, the way so many millions craved him, and to meet his idol in the flesh seemed almost unimaginable.

Engelberg remembers what he wore, making sure it would adhere to the DiMaggio dress code: a dark-blue three-piece suit, a white button-down shirt with a red tie, and black Allen-Edmonds wing tips. He remembers what DiMaggio wore: a white shirt with a red tie, a wine-colored sweater, and a dark-blue blazer. He remembers DiMaggio's first words to him, as if it were Stanley greeting Livingstone: "Mr. Engelberg, I am sorry that I am five minutes late." He remembers how impressed DiMaggio was by what he knew, and he even remembers what DiMaggio had for breakfast that day: a cup of decaf coffee, half of a grapefruit, a sliced banana.

DiMaggio was used to such idolatry. Much of his life had been spent in the company of men who worshiped him and drove for him and paid for him and dumped their wives at home when he whistled for their company. There was always an entourage, and there was always a waiting list to get in, particularly since, as Engelberg learned, friends were largely interchangeable to DiMaggio. As their relationship evolved and Engelberg claimed a place in DiMaggio's life that inevitably meant the shoving out of others, people warned him never to feel too secure. They warned him that one day he would find himself thrown "out of the phone book" because that was DiMaggio's way, to throw people out of his life for some slight or transgression, something to underscore the credo that he uttered to Engelberg one day in the front seat of the car with his head down and his mood foul and snappish, as it so often was:

"I don't trust anyone. No exceptions."

But Engelberg was different, utterly determined to stay in the good graces of DiMaggio regardless of the impact it had on anyone, including his wife, Stephanie. When the three of them went out to dinner, it was DiMaggio and Engelberg who sat on one side of the booth and Stephanie on the other. When the three of them traveled to Los Angeles and went to a Dodgers game, it was DiMaggio and Engelberg who went together in one car while Stephanie lagged behind in another, and it was DiMaggio and Engelberg who sat in the owner's box while Stephanie had a seat somewhere else. When Engelberg and his wife went out to dinner with other couples, it was Engelberg who dominated the conversation with hour after hour of DiMaggio stories. "You monopolized the whole evening," Engelberg remembers his wife telling him. "I'm not going out with you anymore. You're a sick man. All you do is talk about DiMaggio."

"He was married to Joe, not his wife" was the way one person who observed the dynamic put it. "It was sick. There was almost a symbiotic relationship between him and Joe. He wanted to be Joe DiMaggio, assume his personality."

From the very beginning, Engelberg had the complete deference that was a prerequisite for admission to the DiMaggio inner circle. But he also had something else, a sharp financial and legal acumen that DiMaggio coveted, particularly when he found out that Mrs. John Paul Getty was one of Engelberg's clients. They talked for five hours that first morning at breakfast, much of the conversation centered on money, or more precisely DiMaggio's lack of it, given that his net worth was somewhere between $200,000 and $300,000. A short time later, DiMaggio called Engelberg to help renegotiate his contract with the Bowery Savings Bank. He was concerned that the bank was going to reduce his pay as spokesman.

When Engelberg met DiMaggio in New York at the Stage Delicatessen to tell him that the Bowery was actually going to increase his pay, DiMaggio took out his checkbook and removed a yellow check and made it out to Engelberg for $20,000, misspelling his last name. He handed the check to Engelberg, and Engelberg folded it up and returned it to him.

DiMaggio responded to the gesture by also letting Engelberg pay for lunch.

As far as Engelberg could tell, the habit of not paying for anything was long ingrained in DiMaggio. In fact, at the beginning stages of their relationship, Engelberg couldn't remember ever knowing anyone who spent less, around $10,000 a year. He drove a Toyota that had been a gift from a car dealership. When he stayed at his apartment in Florida, he did his own vacuuming in a pair of old army shorts and also his own laundry, with strings of underwear hanging across the shower curtain. Someone else picked up the tab whenever he went out to eat, and virtually all the clothing he wore had been gifts, suits and shirts and boxes and boxes of golf pants. As DiMaggio eventually began stopping by Engelberg's law office in Hollywood three times a week, he complained that his single biggest expense was the cost of gas for the fifty-five-minute drive from where he lived. Engelberg figured he was joking, but there was no point in taking any chances:

He started driving to DiMaggio's apartment.

After that Bowery negotiation, Engelberg realized that DiMaggio, with a little bit of guidance, could be a cash machine. The sports-memorabilia business was beginning to boom, and it was clear to Engelberg that DiMaggio's perfect signature and the various uses of it, on balls and bats and posters and photos and serigraphs and lithographs, could make DiMaggio a very rich man with very little work.

When the two men first met, DiMaggio was getting a flat fee of somewhere around $10,000 for a three-hour signing at a memorabilia show. Engelberg refuses to reveal any of the financial particulars of the deals that he and DiMaggio negotiated. But according to a source familiar with their transactions, the fee went up to $25,000, then $50,000, then $75,000; eventually, DiMaggio was paid for the number of pieces he signed at an appearance, with a guaranteed minimum of $150,000.

In Engelberg's estimation DiMaggio was a simple man, acutely aware of his lack of education and the degree to which various people had tried to take advantage of that lack of sophistication, particularly when he had been younger. His favorite book was the bestselling *The Millionaire Next Door: The Surprising Secrets of America's Wealthy.* He chose his friends and acquaintances in part on the basis of what he could get from them — places to stay when he traveled, free soap, free ice cream. The most pressing moment of most days was figuring out where the next meal was coming from and what it would be, and the only place where he seemed truly comfortable was in the presence of children. He prided himself on his dignity, but sports memorabilia was a nasty business, the subject of frequent criminal investigations for forgery and fraud. DiMaggio wasn't far off when he told Engelberg that "in this business there are only four types of people — felons, forgers, phonies, and liars."

For a man obsessed with his own impeccable elegance, it was hard to think of any atmosphere more degrading. But his hatred of the memorabilia shows was outweighed by the money, not the "need of money," as DiMaggio once put it, since his expenses were so minimal, but the sheer "want of money." In one show alone, at Hofstra University, he made an estimated $350,000 when he signed more than two thousand pieces. In Atlantic City, a private signing reportedly netted him $120,000.

To avoid oversaturation, Engelberg had DiMaggio do only five card shows a year. Engelberg also guided DiMaggio into other areas of the memorabilia business with even more astronomical paydays. (At the time of his death, sources placed the value of DiMaggio's estate at a minimum of $45 million, and some said it may have been as high as $80 million.)

In the early 1990s, DiMaggio signed a deal with a New Jersey–based memorabilia company called the Score Board under which he was reportedly paid between $7 million and $9 million over a two-and-a-half-year period to sign one thousand baseballs and one thousand photographs a month. That meant two days of signing a month for DiMaggio at Engelberg's law office, the equivalent of $160,000 a day.

It was an amazing deal. Even Engelberg himself believed the company had crazily overpaid for the DiMaggio name, and there was little surprise that the company ultimately filed for bankruptcy. After the contract was agreed to, all the parties involved went to the Deli Den. Engelberg picked up the check. DiMaggio and Engelberg then went to a nearby drugstore for a roll of antacids. The druggist became apoplectic at the sight of DiMaggio, heaping free items on him, and as Engelberg watched, he realized that DiMaggio took more pleasure in wangling several dollars' worth of merchandise from the druggist than he had in signing a multimillion-dollar contract. "He got it for nothing, it turned him on," said Engelberg. "Don't ask me why."

After the Score Board deal, DiMaggio signed a reported $3 million deal with a company called Score that required him to sign several thousand baseball cards as well as allow the production of a tin baseball-card holder with his picture on it. After that, Engelberg talked DiMaggio into a bat-signing deal with Pro Sports Services that would earn him a reported payday of between $3 million and $4 million.

Thanks to those three deals, DiMaggio's net worth had grown by close to $15 million in the space of roughly two years. If it was want of money that drove him, that want had been satisfied. But there was still a core of hollowness to his life, a self-imposed emptiness. At the time of the bat deal, DiMaggio maintained an apartment at the Seacoast Towers in Miami Beach. With its threadbare carpet and flimsy hotel-style furniture, there wasn't a trace of a personal touch in it. He apparently liked it because it was near the Fontainebleau Hotel, where he and Marilyn Monroe had once stayed. Its sad decrepitude didn't seem to bother him in the least, as far as Engelberg could tell.

A few years earlier, on New Year's Eve in 1991, DiMaggio had served as the grand marshal of the Orange Bowl Parade, accompanied by Engelberg. It was around 10:00 P.M. by the time the festivities were over. Engelberg took DiMaggio out to eat at the Deli Den, and then he pleaded with him to come back to his house for New Year's.

"It doesn't mean anything to me," said DiMaggio. "It's just another night."

Engelberg drove him back to the Seacoast Towers. Normally Engelberg walked through the lobby with him and then went up the elevator to shake his hand and say good night. But this time he watched from the car, just watched, as his idol, America's idol, tired and slightly stooped, walked into that lobby without a soul around him, as if it were all he ever knew and ever wanted to know.

The money also didn't take away the moods. They came at all times, once or twice a day in the presence of Engelberg, signaled by the downturn of the head — the "bad head," as Engelberg called it. "You would have a great eight hours with him. The last mile he gets moody and you feel like shit walking up the stairs."

Whenever he asked DiMaggio what was wrong, the response was almost always the same:

"Don't you know?" he would say, and Engelberg knew he was thinking of Marilyn Monroe. As far as Engelberg could tell, she was the one person in life that DiMaggio had truly loved, particularly since DiMaggio had a thing for underdogs, and also a thing for blondes, and Monroe exceptionally met both criteria. They had gotten married in San Francisco in January 1954, but early on, when Monroe left him to go entertain the American troops in Korea, the marriage seemed doomed. According to various accounts, he wanted a stay-at-home wife, a role that Marilyn Monroe was totally unsuited for. She in turn wanted a husband who was fun and spontaneous, a role that Joe DiMaggio was totally unsuited for.

When Monroe filmed the now-classic scene in *The Seven Year Itch* in which the wind from a New York subway grate pushes up the dress she is wearing to reveal her bare thighs, DiMaggio silently bore witness and was livid. They had a terrible fight, and the marriage was over after nine months. But he never stopped loving her. In the early 1960s, he rescued her from the depths of drug and alcohol addiction. There was talk of reconciliation and maybe even remarriage. But on August 5, 1962, she died of an apparent overdose, and the loss left him bitter and in some ways forever shattered.

He told Engelberg that he blamed three people in particular for what had happened to her. One was Frank Sinatra, who, he was convinced, had set her up with President Kennedy and his brother Bobby — in effect acting as a "pimp," as DiMaggio put it, in return for possible political favors. The other two were the Kennedys themselves. He despised them to the point that he saw something deserved in their assassinations. His hatred of the entire Kennedy family was such that once, when he was invited to the Kennedy Center to present awards on behalf of a charity, he said he would go only if he received a letter stating that no member of the Kennedy family would be allowed into the event.

Beyond the brooding over the loss of Monroe, there was also the trail of relationships chopped off as if with the stroke of an eversharpened knife because of distrust, or suspicion, or failure to obey the rules of DiMaggio, which had become as familiar to those around him as the Ten Commandments: Never mention Monroe, Sinatra, or the Kennedys. Never be late. Never ask for a signature on something during a meal. Never wear the wrong-color outfit.

Before his marriage to Monroe, DiMaggio had been married for five years to the actress Dorothy Arnold. They had a son together whom they named Joe junior, and the father-son relationship was marked by estrangement. When Joe junior was a student at Yale, a university official called Joe senior to say that his son was having significant difficulties. Because of Joe junior's stature as a DiMaggio, the official also said the university was not inclined to expel him. But DiMaggio said there should be no double standard for his son, and told the official that Joe junior should be expelled if he deserved it. Later on, when Joe junior developed a serious addiction to alcohol and spent lengthy bouts on the street, DiMaggio referred to him as a "bum."

*

DiMaggio's relationship with his brother Dom was also apparently uneasy at times, marked by a falling-out several years before his death. Dom DiMaggio said the "cooling off" had to do with a mix-up over a charity event involving his brother which Dom said he did not attend because he never received an official invitation despite repeated requests. While acknowledging "differences of opinion" over the years, he described his relationship with Joe as being a supportive one, noting that he had been named at one point as the executor of his estate. It was also Dom who gave the eulogy at his brother's funeral. "Dominic was a good brother, and he was a good brother to the end," said Joe Nachio.

But Engelberg and several other DiMaggio intimates maintain that Joe, despite Dom's frequent overtures, wanted little to do with his brother.

There were several reasons for this, says Engelberg, but one in particular had to do with the fact that Dom, in writing a book about his time as a member of the Boston Red Sox during the 1941 season, put his brother on the cover. Joe DiMaggio apparently felt that Dom was capitalizing on the Yankee Clipper mystique for his own commercial interest. In 1994 Engelberg and DiMaggio went to Hernando, Florida, together for the opening of a museum in honor of Ted Williams. Dom DiMaggio was there as well, since he had been a teammate of Williams's. But when Joe saw him initially in the Holiday Inn, he didn't even bother to say hello.

"Wasn't that your brother?" asked Engelberg as they walked to their rooms.

"So what," said DiMaggio.

Dom DiMaggio said he put his brother on the cover because "it looked nice." And any suggestion that he was trying to capitalize on his brother's name was "ridiculous." He also said that his brother was cordial during the Ted Williams Museum festivities when he introduced Joe to a fan who had asked to meet him.

DiMaggio also had a falling-out with his older sister Marie, according to Engelberg. The two lived together in a house in San Francisco that DiMaggio had purchased for his parents when he was still playing with the Yankees. Marie did basic bookkeeping chores for her brother, such as signing checks for his corporation and opening the mail. Engelberg, who spoke to her frequently, described her as one of the "sweetest, sweetest ladies" he had ever met. She spent most of her time in the kitchen drinking coffee and smoking cigarettes. But when DiMaggio became convinced that Marie had taken several items that had been given to him as gifts, he took all bookkeeping chores away from her and then instructed Engelberg to cut her out of his will, even though she was in her eighties. The change became moot when Marie died in 1996, an event DiMaggio considered of such little consequence that he didn't even tell Engelberg about it until he happened to inquire about her one day in casual conversation.

"How's Marie doing?"

"She died a couple of months ago," said DiMaggio.

If DiMaggio imposed rigid rules of behavior on his family, he may have imposed even more on his entourage. On one occasion a New York surgeon named Rock Positano, who was very close to DiMaggio during the last decade of his life and organized a memorial Mass for him at St. Patrick's Cathedral, arrived for dinner at Coco Pazzo in New York with DiMaggio and his two granddaughters. Positano was wearing a blazer and a cashmere shirt, an unacceptable breach of the DiMaggio commandments on proper attire in the presence of women. When Kathie and Paula went to the rest room, DiMaggio informed Positano that upon their return he would say that he had just received a medical page, go to his nearby office, put on a shirt and tie, and then come back. Positano, aware of the strictures of the inner circle, did exactly that.

"O.K., now we can have dinner," said DiMaggio.

The closest Engelberg himself ever came to severing his relationship with DiMaggio was at a card show in Atlantic City. Engelberg had just had a serious eye operation, making it impossible for him to fly. Instead, he took a train from Florida to Philadelphia that took roughly thirty hours because of a breakdown. Engelberg then had to ride in a car for an hour to get to Atlantic City. But far from being appreciative of his presence, DiMaggio at one point slapped Engelberg's hand during the show because he wasn't handing over memorabilia quickly enough for him to sign. Engelberg got up and left. He went back to his hotel room and called his wife to tell her what happened, to which she responded, "You bring it on yourself." Engelberg grudgingly went to dinner that night with DiMaggio and several others, and at the end of it, when DiMaggio put his arm around Engelberg and said, "Sometimes these shows piss me off," all was forgiven and the relationship remained intact.

But others, such as Barry Halper, a minority owner of the Yankees and one of the world's most prodigious collectors of sports
memorabilia (he sold much of his collection at Sotheby's for
roughly $21 million in 1999), were not so lucky. Halper had been a
devotee of DiMaggio's for nearly twenty-five years, to the degree
that DiMaggio had been a frequent guest at his home in Livingston, New Jersey, and attended the bar mitzvah of Halper's son.

Halper worshiped DiMaggio, but after a series of seemingly in-
nocuous disputes — one involving an event at Halper's home to
which the media showed up, another resulting in some apparent
violation of DiMaggio's strict rules on signing memorabilia —
Halper was jettisoned from DiMaggio's life completely, to the point
where, despite phone calls and faxes, he was not allowed to visit the
hospital when DiMaggio became sick. But Halper doesn't blame
DiMaggio for this. Instead, like others, he blames Engelberg, and is
convinced that Engelberg became so pathological in his relationship with DiMaggio that he worked to keep others out.

"Anything that happened was Morris's influence. He just became this ever-present, self-appointed man in charge," said Halper,
and he believes that DiMaggio would have taken steps to sever the
relationship had he not become gravely ill. "[Morris] has alienated
just about everybody who had any affection for Joe. So many people have been burnt by this. I can't talk about it. It's painful to me. I
have the memories."

"Joe suffered from a Stockholm syndrome at the end of his life,"
said another close associate of DiMaggio's who ended up estranged. "The older Joe got, the less he was able to extricate himself from the relationship." This person also believes, like Halper,
that Engelberg was often motivated by jealousy. "Anytime you got
too close to Joe, there was a threat to Morris, [and] he pushed you
out."

Engelberg said that any action to sever a relationship was always ini-
tiated by DiMaggio himself, never by him, and that in the particular case of Halper he actually tried to talk DiMaggio into resuming
their friendship. But Engelberg carried grudges, deep and bitter
ones rooted in possessiveness, and he made no secret of them.
When Halper wrote a heartfelt first-person piece in the *New York
Daily News* shortly after DiMaggio's death, detailing his friendship

with the Yankee great, Engelberg responded with a letter as self-revealing as it was vicious:

"There is something wrong in your personality where you constantly need the attention of playing off Joe DiMaggio for your own self benefit — this will no longer be tolerated, especially when your remarks are full of lies."

By the time the memorial Mass for DiMaggio was celebrated at St. Patrick's Cathedral in Manhattan the month after he died, Engelberg's dislike of Dom DiMaggio and his wife had grown to such a level that he was perfectly content to leave them off the invitation list altogether regardless of their blood relationship. "If you wish to invite them to the mass, that is your choice," he wrote to Joe DiMaggio's grandchildren after they had pointed out the absence on the invitation list. The same went for restaurateur Dick Burke and his wife, whose Fifth Avenue apartment DiMaggio had stayed at during visits to New York. Nor, for that matter, was he particularly crazy about the idea of DiMaggio's own son, Joe junior, going to the Mass. "I do not want to be responsible for him while I am in New York," he wrote.

Engelberg's detractors also wonder if the lawyer is trying to profit from his relationship with DiMaggio now that he is no longer alive. Engelberg never charged DiMaggio for any of the legal and negotiation work he did, fees that would have risen well into the millions had Engelberg charged a standard 10 percent agent's fee. As the trustee of the DiMaggio estate, Engelberg does gain a fee for his work. In addition, Engelberg has hundreds of signed pieces that DiMaggio had given to him as gifts. On April 5, 2000, at Christie's East in New York, an auction was held in which Engelberg attempted to sell dozens of items at prices so stratospheric there were virtually no bidders. Engelberg says that any gains from the sale would go to charity, and his handling of the estate has been praised by DiMaggio's granddaughter Kathie Stein. "I truly believe he has our best interests at heart," said Stein.

Engelberg's opponents also question the propriety of the lawyer's plan to write a memoir about DiMaggio, given the ballplayer's own desire for privacy. "I'm just curious to know how an attorney would take license to publish his memoir when Joe didn't do it," asked Jerry Romolt, who is in the sports-marketing business and did several major deals with DiMaggio. Engelberg said he was not betraying any confidence by writing about DiMaggio. He does anticipate criticism from DiMaggio's two granddaughters if such a book is published. But he said he would offset any feelings of betrayal by sharing the publishing proceeds with them. "You know something?" he said. "I'll give them a chunk of money. They'll stop resenting me."

Around 1994, DiMaggio left Seacoast Towers and relocated to an apartment in a posh residential community in Coral Gables called Deering Bay. It was a sweetheart deal for DiMaggio, as all deals were. He lived for free with furnishings that were worth in excess of $200,000. In return for being a spokesman for the complex and agreeing to play golf there three days a month, DiMaggio also received a yearly fee of $100,000. Although the trappings were luxurious, DiMaggio seemed utterly uninterested in them, except for the size of the televisions. He told Engelberg that he wanted a treadmill, so Engelberg went out and bought him one only to discover later that DiMaggio appeared to be using it largely to hang his shirts.

DiMaggio felt isolated in Deering Bay. Engelberg could sense that, and in 1996 he suggested to DiMaggio that he move into the Harbor Islands complex. The home that DiMaggio settled on, which he lived in for free in return for becoming a spokesman for the developer, was right across the street from Engelberg's. Engelberg bought a golf cart for DiMaggio so he could ride around the complex, customizing it in Yankee blue and decorating the hubcaps in Yankee pinstripes. For quite some time he shopped for him, stocking the kitchen with the food DiMaggio liked: bananas, red peppers, a certain kind of peanut. He basically rearranged his own work schedule to accommodate DiMaggio. He would leave his own home in Harbor Islands at 5:30 A.M. to put in a few hours at the office, return to Harbor Islands around 8:30 A.M. to pick up DiMaggio, take DiMaggio to his office in Hollywood, have breakfast and lunch with him, take him back to Harbor Islands around 5:00 P.M., have dinner and talk with him until about 9:00 P.M., and then work until 1:00 A.M.

DiMaggio continued to do his share of traveling. He still loved going to New York, where he stayed in the Burkes' apartment (he took the master bedroom, and they moved into the guest room) and was squired about by Rock Positano. He was still furiously in demand. On one occasion he went to a birthday party at the 21 Club, his attendance so desperately sought that he was actually paid somewhere in the range of $50,000 for it. When *Time* magazine held its star-studded seventy-fifth-anniversary party at Radio City Music Hall in March 1998, it was a matter of course that he would be one of the key invitees.

The invitation was conveyed to DiMaggio through Positano. DiMaggio said he would be happy to go, expressing to Positano the desire to sit with Dr. Henry Kissinger, a lifelong Yankee fan, and his wife, Nancy. Then *Time* managing editor Walter Isaacson called Positano to say that the organizers of the dinner wanted to place DiMaggio at the same table with President Clinton. Positano conveyed the news to DiMaggio, who had a distinct response.

"I'm not going."

Despite the threat, DiMaggio did go.

And was seated with Henry and Nancy Kissinger.

There seemed little doubt that DiMaggio liked the attention and company of the rich and powerful and famous. He liked his status as a living American myth, as long as the myth was carefully maintained on his terms without any leakage. But in his final years DiMaggio also fell into the rhythm of his life at Harbor Islands. The five-bedroom house, a subtle shade of pink on the outside with a red tile roof, gave him a sense of belonging he had never encountered before. "He was happy, as happy as Joe DiMaggio could be," said Engelberg. He gave willingly of his time to the hospital that has been named after him, the Joe DiMaggio Children's Hospital in Hollywood. He moved closer and closer emotionally to his two granddaughters and their families, and it was they who would ultimately inherit his multimillion-dollar estate. He developed a love for his four great-grandchildren that was deep and true, and he kept a little shell one of them had given him as if it were more valuable than any World Series ring. One Christmas morning, he toiled away in the kitchen making scrambled eggs for everyone, actually cooking. But almost as soon as DiMaggio gained the comfort of Harbor Islands, free of the isolation that had been his cloak, he also discovered something else.

He was dying.

*

On the surface, it seemed to make little sense for the Yankees to suddenly hold Joe DiMaggio Day at the end of September in 1998, with the regular season dwindling down and little time for adequate promotion. But Engelberg kept pushing for it for reasons that would later become obvious.

The weekend had been both exhilarating and grueling, starting in Chicago, where a statue of DiMaggio was unveiled by the city and the National Italian American Sports Hall of Fame. He could hardly eat, and he was in pain, and in private at least there was barely a moment in which Engelberg didn't hold his arm to keep him steady. The schedule was such that he didn't get into New York until early Sunday morning. He had gotten barely any sleep, and he was pale and exhausted, and yet, when it was time to go to the stadium, he looked the way he had always looked — royal and regal in a blue suit and white shirt and red tie, not a wisp of hair out of place.

He arrived at Yankee Stadium early as always, about 11:30 A.M. He rode in a golf cart through an underground tunnel from the dugout to a little section near the right-center-field bleachers. The plan was to keep him there until the stadium filled, at which point he would ride across the field in a white convertible. He was eighty-three years old at the time, and the wait made him livid. Suddenly, Deborah Tymon, who handles marketing for the Yankees, received a call in the dugout from security — DiMaggio was actually trying to leave.

Engelberg himself ran out of the dugout across the field to try to calm DiMaggio down. When the lawyer got there, DiMaggio was as white as a ghost, standing by an exit, railing:

"I don't need this crap. I want to get out of here."

Engelberg gently reminded him that the Yankees were about to present him with the replicas of the eight World Series rings that had been stolen from DiMaggio's hotel room years earlier. Engelberg's presence calmed DiMaggio.

He rode across the field in that white convertible. The rings were presented to him, and he went to the microphone to give a short speech, knowing in his heart that this would probably be the last time he would ever set foot in Yankee Stadium, the scene of his happiest days and his greatest triumphs, when no one in all of baseball had ruled center field with more majesty and splendor. He began with the words "Thank you for the very kind ovation," but something was wrong.

The microphone wasn't on, and his last words would never be heard. DiMaggio waved to the crowd and walked into the dugout runway. Then he ripped into Tymon with such full and angry force that she began to cry — the first time that Engelberg had seen him lose his temper in public.

The next day, DiMaggio flew back to Florida. And fourteen days after that, he was hospitalized for cancer, or the "funny cells," as he called them, because cancer was a word he could not bear.

For more than a decade, Morris Engelberg had done everything that Joe DiMaggio had asked of him. Now, in the final five months of DiMaggio's life, as he lay dying with cancer, Engelberg would be asked to do more for DiMaggio than ever before — not just help make millions for him, or shop for him, but lie for him, and risk his own reputation for him. Engelberg became the battering ram for the wrath of those whom DiMaggio wanted sealed off as he tried to control the act of his death just as he had always tried to control all the acts of his life. "I was his liar. I did his dirty work," said Engelberg, but it was a final role he played willingly, just as he had played all the other roles, as if he had been a member of a cult, the cult of Joe DiMaggio. "I wanted him to love me," said Engelberg in explanation. "He was more important to me than my reputation."

The night before DiMaggio had surgery at Memorial Regional Hospital in Hollywood for the removal of a cancerous tumor from one of his lungs, he made Engelberg promise not to tell anyone about the cancer unless it was successfully removed and there were no complications. But there were complications. For months, Engelberg honored that vow with outright deception.

Word quickly leaked out to the media that DiMaggio was in the hospital. Reporters and camera crews began to gather, but Engelberg's answer was basically the same to their questions whether it was the *New York Daily News* or the *New York Post* or the Associated Press: DiMaggio had been hospitalized for pneumonia. To further the ruse, Engelberg went into the hospital one day with a pizza box.

The box was empty.

*

Roughly a week after the surgery, DiMaggio took a serious turn for the worse. An emergency procedure had to be performed to remove excess fluid from his lungs, and Engelberg realized that, regardless of his oath of silence, he had to tell DiMaggio's grandchildren the truth. But DiMaggio's brother Dom was another story.

He arrived at the hospital, demanding to know what was happening to his brother. Engelberg refused to tell him, saying he would have to hear it from the doctors. Dom reportedly threatened to take the matter to court, and Engelberg still wouldn't tell him, invoking attorney-client privilege. Dom DiMaggio in turn reportedly called Engelberg a "phony, liar, and control freak." Engelberg still wouldn't say anything. Instead, it was the head of the hospital, Frank Sacco, who told Dom of his brother's medical condition.

On January 18, 1999, after ninety-nine days in the intensive-care unit of the hospital, DiMaggio returned home to Harbor Islands. To avoid a media circus, Engelberg arranged to have him taken through a back exit of the hospital with a towel over his face.

Much of the media, depending on Engelberg for their information, painted DiMaggio's return home as a major step in a recovery every bit as epic as the fifty-six-game streak. The word "comeback" was used, as if DiMaggio were climbing just another rung on the storybook ladder of his life and would make it to that Yankee home opener in April.

About a week before Joe DiMaggio died, he rallied briefly when George Steinbrenner came to visit. Steinbrenner adored DiMaggio, appreciating in a way that no Yankee owner ever had the pivotal role that DiMaggio had played in the Yankee mystique. DiMaggio was bedridden most of the time he was at home, but he sat in a wheelchair for Steinbrenner's visit. He wore a white shirt and a blanket covered his legs. He was alert, and he looked regal, as only Joe DiMaggio could look regal, and he took in the story Steinbrenner told of how, as a kid in Cleveland, he would go down to the train station when the Yankees were in town and try to carry DiMaggio's bag.

DiMaggio's performance that day was remarkable, perhaps because he knew it was his last. But after about twenty minutes he was bent forward with stomach pains and said he was tired.

He was on morphine at the end, because the pain was intolerable, and sitting in a wheelchair on the little terrace in the shade of several ficus trees, he told Engelberg how much he regretted that he would never see his great-grandchildren grow up. But he also told Engelberg that he was ready to die. With radiation he could have lived longer, but he didn't want radiation, because he didn't want a nation to watch him die for any longer than it already had.

In the final hour of his life the night of March 7, 1999, there were six people present — Engelberg; DiMaggio's granddaughter Kathie; Jim Hamra, the husband of DiMaggio's other granddaughter, Paula; two nurses; and an official of a local hospice. DiMaggio's hair was combed, and his nails were manicured, and Engelberg gently lifted his head and kissed him on the forehead.

"I can never thank you for what you did for me," he said to him. "I love you, Joe."

DiMaggio's mouth was open, and then, in a whisper, came his final words.

"I'll finally get to see Marilyn."

MICHAEL LEAHY

Swing Shift

FROM THE WASHINGTON POST MAGAZINE

Play it again — and some more, Cal — B.C.

THERE ARE TWO of him these days. There is the nearly mythic figure with his obligation to his legend, and there is the man with his uncertainties. The legend's visage smiles down on him from posters and T-shirts. The man has a back on the mend and a big red splotch in the middle of his forehead and hair that has gone silver on its sides. But there is a small kid across the clubhouse staring numbly at him right now, a glazed look he recognizes. It is that shy, frozen, open-mouthed gaze he often gets, and so he walks over. The child has been collecting autographs on a baseball in the Baltimore Orioles' spring training clubhouse. Cal Ripken bends and points. "Want me to sign that?"

The kid, who comes up to about his waist, can say nothing. An honorary Orioles batboy for the day, he has been too awed even to make his little legs shuffle over.

"What's this?" Ripken says, noticing Eddie Murray's large signature on the ball. "You went to Eddie before me? Before *me?*" He is grinning and teasing now, and the kid is beaming, so thrilled that his mouth quivers. Ripken pats his tiny shoulder, grabs the ever-present pen from his pocket, and signs, his idol's chores done.

In that instant his mood changes. It is as if a switch has been flicked and the lights inside in him have gone off. He steps into a dugout and plops down on the bench, thinking about the uncertainties, looking out on an empty stadium. "My back's feeling okay, getting there, but nothing's for sure," he says. "I don't have the stiffness I did last year and that's great. But you don't know. And I really think I need more functional strengthening in my left leg."

His surgery last year relieved a herniated disk that had rendered his lower back immobile and sent excruciating pain radiating down his left leg, finally leaving him incapable of walking normally. He straightens his back. "My left leg," he repeats. "Did I say that?" There have been days in the last few weeks when Cal Ripken has sounded like any mortal who's gone under the knife and now finds himself in rehab limbo. It's taken something from him. The famous resolve and grit are intact, but the stoicism is gone. The thought of back surgery was "kind of frightening," he admits. There are "no long-term guarantees," he says. In the aftermath, there was a very unsettling moment during a January rehab work-out.

"I felt some slippage," he murmurs.

Slippage?

"Slippage right around here," he says, gesturing vaguely at his mending back. "It was, I don't know, scary, a little scary."

This hangs there.

"I know there isn't any way of knowing anything yet," he says. "I have concerns like anybody who's had surgery. That slippage . . ."

Outside the stadium, behind a chainlink fence, they are waiting for him as the sun falls, the hundreds with their baseballs and scraps of paper and anything else on which they might get a piece of him. "I like sitting here this time of day," he says slowly, looking at cool shadows lengthening on the outfield grass. "It's very peaceful." A long pause. He is already thinking about something else. "So, anyway, things are pretty normal, but not completely, because you just don't know, you can't be sure."

The hagiography of Cal Ripken, with its heavy helpings of solemnly told tales about humility and an ascetic work ethic, always has masked the reality of Ripken — obscured his worries, his fierce pride, his boyish appetites to test himself in contests rough and rougher, his compulsion to win, his zeal for control, his quirks and excesses — as if the glimpse of any of these traits might undermine our apotheosis of him. In a culture run amok with athletic thugs and celebrated antiheroes, fans always have needed his deification more than he. He sees himself as he is. "I haven't got the same speed or some other things that I had at twenty-five," he says. "But I'm here. I have got other things going for me. People should know me well enough to know I'm going to lay it on the line."

In an injury-shortened season, he hit an astonishing .340 last year, which made even Ripken doubters repent and genuflect. But it matters far less to hit .340 at age thirty-nine than at twenty-nine. There are always suspicions that a sterling season and prodigious numbers might be a graybeard's last, that reflexes could dull overnight, that backs might not get better. "I know some people will always have questions from now on," he says.

Sometimes now you feel the urgency in his pauses and the way he clarifies and reclarifies the condition of his back, as if, against his nature, adversity is peeling back his layers and allowing a glimpse inside. There are days when his eyes narrow and he sighs hard and his head swivels toward an empty spring training diamond and it is easy to see clear to that fierceness at his core. "I played with a herniated disk last year, so I don't think anybody could ever question my commitment and ability to play," he says.

Still, he can see the end, at least of his playing days. He does not make much effort to hide his thoughts, dreams, or resentments any longer: his yearning to one day control the team outright and remold an organization that he believes has lost its way; his conflicted feelings over how the frequently changing Orioles management alternately treated him, his father, and brother Bill; his zest to teach baseball to kids the way his father taught it to him; his desire not to lose control over his life like so many retired athletes; his enduring belief in his athletic prowess; his determination to rise yet again from back problems and prove he is young at thirty-nine, no, thirty-nine years and eight months now.

He came in with Reagan. He can hear time ticking now. He is one of those athletes whose career reminds you, against your will, of your own passages, and mortality, of the days fleeing. It can make you a little queasy. On game days when he warms up, the red-faced Fort Lauderdale retirees and snowbirds crowd around the first-base railing to exhort him, watching him jog and stretch carefully. They were young when he started and now they are not, and they good-naturedly shout out back-care treatments and tell him never to leave. He laughs. He has no plans to leave, not really, planning on his post-playing days to be one seamless entry into just another stage of baseball life.

But for now he's a player, and never has he lost a personal challenge, can't conceive of losing this one. Within a week, he will be forced to sit out a game because of a strained neck muscle, and

while the injury is unrelated to his back, it reminds everyone of the
new ailments threatening any player crowding forty. So, even away
from the crowds, in the dugout, he is looking for a way to bolster
his odds. "I think I'm going very well right now, but more structural
strengthening is something I need." He is staring at that patch of
preternaturally green outfield grass. He reaches down and touches
and retouches his left leg. "Right here. Structural strengthening."

The phrase comforts him, in the way a mantra comforts any be-
liever.

He seldom permits himself public expressions of worry. Some of
this is inscribed in his genetic code. His late father, a man tough
enough to repair and drive a tractor after being struck by its fly-
wheel and gushing blood, conceded to nothing. The eldest son,
carrying the added burden of celebrity, has been faithful to the image others carry of him, aware that for a long while he has been
something larger than himself, equal parts American deity and living ethic, less flesh than legend.

The doctors' and trainers' statements about his surgery are sani-
tized and clinical. Their patient talks with undisguised amazement
about what has happened to him, not looking for sympathy but,
just the same, not wanting anyone to minimize what he's gone
through, or to liken his back to a Ferrari that with a little tinkering
can be sent on its way good as ever. His body is not an engine, his
tissue and tendons not pistons and valves. "I . . . got . . . cut . . . on,"
he says, very deliberately.

Not "treated." Not "probed" or "operated on." But "cut on." And
few things are scarier to the great athlete. It exposes him to the
great unknown, the possibility that surgery might cut into his inef-
fable magic — the greatness of his muscles and synapses a mystery
on some level even to him. The only certain thing for Ripken at the
moment is that everything is uncertain.

His back's "slippage" was less a specific pain than a sensation during one of his solitary rehabilitative fielding drills in offseason —
his "scoop movement," as he calls it, normally a routine, unde-
manding exercise where he drops a ball near his feet, bends,
scoops the ball, twists to his left, and, all in one deftly swift motion,
flips the ball to second base, as if he were still a shortstop. But
something felt alien on that afternoon. This wasn't *his* back. Gears

weren't correctly meshing. "Slippage" didn't mean anything as threatening as a slipped disk, simply a lack of synchronicity in his body's different moving parts. But that was frightening enough. To the contorting, pivoting athlete like Ripken who needs his parts working as smoothly as a Rolex's, the strange stiffness spoke of a fluidity possibly gone, irretrievably so.

"I was concerned," he says. "You don't know what to think when that happens — what it might mean, you know? Right away I went to the trainers and said, 'What's happening? Can you tell me? What's *happening?*'"

Even more than reflexes, what a great athlete loses late in his career is control — over his body, over his dominion, over prerogatives and privileges that once felt like his forever but, in truth, were always tenuous, tied to his on-field supremacy. Suddenly, a .128-hitting twenty-one-year-old becomes heir apparent, as a struggling Ripken himself did after the 1981 season when Doug DeCinces was deemed past his prime and traded. When Ripken's new manager and longtime friend Mike Hargrove announced during spring training's opening week that he was working out Jeff Conine as a third base backup and let it drop to reporters that, every couple of weeks, Ripken might give way to Conine and perhaps could even play a little first base, it seemed yet another signal that Ripken's career had entered a new stage.

Eyebrows lifted from Fort Lauderdale to Baltimore, and Ripken expressed puzzlement. The manager quickly rushed to mollify the legend, assuring him nothing of substance had really changed. Under the panting heat of reporters who study the subtext of managerial statements about Ripken the way Kremlinologists once parsed Soviet party leaders' words for clues to coups and purges, Hargrove swiftly backtracked to explain that the reference to Ripken at first base simply was meant as a hypothetical, a tribute to his star's athleticism and versatility. Ripken would play third for as long as he physically could, added Hargrove.

But the moment succeeded only in reminding everyone that the legend's prerogatives are slowly ebbing, like the ground ball that you know, from the time it leaves the bat far away, will be just beyond the grasp, rolling inexorably into left field. No matter how glittering his statistics remain as he enters his forties, people will hereafter see him in twilight, expecting the light to recede. And as his gifts and durability further wane, so too will the deference paid him: It is the single intractable rule of sports. DiMaggio learned it, and Mays, too. With Hargrove's prodding, Ripken already has relinquished absolute claim to third base, losing a measure of control over his professional life, and what Cal Ripken always has loathed most is lack of control over anything. "I like to know where I stand," he says. "I've always had that. And no one likes it when they don't have it."

He's unaccustomed to uncertainty. His record streak of playing in consecutive games was the absolute expression of certainty and control — 2,632 games over seventeen seasons where his resolve as much as his play dictated that his name would be written in the starting lineup every day. He played more than five years without missing an inning, a lesser streak that ended in late 1987 only because his father, then the Orioles' manager, asked him during a game what he thought about the idea of coming out. The son relented. It was a testament to how much he revered Cal Sr. "If you did things right on a field, if you worked hard and had synchronicity, you had control," Ripken says. "My father had drills timed down to the minute. . . . I love to play. But I love even more doing things right on a field. . . . That's when you say to yourself you want to do this as long as you can."

He believes that his .340 last season, even if it hasn't assuaged all worries about his back, should at least muzzle his critics. Around reporters, he has spent the spring honing a slogan that sounds vaguely political in its promotional ring: "Armed and dangerous," as in, "It felt good to be armed and dangerous last year, and I'm feeling that way right now."

It is part of his low-key charm that this doesn't sound like a boast, merely a request that the cynics wait before pouncing, a suggestion that his prospects are high given last year's hard numbers. His eighteen home runs in roughly half a season gave him his highest ratio of home runs to at-bats ever in a year, and his .340 would have been a career high had he compiled enough plate trips. He had a new compact swing and a bat that looked quicker than ever.

His resurgence could be seen in ways never to be found in any box score. In Atlanta, during a nationally televised game, ESPN clocked the swings of Orioles and Braves hitters. Hitting in a group that included Chipper Jones, Ryan Klesko, Andruw Jones, and Brady Anderson, Ripken had the fastest bat, timed at eighty-nine miles per hour on one swing and ninety miles per hour on another. No one among the younger lions was faster than eighty-seven.

To a happy Ripken, the moment served as a sharp retort to skeptics. He is a rabid competitor not above discreetly gloating, and he has a long memory when it involves observers who have questioned either his play or his disinclination during the streak to sit out games. "I downplay it, but I know I have talent and that it matches up well," he says, allowing himself a grin. "Is it like Ken Griffey's? No. But I know what I possess. You get older, you lose an edge in some places, but there're certain things you still have an edge on. I don't want people thinking I don't. You measure your ability against a young player, and when you're successful, well, you cling to that. You've shown you're still armed."

"Armed," he obligingly repeats.

"You know what I can't understand?" he says one morning in Maryland, genuinely puzzled, standing on the indoor basketball court that adjoins his home and, while hardly looking, flipping a baseball backward over his head into a basket like a reverse layup, catching it, and immediately flipping it again over his shoulder. "I can't understand how Michael Jordan could give up playing when he did, not with all that he could still do, *can still do,* you know? I'm not passing judgment on Michael; I'm sure he had reasons that I'd appreciate if I knew them. I'm just saying I could never do what Michael did. It's not because of the attention. The ovations? I don't need those, I don't play for those. I just love playing too much. I'm gonna play as long as I can — until, you know, I can't do it."

No two athletes, contemplating the end, are moved by the same impulses. When his batting average plummeted and his power left him the way it did Samson, Hall of Fame third baseman Mike Schmidt quit in the middle of a season, unable to bear his slide into mediocrity. Ripken's former Orioles teammate Mike Boddicker remembers the weird, vaguely scary, wholly disorienting feeling of waking up from fitful naps just as airplanes were touching down somewhere, not knowing where he was, and realizing it was time to get out. Jim Palmer retired, then attempted an ill-fated comeback, missing nothing so much as the game's "focus," which he defines as "tuning out the whole world's exterior, so that you're at the center of things and concentrating on something very special." What would Cal Ripken miss? "Everything," he says softly.

A shot finally spins out; the baseball plummets past his glove, hits the floor. Ripken stoops to pick it up, bending carefully at his knees, as if to safeguard his back, and scratching his balding pate, its sparse blades spiked straight up. "If Michael had played another season, he just as well could have won again," he says excitedly. He is talking while bounding around his gym. It is his refuge at his manse, and on a cold Maryland day in late February, it is a nice warm place to be. Outside is like a scene from *Christmas in Connecticut:* pristine snow everywhere, and a high sledding hill just around the bend from a neighbor's red farmhouse and other gentleman planters and ranchers. It is an idyll only thirty minutes from Camden Yards.

He is dressed in black — black workout shirt, black shorts, black tennis shoes, very little like the immaculate, white-uniformed, iconic Ripken of cereal boxes or Baltimore Orioles posters. Brown as a nut, he has a feral quality to him away from a ballpark, the sense of a man free — his movements jauntier so that his head bobs in a shamble of sorts, his calves exposed and enormous, his grunts loud, his yells boyishly and coarsely exultant when he hurls baseballs or swings his bats.

The place is Guy Paradise. Richie Rich would covet this court, complete with its glass backboards and a scoreboard and a three-eighths-inch-thick all-purpose rubber floor so that you can play all kinds of games and party on it, too. There's a weight room and a batting cage and, off in the wings, a nicely appointed pro-style locker room, the wood-paneled cubicles reeking manliness and filled with enough basketball uniforms for six different teams. If Ripken and his pals want to be Milwaukee Bucks tonight, there are the Buck uniforms neatly hanging for them.

He resumes flipping the ball into the basket, quite manically, chattering on about Michael Jordan. There is a hyperactive quality to him, the tic of a man in constant need of a game and somebody to beat. Ever so slightly, he bumps you, perhaps accidentally, but more likely semiconsciously, bodying you up, as they say in hoops, looking for a subtle advantage in position around the basket as he puts up another layup. All net.

"But you know what I *really* can't figure out?" he blurts. "I can't for the life of me understand why somebody announces before the start of a season that this is gonna be his last season and then goes all around the different cities."

Farewell tours of the kind made by retiring NBA superstars like Kareem Abdul-Jabbar and Charles Barkley mystify him. "They were great players and I'm sure they had their reasons," he says, "but if they've made a decision they don't want to do it anymore and that their career is over, why not retire right now? Mentally, I couldn't do it. It'd take something out of your effort. And in order to find out if you can still compete, you gotta compete with something on the line. You have to lay it on the line. I'd want to play; I'd *have* to play. Can you think of a good reason for saying you're quitting in advance? Can you? No, really, I want to debate this with you."

You resist. He issues challenges like this often. He has an athlete's physique but a litigator's mind-set, heavy on logic, keen to rhetorical openings, bent on winning the point. Even talking offers the chance of competition. "Come on," he persists genially. "Why say you're quitting before you do? What's to be gained?"

You recall Willie Mays stumbling around in Shea Stadium late in his career. Isn't that among the things that the great athlete who has lost a step or two might wish to avoid by setting himself a timetable? The futile dives for balls? The fastballs, once big as grapefruits, shooting past him like BBs.

"No, that wouldn't be it for me, because I *have* lost a step," he says, looking up to see another ball falling through the net. "I might lose a little more. But as long as I can still help and play at the level I expect, I want to do this. If I retired, whenever it was, it'd come at a time when things were pretty obvious to me and it'd happen pretty fast. . . . I'd hope so. It's hard to know."

He falls silent. For a moment, the gym is as quiet as a morgue. On most February days here in past years, he would have been playing basketball. Seattle Mariner Alex Rodriguez might have stopped by, and Oriole Ryan Minor, too, the Ripken game frequently populated by hotshot major league baseball players and former Division I collegiate basketball players. But the doctors wouldn't allow Ripken to play basketball for five minutes this past offseason, let alone the three hours a day that he expects from himself in winter as part of his conditioning regimen.

"I was tempted to play a couple times anyway," he confesses. "But the risk was too great." So he feels strange, out of sorts, for the first time in two decades. "I haven't been able to prepare for this season like I usually would, so I'm just not sure of things like I'd usually be," he says, gripping a baseball bat hard and then harder still, the veins rising in his forearms like little blue cables, the silence in the air being the void he can't yet get a read on. Then, as if hearing the doubt in his voice, he whips the bat through the air, letting out a yell. "But nobody should make any mistake that I'll be ready to compete," he says. "I know there's always an element of having to prove yourself again. I'm ready to lay it on the line."

If things do not work out, whenever that might happen, he says, he will be able to deal with it. He sees the risks ahead to his status and legacy, and does not care. "I'm different," he says. "Something happened to me last year."

Last year was the year his father died of lung cancer. Last spring was the season when his father's counsel was silenced, when his chronically bad back began searing, when his skills seemed to be eroding, when he went on the disabled list, when more doubters said his time was up, and, finally, when the realization struck him: He did not have forever to enjoy things. What was the worst that could happen? What else could they take away?

"I found peace," he says with no small wonder. "I can't explain how or why exactly. Probably my father's death had a lot to do with it. Something just happened. Something . . ." He shrugs.

His family's two big young Akitas, Halo and Rocks, are sitting at attention outside like gargoyles, looking his way as dumbly mesmerized as everybody else. Unconsciously, his hand drops a baseball at his feet. He dips and backhands the ball without looking, gazing past Halo and Rocks. "Spring training had been pretty bad. My dad had been very ill, my back was stiff, I was taking extra batting practice in the cage to try to work out the frustrations and pressures. It wasn't helping much, I was really struggling in a lot of ways. . . . And then things just changed. I guess when my dad died I lost that person who was always there for me. . . . But there were other things, which is why I'm saying I don't understand all the variables. . . . My worries about my back probably contributed. Maybe this sort of thing just occurs at a certain time in life. You get older, maybe you get a new perspective."

Quite apart from the rest of him, his hand is still doing its thing with that baseball. Like so many celebrities, he lives on several planes of being at once, simultaneously talking, autographing, posing, stretching, spinning a ball in a free hand, regripping it. Fastball grip now. He was a star pitcher in high school, flirted with the idea of going back to the mound during his early struggles in the minors, and believes to this day, like a lot of Orioles, past and present, that he could have made it as a pitcher.

"I think when Dad died . . ." He pauses. There is an unconscious wince around his mouth. The rest of him, especially his blue eyes, glassy and distant, is with his father. "I think I probably realized you just have a certain amount of days, a certain window to play the game, and that helped me see it and get it," he murmurs. "Get some kind of peace. Which I'd never really had, not in that way. . . . I said to myself, 'What do I of all people have to worry about?'"

He decided he would relish whatever time in the game he had left. A week, a year, five years, a single day. He felt liberated. His agonies lifted, his back pain eased with rest, and a prolonged batting slump ended. "The great thing about peace for a hitter," he says softly, "is that it really helps you stay still in the batter's box and wait for the pitch. And I did. And that's when it all came to me."

His brilliance was reborn. And, just as the world seemed right, he and his back ended up under the blade.

Everything ahead now is a mist.

With his new peace, he can see past the horizon to the end now. He lets himself entertain questions about what his life might look like beyond his playing days.

Managing?

"Why not something bigger?" he answers.

Managing does not interest him, because in modern baseball managers are seldom in control, as his father's brief, painful tenure in that position taught him. Cal Sr. took over the Orioles' helm in 1987, after the Orioles had finished last in their division and sixteen games below .500. Senior's fortunes with a rebuilding ball club were no better: a losing season in 1987, followed by rumors at year's end that Orioles owner Edward Bennett Williams had wanted to fire him, only to be talked out of it by Orioles executives. "I don't think my father ever had a real chance," Ripken says. "People were talking [about the rumors] before the [1988] season ever started. Part of what was unfair, I think, was that we had a shortage of talent on the team and people in the organization knew it. That wasn't my father's fault. . . . My father was respected, and terrific at [motivating] players."

Just six games into the 1988 season, with the Orioles winless, Williams and Orioles management fired his father without so much as forewarning Cal or his brother Bill. He heard the news while en route to Memorial Stadium. It was left to a trainer to break the news that his father already had packed his bag and left. Frank Robinson became manager and, as if in proof of the Orioles' dreadful talent, the team went on to lose another fifteen consecutive games.

Managing, Ripken has believed ever since, means always looking over your shoulder. Others can fire you; others provide the team's master plan and expect you to win with it; others determine your players and your minor-league organization; others have control.

Control is his little-known but central need. Virtual control of a franchise — like the kind Pat Riley possesses in coaching the NBA's Miami Heat or Michael Jordan seems to be acquiring with the Washington Wizards — intrigues him, but only so far. Much better, he observes, would be owning a baseball team someday, preferably the Orioles, so he can put all his baseball theories to the test without interference. "I'd set the direction and principles and have a manager who'd work within those principles," he says. "Manager is a job. An owner sets the direction. There's a big difference. You need to have ownership of the team to control the variables. I think I'm going to have that opportunity sometime, somewhere. But the dream would be owning the Orioles — maybe being part of an ownership group and running the baseball side. I have confidence. I have an understanding, a view, and a knowledge of the Orioles and the organization that few people have. I definitely have an interest in someday putting my philosophies to a test here."

That he wants to lead the Orioles — that he has even stayed with them as a player through his father's dismissal and his brother's sudden, unexpected release after the 1992 season; through contentious contract negotiations; through sly, disparaging remarks about the quality of his leadership from an owner and at least one manager — always has been a mystery to Ripken watchers. The explanation certainly does not lie in wanting to remain with a championship dynasty. Since a five-year run of winning seasons at the start of Ripken's career, the club has had mostly losing years, finding itself in the American League Championship Series only twice, and falling short on each occasion. Several times in the '90s, a consensus of observers and Ripken himself viewed the Orioles as nothing more than a mediocre club in the midst of yet another retooling, prompting some of his friends to wonder whether he might flee in the autumn of his career and latch his fortunes to a contender — the Yankees, perhaps. Ripken didn't. His allegiance to Baltimore has nothing to do with an expectation that the Orioles might suddenly reverse their fortunes and capture a title, but rather is reflective of a determination to help them win again, to restore pride and a measure of "excellence" to a franchise that has been his life since boyhood. He takes more pride in his loyalty than anything now. "I made the decision to endure the rebuilding process because I care. . . . And it didn't matter what difficulties I might have had with [management]. I wanted to be here."

"In the difficult times, he's had the skill of separating the conduct of ownership and management from the rest of the Orioles — from teammates, coaches, fans," says his longtime attorney-agent, Ron Shapiro. "He compartmentalizes. I think it's because the concept of the Orioles starts with his dad and his own early time with Senior in the organization. There are bonds there. But he has worked through some things only painfully, and it wouldn't have happened except that the ties and bonds are central to his life. They begin with his dad and a concept of what's right, how to do things, so he wouldn't give any of that up. . . . Ownership always knew that. Sure, it gave them a certain [bargaining leverage] with us. Cal is an Oriole. It's like a family to him."

A dysfunctional one at times, which doesn't matter at all in the end to Ripken. The key to understanding the relationship, believe those closest to him, is to recognize that Ripken views the Oriole ethos as everlasting, and the suits and money men who pull the Orioles' levers at any given moment as merely transitory figures. He will outlast them, his friends say anonymously. It is a quiet belief rooted in his sense that his claim to the team, not theirs, is the purest, the one rooted not principally in dollars but in the game itself, to be played the way his father espoused it. He, not the suits, best knows the ethic, and how the Orioles organization works, from bottom up. He, not they, will be teaching baseball for a lifetime.

It is an attitude, even conceit, born of the knowledge that he has been with the organization longer than any of them, dating back to scorching summer days helping his father's farm teams and lazy, balmy nights in North Carolina when he was an eleven-year-old batboy at Double-A Asheville shyly sidling up to Doug DeCinces and looking for fielding pointers.

"When my father managed in the [minors], it was an era when people always spoke about 'The Oriole Way,' because the Orioles were the model of what a baseball organization should be," he says. "There was a right way to doing things on the field, a synchronicity, and everybody learned it. My dad epitomized Oriole pride and the right work ethic, and his ethic mirrored that of an organization. 'The Oriole Way' is much more of a slogan now. That's not a knock against anyone. Maybe it represents a change all the way around baseball — more to the entertainment and money. Can I say the Oriole Way is being restored? Is there the same philosophy around here and in the minors as there used to be? I'd have to say no. . . . Very few people know how to do it now, as we get farther removed from that era. So I would like the opportunity. I hope it's there someday."

But even Cal doesn't know when that day will come — or if it ever will.

Several mornings a week, he practices hitting in his batting cage against pitches coming in at sixty miles per hour, which is glacially slow for a major leaguer. "I can hit five hundred pitches in fifty minutes off this machine," he says. Or ten a minute. Or one every six seconds. The numbers roll off his tongue.

He hits a rocket into the net, one-handed. "Yeeeeeaaah," he howls, delighted.

Another swing leaves him groaning. He has cracked his trademark black bat. "Man, I really liked that stick," he mutters, knowing, in that instant, that the bat is destined to become somebody's high-priced souvenir. Virtually anything he cracks, as well as anything he wears and discards, becomes marketable. His signature makes it eternal — to be housed perhaps in the museum that bears his family's name in his home town of Aberdeen, or in some collector's case that he'll never see, a form of veneration baffling even to him sometimes. Ripken Under Glass. "Another bat for a charity auction," he says wryly, gently leaning it against a wall.

He grabs a new black bat, the clone of every other here — thirty-five inches long, thirty-three ounces — and resumes smacking balls one-handed, a drill he adopted last year on the advice of the Orioles' new hitting coach, Terry Crowley, who believed it would help a slumping Ripken shorten his swing and move him more directly toward a pitch. Before the arrival of his old teammate, Ripken's variety of contorted batting stances had evolved into a vaguely hunchback look. Crowley placed his back into a neutral position, got him to stop jumping at the ball, and helped him relax. Ripken's average jumped sixty-nine points and, overnight, Crowley became a swing guru. "I just got Cal comfortable," Crowley says, downplaying his role, which is much of the reason Ripken so likes him.

But was Crowley the major difference between a scintillating '99 and a sub-par '98?

To Ripken, the question threatens to redistribute kudos that belong to the player, not his coach. "Terry's very good and important, but he's no savior," Ripken declares. "Remember, I won two MVPs before Terry ever was doing this." He pauses. He is already reformulating his words. "Terry is terrific. There's trust there and he has no agenda. He's very patient, which is very important. But my father worked with me, Frank Robinson worked with me, and I like to think I brought something. All I'm saying is Terry's not a savior. I brought .300 seasons to this."

He is not a self-effacing man. He will tell anyone who asks that he personally edited all ten drafts of the autobiography drafted for him by a New York writer. That the book's voice is his alone. That a certain celebrity whom he played against is a lousy basketball player. That he never ducked out of the way when a strapping rival like Kirk Gibson tried breaking up a double play.

He doesn't want to sound conceited, but he doesn't wish to be shortchanged by history either. One of the many nice things about being Cal Ripken Jr. is that he actually gets points in these moments for candor. "I worked very hard to get to .340," he says. "And I'm still dangerous."

He competes almost always. You might not see it, but it is happening, in ways big, small, subtle, unseen. He shakes hands hard. He wants to hit a batting-practice homer one-handed in Camden Yards. He says unabashedly that he aimed to hit line drives off the shins of Crowley one day during a batting drill, and exulted when he finally nailed him, with the victim having to limp off to get an ice pack. Just a year ago, when goaded during friendly pickup basketball games by younger players calling him "old man" and questioning his jumping ability, he would dunk on thirty-eight-year-old legs.

There is a story he tells about himself that reveals more about his nature than any bromide about discipline ever will, that reveals a competitive fury so volcanic on occasion that it befuddles even him. Once, during a charity basketball game, after an opponent hit him in the back, he complained loudly to a referee, who made the mistake of addressing him like a mortal, telling him to quit complaining and play.

Ripken exploded. "The rage just came out of me, I really let him have it," he recalls, shaking his head in wonder.

Thereafter, anytime Ripken scored a basket, he looked for the referee and berated him more. After the game, a perplexed trainer sat down next to him and dared to chastise him: "Didn't you know how much that ref admired you? That guy loved you before you did that. What happened to you out there?"

Ripken had no answer. "I knew I'd lashed out at the ref," he remembers. "I knew the guy was stunned. I can't explain what I did. . . . A lot of people say they have a different view of me on a court. I'm definitely more physical, more intense. People will say, 'Can you still dunk, old man?' And then I gotta prove I can dunk. That's me — or at least a part of me. I guess I don't back down, which carries over. . . . I always keep trying to fight my way through things, which can hurt you in baseball. Baseball's all about staying back until the right moment; it's all about approach. Last year's success was all about good approach merging with relaxation. And that's always the battle for me. Approach and relaxation. . . . I want it too much sometimes, I guess."

None of this comes as a surprise to those who know him best. As a young boy, he played card games like hearts so ruthlessly against his siblings that they finally ganged up on him, leaving his brother Bill to say a quarter-century later, "What's driven him isn't just that he loves winning but that he hates losing more than anybody."

During his minor-league days, he compulsively wrestled teammates, just pounced on them and threw them in headlocks, despite their protests. His roommate during his first year in the minors was a twenty-two-year-old pitcher out of Florida State named Brooks Carey, who would never make it to the majors but whom Ripken turned into his unwilling wrestling partner. "You'd be walking around with him and, without warning, he'd just put your head in a headlock and say, 'Let's go,'" Carey remembers, groaning at the memory. "I love the guy, but you could be anywhere, in the room, in a parking lot, anywhere. Headlock. Bam. If I said, 'I don't feel like it,' he'd say, 'We're going anyway,' and he'd throw you down and pounce on you. I'd say, 'Hey, dammit, you're hurting my chest.' He didn't care; he'd just beat you to a pulp. I finally told him, 'I'm tired of your crap and I'm going to the coaches and tell them I can't pitch today 'cause of you.' He talked me out of it. But, man, I was angry."

Ripken shrugs at the story. Oh, God. Long sigh. They're old friends. Sometimes he's as mystified as anybody else by his needs and impulses. "I don't know why I did that to Brooks, I don't exactly know why I've ever done it," he says. "I guess it's a physical need of mine." Another sigh. "It's a matter of measuring myself, I guess. I *think* it's playful, I don't know what other guys thought. I don't know, I wanted to win, I guess."

Carey saw a compulsion in Cal, a need to prove to everyone else that he was better in every contest. "He liked to be dominant," reflects Carey. "And he was the big dog, even when he was seventeen. He expected that he was going to the majors and be a star. He had a vision of himself. He saw his future a whole lot more than I saw mine. He's the most dominant guy I've ever met. That's why the headlocks, man."

Terry Crowley sees Ripken still tossing some teammates around the clubhouse, champion of all he sees. Cringing coaches always have looked the other way. Another Ripken sparring partner, former Oriole and minor-league teammate Floyd Rayford, who was frequently lured by Ripken into trading body punches, laughed years later when asked whether Ripken took special precautions in the interests of preserving his streak. "I always was amazed by the ignorance about Cal's basic personality," Rayford remembers. "He wasn't careful, least not in that way. He's just a strong, tough guy. He *took* what he wanted, you know. And he could do that, because nobody else was doing on the field what he was."

At first Ripken chuckles when he hears of Rayford's tale, reveling in the assessment of himself as strong and tough. But, in the next second, he wonders whether such stories from his friends unwittingly slight his baseball skills. "You know, I've done some things in this game," he murmurs plaintively.

The "things" have been obscured by the streak, without which, detractors argue, the .278 lifetime hitter might never be a Hall of Fame candidate. It is a perspective stubbornly dismissive of Ripken's more lasting numbers. His two MVP awards and two Gold Gloves (his fielding percentage in 1990 remains the highest for a shortstop in major-league history) are among the least of these. Before last year's back injury prematurely ended his season, he swatted his 400th career homer and stroked his 2,991st lifetime hit, en route to another milestone early in 2000, barring injury. Only six players in major-league history have amassed 400 home runs and 3,000 hits.

Like Babe Ruth, Ripken did nothing less than revolutionize a position, making it acceptable to consider the possibility that a heavily muscled, 6′4″ 220-pounder might have the requisite nimbleness to flag down bullets in the hole and leap with élan over base runners on the back end of double plays. "Before Cal and somebody like Robin Yount, nobody really thought about letting a big man play shortstop," says former second baseman and current ESPN analyst Harold Reynolds, a Ripken teammate in 1993. "The big young guys now at short — Nomar [Garciaparra], [Derek] Jeter, and A-Rod [Alex Rodriguez] — they wouldn't be there except for what Cal did."

Adds the irascible former Orioles manager Earl Weaver: "Cal had such great size and reach that he could get to balls in two steps that it'd take four steps for the little guy from St. Louis [Ozzie Smith]. And he had the work ethic."

"Work ethic" is always a phrase associated with Ripken. It means, in its subtext, that he's not flashy; that he toils at maximum effort in contrast to those whose gifts enable them to get by on half his effort. It is said that Larry Bird had a "work ethic," too. It is no coincidence that both are white.

The label frustrates Harold Reynolds. "Cal was, he *is,* an unbelievable athlete, which has always gotten shortchanged," says Reynolds. "In Oakland once, I saw him hit a ball 450 feet off a tee. He threw lasers from the outfield. Amazing."

Race has influenced impressions, believes Reynolds: "Think about Junior [Ken Griffey Jr.] and Cal. Each came up with baseball dads. Each is an extraordinary specimen and a thinking ballplayer who can figure out any pitcher. Junior gets dubbed the Natural. Cal becomes Mr. Work Ethic. The nicknames miss the reality. Cal is as talented an all-around shortstop as there's ever been. . . . He just didn't have to be flashy."

Ripken's style never has been the stuff of highlight reels. No pennant-winning homer; no fence-scaling catches; no barehanded acrobatics, à la the retired Ozzie Smith, whose nickname alone — the Wizard of Oz — oozed flash. He has left no indelible image in our mind's eye. We forever see Willie Mays, with his back turned to home plate, running furiously and seizing immortality as he snatches Vic Wertz's long drive in the cavernous Polo Grounds during the 1954 World Series. We picture Mickey Mantle corkscrewing himself into the ground while launching a white speck into the steamy Bronx night. They are forever young and supreme in our heads. What we carry of Ripken, when we see him at all, is simply the image of a man effortlessly slinging a ball across a diamond, again and again. He is the antithesis of flash, the personification of a quiet, unadorned mastery, the product of his father's ethos realized. "Cal did everything right and just made it look too easy sometimes," says Reynolds. "He's been *too* good."

Ripken's stature has given him an on-field license unthinkable even to other stars. Harold Reynolds remembers Ripken taking over pitch-calling duties from uncertain catchers and pitchers. "He'd go to the mound," Reynolds recalls, "and he'd say, 'I see you two are having a difficult time making a decision. Well, I'll help you. I'll call 'em.' And then he'd start signaling the catcher from out at shortstop."

In the early '90s, Ben McDonald, a talented young pitcher frustrated by a skein of tough losses, had begun moaning to Ripken after landing himself in yet another jam. "He didn't know what to throw," Ripken remembers. "So I just said to Ben and [catcher] Chris Hoiles, 'Let's throw a fastball on the outside corner, then a hook, and another hook, and we'll be out of here.' And we were. I called all of Ben's pitches in a couple of games. I think they were both shutouts." He laughs and the blue in his eyes lights up like a Tiki lamp.

Ripken loathes talking about what role he plays in guiding or admonishing his current teammates, a highly paid roster that includes the eccentric and underachieving, the estranged and occasionally poisonous. The dominant impression of the Orioles in 1999 was simple and unflattering: a collective bitching about having to play exhibition games against Cubans and minor leaguers in between lengthy losing streaks. The famously mercurial Albert Belle, who, already renowned for raising his middle finger to fans and failing to run out some ground balls, spent the second half of '99 declining to take batting practice with the team and waiting for manager Ray Miller to be fired. Ripken won't be drawn into public scrutiny of Belle or any other teammate, scornful of players and managers who think there is some virtue in discussing touchy personnel issues with ESPN *SportsCenter.*

He is sensitive to the suggestion that he has failed to assume leadership within the Orioles' sometimes lethargic and fractious clubhouse. It was a notion encouraged off and on over the years by anonymously speaking players and owner Peter Angelos, who later reversed himself, but too late. "What is leadership?" Ripken asks, bristling a little. "No, I really want to debate this. . . . I want to play devil's advocate against this idea that I'm supposed to get people to produce. It's a manager's job to get people to produce. Leadership from a player should be about inspiring, showing direction. If they want me to do the other thing, then give me the responsibility. I think I do lead in my own way. It's just I'm not a cheerleader. If people want a cheerleader, that's not me."

Over the years nothing has infuriated Bill Ripken more than the suggestion that the streak and other individual accomplishments have mattered more to his brother than seeing the Orioles win. Like so many others in Cal's shadow, Bill stands in awe of the man he calls Junior. "Nobody cares more about his team than Junior," he says. "There are players who, if they get their two hits, go home happy as pigs in slop even if the team loses. Not Junior. He's upset. The losing is all he can think about."

Ripken himself frames the issue as the difference between offering discreet advice and pursuing self-aggrandizement; between real leadership and the mere perception of it. "Being loud and being on TV is not being a leader," he says, but hold on. His tongue juts in his mouth; his lashes beat hard in thought. "I've talked to some people, sure. But leadership doesn't come with standing on the steps of the dugout and yelling at some player: 'Why didn't you run out that ball?' That's negative. . . . I'd say to the player, 'Are you injured?' And if he said he wasn't, I'd say, 'It seems to me you haven't been running out balls.' . . . I'd explain why running it out is important. And nobody else would need to know. . . . If you talk, you lose your credibility with people."

Although he won't discuss it publicly, he didn't like it when then-Orioles manager Davey Johnson suggested that his devotion to the streak made it impossible for him to be benched. It was an increasingly common refrain among Orioles managers and, by 1998, under Ray Miller, Ripken had had enough. "Managers were saying they couldn't take me out even if they wanted to," says Ripken. "Any time we lost some games, it was brought up. I was tired of it. So I made the decision: End it. I was just not going to listen to that stuff anymore."

Sometimes it seems as if everything might sour. When he missed a team flight last year and the general manager, Frank Wren, ordered the plane to take off, it was a reason cited to justify Wren's firing. Ripken hated being placed in the center of the controversy.

The firing briefly revived an old issue as to whether Ripken received preferential treatment from Orioles management. Wanting privacy from the hordes, he does not stay in the team hotel; he does not ride the team bus. So he no longer needs to worry about walking out of his hotel and having half of New York following him as he buys underwear. "Say I have a personality flaw," he says drily. "But I don't want people hanging outside in the hallway. I wish people who had criticisms would come to me directly with them. I'd explain to them that I get more time with my teammates now because I don't have to live like a recluse."

He takes a deep breath. It's spring, and nothing can get under his skin too much at a time when he has his game again in Fort Lauderdale, not when it's eighty-plus degrees and all the children and sun-baked retirees are shouting his name.

True to his word, he is doing his best to relish the moment. Even if his back never fails him again, one spring soon his bat will no longer knife the air at ninety miles per hour; one spring soon he will be up in a booth scouting talent. He waves at fans; he does his little scoop drill. Characteristically, his swing looks jumpy. He is out in front of pitches, his arms ahead of the rest of him, in need of a spring tuneup.

"I'm laying it on the line," he says for the fiftieth time. "Armed and dangerous." In a quieter moment, he says, "I'm trying to enjoy it, too. I know this isn't forever."

He is looking ahead, beyond third base. One gets the sense of a man determined not to be eclipsed by his younger self, already preparing for the second half of his life. He will be more than a baseball man. In a world where athletes frequently sacrifice control over the business side of their lives in exchange for escaping the mundane responsibilities of overseeing ledgers and investments, Ripken long ago signaled that he wouldn't be blindly deferring to advisers. Characteristically, he seized the reins in the early '90s from agent-attorney Shapiro, telling him he wanted to feel more in control. The Tufton Group was born, a company solely dedicated to marketing the man and legend, with Ripken himself calling the shots. "I saw a desire on his part to assume authority," remembers Shapiro. "A lot of players would have wanted to feel safe and dependent forever. Not him. Control is what makes him comfortable."

He operates adult and youth baseball camps stretching from Florida to Hawaii, with plans for expansion. He has purchased a share of a minor-league baseball team, as yet unnamed, to play in Aberdeen, to go along with his part-ownership of the minor-league Baltimore BayRunners of the International Basketball League. He and his wife, Kelly, contribute to a Baltimore literacy foundation that bears their names. Without telling the press, he will sometimes slip away to help somebody, just as he did two years ago, when he went down to Key West and signed free autographs for hours, helping to solicit contributions toward the medical expenses of Brooks Carey's brother, who had undergone brain surgery. Most notably at the moment, he has given his aura, money, and his name to the Babe Ruth baseball league; Ripken has volunteered to help finance the construction of six youth baseball fields near the Aberdeen minor-league baseball stadium. The fields will be scale models of famous major-league stadiums past and present.

He will never want for money. There is, just for starters, the memorabilia market that will never dry up for the twenty-first century's Gehrig. Ira Rainess, the thirty-two-year-old president of the Tufton Group, presides over a marketing strategy that includes endorsement deals with Nike, Chevy trucks, Six Flags amusement parks, Oakley sunglasses, Rawlings, Louisville Slugger, Franklin, Esskay hot dogs, the milk producers, and Century 21 real estate, which features him in a modest television commercial. "We are selling who he is and what he stands for," says Rainess, who believes that people identify with Cal's dedication and dependability.

Well, some do. Rainess is selling Ripken the Ethic, which for the moment, on Madison Avenue, looks out of season. Nike, which has half a dozen promotional campaigns running at once on TV, has no commercial featuring Ripken, evidence that young shoe-buyers are gravitating toward a different kind of athlete: younger, brasher, unpredictable, the sullen antiheroes. "Nike never created a big campaign for Cal, because he doesn't fit what's becoming the brand's image . . . and a lot of brands' image," says Rainess. "He's not controversial enough."

Ripken is unbothered in that way of men who know who they are and what they want. Then the moment arrives, the first game of the exhibition season, against the Cincinnati Reds, and he raps a single to left. In the field, he leaps and twists to pull down a high bouncer over the third base bag, robbing the hitter of a double and so easily throwing him out at first that somebody from the Orioles dugout shouts, "Routine."

The crowd is roaring, standing, wondering. Instinctively, he touches his back. He looks a little sheepish. I'm okay, he seems to be saying. I'm okay. In the next instant, he has dipped toward the dirt to scoop one of his imaginary balls, another test performed while the ovation is dying.

DAVID OWEN

The Chosen One

FROM THE NEW YORKER

The golfing menagerie belongs to a Tiger — B.C.

ON A HOT Sunday afternoon last May, Tiger Woods conducted a golf exhibition in Oklahoma City. During the hour before he appeared, while a large crowd baked in the bleachers, a member of his entourage held a trivia contest, with T-shirts for prizes. One of the questions: In what year was Tiger Woods born? The first guess, by a very young fan, was 1925. That's off by half a century, but the error is understandable. Woods has accomplished so much as a golfer that it's easy to forget that he's only twenty-four. In a sport in which good players seldom peak before their thirties, and often remain competitive at the highest levels well into their forties, Woods is off to a mind-boggling start. Most recently, he won the British Open with a record-breaking score of nineteen under par. After that blowout, Ernie Els, a terrific young South African player and the winner of two United States Opens, said with a resigned smile, "We'll have to go to the drawing board again, and maybe make the holes bigger for us and a little smaller for him."

When Woods eventually appeared for his Oklahoma exhibition, his entrance was appropriately dramatic. A small convoy of golf carts bore down on the bleachers from the far end of the driving range, while martial-sounding rock music blasted from the public-address system. The exhibition was the final event in a two-day program sponsored by the Tiger Woods Foundation, a charitable organization whose goal is to inspire children — especially underprivileged children — and "to make golf look more like America," as Woods himself says. Forty-two cities had applied to be visited by Woods and his team in 2000, and Oklahoma City was the first of just four cities to be chosen. Among the reasons for its selection was the existence of this particular facility: a low-fee public golf course, with free lessons for children on weekends, situated in an unprepossessing neighborhood not far from Oklahoma City's unprepossessing downtown.

Before stepping up to the practice tee, Woods answered questions from the audience, whose members differed from golf's principal constituency in that many of them were neither middle-aged nor white. One of the first questions came from a junior-high-school-aged fan, who asked, "How do you maintain your personal life and your golf career at the same time?"

Woods, who was leaning on his pitching wedge, said, "That's a great question. When I'm off the golf course, I like to get away from everything, and I like to keep everything private, because I feel that I have a right to that." There was heavy applause from the crowd. "There are exceptions to that, where the press likes to make up a few stories here and there. But that's just the way it goes."

When he said that, I shifted uneasily on the small, roped-off patch of ground from which members of the press had been asked to view the proceedings. Woods doesn't think highly of reporters. Particular journalists have annoyed him at various times over the years, and photographers always seem to click their cameras in the middle of his backswing. To be sure, chilly exchanges between Woods and the press have become less frequent as he has resigned himself to the public-relations side of his job. He now knows many of the press-tent regulars by name — even by nickname — and he sometimes goes out of his way to be courteous and helpful. But he has always been impatient with people who don't work as hard as he does, and most of the questions we ask are lazy, repetitive, and dumb. (Earlier in the day, on another part of the course, an eight-year-old golfer had hit a shot that clobbered a photographer, and Woods got a big laugh by saying, "I've been trying to do that for years.")

The night before, at a fund-raising dinner for the benefit of the foundation, I had stood glumly for half an hour at one end of a corridor with a group of other glum reporters, awaiting a promised opportunity to observe Woods's arrival at the dinner (but not, we were reminded several times, to ask him any questions). As it turned out, he arrived by a different route. Later, we were offered a chance to look down upon the evening's festivities in silence from a steel catwalk high above the crowd, a hugely unappealing prospect. I avoided that fate by managing to pass for nonmedia — I had had lunch at a barbecue joint earlier that day with several people connected with the foundation, and they arranged for me to fill an empty seat at a table at the actual dinner — but I never shook the slightly shameful feeling that I was unwanted and didn't belong.

Many very famous people become very famous because, for some compelling and probably unwholesome reason, they crave the approval of the rest of us. That's why they put up with the media, among other things. Even the ones who vigorously defend their privacy seem to do so in a way that attracts an awful lot of publicity, suggesting that their aversion to celebrity is more complicated than they let on. With Woods, though, you get the feeling that his fame mostly gets in the way. We intrude on his golf when he's playing golf, and we intrude on his private life when he's not. He can be a dazzlingly emotional and telegenic performer, and he surely finds it thrilling to walk down fairways lined with thousands of deliriously happy admirers shouting his name, but he conveys the impression that he would play every bit as hard if the cameras and the microphones and the galleries simply disappeared.

That's an awe-inspiring character trait, but it's also a chilling one. Part of the fun of being a sports fan is harboring the delusion that great athletic achievements are in some sense collaborations between athletes and their rooting sections. Woods's accomplishments are so outsized that it's hard to conceive of them as belonging to anyone but himself. As Tom Watson said of him after the British Open, "He is something supernatural."

Before Woods turned thirteen, he had researched and memorized the main competitive accomplishments of Jack Nicklaus because he already intended to exceed them. Between the mid-1970s and a month or two ago, sportswriters viewed Nicklaus's remarkable career (which was crowned by eighteen victories in golf's four major championships) as the permanent benchmark of greatness in golf; the new consensus is that Woods is capable of breaking all of Nicklaus's records, unless he loses interest in the game or injures himself or decides to run for president instead. Nicklaus himself has always been one of Woods's most enthusiastic cheerleaders. In 1996, he said that Woods could ultimately win the Masters more times than he and Arnold Palmer had combined — more than ten times, in other words. That statement seemed like crazy hyperbole at the time; it doesn't any longer.

Here in Oklahoma, though, Woods wasn't focusing on the record book. Earlier in the day, he had worked one on one with twenty-five young local golfers, most of whom were members of ethnic minorities. He watched them swing, offered advice, teed up balls for them, and made them laugh. The kids all looked nervous while they awaited their turns, but most were smiling by the time he moved on. One of those golfers was Treas Nelson, a high-school junior from Lawton, Oklahoma, who had just won the Class 5A Girls' State Championship; she is the first black golfer in Oklahoma to win a statewide high-school title. After she finished her session with Woods, I violated a ban on over-the-rope media fraternization — a ban that was enforced not only by roving public-relations personnel but also by Woods's cadre of Schwarzeneggeresque bodyguards — and asked her what Tiger had told her.

"He said I have the pizza-man syndrome," she told me. "I get my right hand too much like this." She lifted her right arm with the elbow bent, as though she were holding a pizza on a tray at shoulder height. "He said he has the same problem." She was beaming. Like almost all the kids who received individual instruction, she was wearing Nike shorts and a Nike shirt — goodies provided by Woods's biggest commercial sponsor. She had supplemented this uniform with a pair of Nike earrings. "I don't know if he noticed that," she said. But she hoped he had.

"I can relate to these kids," Woods said a little later that day. "I'm not too far from their age. If these kids saw Jack Nicklaus, I don't think they would have an appreciation for what he's done in the game or what he has to offer, just because of the fact that it's hard for a person of Nicklaus's age to relate to a kid. But I'm not too far removed from my teens. I can say 'Dude,' and that's cool — that's fine."

It's only because of Woods that most of these kids even know who Jack Nicklaus is. Woods spends almost as much time studying golf's history as he does making it, and he goes out of his way to share his knowledge of that history with the youngsters who idolize him. In answer to a question from the audience at his exhibition, he said, "When I was young, I looked up to a lot of different players for a lot of different reasons. Obviously, Jack Nicklaus was the greatest of all time. Ben Hogan was the greatest driver there ever was. Seve Ballesteros probably had the best short game. Ben Crenshaw putted the best. So what I did was analyze every different player's game and try to pick the best out of each and every player and try to look up to that. I wasn't going to look up to just one person." For young golfers twenty years from now, however, looking up to the best player in each of the areas Woods mentioned may be no more complicated than looking up to Woods himself. He leads the tour in most of the several dozen statistical categories that tour officials keep track of, including career earnings. (His tournament winnings during the first seven months of 2000 alone exceeded Nicklaus's lifetime earnings.)

During Woods's exhibition, the younger members of the crowd weren't thinking about statistics. What they really wanted to see was a trick they had watched him perform in a hugely popular Nike television commercial: they wanted to see him bounce a golf ball on the face of his wedge while passing the club from hand to hand and between his legs and behind his back, and then hit the ball right out of the air as easily as if it were teed up on the ground. (That commercial arose by accident, when Woods, feeling bored between takes on a shoot for another Nike commercial, began amusing himself with a stunt he had taught himself as a kid, and the director, entranced, asked him if he could do it again.)

"I heard a rumor that this thing I did on TV was all computerized," Woods said, as he began bouncing the ball. "It's kind of a vicious rumor." He passed the club between his legs. "Now, I don't know where that rumor started, whether it was the public or the press, but they obviously hadn't seen me do this before." He bounced the ball up high. "And catch it like this." He stopped the ball, frozen, on the face of his club, let it sit there a moment, then began bouncing it again. "Or I can start out doing it left-handed, if you want me to." Bounce, bounce, bounce. "Or go back to the right." He bounced the ball up over his shoulder from behind, and caught it on the club face in front. "Now, I didn't put this one in the commercial, because it's the hardest one — it's when you hit the ball off the butt end of the club." He bounced the ball high again, twirled the club so that its shaft was perpendicular to the ground, bounced the ball straight up off the top of the rubber grip, twirled the club back to its former position, and resumed bouncing the ball on the face. "Let's see — it took me four takes to do the Nike spot. Let's see if I can do this out here." He bounced the ball high, took his regular grip on the club, planted his feet, and, just before the ball fell back to earth, smacked it more than a third of the way down the range.

A few hours before Woods's exhibition, I sat with the all-black congregation of the St. John Missionary Baptist Church (motto: "We Strive to Be 'The Best Church This Side of Judgment'") while Tiger's father, Earl Woods, gave a guest sermon. His talk was preceded by hymns, prayers, and half a dozen full-immersion baptisms, which were conducted in a large tank that was visible through an opening in the wall above the altar. His subject was his only subject. "Tiger was not created to be a golfer," he said. "Tiger was made to be a good person, and that was first and foremost in our family." Earl is shorter and considerably wider than Tiger. He has a good preaching voice, which caught in his throat a couple of times, despite the fact that he had given essentially the same presentation dozens, if not hundreds, of times before. "Sometimes when I talk about my son, I get very emotional," he explained. "So bear with me."

Earl divides his life into two distinct phases, the first of which he now considers to have been a divinely directed training mission for the second. In the first phase, which began during the Great Depression, he grew up poor in eastern Kansas, lost both parents by the time he was thirteen, attended a mostly white high school, became the first black baseball player in what is today the Big Twelve, spent twenty years in the Army, served two widely separated tours of duty in Vietnam (the second as a Green Beret), and endured an increasingly loveless marriage for the sake of his three children, to whom he was a remote father at best. In the second phase, which began in the late sixties, he divorced his first wife, married a Thai receptionist named Kultida Punswad (whom he had met in Thailand during his second Southeast Asian tour), took up golf, and produced Tiger Woods — whose real first name is Eldrick, and whose nickname Earl had given first to a South Vietnamese lieutenant colonel named Vuong Dang Phong, who was his colleague, close friend, and protector during the war.

Earl was determined to be a better parent to the last of his four children than he had been to the first three, and after he retired from the Army, in 1974, he had more time to be attentive. His one significant distraction — other than his job, as a contract administrator and materials manager at McDonnell Douglas, in Huntington Beach, California — was golf, a game at which he had become remarkably proficient despite having taken it up just four years earlier, at the age of forty-two. He worked on his swing in the evenings, by hitting balls into a net in his garage, and he often placed his infant son in a high chair beside him so that the two of them could commune while he practiced. "It was a way of spending time together," he told me recently. The baby, far from being bored, was captivated by the motion. One momentous day, when Tiger was still young enough not to have mastered all the finer points of walking, he astonished his father by climbing down from his high chair, picking up a club, and executing a passable imitation of Earl's (quite good) golf swing. At that moment, his father realized he was the steward of an extraordinary talent.

Earl also began to believe that the birth of his son had been — as he told the St. John congregation — "the plan of the man upstairs." Looking back on his life, he detected a pattern of trials and tests and close escapes from tragedy, and he decided that God had been grooming him all along for something big. As the child grew, Earl was struck more and more by what he described in church that day as "the charismatic power that resides in my son Tiger" — a power that he had otherwise noticed only in Nelson Mandela.

Even to someone sitting in a church pew, this might sound sort of mystical and wacky — and yet the more you learn about Tiger Woods's preternatural relationship to the game of golf the easier it becomes to understand why terrestrial interpretations seem inadequate to Earl. When Tiger was still a toddler, Earl says, the child was able to identify the swing flaws of adult players. ("'Look, Daddy,' Tiger would say, 'that man has a reverse pivot!'") Tiger putted with Bob Hope on *The Mike Douglas Show* at the age of two, broke 50 for nine holes at the age of three, hit golf balls on *That's Incredible!* at the age of five, and received his first autograph request when he was still too young to have a signature. Before he had learned to count to ten, Earl says, Tiger could tell you, on any golf hole, where each member of a foursome stood in relation to par. While his grade-school contemporaries drew pictures of racing cars and robots, Tiger sketched the trajectories of his irons. He came from behind to win the Junior World Championship, in San Diego, against an international field, when he was eight.

Tiger first beat his father in golf, by a single stroke, with a score of 71, when he was eleven. That same summer, he entered thirty-three junior tournaments, and won them all. ("That's when I peaked. It's been downhill since.") At fifteen, he became the youngest player ever to win the United States Junior Amateur Championship — and then the only player in history to win it three years in a row. At eighteen, he became the youngest player ever to win the United States Amateur Championship — and then the only player in history to win it three years in a row.

When Tiger first began to attract national attention, people often assumed that the real force behind his game must be the oldest one in modern sports: a pushy father with frustrated athletic aspirations and a powerful yearning for unearned income. In early 1998, the sportswriter John Feinstein published a short, mean-spirited book called *The First Coming*, in which he compared Earl to the manipulative father of the tennis prodigy Jennifer Capriati, who burned out on the women's tour at seventeen. (She has since returned.) But Feinstein was clearly wrong. It has gradually become apparent that Tiger's drive has always been internal, and that while Earl and Kultida may have been its facilitators they were not its authors. When Tiger was still very small, for example, he memorized his father's office telephone number so that he could call Earl each afternoon to ask if the two of them could practice at the golf course after work. Earl was a tireless (and innovative) practice companion and coach, but he believed that the initiative must always be taken by the boy.

Rather than pushing their son, the Woodses sometimes worried that his infatuation with golf was eclipsing other parts of his life. "In junior golf, I was all-out," Tiger said in Oklahoma. "My parents would say, 'You can't play, you're playing too much.' But I wanted to play every tournament, and play twice in one day." Earl repeatedly urged him, with little success, to try other sports. Kultida used golf as an incentive — for example, by forbidding her son to hit practice balls until he had finished his homework. ("My wife was the disciplinarian in the family," Earl told me, "and I was the friend.") Earl once fretted that Tiger was so focused on winning that he had ceased to enjoy himself on the golf course. Tiger replied curtly, "That's how I enjoy myself, by shooting low scores." After that, Earl kept his opinions to himself.

Although Earl and Kultida did not force Tiger to become a golfer, they both made enormous sacrifices to help him realize his ambition. Earl estimates that the family's annual travel expenses during Tiger's junior-golf years amounted to as much as $30,000, a sum Earl couldn't have covered without the help of a succession of home-equity loans. Kultida was an infinitely patient chauffeur, rising long before dawn to drive Tiger to distant tournaments (and reminding him to bring his pillow so that he could go back to sleep in the car). Both parents believed that their son's needs must always come before their own, and they were determined that the only impediment to his success — in golf or in whatever other field he might choose to pursue — would be the level of his own desire.

Earl and Kultida's sacrifices took a toll on their marriage; they have lived apart for several years now, although they have not divorced. Their living arrangement inevitably comes to mind when Earl says, as he did in church in Oklahoma that day, "The family is the most important institution in the world." But Earl doesn't view his own domestic situation as conflicting with his beliefs. The family as Earl conceives it is mainly a relationship between parents and their children. He told me recently, "Tiger has a mother and a father who love him dearly, and who have always supported him and always will. He is the top priority in the family. There is no bitterness between his parents, and there is no animosity. The only thing is that we live in separate places. My wife likes a great, big-ass house, and I like a small house. That's all." Still awaiting Tiger is the challenge of raising a family of his own — an achievement, Earl says, from which Tiger must not allow himself to be distracted by his golf.

Tiger's obsession was obviously indulged by his parents, but the child wasn't spoiled. Almost from the beginning, he was made to take responsibility for his own aspirations. Starting when he was quite young, for example, he was put in charge of making the family's tournament-related travel arrangements, including hotel reservations. When he was asked what he intended to study in school, he would say that he hoped to major in accounting because he wanted to know how to keep track of the people who would one day keep track of his earnings. He went by himself to check out the colleges that had recruited him, and he went by himself when it was time to enroll at Stanford, the college he ultimately chose. (Tiger's best friends today include three former Stanford teammates: Notah Begay III, who is the first full-blooded American Indian to play on the PGA Tour; Casey Martin, who is physically disabled and won a court decision allowing him to use a motorized cart in PGA Tour events; and Jerry Chang, to whom Tiger quietly returned a favor by serving as his caddie during a thirty-six-hole qualifying tournament the week following his own victory in the U.S. Open.)

The real purpose of the Woods family's lifestyle, both parents have said, was not to turn Tiger into a professional golfer but to strengthen his character. "Golf prepares children for life," Earl told me recently, "because golf is a microcosm of life." According to Earl, the truly important lessons he imparted on the golf course had to do with things like honesty, etiquette, patience, and discipline — virtues for which golf provided handy talking points. (Golf is the only competitive sport, for example, in which the players call penalties on themselves.) Earl also stressed to Tiger that his athletic gift, if he continued to pursue it, would always entail outsized public obligations — not least because of his racial background. Tiger lived in a mostly white neighborhood in Cypress, California, and he attended mostly white schools, and he was sometimes harassed by bigoted bullies — one of whom tied him to a tree one day when he was in elementary school — but both his parents taught him to rise above such incidents and to understand that racism is evidence of a defect in the racist, not in the racist's victim. Kultida urged him to be remorseless in competition, but she also steeped him in the Buddhist tradition in which she herself had been raised.

It appears that Earl and Kultida provided their son with exactly what he turned out to need (competitive focus, immunity to intimidation, a cut-down 1-iron) at every critical juncture in his development. But I sometimes wonder whether Tiger didn't in some sense "create" his parents as much as they "created" him. From the moment he climbed down from that high chair, he seems to have been phenomenally well equipped — temperamentally, emotionally, intellectually — to exploit the physical gift that he was born with. Is it outlandish to wonder whether part of his genius didn't lie in an ability to inspire his parents to conduct their lives in perfect harmony with his ambition?

I first saw Woods in person at the Augusta National Golf Club, in Augusta, Georgia, during the week of the 1997 Masters Tournament. He had turned pro just seven months earlier, after winning his third United States Amateur Championship, and he had dominated the tour almost from that moment. I was standing near Augusta National's first tee late one afternoon early in the week when he emerged from the clubhouse to play a practice round. I didn't see him at first, but I quickly guessed that he was near, because the crowd loitering between the clubhouse and the first tee suddenly convulsed. He was moving fast, and he was encircled by guards. "Tiger! Tiger! Tiger!" The ardor of those fans I can think to describe only as ferocious. Their supplications sounded almost angry. Woods's face, meanwhile, floated expressionless among the grimaces of his protectors.

The 1997 Masters provided Woods's formal introduction not only to many golf fans but also to some of the best golfers from outside the United States. In the third round, which he began with a three-stroke lead, Woods was paired with Colin Montgomerie, who had played well enough the day before to have shared the lead himself for a short time. He was now tied for second. Montgomerie, who is Scottish, was (and still is) the best player on the European PGA Tour, and he had been a star of the European Ryder Cup team. He had never won a tournament in the United States, but he had come close several times, and he was especially optimistic about his chances that week in Augusta.

Playing side by side with Woods, however, was a transforming experience for Montgomerie. He shot 74 — a score that ordinarily wouldn't have been disastrous at that stage in a major tournament, except that Woods shot 65, and thereby increased his lead over the field to nine strokes, and his lead over Montgomerie to twelve. When their round was over, Montgomerie was taken to the press building for a postmortem, as the top players always are. He looked frazzled and discouraged as he stepped onto the stage, and he didn't wait for anyone to ask a question.

"All I have to say is one brief comment today," he began. "There is no chance. We're all human beings here, but there's no chance humanly possible that Tiger is going to lose this tournament. No way."

"What makes you say that?" a reporter asked.

Montgomerie looked at the reporter with palpable incredulity. "Have you just come in?" he said. "Or have you been away? Have you been on holiday or something?"

Montgomerie was clearly shaken by what he had witnessed at close quarters. In his encounter with Tiger Woods, he had crossed from the first stage to the second stage in the process described by Emily Dickinson as "First Chill — then Stupor — then the Letting Go." In the fourth and final round, he shot 81, a dismal score, which left him in a tie for thirtieth place. When he finished, he looked as though his body had been drained of blood.

Weekend golfers who attend professional tournaments for the first time are almost always struck by the breathtaking quality of the pros' shots, and they end up realizing sadly that professional golf and weekend golf, despite superficial similarities, are very different games. I had been to tournaments before the 1997 Masters, and I had even played golf with a couple of touring pros, so I had no remaining illusions about my own abilities. But some of Woods's golf shots during that tournament seemed almost as different from an average pro's shots as an average pro's shots would seem from mine. They belonged in a category of their own. David Feherty, a former tour player from Ireland, who now works mainly as a television commentator, told me recently, "I've played with just about everybody, and I think I can say now that Tiger has hit virtually every truly great shot I've ever seen. As we speak, he is deleting some of my greatest memories and replacing them with his. He simply does things other golfers can't do. He's like the Heineken in the commercial: he refreshes the parts other beers cannot reach."

Woods's swing is so powerful that it is difficult to capture on film. For many years, *Golf Digest* has published detailed photographic sequences that anatomize the swings of the game's best players — sequences that are descended in spirit from the studies of running athletes and galloping horses which were made in the late nineteenth century by the photographic pioneer Eadweard Muybridge. Since 1973, the magazine's photographers have shot their swing sequences with a high-speed camera called a Hulcher, which was originally developed, at the request of a government agency, to take stop-action photographs of missiles. The camera can shoot hundreds of high-quality images at a rate of sixty-five frames a second — plenty fast enough to break a golf swing into its constituent parts.

Woods performed for the Hulcher a few months after his Masters victory. The camera recorded fifteen driver swings from five different angles. When the prints came back from the lab, the magazine's editors discovered that only five frames among the hundreds taken during the shoot had captured Woods's swing at the approximate moment his club head came into contact with the ball — a problem they had never encountered before. "With other tour players, we almost always get a picture of impact with every swing," Roger Schiffman, the executive editor, told me. When Woods makes his normal swing, the head of his driver moves at about a hundred and twenty miles an hour — a good fifteen miles an hour faster than the club head of a typical touring pro, and about thirty miles an hour faster than the club head of an average amateur. Between one Hulcher frame and the next, Woods's driver traveled through roughly two hundred degrees of arc, which means that a ball sitting unthreatened on the tee in one frame would be long gone by the next.

That *Golf Digest* swing sequence was photographed two days before the start of the 1997 Western Open, which Woods went on to win. "When he saw the pictures later, he said, 'No wonder I won,'" Schiffman told me. "He said his swing looked almost perfect." It was quite a surprise, therefore, when Woods decided not long afterward that his game required a major overhaul. With the help of Butch Harmon, a former touring pro who has been Woods's teacher since he was seventeen, Woods spent more than a year taking apart his "almost perfect" swing and putting it back together.

The eyes of nongolfers glaze over when golfers fret about their swing, as they do when offered the least opportunity. If you play golf, though, you understand the fascination. The golf swing may be the most frustrating motion in sports. It's all angles and levers and timing and voodoo, and, because it starts from a dead stop and is directed at a stationary object, it permits, and even encourages, a dangerous level of intellectual interference. Most athletic actions work best when the attention of the athletes executing them is directed somewhere else — on a rapidly approaching tennis ball, for example, or on the footsteps of a furious linebacker — but golf is a highly self-conscious game. As a result, golf instruction often veers in the direction of pop psychology, and the advice offered in countless books, magazines, videos, infomercials, television shows, and weeklong swing schools can begin to seem slightly oracular. ("Swing easy as hard as you can"; "Don't be tight"; "Don't be loose"; "You can play well with a bad swing as long as you make an even number of errors.") Golf is so unnerving that longtime players are susceptible to a host of bizarre and virtually incurable mental disorders, among them a putting problem known as "the yips," and a calamitous swing breakdown known as "the shanks" — a condition so devastating that many golfers superstitiously refuse to utter its name.

At the Ryder Cup in 1993 — which was held at a club in northwest England called the Belfry — I stood by the driving range for half an hour while the British player Nick Faldo worked on swing minutiae with his teacher, David Leadbetter. Faldo would address a ball, then sweep his club halfway to the top of his backswing and freeze; Leadbetter would modify the position of Faldo's hands by an inch or so; Faldo would readdress the ball, then sweep his club halfway to the top of his backswing and freeze; Leadbetter would modify the position of Faldo's hands by an inch or so. They repeated this exercise again and again and again. (The real proof that golfers are mentally unbalanced was provided not by Faldo and Leadbetter but by me: I stood there and watched. And took notes!) For most players, this sort of incessant meddling is necessary yet perilous. Faldo himself suffered a swing collapse a few years ago, and, indeed, he is still trying to rediscover his old touch.

Woods's dissatisfaction with his swing in 1997 therefore seemed, to an outsider, almost reckless — especially since it concerned a problem that is beyond the ability of most golfers to conceive of as a problem. I saw an example of this dissatisfaction once in a tournament on TV. Woods had driven his ball beautifully on a par-4, leaving himself just a short iron to the green — an easy shot. He swung, and his ball soared through the air, and, sure enough, it ended up just a few feet from the hole. (He later sank that putt, for a birdie.) But Woods reacted as angrily as if he had just bounced his ball off a car in the clubhouse parking lot.

He later revealed what had bothered him. He had intended to

play a fade — that is, a shot that starts left of the target and curves back toward it, to the right. At some point during his downswing, however, he had sensed that his club was in the wrong position in relation to his body, so he manipulated his hands in such a way that the club head rolled over at the bottom of his swing, imparting side spin to the ball in the opposite direction and causing the shot to curve from right to left instead — a shot known as a draw. Because of the speed of his swing, and the time it takes for electrical impulses to travel back and forth through the human nervous system, that sort of midcourse correction, given its end result, is almost impossible to comprehend. In any event, Woods didn't like having to rely on his hands to twist his club into the right position, so he decided the time had come to tighten up his swing. That process took more than a year, and it coincided with the only relative dry spell in his career thus far — a period, which ended late in 1999, during which he won only a tournament or two. Since then, he's won roughly half the tournaments he's played in.

I won't bore you with the details of how Woods and Harmon did it — and the details are definitely boring — but the process included hitting thousands upon thousands of practice balls, enduring countless hours of tedious drills, and adding several brick-size slabs of muscle to what was already a virtually fat-free physique. Woods has always loved to practice, and he is a fascinated and deeply analytical observer of his own swing. "He is the best student I ever had," Harmon told me recently. "He is like a sponge — he soaks up information, and he always wants to learn and get better." That notion is deeply disturbing to other tour players, who had more than enough trouble with the old Woods — the one with the allegedly terrible swing. Even worse, Harmon describes his student as "a work in progress," and they both say that the Woods we have seen so far is only 75 percent as good as the Woods they both believe we will see at some point in the future — and probably sooner rather than later. "He can get a lot better," Harmon told me. "Scary thought."

"I've worked countless hours," Woods himself said shortly before his Oklahoma exhibition (during which he demonstrated a new low-flying shot with his driver which he and Harmon had spent a year developing specifically for the hard fairways and high winds of the British Open). "People have no idea how many hours I've put into this game — and they don't really need to know, either — but I've put in a lot of time and a lot of effort. My dad always told me that there are no shortcuts, that you get out of it what you put into it, and that if you want to become the best you're going to have to be willing to pay your dues."

In paying his dues and becoming the best, Woods has changed almost everything there is to change about golf. The conventional wisdom among sportswriters used to be that the PGA Tour had become so deep in talent that no modern player could hope to dominate it the way Palmer or Nicklaus or Watson did in the sixties and seventies and eighties, or the way Snead or Nelson or Hogan did in the thirties and forties and fifties. Now, though, Woods becomes the favorite in any tournament simply by signing up, and professional golfers all over the world have begun lifting heavier weights, eating healthier food, and going to bed earlier, in the hope of becoming good enough to be considered second best. "He's in their heads," the sportswriter Tom Callahan told me. Callahan recalled the corrective eye surgery that Woods had last year. "The first thing he said afterward was, 'The hole looks bigger.' Now, if you're Davis Love, is that what you want to hear?" More than a few pros once viewed Woods as dangerously overhyped; nowadays, like most of the rest of his awestruck admirers, they tend to stop what they are doing and watch — perhaps thinking ahead to a day when they'll be able to brag to their grandchildren that they once got personally whomped by the "Chosen One" (as the tour player Mark Calcavecchia called him at the British Open).

Woods has also changed golf's public image, which has suffered for decades from the game's suburban association with saddle shoes, cigars, and miniature electric cars. "Golf was called a wussy sport when I was growing up," he said in Oklahoma. "You weren't supposed to play it unless you were a wuss." No longer. Twelve-year-olds who used to dream only of becoming professional basketball players now sometimes decide that they might like to give the PGA Tour a try, too, at least in the off-season. Tubby middle-aged hackers now stand a little taller at cocktail parties, because Woods, miracle of miracles, has made golf seem kind of cool. When a teenage checker at my local grocery store discovered that I played a lot of golf, her eyes lit up, and she asked, "Have you met Tiger?" Woods has even taken the most shameful aspect of the game's long history

— its legacy as a decadent pastime for white people with too much time on their hands — and turned it inside out.

Between 1934 and 1961, the constitution of the Professional Golfers Association of America — the direct predecessor of the modern PGA Tour — explicitly limited that organization's membership to "Professional golfers of the Caucasian race." The Caucasian-only clause was not some esoteric historical artifact; the rule merely formalized a policy that had always been followed, and the PGA apparently bothered to put it on paper only after discovering that a light-skinned black man had managed to work as a club pro since 1928. The PGA methodically fought efforts by black players to overturn or circumvent the rule, and it didn't amend its constitution until it was forced to do so by the attorney general of California, who threatened to ban tour events in that state and to encourage other attorneys general to do the same. The pressure for change did not come from the white pros of that era; the vast majority of those men were happy with their world the way it was.

When Tiger Woods was born, in 1975, the Caucasian-only clause was no more distant in time than the stock-market crash of 1987 is from today — and the mind-set that had fostered it was very much a part of the landscape of golf. One winter in the early seventies, when I was in high school, someone from the Midwestern country club that my parents belonged to asked me to suggest other young people who might be invited to the club's upcoming Christmas dance. I in turn asked what would happen if my list included the names of one or two of the three black members of my high-school class. Shortly afterward, the dance was canceled.

Less than nine months before Woods's birth, Lee Elder became the first black golfer to play in the Masters. Elder's appearance at Augusta has been celebrated ever since as an early milestone in the drearily slow enlightenment of white Americans, but it did not herald a new generation of black golfers. Like most of the few other black tour players of that time, Elder was a veteran of the old United Golfers Association, golf's equivalent of baseball's Negro leagues, and his athletic prime was mostly behind him. (He was already forty-one.) A black player named Calvin Peete, who was born in 1943 and took up golf too late to have been involved with the UGA, became one of the truly dominant players on the PGA Tour in the eighties, a decade during which he won more tournaments (eleven) than any player except Tom Kite. But Peete was virtually the end of the line; Woods is the only black member of the PGA Tour, and he is the first in a very long time. In the past fifteen years, only one African-American golfer has won a PGA Tour card by way of the tour's qualifying "school" (actually, a notoriously arduous six-day tournament). That was a now forgotten player named Adrian Stills, who qualified in 1985. "We're a dying breed," Lee Elder told me last month.

Why did the black presence on tour shrink to the vanishing point between the mid-seventies and the mid-nineties, just when one would have expected the opposite? Pete McDaniel — who is the author of *Uneven Lies*, a cultural history of black golf in America, which will be published this fall — recently told me, "It was the golf cart. The rise of the motorized golf cart marked the beginning of the end of minority golf, especially among African-Americans, because golf clubs that had carts didn't need caddies, and most of the black professional players had come from the caddie ranks." Golf carts, in addition to being a typically American response to the threat of mild physical exercise, eliminated what to golf clubs had been the unappealing necessity of maintaining on their premises large pools of mostly young, mostly disadvantaged workers. As carts displaced caddies, kids whose families were excluded from private clubs lost their principal avenue of access to the game.

Of course, a world in which a handful of black men managed to claw their way into mostly marginal professional careers as a result of having lugged the weekend baggage of wealthy whites was hardly a utopia. The real problem with golf in America, as far as race is concerned, is not that caddying declined as an occupation but that the game, over the course of more than a century, has only grudgingly made room for more than a privileged few. Given the inexorability of the cultural forces at work, it seems almost unbelievable that Tiger Woods emerged as a golfer at all, much less as a golfer who has a decent chance of one day being remembered as the greatest of all time. As Earl says, his son is the first "naturally born and bred black professional golfer" — the first whose initial exposure to the game did not come through the service entrance. For Woods simply to have earned a tour card and kept it for a couple of years would have made him a pioneer. Doing what he has actually done moves him into the category of myth.

*

Woods's own views about race are attractively complicated. He dislikes being referred to as "African-American," because he regards that term as an insult to his mother — and so does his mother — who, after all, is Asian. Earl's ancestors were black, white, American Indian, and Asian, and Tiger once referred to his own ethnicity as "Caublinasian," a word he made up in an effort to suggest the diversity of his genealogy. He often seems inclined to concentrate on golf and let American race relations look after themselves, but he has invested a great deal of his increasingly scarce and valuable time in reaching out to disadvantaged children through his clinics.

Woods has been conducting clinics for young golfers since he was in high school, when he and Earl set up exhibitions in cities where Woods was playing in tournaments. The clinics ended when Woods was at Stanford, because the National Collegiate Athletic Association held that they were in violation of a rule concerning individual college athletes and public exhibitions. (Earl and Tiger had several running battles with the NCAA during Tiger's two years in college, and Earl says those battles contributed to Tiger's decision to turn pro shortly after the beginning of what would have been his junior year.) After Woods left the aegis of the NCAA, late in 1996, he and Earl established the Tiger Woods Foundation to continue their mission.

The foundation has been accused by some of creating unrealistic expectations among children who have limited opportunities for becoming even recreational golfers, and virtually no chance at all of becoming touring pros. ("You wonder if it's false hope," a skeptical sportswriter said to me recently.) What good does it do — the critics have asked — to introduce an inner-city kid to a game that, for all practical purposes, can't be played in an inner city? And, indeed, if the goal is to turn more members of ethnic minorities into golfers, a simpler approach might be to concentrate directly on transforming ghetto youngsters into middle-aged Republicans — the kind of people who seem to take up the game as a matter of course. There's a public-service commercial on television which shows a black child using a hammer to drive a tee into the pavement on a dark urban street, so that he can tee off in his neighborhood. Well, exactly.

Although it's true that playing on tour is an unreasonable ambition for almost everyone — the PGA Tour has only 125 fully exempt playing spots, and many of those are locked up by golfers whose careers will ultimately be measured in decades rather than in years — earning a different kind of living in the world of golf is within reach for many. Unlike most other spectator sports, golf is played by millions of nonprofessionals, whose needs are served by a large industry that comprises equipment manufacturers, clothing retailers, agronomists, golf-course maintenance workers, traveling salespeople, teaching professionals, scuba-diving golf-ball recyclers, and others — even journalists. Within that industry, there is now a widespread conviction that if golf is to grow significantly as an economic enterprise it needs to extend its reach far beyond white suburban males. Woods's foundation, in connection with its clinics and exhibitions, conducts seminars for children and parents in which such job opportunities are described and explained. Woods himself has estimated that as many as 5 percent of the children who pass through his foundation's programs will one day end up in jobs that are somehow connected with golf. That seems like a lot, but who knows?

Even for kids who have no interest in golf-related careers, the game as a pastime has virtues that its more grotesque attributes have often obscured. Golf has a work ethic (the driving range and the practice green), a dress code (no jeans or T-shirts), and a tradition of etiquette based on personal responsibility and consideration for others (replace your divots). Spectator behavior that is tolerated and even encouraged in other sports — the frantic waving of plastic-foam tubes in an effort to fluster free-throw shooters in basketball games, for example — would be considered grounds for arrest at golf tournaments, where fans are expected to keep even their shadows under control. Aspiring golfers who set out to be just like Tiger Woods may never make it to the tour, but they will inevitably end up learning something about what it takes to find and keep a job more demanding than that of filling orders at a drive-through window. "The first thing they learn is to play by the rules," Earl told me, "and we have a lot of knuckleheads in prison today who never learned to play by the rules."

White golfers also tend to underestimate the emotional impact that Woods's racial background has had on non-Caucasians. For upper-middle-class white fans, a big part of Woods's appeal is that he seems to negate racial issues altogether — he's just Tiger, the best golfer in the world. I've seen sixty-year-old white chief executive officers with their own personal jets who were as excited as a ten-year-old kid would be about having a chance to see Woods in person. Their excitement was genuine, and, to the extent that such a thing is possible, it was color-blind. When white golfers do think about Woods's racial background, it's often with a sense of relief: his dominance feels like an act of forgiveness, as though in a single spectacular career he could make up for the game's ugly past all by himself.

For many of the young players I saw in Oklahoma, though, Woods's appeal had everything to do with race: the color of his skin was the bridge they were crossing into the game. Dennis Burns, who works for the Tiger Woods Foundation and is one of a handful of black American golf professionals (the kind who give lessons and work at golf clubs rather than play on tour), told me, "Kids walk away from Tiger's clinics with a sense that here's a guy who looks like me and has done it. It's a feeling of confidence — and it doesn't just have to do with golf." Children generally admire great athletes for most of the same reasons they admire cartoon superheroes: the constraints of the adult-ruled world don't seem to apply. But, for teenagers who are outside America's cultural mainstream, Woods has meant incalculably more. He is the fearless conqueror of a world that has never wanted anything to do with them.

A lesson in fearlessness may be what professional golfers need as well. Woods has upended their universe. Ernie Els has finished second to him five times now, twice in major tournaments. Els is one of the very nicest people on any golf tour — and he has made nothing but generous, flabbergasted remarks about Woods — but surely it must have occurred to him that if Woods had spent four years at Stanford and then gone to graduate school, he himself might today be considered the best player in the world. He and the other young golfers who used to contend for that position, including Phil Mickelson and David Duval (who briefly supplanted Woods at the top of the world rankings around the time that Woods was making his big swing change), have to wonder if their moment in golf history passed before it arrived.

Superb athletes fascinate in part because they seem like proxies for ourselves in a metaphorical battle with the eternal: broken records arc death-negating acts. Even Woods's most lopsided victories have been thrilling to watch, because his efforts have seemed so effortless — as though he had found a way to win the game that can't be won. But will we feel the same way five years from now if no player has stepped forward to challenge him? Nicklaus had the considerable advantage during his career of being chased and, not infrequently, elbowed aside by other great players, among them Arnold Palmer, Billy Casper, Gary Player, Lee Trevino, and Tom Watson. Woods's principal rival, so far, has been the record book. If that doesn't change, then those of us who can only watch — sports fans, television commentators, sports reporters — may someday come to view his triumphs with the same dispassion that he seems to feel toward us, until the passage of time erodes his powers and makes it all seem like a contest again.

TOM FRIEND

The Natural

FROM ESPN: THE MAGAZINE

Is Daddy watching his little girl from afar? — B.C.

WE MUST remember that she's only nineteen. That she never misses *Buffy the Vampire Slayer.* That she has it taped when she's in Europe. That her bedroom is three shades of pink. That she's never been kissed. That she's never sipped an ounce of alcohol. That she prays every night from her knees. That she can't go three sentences without laughing like hell. That she attended exactly one high school party. That her mom called at ten that night to say hurry home. That she has a crush on Derek Jeter. That her favorite expressions are "As if . . ." and "That's so retarded." That she always wanted to be a cheerleader. That she wishes for Gabrielle Reece's legs. That she doesn't wish for Lindsay Davenport's.

We need to remember all of this because the rest of her world is a nauseating one. Like the father who ignores her. Or the tennis tour that ostracizes her. Or the coach who's in jail for child molestation. Or the lesbian players who glare at her mother. Or the player who called her fat. Or the player who called her "nigger."

She used to draw herself white as a child, because that is how she saw herself. She used to dream she was blue-eyed and blond, and she still crinkles up any newspaper that calls her African-American. For years, she'd hear people ask who her father was. They'd guess Wilt or O.J., until some reporter actually bought her birth certificate last year with company money. And then the sordid family secret was out, and it was all fair game, and now she cannot sail through an airport without grown men shouting, "Hey, Dr. J's daughter!"

She wants to tell them, screw you, I'm Alexandra Stevenson. But she avoids them because Julius Erving — basketball Hall of Famer — is a name she chooses not to hear. He is undeniably her father, and she has his face to prove it, but her feelings for him are cold and raw, and the events of these last few weeks do not help. Just recently, Erving stood at a podium to discuss his missing nineteen-year-old child — and he wasn't talking about her. His son Cory, a long-time drug user, had disappeared, and Erving was there begging a sympathetic public to help find him. But the natural response of the daughter was, I feel your pain, but why not come and find me? "People keep asking how I feel about the boy who's missing," she said that day. "Well, I don't even know my father. How can I know his kids?"

And so if Julius Erving is in a private hell, so is Alexandra Stevenson. He has a son who has vanished, and she has a father who has essentially vanished. Four children grew up under Erving's roof, but only she, who grew up estranged from him in a one-bedroom condo, has demonstrated his athletic genius. That is why the world is fascinated by her, but the world also needs to know she is not so fascinated by him. "He didn't change my diapers," she says.

Her white mother did all that — gave birth to her, raised her, schlepped her, shared a bedroom with her, explained her affair with Dr. J to her. "I'm my mom's daughter, not his daughter," she says. Alexandra doesn't intend to sound callous, not as he holds vigil for his son, but as far as she's concerned, "I don't want to be in the same sentence with him. I don't want it to say 'daughter of Julius Erving.' It's not who I am. It's annoying. I don't like being labeled. It's like being called African-American. I mean, part of me is African-American, but not all of me. Just like he's part of me, but not all of me."

Perhaps this is why she hates basketball, the sport her father transcended. Her coach, the one in jail, used to ask her to play H-O-R-S-E, and she'd lose every time. He'd say, "You're not very good at this," and she'd say, "Thank you." Instead, she played tennis, and tennis soon became her joy, and also her curse. If she hadn't been the first female qualifier to reach the semis at Wimbledon last July, she wouldn't have her new villa right now or her new Nike contract or, for the first time ever, her own room. But if she'd lost in the first round, no one would care who her father is, and she wouldn't feel an ounce of pressure. She wouldn't have everyone wondering why she's kept losing in the first round since then. She'd be at UCLA. But instead, here she is at Wimbledon one year later, wishing she could just be Alexandra Stevenson. Wishing the other players would stop hazing her. Wishing the press would stop asking about a missing half-brother she never knew or a father she's never embraced. Wishing they would see her and not think Dr. J.

"Yeah, right," Alexandra says. "When monkeys fly out of my butt."

The pregnant woman would have this awful dream. She'd dream she was in labor and that her baby had come out green, absolutely green. This was the spring of 1980 and the pregnant woman was a blonde sportswriter named Samantha Stevenson, and she was not sure if her baby needed to be born. It was so complicated: her relationship with Julius, the colors of their skin, the color their baby's skin would be. They had met in Philadelphia, circa 1976, and in those days, athletes and sportswriters weren't archenemies. She was in Erving's circle. "We were friends like you were friends in the '70s," she says. "You go have a glass of soda, you share lunch, you share a conversation."

She was flashy and opinionated. She'd demanded equal access to the 76ers' and the Phillies' locker rooms, and the players' wives did not want her near their men. "We'd never seen the likes of a Samantha Stevenson," one former Sixers executive remembers. "She'd come in the locker room dressed provocatively. I remember it got to the point where Bobby Jones wouldn't shower. He'd be across the bridge to New Jersey by the time the locker room doors opened."

But Erving connected with her. He was spending his basketball seasons apart from his wife, Turquoise, who preferred to remain in their home on Long Island, and this left Erving unattached. Confidants of Erving say his marriage was in trouble at the time, and one thing led to another. "The intimacy wasn't as important as the friendship," says Samantha. "We talked about everything; we were friends the moment he arrived from the ABA."

But theirs was an on-again, off-again affair, and he already had young children, and Stevenson became convinced he would not leave his wife for her. When she learned she was pregnant, she decided to have an abortion, but a small outbreak of Legionnaires' disease had hit the city and she was reluctant to go to the hospital. She had time to rethink her decision. She was certain she and Erving were still in love, and at the urging of some of her more religious friends, she kept the baby. Alexandra was born in Samantha's hometown of San Diego, on December 15, 1980, and Erving, who declined to be interviewed for this story, telephoned that day to say congratulations, and to ask what the baby's name was. He also told her he was coming to see them soon, real soon.

"I never doubted him," she says. "I waited. I always thought he'd come. I waited nineteen years."

Mother and daughter managed. It was the two of them and their Volvo station wagon against the world, and in the two decades that followed, the daughter saw her father only twice — once on a day she cried, and once on a day he did.

From the start, it was Samantha's idea to raise her daughter as an athlete. The child tried swimming, gymnastics, ice-skating, ballet, and soccer, and before she was four, she was gripping her first tennis racket. To outsiders, who now have the benefit of hindsight, this was her mother's grand scheme to cash in on Erving's genetics. But the truth is, Samantha was having a hard enough time just dealing with the covert racism. At grocery stores, the checkout clerks would say to her, "Are you babysitting?" And one day, a playmate's parent came to their La Jolla apartment, fingered Alexandra's hair, and said, "This must be difficult to brush." Samantha said, "Actually, it's easier to brush than my hair, and, to be honest, do you see me touching your daughter's hair? I'd like you to leave my home."

She realized any child of color would need protection, and so she wrapped herself up in her daughter's life. Over the next nineteen years, she went out on exactly one date, and that date ended with three-year-old Alexandra tossing ice water on the gentleman's lap. Theirs was a tidy cocoon, and if sports was their avenue to a better life, so be it.

In the interim, she had not much money, even with an undisclosed income from Erving, and she began writing for *World Tennis* magazine. The editor proposed that she do a diary about raising a child in tennis, and her journalist friends, knowing she needed the cash, urged her to be bold with it. So she wrote that she envisioned her four-year-old daughter being on Wimbledon's Centre Court someday. It was a line, not a manifesto, yet it would come back to haunt her.

It was around this time that Alexandra began asking if she had a father somewhere. It became a sore subject when all the students in her class were asked what their fathers did. Alexandra's response was, "That's my personal business, not yours." She was only regurgitating what she'd heard at home, but the incident forced Samantha to break out her Seventy-Sixers pictures. "I said, 'This is your father, and he plays basketball, and he's a very nice man, but he doesn't live with us,'" Samantha says. "She'd look for a minute, and then go back to playing with her Barbies."

Actually, father and daughter had already laid eyes on each other, when Alexandra was eighteen months old. Samantha was still in Philadelphia, and was walking with her baby when a limo pulled up. It was a surreal moment. The baby's bawling, the limo's window rolls down, and it's Erving. "I look right at him," Samantha says. "And he looks right at her, screaming away. I was, like, paralyzed. And he rolled up his window and drove on. It was like someone throwing ice water over me."

It was seven years before father and daughter met again, one final time, at a San Diego basketball clinic. Alexandra was eight, and was upset that the boys at school were abuzz over Julius Erving's one-time-only appearance. She asked to go see him for herself, and Samantha reluctantly agreed. Samantha wouldn't go, and asked her own mother and a family friend, Geneva Kandel, to accompany Alexandra. The two women made sure to write "Alexandra Stevenson" on a name tag in huge, block letters.

But Alexandra's demeanor soured the moment she eyed Erving. As soon as they were face to face, she snapped, "I don't want an autograph." Erving instead extended his hand to say, "Nice to meet you," but she glared and walked away. He told one of the boys to give her a signed ball anyway, and that was the end of it.

"Geneva told me that when Alexandra got to the front of the line, he looked at her and realized he was looking at himself," Samantha says. "She said that when Alexandra walked away, he just sat there with tears in his eyes. Geneva said she knew then he could never do anything."

People close to Erving say he kept his distance that day out of respect for his wife. They say Erving simply felt it was in everyone's best interest if he supported Alexandra financially, and left it at that. But they say that deep down he cared. Of course, this was no consolation to Alexandra, and after that clinic, she wrote him out of her life. Samantha still felt that her daughter needed a male role model, but tennis soon took care of that.

Samantha began freelancing for the *New York Times* and was tipped off about a ten-year-old tennis phenom from the streets of Compton named Venus Williams. Venus was playing a tournament that day in a San Diego public park, and Samantha took nine-year-old Alexandra along. Venus was tall, powerful, and dark-skinned, and the parents at the public park were clearly threatened by her. One woman asked to see Venus's birth certificate, and the confrontational Samantha intervened to say, "Well, why don't we get your daughter's birth certificate? You are so racist." The parents backed off. And while Samantha was bonding with Venus's parents — Richard and Oracene — Alexandra, Venus, and Venus's little sister, Serena, played on the jungle gym.

Samantha soon wrote the first major story about Venus in a national publication, and the *Times* began using her more. She would bring Alexandra on her assignments — she didn't believe in babysitters — and one story took them to Palos Verdes to interview Pete Sampras's childhood coach, Pete Fischer. After the interview, Samantha mentioned she needed a tennis coach for her daughter, and Fischer offered to take a look. After one session, he announced she could be number one in the world someday, and they began negotiating. Fischer, a pediatrician, wasn't going to come to La Jolla, so Samantha would have to make the five-hour round-trip drive to Palos Verdes. Samantha asked Alexandra if she was willing to make this sacrifice, maybe miss out on school dances and dates with boys. Alexandra had just seen Martina Navratilova on TV saying, "There's some eleven-year-old out there who's going to serve and volley like I do someday," and she'd sprinted around the house shouting, "That's me! That's me!" She was all for it.

So mother and daughter practically lived in their white Volvo. That car had clothes and food and Band-Aids and shampoo inside. They drove it to L.A. even during the Rodney King riots, with Samantha often ordering Alexandra to hide on the car floor. "In certain neighborhoods, if they saw she was in a car with a white woman, we might get shot at," Samantha says. And they did have a close call. A man almost ran them off the road one day, and when Samantha raged at him, he pulled a gun. Alexandra dove to the floor, her peanut butter sandwich flying, and the whole time Samantha was howling, "Put down that gun. It's people like you that make this a bad country."

This five-hour commute not only bonded mother and daughter, but Alexandra finally had her male role model. Fischer helped her with homework, took her to the opera, attended her school plays, and never let her mom speak during tennis lessons. His coaching partner, Robert Lansdorp, taught her a lovely one-handed backhand and Fischer turned her serve into a one-hundred-mile-per-hour weapon. If she ever asked if she could skip conditioning drills, Fischer would say, "When monkeys fly out of my butt." That was his favorite saying. She adored him. Before every match, he'd say, "Remember, you're not playing Steffi Graf," and if she lost, he'd say, "Well, you lost to a suckpot." That was his other favorite saying.

She began dueling it out with Venus, although Williams always won. "Don't feel too bad," Venus would say. "Someday you'll beat my sister." Richard Williams, impressed with Venus's rapid progress, asked Fischer if he would coach his daughters exclusively. "No," Fischer said. "I've got the better athlete." And the truth was, Fischer knew who Alexandra's father is, knew she had the genes. Fischer and Sampras — who used to come home to Palos Verdes at Christmas and play against Alexandra — had each guessed early that her dad was Erving, which is why Fischer always wanted her to shoot baskets. But neither Samantha nor Alexandra would fess up. "We used to say, 'My father's dead,' that he died in the war," Alexandra says. "We really hammed it up. We'd say he was a famous sheik in the desert, that he was lost in Kuwait. We'd say that when I turned twenty-one, I'd inherit millions."

Alexandra and Fischer put in seven years together, and by the time she was sixteen, she was 6′1″ and had more junior trophies than Sampras, and Fischer had drawn up a manual for her on how to beat the top ten players in the world. Then came the police report. Fischer had been arrested and charged with child molestation. Mother and daughter were mortified, because they had never once felt threatened by him. He eventually pleaded guilty and accepted a six-year jail term. And on the day he went to prison, in February 1998, Alexandra rushed through a tournament match in Michigan, just so she could phone him before he left. "I won, Pete," she said. "I played a suckpot." She then handed the phone to Samantha, who could tell Fischer was weeping. He told her, "You're the coach now," and she knew what he meant.

So once again, it was mother and daughter against the world. Except by this time, the Volvo had 250,000 miles on it.

The N-word changed everything. A foreign player — neither mother nor daughter will say who — called Alexandra a "nigger" during the 1998 Roehampton junior tournament in London, and Samantha knew the hate was on. Oracene Williams intervened and told Alexandra, "Listen, girl: Next time someone does that to you, go up to the net and start singing, 'Nigger, nigger, nigger.' And you say, 'Does that make you feel better? Come up here. I'll help you say it.' Because, girl, you're a beautiful person, and don't you let anyone ever do that to you." But it was still a difficult stretch. That same summer, at Wimbledon's Junior Championships, a reporter for the *Fort Lauderdale Sun-Sentinel* asked Alexandra, "Who's your father?" Samantha shooed him away, saying, "If you ever try to hurt my child again, you'll have to deal with me."

But the hurt stayed with Alexandra, and the following June she learned she'd have to return to Roehampton. Wimbledon qualifying was being staged there, and she was ranked too low to go straight into the main draw. She either had to return to the scene of the N-word or skip Wimbledon. She didn't want to go at first. But Fischer wrote from jail, urging her to have a "big Wimbledon," and because she loved grass-court tennis, she acquiesced. The events of the ensuing fortnight were mind-boggling.

It started when the Roehampton N-word incident hit the British tabloids. Samantha mentioned in an interview that she wanted to protect her daughter from racism and from the odd cliques on the tour. Egged on, she said she wanted her daughter to marry and have kids, and the tabloids inferred she was attacking the lesbians on the tour. One headline, she said, was "Keep Your Filthy Hands Off My Daughter." The gay players were livid. When Alexandra played her fourth-round match, several lesbian players came to root against her, and during the changeovers, some stood and stared at Samantha.

The press began portraying Samantha as an evil tennis mom

and, if that wasn't enough, the *Sun-Sentinel* purchased Alexandra's birth certificate, which stated Erving was her father. Erving at first denied the story, which tore Alexandra up. "How weak was that?" she asks. Two days later, he admitted it.

While all this was happening, she became the first woman qualifier to reach the Wimbledon semis, tying John McEnroe, the only other qualifier to do it. Nike's Phil Knight — whose tennis people had cut Alexandra a few months before — personally flew in to re-sign her. But her shoulder was gone — she'd already played eight matches — and Davenport routed her, 6-1, 6-1. Samantha — who all week took pictures of Alexandra for her baby book — told writers she'd heard Davenport feared Alexandra's serve, and Davenport reacted by ripping Samantha as an ogre tennis mom. Even Alexandra's Wimbledon coach, Craig Kardon, came out later and said Samantha should step back and let her daughter be the star.

Samantha took the hit. She'd always thought that if her relationship with Erving surfaced, it would be a blip. But she was dead wrong. She was criticized for sleeping with an athlete she'd covered, and the *Times* stopped publishing her, citing a potential conflict of interest because her daughter was now a prominent player. And the same female sportswriters she had once fought for turned on her. Some of them were particularly livid when they heard she'd dressed provocatively while interviewing players in the '70s. "That's how we dressed in the '70s," Samantha says. "We didn't wear bras. Miniskirts were in. It was just the era. Everybody was doing it."

As for Alexandra, her world ranking climbed as high as number thirty-three, but life on the tour, she found out, was vicious. She says Jennifer Capriati called her fat. "She should look in the mirror," Stevenson says. "The girls are catty. Like a high school locker room. Or worse. In high school, they weren't mean or didn't ignore you. They love to say I'm overweight and fat and can't move. I guess because they're not used to tall girls. But Lindsay's tall and not muscular, either, and I don't hear it about her. Lindsay doesn't have muscles. Look at her, she's flabby."

Her only true friend on the tour was Venus, who promptly nicknamed Alexandra the Big Baby. "Well, she's an only child," Venus explained. "And she's kind of spoiled." But the truth is, Venus knew how Alexandra felt. She and Serena had been similarly ostracized when they joined the tour — players even left dirty underwear in front of their lockers. That's why Venus and Alexandra began giving unflattering nicknames to a lot of the tour players. "Like, we call Martina Hingis 'Little Martin,'" Alexandra says. "Because she's like a little Martin who walks around gawking. She's a dork. She's a nerd. She tries to be cool." At the '98 U.S. Open, Alexandra says, Davenport crossed Stevenson's name off the list for massages and replaced it with her own, saying, "Get this [bleeping] junior out of here." She then kicked Alexandra's bag, at which point Venus told Alexandra, "Just let me know; I'll beat her up for you." Davenport won't comment on the incident.

It didn't help that after Wimbledon, Alexandra kept losing. The expectations after Wimbledon had been too high, considering how inexperienced she was — she was one of the few rookies who'd finished high school, and her body wasn't truly toned yet. Plus, she'd had no steady coach since Fischer, and no one had ever taught her how to construct a real tennis point. She would just blast away, never changing pace, and while that had worked at Wimbledon, she was now spraying unforced errors everywhere. "Losing Pete crushed us," Samantha says. "We had spoken to him every day from the time she was nine, and now he was gone at such an important time."

She lost thirteen of the next twenty-one opening-round matches after Wimbledon, crying after virtually every defeat or telling her mom, "I can't play tennis." She eventually moved to Florida to train with Nick Bollettieri, who predicted it would take six months to a year to get results. He told her she just had to learn to control her raw power, like Davenport and Venus had learned to do. And she also had to learn to stop pouting.

But the tour was almost swallowing her whole. At a tournament in Strasbourg, France, in May, Alexandra was playing France's Amelie Cocheteux, and she says Cocheteux repeatedly made racist and vulgar comments during changeovers (which Cocheteux denies). Then at the French Open, Alexandra says Cocheteux tried to bump her in a hallway (which Cocheteux also denies). "They're big bitches," Alexandra says of the players she believes are harassing her. "I think some girls are jealous. And others are so in their cliques that they don't talk to you and give you dirty looks. Next time someone bumps me, they're gonna be knocked out."

The Stevensons mentioned the French incidents to tour officials. Alexandra says it was dismissed as rookie hazing. But this is why they don't stay at the tour hotels, why Alexandra now dresses in the coaches' locker room. "It's a war out here," Samantha says. "If I'd known it was such a battle, I wouldn't have opened these doors for my daughter. I would've steered her to an academic life. I'd have her in college athletics. They try to take your soul out here, and I worry about her spirit. I think I could've given her a better life than this. I used to tell her about the glory of the sport. I was naive."

In fact, she is trying so hard to restore Alexandra's sagging confidence that she has done the unthinkable: She has brought up Erving. Several years ago, Samantha had shown Alexandra a film of him playing, just to show her how graceful he'd been in the last two minutes of games. And now she has mentioned him again. She wants Alexandra to know that she is Dr. J's daughter. That she can be as graceful as he was. And not to discount that. Never. "She has the same aura he had," Samantha says. "I can see it. And I want her to know that. It was not her choice to be born into this world. It was my choice."

This is all so hard for Alexandra to hear. Her father never called after Wimbledon, and her response now is, "It's his problem. I'm a good person to know, and if he doesn't want to know me, he's missing out." But then again, she is only nineteen. He may be wrapped up in his missing son, but she's determined not to be wrapped up in him. She simply denies his existence and plays her Wimbledon, and hopes someday to get her date with Yankee shortstop Jeter.

"Me and fifty thousand others," she says. "I met him after Wimbledon. He said, 'I'm a big fan of yours,' and I said, "Me, too.' I was so retarded."

It's her mother who worries. It's her mother who speaks with Erving's lawyers, but never with Erving. It's her mother who prays Cory is found safe. It's her mother who thanks God she didn't have the abortion in 1980.

They sit at lunch, just the two of them, one white face and one brown face, and they talk about the last nineteen years.

Samantha: "I did the best I could do."

Alexandra: "Yes, you did, Mom."

"I tried to have men around you — like Pete."

"Yeah, Mom, but hardly any women."

"But you had me — you didn't need any women. I was enough."

"I didn't need any men. You were enough."

JAMES McMANUS

Fortune's Smile

FROM HARPER'S MAGAZINE

*Penny ante it ain't. A determined lucky guppy
survives among sharks* — B.C.

I FLEW IN on American Airlines, the nickname for two pocket aces,
and I take that as a very good sign. I've got my poker books, sunglasses, and lucky hats, including the White Sox cap I got married
in. My room at Binion's Horseshoe overlooks downtown Las Vegas's dolorous, last-gasp attempt to keep up with the billion-dollar
resorts five miles south on the Strip, which in the last few years have
siphoned off most of the city's 34 million annual tourists with
pixilated facsimiles of Paris and Bellagio, Imperial Rome and Re-
naissance Venice — all the more reason to be happily ensconced
way up here at the Horseshoe. Even better this evening is that the
2000 World Series of Poker is in full swing downstairs. Tomorrow,
with a $4,000 stake, I'm going to try to win a seat in the million-dol-
lar championship event, due to begin in five days.

I ain't superstitious, as Willie Dixon once sang, but my second
daughter, Beatrice, was conceived in Bellagio, Italy, so my lucky
hats include a sun visor sporting the logo of the local version. I've
also been playing poker for thirty-nine years now, everything from
penny-ante family games in the Bronx to $80 to $160 hold'em at
the Bellagio, but never at anything close to this level. The championship event costs $10,000 to enter, and always draws the top two
or three hundred pros in the world. I'm good, but not that good. I
was taught by my uncle and grandfather, both named Tom Mad-
den, then got schooled in caddy shacks by guys with names like Doc
and Tennessee. My current home game in Chicago involves day-
traders, attorneys, a transit-systems planner, and a pizza delivery

man. It's a game that I fare pretty well in, but I still have no reason to doubt T. J. Cloutier, the former Canadian Football League tight end who is now one of poker's best players, when he says: "The World Series is a conglomeration of local champions. There's Joe Blow from Iowa who's the champion in his game at home; hundreds of local champions like him come to Vegas to play the World Series. But it's like the difference in going from playing high school football to college football: It's a big step up."

To reduce the long odds that I'll only embarrass myself, I've spent the last year practicing on a computer while studying the four poker bibles: Cloutier's *Championship No-Limit & Pot-Limit Hold'em*, cowritten with Tom McEvoy, the 1983 world champion; David Sklansky's seminal *Theory of Poker* and *Hold'em Poker for Advanced Players*, the latter cowritten with Mason Malmuth; and Doyle Brunson's *Super/System: A Course in Power Poker*, cowritten with (among others) Sklansky, Chip Reese, and Bobby Baldwin, the 1978 champion and currently president of the Bellagio — which is good luck right there, I figure, as I switch on the light in the bathroom. These little yellow horseshoes on the shampoo and soap might help, too.

The crowded main tournament area has forty-five oval poker tables, each surrounded by ten or eleven chairs. The size of a grammar school gym, the room has an eighteen-foot ceiling fitted with cameras and monitors but not quite enough ventilation for the number of players who smoke. Posters along the walls give results from previous events, including a color photograph of each winner. There's precious little else in the way of adornment, no music besides the droning announcements of poker activity and locust-like clacking of chips. Shangri-la!

The $3,000 no-limit hold'em event starts tomorrow at noon, so that's when I'll play my first satellite — while the best two or three hundred players are otherwise engaged. Before I go to bed, though, I need to take a few notes on the action. In satellites for the Big One, ten people pay $1,000 apiece and play a winner-take-all freeze-out. Which will make me a 9–1 underdog tomorrow, assuming I'm evenly matched with my adversaries, and of course I will not be. But a night's sleep and diluted competition will give me the best, or least bad, chance of winning.

Most of the satellites have $300 buy-ins and generate a seat in to-morrow's event, but one table along the near rail is reserved for $1,000 action. A harried blond floorperson with a microphone — her nametag says CAROL — is trying to fill the next one. "Just one more seat, players! Chance to win a seat in the Big One . . ." Nine hopefuls already have chips stacked in front of them, along with their Walkmans and water bottles, ashtrays and fans. As Fyodor Mikhailovich confessed to his second bride, Anna Grigoryevna, who'd conquered his heart while taking down *The Gambler* in short-hand: Once I hear the clatter of the chips, I almost go into convulsions. Hear hear! Down I sit, forking over $1,015, the $15 being the juice. Tired schmired. Once I receive my own $1,000 stack of green ($25) and brown ($100) chips and the dealer starts shuffling, I've never felt any more ready.

Hold'em involves nine or ten players receiving two facedown cards each (called "the pocket"), followed by three faceup shared, or "community," cards ("the flop"), a fourth community card ("the turn," or "fourth street"), and a fifth community card ("the river," or "fifth street"). Two rotating antes called "blinds," small and large, initiate a round of betting before the flop, with a round of betting after the flop, after fourth street, and after fifth street.* Starting at $25 and $50, the blinds double every twenty minutes. Since the game is no-limit, a player may bet anything from $50 up to all his chips at any point in the sequence. No-limit action seldom reaches a showdown on fifth street, where, if it did, the best five-card poker hand wins. Most often, an intimidating wager before or just after the flop gets no callers, and the bettor receives the whole pot.

Things get much trickier when factoring in your position. Acting last from the dealer's button (which rotates hand by hand) is the strongest position, since you see everyone else's action before deciding whether to fold, call, or raise, and can therefore get away with playing slightly weaker hands; whereas only big pairs, ace-king, or suited connecting face cards (Q♦J♦, for example) are likely to make money played from an early position. As early shades clockwise into middle, then late position, the valences of wagering assert themselves and less savvy players get soundly outmaneuvered.

---

* See the "Ranking of Poker Hands" and "Glossary of Poker Terms" on pp. 184–85.

My satellite rivals are mostly middle-aged guys of all stripes: the anxious, the collected, the pocky, the sleek; ex-beatniks, ex-jocks, and ex-hippies. So I feel right at home on all counts. Although one of us will stroll off with everyone else's money, the table has a friendly, if not quite munificent, vibe. When someone gets edged at the showdown, the usual response is, "Good hand." We also tip the cocktail waitress for one another. None of this fools me, however.

A gray-haired Vietnamese woman in round mirrored shades has taken the lead, winning three of the first eleven pots. Doing less well is the toothless varmint in seat one, just to the left of the dealer. His scraggly beard starts high on his cheekbones and covers his Adam's apple, with scalp hair of similar aspect, the entire gnarled package tentatively winched together by a powder-blue UNLV cap. Yours truly sports poker face, titanium shades, and Bellagio visor but still hasn't entered one pot. Him too scared.

Most of my no-limit experience is on Masque's World Series of Poker program and Bob Wilson's Tournament Texas Hold'em. By playing hundreds of thousands of hands (and winning three virtual tournaments), I've sharpened my card sense and money-management skills, and developed a not-bad sense of no-limit wagering rhythms. Yet computer play affords no opportunity to read faces and body language for "tells," and may actually diminish the mental, fiscal, and physical stamina required for live-action poker. The $1,015 I'm risking is real, with 9–1 odds that I'll lose every cent. I can't sit here with T.J. and Brunson and Sklansky open in my lap, thumbing an index or two for advice about playing an unsuited ace-jack.* The main thing I need here is feel, and for this, books and computers can't help much. Right now the pot has been raised by the muscular Arab in the salt-stained tortoiseshell Wayfarers, not Masque's "Player #4." What is Stains thinking that I'm thinking that he's thinking? Is his visceral aplomb all an act? The only things I'm sure of is that he wants my money more than Player #4 ever could and that he's already knocked out Madame Ho. But if I can't look into his eyes, at least I can observe how hard his lungs are working. If I've tuned him in right, I can feel it.

Right now from middle position I'm playing A♦J♥, having called

---

* In a poker tournament one plays hundreds of hands a day; the hands discussed in this article have been reconstructed as accurately as I and others can recall.

Stains's $200 preflop raise. The flop has come ace, five, king — all
of spades. With flushes abroad, there's a bet and three calls ahead
of me. That no one has raised makes my pot odds about 12–1, with
my shot at a full house a lot worse than one in thirteen. But I call,
God knows why, and fourth street comes up J♠, giving me aces and
jacks. After Stains bets another $200, two hands get folded, but the
guy on the button reraises. Two other calls on my right, then a fold,
then . . . the next thing I know the dealer is staring at me. So is
Stains. So is the Pakistani guy to his left. With only four outs (the
two remaining aces and jacks), folding aces-up makes me groan
with irrational pride, but when the dealer turns over J♣, I no
longer have a good feeling.

I need to take a piss about now, but I hold it, and the poker gods
deem fit to reward me. Fifteen hands go by in which I can do no
wrong. I win six good-sized pots, three in a row toward the end, using check-raises, semi-bluffs, traps — the whole works. By midnight
I have $4,900, almost half the chips on the table. The slender Paki-
stani guy, who's named Hasan Habib, has roughly $2,700; a big,
bearded guy named Tom Jacobs about $2,400.

With the blinds at $400 and $800, Jacobs moves all-in on the
third hand we play. Habib calls, turning over two sevens. (In heads-
up action, when one player goes all-in usually both expose their
hole cards since no more betting is possible.) When Jacobs flips
over A-10, Habib becomes an 11–9 favorite, and I get to watch the
do-or-die "race" from the sideline: J-J-3, followed by a trey, then a
deuce. I'm down to one adversary. The only problem is that it's
Hasan Habib, who finished second last month at the World Poker
Open no-limit event down in Tunica, Mississippi. And he now has
me slightly outchipped.

We fence for a half-dozen hands, neither of us willing to call
preflop bets, before I discover a pair of queens peering back up between my thumbs. Betting first, I can try to trap Hasan by (1)
merely calling his big blind, (2) putting in a modest raise, or (3)
moving all-in, hoping that he (a) calls, and (b) doesn't have aces or
kings. I decide to try door number three. And he calls, then puts
the frighteners on me by turning over K♦ and . . . 10♦. When the
board fails to improve either of our hands, the dealer yells, "Winner on table 64!" Yawning yet flabbergasted, I sit back and try to relax. Carol takes my name and address, then issues a printed receipt

for $10,001, the last buck being the token entry fee. *Event 25,* it says, *World Championship, 5/15/2000,* and assigns me to Table 53, Seat 6. I'm in.

Besides drawing record numbers of entries, the 2000 WSOP, I've discovered, has already produced a few of what might be called cultural achievements. The $1,500 seven-stud bracelet, along with the $135,975 first prize, went to Jerri Thomas, a forty-one-year-old from Cincinnati who had given birth only three months earlier. She and her husband, Harry, are now only the second married couple with a WSOP bracelet apiece. The following event, limit Omaha, was won by Ivo Donev, a former chess pro from Austria who'd spent the past two years reading Sklansky and McEvoy and practicing on Wilson software.

A week ago, on May 4, Jennifer Harman won the no-limit deuce-to-seven event. Because of its steep degree of difficulty, the event drew only thirty entrants, but the deuce (in which the lowest hand wins) is the title poker professionals covet almost as much as the Big One. No satellites get played for it, so only by putting up $5,000 can the cockiest, best-bankrolled players compete. Harman is a blond, thirty-twoish, dog-crazy gamine who plays high-stakes lowball games every night with the likes of Brunson, Chip Reese, and Annie Duke, but she'd never played no-limit deuce. Neither had Duke, for that matter, but that didn't faze either of them. They took a ten-minute lesson from Howard Lederer, Duke's brother, and ten hours later Harman had the bracelet and $146,250. And then, on May 5, Phillip Ivey took home the Omaha bracelet, defeating Thomas "Amarillo Slim" Preston with a series of fifth-street miracles at the final table, coming back from a 5–1 chip deficit. In thirty years of World Series play, during which he's won four bracelets, Slim had never lost at a final table. Playing out of Atlantic City, the twenty-three-year-old Ivey has been on the tournament circuit for less than six months but is now the only African American with a WSOP bracelet.

The World Series of Poker (and tournament poker in general) was invented by Benny Binion in the spring of 1970. He simply invited a few of his high-rolling cronies to compete among themselves and then vote for the best all-around player; the winner, Johnny Moss, received a small trophy and whatever money he'd earned at the table. The current freeze-out structure, which continues until one player has all the chips, was instated in 1971, and Moss won again, this time taking home $30,000. The next year's winner, Amarillo Slim, won $80,000, wrote a book, and went on the talk-show circuit, boosting the public's interest in tournament poker. By the time Brunson became the second repeat champion in 1977, first prize had quadrupled to $340,000. It was up to $700,000 by 1988, the second year Johnny Chan won. From 1991 until last year, first prize was an even $1 million, with the number of entries and total prize money steadily climbing. Last year's championship event drew 393 entries, with second place paying a record $768,625. Almost from the WSOP's inception, the total prize money awarded has dwarfed the purses of Wimbledon, the Masters, and the Kentucky Derby. There are now twenty-four preliminary events. The buy-in to the Big One remains $10,000, but these days the majority of players gain entry by winning satellites or super-satellites, mini-tournaments designed to democratize the competition; they are also thought to be the most legitimate route in, since they reward poker skill instead of deep pockets, though the two often work hand in hand.

T minus seventy minutes, and counting. After half an hour of lazy backstroke in the rooftop pool, I open my Cloutier and start cramming for my first big exam since I was an undergrad twenty-seven years ago. I'm reviewing all twelve of T.J.'s practice hands, poring over underlined phrases to see if I've absorbed the logic of his analyses. "Cardinal rule number one in no-limit hold'em is: If you limp with aces, you will never get broke with aces." And this, on the luck factor: "You can set up all the plays in the world, you can play perfectly on a hand, and you can still lose. And there's nothing that you can do about it." The rest of his advice I've tried to reduce to four memorizable aphorisms.

1. Don't call big bets; fold or raise.
2. Avoid trouble hands like K♦Q♣, K♥J♣, or any ace with a kicker smaller than a king in the first four positions.
3. Don't always steal-raise in obvious bluffing positions (the small blind, the button), and play big hands (even A♦A♣) slowly from them.
4. Drawing hands are death.
This last one means: don't risk your tournament life chasing big

pairs with small ones or medium suited connectors, as is often correct in a limit game. You'd win a big pot if you filled your straight or flush, but aggressive no-limit players make you pay too high a price to draw against them. Mistakes in no-limit tend to be costlier by an order of magnitude, and the chips that you lose in a tournament can't be replenished by digging into your pocket. Amen.

Furious satellite action is still under way as I arrive in the tournament area just before noon, with the overflow crowd getting denser by the second. Judging from their faces, a few of these hombres have been playing all night. Dealers raise the betting levels every three minutes instead of every twenty, eliminating players *tout de suite* but reducing the caliber of poker to little better than all-in crapshoots. Railbirds are six or eight deep, clapping and whistling when their hombre survives, as four camera crews roam the aisles. One guy they're focusing on is tournament director Bob Thompson, a silver-haired cowboy with a dulcet basso drawl. With his big jaw and narrow-eyed gaze, he effortlessly personifies the American West, Texas hold'em in particular. And that's what we came here to play: cowboy poker. Thompson runs the floor with his son, Robert, and Tom Elias; his daughter, Cathi Wood, coordinates the administration. Her fact sheet says that if five hundred entrants sign up, nine players more than the usual thirty-six will be paid; first place will pay $1.5 million, second will pay almost $900,000, and all other payouts will escalate. Her father just announced that last year's record of 393 has been shattered, then pointed to the line of new entrants with ten grand in their pocket still snaking three-players thick out the door. Clearly no cards will be in the air for a spell.

In the meantime, Puggy Pearson, the 1973 champion, holds court in a gold-and-lemon silk Genghis Khan outfit, including a crown with tasseled earflaps to go with his broad smile, eponymous pug nose, and Abe Lincoln mustacheless beard. Elsewhere I see little black dresses, tuxedos, and a short, wild-eyed black guy in a cloth airman's helmet hung with a dozen pink or yellow rabbit's feet. The leading sartorial choice, though, is Poker Practical: baseball cap, sunglasses, sateen casino jacket. Among so many corn-fed middle-aged guys in goatees and Levi's, Slim still looks clear-eyed and rangy at seventy-seven, bedecked in pressed khaki trousers, platinum belt buckle, mother-of-pearl buttons on his crisp cowboy shirt.

However unlikely this sounds, the World Series of Poker has

evolved from its good-old-boy roots into a stronghold of, yes, functional multiculturalism, proving, if nothing else, that there is such a thing. The field is an ecumenical crazy quilt of players from twenty-three countries on all six inhabited continents, among them Scotty Nguyen (the gold-bedecked 1998 champion) from Saigon, Hasan Habib from Karachi, and, from Pamplona, a Carlos Fuentes. Any all-name team would also have to include Tab Thiptinnakon, Jesus Ferguson, Exxon Feyznia, David Plastik, Chip Jett, Spring Cheong, Sam Grizzle, Lin Poon Wang, and Huckleberry Seed, the 1996 champion. Among toned jocks like Seed and Layne Flack and Daniel Negreanu we have equal numbers of the obese and the skeletal, plus plenty of folks who are youthful or ancient, wheelchair-bound or in dance shoes. Evangelical Christians are competing with Larry Flynt, CEOs and dot-com millionaires against call girls and poker dealers, gay men and lesbians, cowgirls and golfers and artists, black poker professionals and Jewish physicians, Jewish pros and black docs, at least one Aramaic scholar, and several Vietnamese boat people. All told our number is 512, breaking last year's record by 119 and bringing the purse to a staggering $5.12 million.

I fail to recognize any stars at my table, cause enough for slightly less pessimism. After showing our receipts, we each receive a stack of $10,000 in chips: one orange five-thousand, three white-and-royal-blue "dimes," two black-and-yellow five-hundreds, and seven slate-colored "ones" topped by a dozen green "quarters." The cards finally go in the air at 1:35, with the blinds at $25 and $50, no antes. Our dealer flicks out a card apiece to determine who starts on the button — and, with the sad-eyed king of spades, that would be *moi*. On the first hand, I look down and find A♣6♣. No less than five limp in front of me; i.e., they call the big blind by tossing $50 each into the pot, trying to get a cheap look at the flop. Not on *moi*'s watch! I make it $250 to go, get no callers, and, with $10,325, take the lead.

Not for long, of course. I start playing far too impulsively, overriding my own blueprint by entering pots with small pairs, K♥J♦, or 5♥4♥, getting smoked. Is someone else pushing my chips in or making my mouth say, "Let's raise it"? The main person making me pay is an unfearsome cowpoke five seats to my right. Wearing the same puzzled grin, he rakes in pot after pot. The worst hammering comes when I turn an overset of queens — make three queens on fourth street, that is, with no higher card on the board — and bet $2,000. Henrik calls. Even when I fail to improve on fifth street, I feel that six titties, or three queens, are worth another $2,000, a foolish amount at this stage. My logic is that if I could only get Henrik to call — I'd put him on two little pairs — I'd be back up to even: lesson learned, tabula rasa, ready to start playing solid. But not only does the little shit call me, he shows me a seven-high straight.

By the first fifteen-minute break at 3:35 I'm down to $2,200 and change. I skulk up to my room and call my wife, Jennifer, in St. Louis. I give her the ball-crushing news, and she sighs. What I need is a kiss and a head rub, she says, but all she can provide is a suggestion to page through my brag book, the four-by-six photo album with pictures of our girls and my two other children. "Just keep it in your pocket and think about us." It's truly a sorry idea, but since I don't have a better one I take the book with me downstairs. My goal all along has been to go to bed tonight still alive, and it looks like I'm not gonna make it. Yet I have absolutely zero reason to be surprised by this turn of events. Competing against inspired professionals, I'm not even heeding my pedigreed battle plan. Entering this event was an act of mind-bending hubris, so the only surprise is that I still have some chips to my name.

As we're sitting back down to the tables, word comes that Harman, Ivey, Seed, and Flack have already bitten the dust. So that's something. But have I "beaten" these people? Not really, since we only have to take on eight players at a time. What I've done is outlast them. I should therefore be thrilled to be stroking my orange-free stack while Geraldo yucks it up for the cameras.

The players I'm sitting with couldn't care less. All they want is to eliminate me and one another. But not me! Because as soon as I put the brag book next to my chips and open it to the page on which Jennifer reads *The Little Mouse, the Red Ripe Strawberry, and the Big Hungry Bear* to our daughter Beatrice, my pocket cards start to get better. I manage to steal a few blinds, then take down a decent-sized pot when two pairs hold up over kings. More important, I've persuaded myself at long last to fold all my trouble hands. With my new leather ass and my talismans, I manage to hang around until the nine o'clock dinner break, when I've scratched my way up to

$16,450. I dash to my room, call Jennifer again in St. Louis, and brag. And she lets me.

Back at the poker table, I grab myself by the collar and demand that I wait for big hands in all but the last three positions; and I listen. But escalating blinds and a stretch of cold cards grind my stack down to $13,825 by midnight. We're still at Level 4, anteing $25 a hand with $100 and $200 blinds. Down to $11,700, I can't wait forever for a hand. With the blinds at $200 to $400 and $50 antes, it's costing me $1,050 a round just to sit here and fold all my rags. But finally, one off the button, I peek between my knuckles and discover J♥J♦. Ooh la la. Raising to $1,000, I get three callers, and the flop comes K-J-8 rainbow. Even with the overcard (king) and all these damn callers, I bet $1,500. Seat 7 folds, but the Japanese yuppie in Seat 8 makes it $3,000. Then the shaved head in 1 cold-calls both bets. Jesus Christ! It's gonna cost me every last chip to keep playing this hand, and without the mortal nuts (at this point, a "set" of three kings) I'm petrified of set over set; even worse are the obvious straight draws. Yet if I don't get my chips in with this hand, when am I going to? Never, I decide, as I call, then watch fourth street come a darling, a beautissimous, a sideways-infinity 8, providing my first full house of the day — in two days, actually. I nudge the rest of my chips ten inches forward. "All-in." Japan meditates on his options for a minute, then folds, flashing two queens in disgust. Sayonara! Shaved Head, however, smooth-calls me. Since I'm all-in, no further betting is possible, so we both turn over our hole cards. His are 10♣9♣, *not* the cowboys or the other two eights, so it's over: any straight he might make will still lose to jacks full of eights — a full house. The pot comes to $36,900. Stacking it next to my brag book, I'd love nothing better than to trudge off to bed, but we still have fifty-two minutes left at Level 5. I order hot chocolate and sit tight, once folding pocket sevens from middle position even though no one had raised yet. Me solid!

Bob Thompson calls a halt to our match at nine after two. Sheets are passed around with places to record our chip count. Mine comes to $35,325. Tom Elias recounts them, signs my sheet, stuffs chips and sheet into a Ziploc bag, staples it shut. Done. Still alive. It's too late to call my wife, but my rush while it lasted — one hand! — has gladdened my heart as much as any sonnet or fuck or narcotic or shot glass of silver Patrón, as much as any three of those things, though it still takes 150 milligrams of Trazodone washed down by room-service cabernet to finally fall off, I'm so wired . . .

Tuesday morning, after thirty-six laps in the pool, a fast shower, room-service oatmeal and OJ, all in the service of tuning my nerves, muscles, and glucose, I arrive back downstairs to the sunlit fact of my name on page one of the five-page, single-spaced leader board. Two hundred fourteen still have chips, and my $35,325 is good for thirty-eighth place. With par at $23,933, this puts me in pretty good shape, though Mehul Chaudhari, the leader, has me almost tripled with $92,500. My satellite rivals, Hasan and Tom, are in fifth and sixteenth, respectively. Rising star Kathy Liebert is seventh, T.J. nineteenth, Noel Furlong right above me in thirty-sixth. Bunched near the middle are Hayden, Duke, Enright, and Erik Seidel, runner-up to Chan in 1988. All of these folks are my heroes.

By the end of today we'll have to lose 169 more of us, but every survivor will be guaranteed at least $15,000. Am I ready for this? Maybe not. My first big mistake is walking pocket kings, failing to protect them by raising in hopes of building a pot, then getting caught by a straight on the river. Exactly when, I have to wonder, did I become a person on whom everything is lost? This game is *designed* to blast draws from the battlefield, imbecile! Down to $28,000, I resolve, for the umpteenth time, to play solid poker — to stay out of pots until I find what Sklansky calls the Group 1 or 2 hands (aces or kings down through suited K-Q), then attack. For the next ninety minutes, it works. I also manage, from later positions, to slip into a few unraised pots with suited connectors, two of which turn into flushes. Bottom line? Ninety-eight grand. If I hadn't wasted a call with A♦3♣ on the previous hand, I'd now have the magic one large.

After dinner I get moved to Seat 2 of a table with Hasan in Seat 1, J. J. Bortner in 3, Kathy Liebert in 4, Mickey Appleman in 6, and Daniel Negreanu in 8. Scary, but also more fun. Bortner keeps a plastic baby rattler coiled atop her stacks that she's quite fond of shoving toward the pot, snake and all. Appleman is one of the game's veteran pros and melancholy philosophers. He used to work with alcoholics in Harlem, but he's been on the pro poker circuit for twenty-five years now. He's wearing a white Massada baseball cap over his ash-blond Groucho Marx moptop, and losing.

The goateed Negreanu is whippet thin under his Sharks jersey and ultimatebet.com hat. Fresh off a win at the U.S. Poker Championship, he's brimming with humor and confidence. "Let's be honest here," he tells Hasan, after a flop comes off A♣7♠7♥. "You've got the seven. Why walk it?" As Hasan tries to keep a straight face, Daniel grabs a dozen orange chips, winds up like he's getting ready to throw a left hook, and *wings* the chips into the pot, which he goes on to win with A♦10♣.

With sixty players left, I'm back down to $82,000, so I play extra-tight for a stretch, waiting for a monster I can sic on these big shots. The leaders are Duke, Liebert, Habib, and a guy called Captain Tom Franklin, all with around a quarter of a million in chips. With the blinds at $1,500 to $3,000 and $500 antes, it's costing me nine grand per round. So the last thing I'm in the mood for is a photo op, but here, as the cameras shark in, we have Slim standing up behind Liebert, holding a butcher knife to his throat. Turns out that back in 1972 Slim reportedly threatened to cut his throat if a woman ever won the tournament. (What he said was that he'd do it if a particular woman won, but the misquote makes much better copy.) I'm sure Kathy wants to concentrate on poker, but she's being a pretty good sport, though I'd be smiling, too, if I had big straight white teeth and $270,000 in front of me.

With a dozen eliminations to go till we reach forty-five, I basically hang around for two hours, actively avoiding confrontations. Doesn't work. By the time we're down to forty-seven, I have only $36,000 left, almost exactly where I started the day. But if I can only survive two more ousters, I'll not only be good for $15,000 but will be on a freeroll for the $1.5 million.

At this stage we're forced to play hand for hand, holding up the next shuffle until all six tables complete the previous hand, this to keep short stacks from stalling. My table is already a terrifying convocation, but when the player in the 8 seat goes out, he's replaced by — oh, shit — T. J. Cloutier. It gets worse. More than content to just sit here and wait, I somehow get forced into a series of make-or-break jousts. The first comes when, one off the button, I find A♣J♥. T.J. has already raised it to $5,000, and both the tanned, blond cowboy in 9 and Hasan have folded. *Don't call big bets,* I remind myself. *Fold or raise.* Yet I'm also aware that strong players target weak players, especially when the pressure is on, and my guess is that this is what T.J. is up to. I call. Jerry, the mustachioed Latin dealer, raps the felt, turns the flop: A♦9♣6♥. T.J. stares at me, checking. If he's got a bigger ace I am cooked, ditto for A-9 or A-6, but with top pair and a decent kicker I still have to bet $20,000, having put him on an ace with a medium kicker. I meet his warm glare for a second or two, then study the smoke-marbled distance. I must appear terribly frightened, however, because T.J. moves in with alacrity. His stack is smaller than mine, but only by three or four thousand. I call.

Now it's old T.J. who don't look so happy. "I think you've got me outkicked," he growls hoarsely, then exhales a yard-long plume of smoke as I show him A♣J♥. He makes me wait while snuffing his Salem, then turns over . . . A♥10♠! My heart hurdles four of my ribs.

The turn is 9♦, giving both T.J. and me aces up, with my J♥ still outkicking his 10♠. Only a ten will beat me, I figure; any other card comes on fifth street, I win. Instead of going out two off the money, I'm a 44–3 favorite not only to win a big pot but to punch out the number-one badass. Jerry raps the felt, turns over . . . an ace. Whew! The crowd around us gasps, and I hear Liebert say, "Oh my God!" With so much hot blood in my head, I'm able to parse neither the buzz of commentary nor the looks on the other seven players. All I know is that T.J. is grinning. Even after Jerry announces, "Split pot," and is echoed by dozens of railbirds, it takes me a moment to fathom that we both just made aces full of nines. Jerry shoves me my measly half-share of the chips. I try to restack them by color, but my fingers don't work very well.

For the next thirty minutes, Liebert keeps the table pretty much under control, maneuvering her $300,000 stack like Rommel in a short desert war, blitzkrieging our antes and blinds, setting us all-in when we draw. Down to forty-six we are still hand for hand, and sometimes the suspensions last eight or ten minutes. When I try to stand up, the tendons in my legs yank me forward. As I hobble into the men's room, Jesus Ferguson is manning a urinal in his trademark unreadable getup: full beard and yard-long auburn locks under black cowboy hat slung low over wraparound shades. "Still have chips?" he asks cordially. Sort of, I tell him. What about you? "I guess I'm still doing all right. Hey, good luck." Heading out after washing our hands, I notice that his feet are adorned with elegant little black dancer's shoes. Strange! Before I sit back down, I try to survey the other five tables. Jacobs and Duke have big stacks, though Liebert still rules the whole tournament. The tiniest stacks are at my table, where Appleman is down to $4,500. Another round of blinds and he's through.

Three hands later I flop two pair in a heads-up pot with Hasan and get elated all over again — until Hasan sets me all-in. The two diamonds on board are what scares me. If he makes his flush while I fail to improve, it'll be I going out instead of Appleman, and in the worst of all possible places. I've put Hasan on flush draw and inferred that he's semi-bluffing before his own hand gets made — or does not. Only a fool wouldn't do so with those scary-looking diamonds out there, and Hasan is no fool. So I call. And my sevens and sixes hold up, doubling me through to $78,000.

During the next break I notice that Andy Glazer, the *Detroit Free Press* gaming columnist, is talking to Jesus. When I introduce myself and ask for a cigarette, it turns out that neither of them smokes. I tell Ferguson that I'm shocked: in spite of the dance shoes, he looks like a Marlboro Man all the way. In fact, he's a gentle-voiced, day-trading wonk with a new Ph.D. in computer science from UCLA who happens to love ballroom dancing; the outfit is "just for disguise." Does he prefer to be called Jesus or Chris? "Both." Both? "Either one. I like them both the same." Helpful! Andy now suggests that I might want to slow down at this point. I tell him that the last thing I want is to keep mixing it up, but the table's not giving me much choice. "Plus my hand keeps grabbing the chips and tossing them into — "

"Almost as though you've been hypnotized."

"Ri-i-ight . . ."

"We understand perfectly," says Jesus.

With me on the button and Liebert in the big blind, Appleman folds one more hand, leaving him with barely enough to post the next blind. The next player, Roman Abinsay, pushes his entire $10,500 into the pot. Appleman, of course, desperately wants someone to knock out Abinsay, in forty-sixth place, but no one ahead of me can call; neither can I, with 7♠4♦. Which leaves it up to Liebert to play sheriff, especially since she already has $3,500 invested in the pot. And that's what she does, calling and turning over K♣Q♦. Appleman's long face never once changes expression, even when Abinsay turns over . . . aces. Liebert sighs. The flop comes Q♣7♥3♥, leaving her dead to either of the two remaining queens. The turn comes a seven, apparently helping neither of them. When a king comes on fifth street, some overexcited rail-birds start chirping that we're done for the night, and I'd love to believe them. But another quick look at the board makes it clear what Liebert already knows: that kings and queens loses to aces and *whatever* pair.

On we play. I'm more determined than ever to stay on the side-lines. Even when under the gun I find aces, I think about mucking them, but it's too easy to imagine kicking myself fifteen minutes from now, let alone fifteen years. Deciding to walk them, I bet "only" $10,000 and get called by the cowboy. When the flop comes J♠4♥2♠, I bet $12,000 more, expecting to win a nice pot then and there, though with part of me hoping he'll raise. When he smooth-calls again, it finally dawns on me that I may well be trapped by three jacks. Fourth street is 5♥, giving me an inside straight draw to go with my aces. I can't put the cowboy on anything higher than jacks, since he wouldn't have called $24,000 with A-3. I almost pre-fer he has jacks as my right hand picks up fifteen blue chips, break-ing them down into three piles . . . and Cowboy smooth-calls me *again!* Thank God the river card is 3♠, backdooring me into a wheel (giving me, in other words, an unexpected five-high straight on the final two cards). No way is Cowboy holding 6-3, and since the board hasn't paired, he couldn't have filled his three jacks. I check, hoping he'll at least represent the 6-3 and I can raise him all-in. He had me trapped back there on the flop and the turn, but now I believe I have him. When he shows me two pocket jacks, I turn over one ace for the wheel, and then, for good measure, the other one, which Cowboy doesn't seem to appreciate.

All of a sudden I have almost $200,000, second at this table only to Liebert's four large. I'm reminding myself to avoid her, in fact, when, back on the button again, I find A♦Q♠. When it gets checked around to me, I raise it to $12,000. After Bortner folds, who else but Liebert reraises to $24,000. She does this, of course, with an absolute minimum of anima. Zero. She could care less, she couldn't care less: take your pick. Assuming again that the big-time pros want to push me around, but failing for the dozenth time to heed T.J.'s advice about raising or folding, I call. The flop of

2♠7♣Q♣ bails me out, in a way. Because when Kathy, the reraiser, taps a slender pink finger to check, I catch a faint whiff of check-raise. As the odor becomes more insistent, my overmatched brain seizes up — *chcheckcheckch* — but my thumb and middle finger somehow manage to bet $20,000 without even pausing to consult with their boss. Kathy stares me down through my polarized lenses like some chick laser surgeon zinging my capillaries. Do they smoke? Do they twitch? I don't know. The hand I'd put her on was a medium pair, but now I ain't so sure — not that I was sure in the first place, though I doubt she reraised me preflop with Q-2 or Q-7. Whatever queen she's playing I've got her tied or outkicked, but what if she's slow-playing two of them? After weighing and squeezing her miniature blue-and-white soccer ball for over a minute, she cuts out a stack of fifteen orange chips, fondling them as though ready to move them forward, all the while watching me closely. Zzzt . . . zzzzzzt . . . I stare away from the table for ten or twelve seconds, then pointedly look back at her. I like her a lot, and she knows that.

When she finally mucks, I flash her my Q♠ in what I hope will be taken as a comradely gesture. "Show one, show all," Abinsay demands. I pick up both my cards from the edge of the muck and flip them over. Kathy nods twice but doesn't look happy. She also makes a point of sliding her own cards facedown toward the dealer.

Two hands later, after T.J. has raised to $10,000, I find an eminently foldable A♠5♥, but I can't shake the feeling that my new favorite author wants to pilfer our antes and blinds. The longer I think about it the more convinced I become, so I call. My heart thumps out signals visible all over my body — fingers, neck, pupils, complexion — of how nervous I am, so I try to persuade myself that they can also be read as elation, as in, "Yes! I'm finally gonna get T.J.'s chips!" I camouflage my relief when the flop comes A♦3♦2♣, giving me an inside straight draw to go with top pair and pitiful kicker. When T.J. raps his fist on the table I'm convinced I'll be check-raised, but even if he comes back over the top of me I've got enough chips to survive. I pluck two pink $10,000 chips from the top of one stack and toss them forward. Take that!

Now it's T.J. who's staring me down, an altogether more visceral experience than my face-off with Kathy. While there's nothing overt about it, the man comfortably embodies a lethal threat, even from the seated position. If it happens to suit him, he can reach across the table and rupture key vertebrae with his bare hand, and everyone sitting here understands this down in our helical enzymes — my helical enzymes, at least, not to mention my looping and straight ones. Doing my best to meet his jagged scrutiny, I decide not to taunt him about his run-on sentences or the stench from his Salems. The best way to take care of that is to break him and make him go home.

And he mucks it, God love him! Showing me Q♣Q♠, he seems both proud of his laydown and irked at the gall of me, slick little East Coast book-learned weasel that I am, even if it's *his* goddamn book I've been learning from. It's impossible not to think of Jack Palance staring down Billy Crystal: *I crap bigger'n you . . .* Amid the ensuing buzz, I overhear Andy Glazer speaking about "how spooky things are getting. A few minutes ago he was a writer trying to hang on, and suddenly he's messing with T.J. and Kathy?!" With T.J. perhaps. I certainly didn't think of myself as messing with Kathy. I read them both as messing with *me,* each time with less than a premium hand. All I did was refuse to lay down my strong hands just because they were who they were and I didn't have the absolute nuts. So even after I get pocket kings cracked by Appleman's K♣10♥ when the board makes him a straight, everything's still copacetic. A few hands later an unfortunate gentleman at another table gets busted in forty-sixth place and it's time to call it a morning. And this time I do wake up Jennifer.

Eight and a half hours later I have unwelcome company in the pool on the roof. The strong swimmer splashing away my tranquillity is a big, dark-haired guy with a mustache. When he finally climbs the hell out, I recognize him as Umberto Brenes, a Costa Rican player I met, along with his younger brother, Alex, back on Monday. He'd shown me his World Series bracelet, for the 1993 seven-card stud event, and invited me down to his poker club in the Hotel Corobici in San José. I saw him at Ferguson's table last night, so I knew he was still in the running. It turns out we're both in our forties and have kids. I have four, Umberto has two; he has a World Series bracelet, I don't. But my $276,000 is good for third place, just behind Liebert's $283,500 and Englishman Barney Boatman's $282,000.

Downstairs we learn that Umberto, with $101,000, is at Table 48, the most hazardous of the five — plenty of chips to win if you catch cards and play well, but with Boatman and Liebert wielding big stacks, you risk being set all-in each time you enter a pot. Tom Jacobs's $229,000 makes him the bully of Table 47, which has four stacks under $39,000. Duke, Habib, and Mike Sexton are all at Table 54, the second most chip-laden group and perhaps the most talented. Duke and Habib are both hot, and Sexton is fresh off a victory at the European No-Limit Championship. In Seat 6 of Table 55 sits its putative bully, yours truly. I've fantasized for decades about having a World Series stack big enough to make brutal sport of my opponents, but I have zero actual experience in the role. I spent the first two days gasping and thrashing to keep my nose above water, and it isn't so obvious how to skim along the top with the current. Another problem is that my four most chip-laden opponents sit immediately to my left. Larry Beilfuss in Seat 7, with $121,500, is a bespectacled, all-business guy around my age. Then comes Dae Kim in 8 with $127,500, Meng La in 9 with $197,000, and Anastassios Lazarou in 1 with $125,000. Since chips tend to flow clockwise around the table, I'm in lousy position to kick any serious butt. On my right, I have a curly-haired Parisian by the name of Angelo Besnainou, who has what sounds like Cuban salsa leaking from his earphones. He's about the sunniest person I've met in Las Vegas so far. Even sunnier is the fact that he has only $64,000, which I plan to relieve him of stat.

At Level 11 the antes alone are $1,000 (five times the buy-in for my home game) with blinds of $2,000 and $4,000. My stacks now consist of sixteen blue-and-white dimes, twenty-four orange five-thousands, and fourteen hot-pink ten-thousands. We've been told to keep our pinks at the fore so that opponents can gauge whom they do or do not want to tangle with.

As expected, the first player eliminated, over at Table 62, is Eric Schulz, who started with a single $500 chip. An old poker adage says that all you need to win is a chip and a chair, but starting from so far behind at a table with Mel Judah, T. J. Cloutier, and Jesus Ferguson, that's what it remained for Mr. Schulz — an old adage. Yet that yellow-and-black chip of his just earned him $15,000, the same prize the next eight eliminatees will receive. Meanwhile, at our table, Appleman has just raised all-in. Angelo folds, and I'm not playing trooper with Broderick Crawford. After mucking, I have to brush away what looks like cocaine or powdered rock salt from the baize between my stack and Angelo's. Beilfuss calls Appleman, but Kim, La, and Lazarou all fold. (Was someone snorting lines or noshing saltines here last night?) Pair of fives for Appleman, A♦9♠ for Beilfuss. The flop comes A♥A♣5♥, ruining Beilfuss's day while doubling Appleman through to $180,000. It seems like he was down to felt only a few minutes ago.

The white mess turns out to be sugar, and the culprit turns out to be Angelo. I discover this by watching him sprinkle out more of it. I stare at him, shaking my head. "For sweet life," he tells me. "You know?" He goes on to explain that Tunisian Jews, of which he is one, have a tradition of adding sweetness to life by sprinkling sugar on portentous objects: a new house, a tractor, a child. . . . I have to admit it's a wonderful concept, but as its substance combines with the moisture on our fingers we're sugarcoating the cards as we play them. Isn't it bad enough that I've got either the suddenly ill-tempered Beilfuss or the ever inscrutable Kim snapping me off with reraises each time I try stealing blinds? Have they no damn respect for the Bully? A few hands later Meng La comes over the top of me, all-in, this after I've made the heaviest wager of my life by raising his big blind eight pink — eight pink $10,000 chips. I'm forced to lay down the same red jacks that came to my rescue on Monday.

After licking my fingers and wounds for a round, I'm only too happy to call, with K♣K♦, the last $28,000 of Ron Stanley, the player in Seat 2. Stanley turns over K♥10♠. Oh yeah, I gloat, mentally pumping my fist. Time to get back in the lead! But the Q♥9♦3♦ flop gives Stanley a belly straight draw, and when, sure enough, the beardless jack of clubs arrives on the turn, my stack and my confidence plunge to $97,000, a piddling sum at this stage. Just in time, too, for Level 12, when the blinds jump to three and six grand. Worst of all, I get high-carded to a table with Habib, Sexton, Jeff Shulman (the chip leader, with almost $500,000), Jacobs, and Cloutier. In my humble opinion, it's over. Not that I've given up, but I have to be realistic before I get blinded to death. My only chance is to wait, not too long, for a monster to materialize between my knuckles, hope I get called by a worse hand and don't get sucked out on, and so double through. And then I have to do it *again*. And then I have to do it again. At least we have a ravishing dealer named Red, presumably because of her fox-colored shoulder-length locks, to go with wide hazel eyes and a sly grin.

T.J.'s $400,000 threatens to make him boss hoss, a role he was surely born to play. And with Shulman's vast stacks on my right, I'm developing a severe case of big-stack envy. A half-hour later we lose Kathy Liebert. She entered a big pot with queens but lost to K♥10♦, then got bounced five hands later when someone called her K♦10♣ raise with a pair of queens, and that time the queens *did* hold up. Very brutal. But now I can barely keep from whooping when, sitting in the small blind, I find K♠K♦. Even better is that Annie Duke, who's playing without shoes or socks, has already raised it four pink. I reraise eight more and flash her what I hope is a friendly but confident smile. Her response is to say, "I'm all-in." Terrified of aces, I call, timidly flipping my kings as Duke snaps down . . . Q♣Q♥. This is good. What's bad is that our table has suddenly become the matrix of Annie Duke fandom, all of them training a miasma of estrogen on to my innocent cowboys, willing them to be bushwhacked by ladies. Bob Thompson's reminder that Annie's the last woman left only whips them up further. *Annieee! . . . You go, girl! . . . C'mon, queeeen!* Yet in spite of all this, my brag book decrees that the cowboys stand up.

We come back from dinner to antes of $2,000, blinds of $5,000 and $10,000, with the final fourteen reconfigured as such:

Table 1

1. Mark Rose, $223,000
2. Annie Duke, $130,000
3. Hasan Habib, $330,000
4. Chris Ferguson, $305,000
5. Jim McManus, $450,000
6. Steve Kaufman, $400,000
7. T. J. Cloutier, $540,000

Table 2

1. Mickey Appleman, $540,000
2. Roman Abinsay, $330,000
3. Angelo Besnainou, $70,000
4. Tom Franklin, $450,000
5. Jeff Shulman, $440,000
6. Anastassios Lazarou, $105,000
7. Mike Sexton, $385,000

What a player Appleman must be, having started the day with $6,000! I'm glad that he's not at my table as, once again, we play hand for hand, aiming to get down to six. Between shuffles I get up and watch Angelo get bounced when his A♣6♠ goes down to Shulman's A♦10♣.

I remind myself how much seven-handed action changes the value of pocket cards. Trouble hands like K♠Q♦ or small pairs become cautiously playable, even from an early position. It's crucial that I not only adjust but account for the fact that my opponents will, too. The amazing thing to me is how calm I now feel, as though vying for the lead late on day three of the Big One is all in a night's work. I can't see the stacks on the other table, but I figure I'm in fourth, third, or second, and I understand that I can win.

I watch as Chris Ferguson makes what has become our standard preflop raise, $60,000, and with J♥J♠ I am happy to call, especially since I've read Chris's raise as positional. Kaufman and T.J. and Rose and then Annie all fold, but Hasan, in the big blind, calls, too. This triggers the blend of *oh, shit* and *oh, well* that's been percolating down through my brain each time I play a big pot. I've risked only sixty so far, but we're likely to take it much higher. When the flop comes A♦Q♦2♣, it's more like *oh, shit* and *oh, shit*. The fecal sensation becomes more pronounced as Chris moves both hands behind his stacks, clasps them together with pale, bony fingers, and pushes them slowly toward the pot, making sure not to topple any of his precious pink towers. I ask him to count it. "Two-fifty," he says, without counting. I believe him, and the dealer confirms it. Do I call an all-in bet with two overcards already on board? I don't think so. At the same time, I don't want no Fred Astaire wanna-be shoving me off my two jacks. T.J. and Annie and Slim all have their share of the photographers' attention, but Jesus of late has become the new darling. Both the still guys and film people regularly zoom in on his badass Black Stallion hat with silver buckles adorning the brim, his wraparound shades whose convexity must make for some swank photographic effects — Fred Astaire meets Richard Petty, along with the Youngbloods hair and beard, the bona fide Jesus-esque features. I'm sure they're all pulling for him to win the whole thing, as opposed to some puffily unphotogenic dad-type like me. But darn it all, I'm bad as well! Haven't they noticed my space-age titanium shades, or the stain on my top right incisor from smoking Cambodian opium? And what about the four-color tatts of Sade and Genet on my scrotum? . . . I flip my jacks into the muck. Too many overcards, plus no read whatever on Chris.

But I only have to wait three more hands till I get my first chance at redemption, looking down to find what certainly looks like Big Slick. I peer in again to make sure. Yessiree, it's A♦K♣. Swallowing as discreetly as possible, I wait my turn before pushing ten orange toward the unraised pot. The instant that Steve Kaufman mucks, T.J. shoves forward a tall stack of pink, snarling, "Raise." He may not have actually snarled, but that's how it registers in my soul. And whatever the participle or verb, it's another $100,000 to me.

In the final chapter of *Super/System,* Brunson claims that A-K are his favorite pocket cards because you win more with them when you make a hand and lose less when you don't; whereas A-Q, just one pip below it, is a hand he famously refuses to play under any circumstance. T.J.'s book stresses that you have to win both with and against A-K. "It's the biggest decision-hand in a tournament." He considers it so decisive that in four of his twelve practice hands, the reader is given A-K. And be still my computerized, book-learnin' heart and suck in my un-Christlike cheeks, but I just have a feeling that T.J. is making a play. And I want him to go on making it. Yet with four hundred large in the pot, what the hay is a feeling? The short answer runs something as follows: T.J. writes that when he gets raised holding A-K, his response depends on *who made the raise.* I've studied the passage so obsessively, I believe I can quote it verbatim. "There are times when I will just flat call the raise. There are times when I will try to win the money right then by reraising. And there are times when I will simply throw the hand away. It all depends on what I know about my opponent." Not to get overly granular here, but I think T.J. thinks he can push me around, so I *feel* I should give him a call. Playing against him these last two nights has made it clear he's a guy on whom nothing is lost — just his chips in this case, if I'm right. If I'm wrong, I'll be out of the tournament.

"Call."

The flop of my life comes a baby rainbow: 2♣5♥4♦. I still have boss overcards, plus a nice belly draw to a wheel; but I also have nada. Same draw for T.J., I'm guessing, since I've put him on a medium ace. He's not the kind of guy to reraise with A-3 — unless he has Kryptonite testes or assumes he can bluff me with garbage, both of which are probably operative. I recall that in Practice Hand 4, the flop comes three babies. If Player A bets, T.J. quizzes the reader, what do you do? "You throw your hand away. Why? Because you have nothing. In no-limit hold'em, you never chase" — about the dozenth time he's restated the never-chase maxim. Assuming he knows that I know this, I chase. The instant I tap the felt checking, T.J. mutters, "Two hunnerd thousand," and his entire stack of pink chips disappears into his hand, to be deftly redeposited between him and the pot in four stacks of five. His fingers don't seem to be trembling.

"Call," I croak finally, making a virtue of necessity by trying to sound like I've lured poor T.J. into my trap, an impression I hope isn't risibly belied as my vibrating digits fumble to count twenty pink. I can't bear even to glance in T.J.'s direction, so I cannot say how he reacts to the turn card, the seven of diamonds, which as far as I'm concerned changes exactly nothing. I check.

"I'm all-in," T.J. says. No surprise here, since he's been trying to buy the pot all along. A third enormous bet doesn't scare me any less, or any more, than the first two did. Except now he has put me all-in.

"I call."

Thompson notes for the gallery that T.J. has me covered by a hundred thousand or so. What he doesn't say is that if his fellow Texan has even a pair of deuces, I'm finished. T.J. turns over an ace and a nine, muttering something I can't quite make out because of the buzz off the rail. When I turn over macho Big Slick, there are oohs, aahs, applause, and T.J. appears mildly shocked. Amid the gathering uproar, Thompson announces our hands. A trey will give us both wheels, a nine and I'm kevorked. Anything else, the pot's mine. My sense, as the dealer's right fist thumps the table, is that T.J. is going to catch . . .

"Jack of clubs on the river," drawls Thompson. "Jim McManus wins eight hundred and sixty-six thousand and becomes the new chip leader." Benny Behnen and Amarillo Slim have been standing behind the table for the last several hands, and Benny now drawls, "Jesus Chrahst!"

"Ah'd bet on that boy," Slim drawls back. "He's got the heart of a cliff divah."

"T.J. taught me everything I know about this game," I announce. "Read his book and you'll see." If I had my copy on me, I would brandish it aloft for the cameras. T.J. stubs out a Salem, not pleased. "It didn't teach you that, boy," he growls, with what I hear as a trace of contempt. Now, the last man on earth I would taunt is T. J. Cloutier. I also remember how showing my queen to Kathy Liebert didn't seem to assuage her. Not that it's my job to assuage either one of them . . .

This *former* cliff diver, though, is gonna sit good and tight with his chip lead. After thirteen hours at the table and staring down T.J.'s three barrels, he's got cobwebby spermatozoa floating through his vitreous humor. So he's not even tempted to play a 3♦8♥, J♥5♣, or even A♥7♥. No, sir. He also decides not to raise but to limp. And Duke, one off the button, cooperates beautifully, raising to $60,000. Hasan and Chris fold. Hasan stands up, yawning and stretching, to watch. And then I'm yawning, too, just as I happen to start moving $150,000 toward the pot; judging by the size of Duke's stack, it's enough to have set her all-in. The next thing I know, both Kaufman and the dealer are citing me for a string raise, claiming I went back into my stack for more chips without saying, "Raise." I realize they're right and apologize. The dealer determines that the amount in my hand as it started forward was $60,000, which happens to be the minimum allowable raise of Annie's original bet. And boy, she's not happy. My raise doesn't set her all-in, but since she only has $140,000 left, she's been priced in. She turns to her entourage. "This is the worst thing that's ever happened to me in a tournament!" she shrieks — and *shrieks,* I'm afraid, is the word. "Let me call that myself," she chides Kaufman, and for a moment I'm cheering her on, till she adds, "I would've been glad to let him go to his stack for more!" She runs a hand up through brown bangs, jangling her wrist load of beads, braided leather, plastic bangles. That she would have been "glad" to let me put her all-in suggests she has a premium hand, and that she was so overwrought when she said it makes it impossible to believe she was acting. I have to put her on something better than a lousy pair of jacks, do I not? But so why, after my raise was scaled down to sixty, didn't she simply reraise me?

The flop comes A♣Q♣8♣, about as bad as it can be for my jacks, so I check to the shrieker. "All-in," she says, sliding her stacks in. She has a live human being inside her — her third — but that's not the reason I fold. No way can I call even a hundred grand more, though the pot odds declare that I should. Not with them overcards squatting pregnantly on the baize. It isn't the toughest laydown I've made, but it still smarts to have to muck johnnies again. This is, after all, two-card chicken we're playing, and things can change fast on fourth street and fifth street. . . .

"I changed my mind," Duke announces, then graciously shows me an ace before mucking. "That's the best thing that ever happened to me in a tournament." Big applause from the rail. *Hang in there, Annie! . . . Chicks ruuule!* Yet who can I blame but myself and Steve Kaufman? If I'd been competent to set her all-in before the flop, when all she probably had was a medium ace, she almost certainly would have folded; but for only $60,000, she was still sufficiently tied to the hand to make a crying call correct. Then she caught that huge piece of the flop. So my little snafu while trying to put her all-in cost me $120,000 and handed Jeff Shulman the lead. If I'd simply said, "Raise," I'd be sitting on over a million.

To stem this new ebb tide, I resolve to enter no pots for the next fourteen hands unless I find aces or kings. I watch two rounds go by without a flop, a single raise being enough to capture the blinds. Meanwhile, at the other table, Sexton and Lazarou get bounced on consecutive hands.

Level 15 brings with it $3,000 antes and $15,000 and $30,000 blinds, but my chips are still copious enough to let me relax, await monsters. Anyone in his right mind would follow this plan, yet when I find A♣9♦, I flash back to what Annie just did to me and call Chris's raise to $60,000. Hasan calls as well. When the flop comes A-Q-5 rainbow, Chris says, "All-in."

"Jim has about $700,000 in chips," declares Thompson, "Chris and Hasan, oh, I'd say about half that."

If I call and lose I'm out of the tournament; if I win I'll not only guarantee playing tomorrow but I'll have a huge lead in the sprint for the $1.5 million. Yet every last piece of advice I've received says no way do you call in these situations unless holding the absolute nuts. I do have top pair, but I lose to any kicker above nine. I wish I had some kind of read on this Jesus character. He's certainly capable of bluffing, but he's also extracted quite a few fishes and loaves from his butt in the last twenty minutes. My mouth for some reason says, "Call," and Chris turns over . . . A♥9♠. I pause long enough to give him decent psychological scourging before I let him off the hook and show mine. Shaking our heads as the crowd goes bananas, we triple-check the board for a flush draw; finding none, we both burst out laughing. His slender blond wife stands behind him, wrist to her forehead, recounting the split on her cell phone. In the meantime, on the very next hand, Annie goes all-in again, only to have Chris call and show pocket aces. Revealing the fateful A♠9♠, Annie never catches up, so she's out. As she slowly gets up, Thompson announces that Annie's tenth-place finish is the highest by a woman since Barbara Enright came in fifth in 1995, and the $52,160 makes Annie the leading female money winner in World Series history. After watching her play for a week, I doubt this will cheer her up much. She's a cowgirl.

Down to nine men, we are ranged around one table: Ferguson in Seat 1 with $800,000, then Habib with $400,000, me with $950,000, Cloutier with $550,000, Abinsay with $420,000, Appleman with $240,000, Jeff Shulman with $1,000,000, Captain Tom Franklin with $600,000, and Steve Kaufman with $220,000. Sitting just to my left, T.J.'s in perfect position to hammer his student, like he's been trying to do for two days. Plus he now has revenge as a motive.

For the next hour or so, the standard preflop raise is ninety or a hundred thousand, usually enough to take down the blinds. From time to time one of us reraises all-in, but in each case the original raiser gives the reraiser credit by folding. Then, in very short order, this happens: Abinsay, from under the gun, brings it in for $60,000, and Appleman calls with his last $58,000. With the J♠10♠, I'm tempted to make it a three-way, but I follow the no-chasing dictum. Thank God and Cloutier, too, because none of my straight or flush cards appear on the board as Roman's A♠K♠ easily holds up over Mickey's A♦10♣. Two hands later Captain Tom wagers his last $118,000 before the flop, and Ferguson calls him with tens. When the Captain shows fours and the board gives no help, we are seven.

One more unfortunate bet and it's bedtime, but nobody wants to finish in seventh. As in every WSOP event, the last nine players receive commemorative final-table jackets; there's also a hefty difference in prize money ($146,700 for seventh versus $195,600 for sixth); but the main reason for our lull in aggression is that tomorrow's final table will seat only six, owing to the Discovery Channel's need for compressed action in their documentary. Since we all want to be in the movie, not one all-in bet gets a call for the next forty minutes. The guy forcing most of the action is Jeff, and he steadily builds up his stack. I'd love to know whether he's doing it with legitimate hands, but I'm not catching cards to find out with. One mistake against Jeff and you're gone, whereas he can guess wrong and still play.

Finally, *finally*, one off the button, I find aces, the first time I've seen them all day. But my ecstasy ratchets down notch by notch as Kaufman, then Chris, then Hasan, muck their hands. At this point I'm tempted to limp, though I know it would be read as a trap. The $66,000 in antes and blinds I'll win by raising is hardly chump change, but when you find pocket rockets you want to *eviscerate* people. Masking my chagrin, I make the minimum raise to $60,000, hoping someone will come blasting back over the top of my show of timidity. Not this time. T.J. even shoots me a rare little smile as he folds, and Roman and Jeff are also untempted to call.

Three hands later, Jeff raises $200,000 from the button. Kaufman ponders defending his $15,000 small blind for a moment, then passes, leaving Chris, in the big blind, to reflect on his options for another thirty seconds. "What would Jesus do?" a shrill railbird wonders aloud, getting laughs. The answer is: move all seven of His tidy stacks toward the pot, reraising $650,000. Hasan and the rest of us scram. Jeff stares at Jesus for maybe ten seconds, then shrugs almost meekly and calls. When he turns over 7♥7♣ — not really much of a hand to be calling a big stack all-in with — there are whispers and cries of astonishment. Then Chris shows us . . . 6♣6♠! In absolute crunch time, the twenty-three-year-old Shulman has somehow made a veteran read of his opponent, leaving Chris with two outs. As auto-advance cameras fire away and the railbirds go silent, the flop comes 10♥3♥ . . . 6♥! Having flopped a miraculous set, Jesus vaults from his chair. And yet Jeff, for all his hellacious bad luck, has a flush draw — nine outs right there, to go with the two other sevens. Jesus's lean, foxy wife, Cathy Burns, has her palms on her ears, a Munch screamer, as voices call out for sixes or sevens or hearts. When 5♣ hits on the turn, Jeff has a straight draw as well, though Chris is still the 2–1 favorite. The dealer turns fifth street: a ten. No heart flush, no seven. As Jeff slumps back in his chair, Chris dances out of his, the sooner to be locked in a tango embrace from Ms. Burns. No celebratory peck for these two, but a lingering soul smooch while they twirl one another around.

"Jesus Makes 6–6–6," I proclaim. "Takes Over Chip Lead, Molests Wife in Public."

"Molests Girlfriend in Public," a railbird amends me.

"Even better," I say. But the truth is, I'm dying inside. Not only is Jennifer not here to cheer me but it's starting to sink in that to win this damn thing I'll not only have to catch a few monsters; I'll need to catch them when someone else holds one a single pip lower. I'll have to play well for four days just to be in a position to get lucky when the big money goes in the pot. If only, if only, I snivel. If only I'd caught aces on this hand . . . till it dawns on me that if I had, I would've lost every one of my chips. But of one thing I'm certain: Smooching Jesus is due for an epic correction. Having bounced Duke with aces and Franklin with tens, he now spikes a two-outer and doubles through Jeff to the lead. What he needs is a quick crucifixion, if only to give his strawberry-blond Mary Magdalene something to hug him about. Everyone at the table would love to just nail him right now, yet we're terrified of taking him on. Not only does he have the big stack but he's got my old horseshoe lodged miles and miles up his ass.

T.J., of course, isn't terrified. He'd seen hundreds of rushes like this before Chris was even born. I fold Raquel Welch (3–8) in a hurry. "Raise," T.J. mutters as soon as the action gets to him, pushing in $290,000. Abinsay folds, but Shulman reraises all-in. Then Jesus not only calls Jeff and T.J.; he, too, reraises all-in! The big guy can't seem to believe what has happened, but he manfully lays down his hand, claiming it was jacks. We believe him. What are jacks, after all, once Jesus H. Christ gets involved? Turns out to be a pretty shrewd laydown when Jeff shows two kings, and Chris has . . . the aces again! Get the fuck outta here! The board renders no poetic justice either, because this time the best hand holds up. Just like that, Jeff is out. A couple of minutes ago he was running the table. He congratulates Chris and the rest of us, and then, with his dad's arm around him, walks away like a man with a future.

Ten hours later, the Horseshoe's vast tournament room has been converted to an intimate poker studio, if there is such a thing. In place of last night's four tables there are twenty rows of seats facing a thirteen-foot monitor. Bleachers were erected along one side of the final table, flanked by more rows of seats at both ends. The table is lit with four banks of lights, surrounded by cameras and monitors. Everyone else wants to interview the finalists, but the Discovery director has first dibs because of the shoot. One of his tech guys wires me for sound, winding the line up through the fly of my pants and clipping the mike to my collar.

Back behind the bleachers, I peruse the new sheet with Hasan.

Chris is in Seat 1 with $2.853 million, Hasan is in 2 with $464,000, I'm in 3 with $554,000, T.J.'s in 4 with $216,000, Roman's in 5 with $521,000, Kaufman is in 6 with $511,000. Between us we have $5.19 million in chips, with which we'll be vying for $3.74 million in prize money. The other $1.38 million has already been awarded to places forty-five through seven.

"Good luck to you, buddy," says Hasan in his buttery lilt.

"And good luck to you." We embrace. I'm startled to realize that I meant what I said. For eight days now, we've been throwing haymakers at each other over critical pots, but that makes me love him a little. Plus we'll both need some luck from now on.

Finally, a little after noon, Thompson introduces us one by one. Chris, at thirty-seven, has already won the $2,500 seven-card-stud event, to go with the 1999 Best All-Around Player at the California State Poker Championship and his new Ph.D., but lists his occupation as "student." I hear Andy note that his nickname stems not from delusions of grandeur but from his hair and the kindness of his features. I also hear that Hasan used to own a video store but has now, at thirty-eight, been a pro for four years; just last month, at the World Poker Open, he finished second in the $1,000 no-limit event.

Now me. On their live Internet broadcast, Glazer and Phil Hellmuth, the 1989 champion, are calling me the "family man's family man," mainly because of my brag book and frequent calls home. Thompson says I'm playing in my first poker tournament and that most of my no-limit strategy comes from T.J.'s book. Down I sit. T.J. needs no introduction but gets a rather lengthy one anyway, followed by a standing ovation. This is his fourth final-table appearance at the Big One; he's won four other WSOP titles, fifty-one major championships altogether. At sixty, he's the sixth-leading money winner in series history, but by placing first or second today, he'd move past Johnny Chan into first. Abinsay, a fifty-two-year-old Filipino now living in Stockton, California, has already placed second in the $2,000 limit hold'em event, so he's hot. Kaufman, fifty-four, is a rabbi as well as a professor of languages (Hebrew, Aramaic, and other Semitic languages) at Hebrew Union College in Cincinnati, sufficiently high-powered as a scholar to be a consultant on the Dead Sea Scrolls. After playing big tournaments since 1997, he made the final table at Tunica. He's also a bit of a noodge.

I may have the second most chips, but we're all basically tied for second behind Ferguson. And with a stack less than half the size of mine, T.J. is at least twice as dangerous. He sits bolt upright and smokes, his gray Binion's polo shirt tucked into beltless beige slacks. I let him know one more time how terrific his book is, but he doesn't want to hear about it. He seems to think it's some kind of gamesmanship, and maybe he's right. Yet it's obvious to him and everyone else who the novice is here, the book-learned tournament virgin. No question, these five other guys see my $554,000 as the most plunderable stack.

The blinds are still $15,000 and $30,000, with $3,000 antes, and will be for the next eighty-one minutes. T.J. can't wait long to make a move, but it's Hasan who puts in the first raise, to $70,000. I'm tempted to call with 2♦2♥ but come to my senses — duh! — in time to pass. When T.J. and Roman pass, too, it looks like Hasan may have executed the last day's first steal. But then here comes Professor Kaufman blasting over the top of him in a language we all understand: twenty pink. Once Jesus folds, Hasan has the day's first gulp-worthy decision. After gazing at Kaufman for maybe ten seconds, he lays down his hand with a sigh.

Hand 2: from the button, Roman makes it $100,000 to go, a likely positional raise. Chris says, politely but firmly, "All-in." Roman calls, pushing his entire half-million, then turns over A♣Q♣. Chris shows 8♦8♥. I want to observe Roman's face, but T.J. is blocking him out as Thompson narrates the 7♥2♦7♣ flop, followed by a jack and a trey. Roman stands up from the table to abundant applause. His ouster has just guaranteed me fifth-place money, though it's the last thing I care about now. What I want is to cast Jesus and the rest of these money-changers from the temple and rake in the *serious* shekels. What I don't want is to glance at a monitor and be forced to wonder who's the little homunculus hunched in the seat next to T.J. — this as, on Hand 4, T.J. is moving all-in. No one calls him, certainly not the homunculus with his measly J♦5♣. T.J. shows us A♠10♠. And now, on Hand 5, here comes Hasan moving in. I can't call with 7♠6♥, and neither can anyone else. Am I playing too passively? I've already bled away 10 percent of my stack while the others are letting it rip.

On my next hand Chris raises $50,000, Hasan folds, and with 8♣6♣ so do I; so do T.J. and Roman and Steve. We've thus let Chris extend his lead by $63,000. His chips are arranged in two massive triangles, one on top of the other: ten pink twenty-chip columns in a 1–2–3–4 configuration, topped by six of less regular color scheme arranged 1–2–3. Very scary.

My next few hands are unplayable, but on Hand 9 I find A♣Q♣. Hasan, in the small blind, has raised it all-in once again. Suited A-Q is a better hand to raise than to call with, but still. Five-handed, it can fairly be called, pace Brunson, a monster. Granted that Roman's A♣Q♠ just got him beheaded, but my read of Hasan is that he's caught up in a spasm of all-in steal-raises. In the end I am happy to call him. Pushing my seven stacks forward, I believe that this puts me all-in. Hasan shows A♥4♥. I was right. When I flip up my A♣Q♣, everyone sees why I'm thrilled. What a call!

But now comes the flop of Hasan's and my life: 9♠6♠K♠. So far, so fantastic. Dead to the three remaining fours, Hasan groans, shakes his head. The other forty-two cards in the deck give me a $900,000 pot and a real shot at taking down Chris. The crowd's yelling hundreds of things, but all I can hear is the Habib Society pleading for fours. "Ha-san Ha-beeeeeeeb!" someone croons. They outnumber my own fans, such as they are, plus they have a specific card to pray for, but I've come to understand that I'm gonna win not just this hand but the tournament. One and a half million dollars. The heavyweight championship of poker. My faith is confirmed when fourth street arrives as the sacred, the numinous, the preternaturally chic five o'diamonds. *Close* to a four, I gloat to myself, but no sucking-out-on-me cigar. Hasan has stood up, getting ready to shake hands. My heart pounds spasmodically, but I'm still feeling thoroughly confident. So that when the fifth street card — *what?* — is — *what!* — 4♥, I "reel," according to Glazer's column that night, "in stunned silence," even though a chorus of f-words and blasphemies and fours is howling like a squadron of Pakistani banshees on tilt through my skull. Glazer will also write that "Jim hadn't suffered too many indignities at the hands of fate in the last couple of days. Most of his leading hands had held up. But now, at the worst possible moment, he'd taken a punishing blow." Punished and reeling, then, away from the table, I have to be told by Hasan that I had him covered. "You'rrre still in therrre, buddy. I'm sorrrry. Keep playing. I'm sorrrry. . . ." Although it feels like I died, I have life, if only $105,000 worth. Hasan and I are still clasping hands, shaking our heads in amazement. We realize that this is what happens in poker sometimes, that it could have just as — *more* — easily gone the other way, the towers of pink and orange chips being raked a foot to the left instead of a foot to the right.

A round or so later I find A♠2♠. I have barely enough chips for the blinds, so I probably won't see another ace, let alone a big pair. I move in. Kaufman — who else? — not only calls but moves in himself, trying to knock me out on the cheap while making sure it stays heads-up between us. Once Chris and Hasan muck their hands, Kaufman turns over ... A♦Q♠. It's perfect. That I'm now in the same spot Hasan was just in somehow inspires an ever more bottomless gloom. Yeah, sure, when Dante was spiraling down into the frozen bowels of Hell he may have also been ascending, without realizing it, toward Paradise, but here in Las Vegas, another frigid desert peopled by faithless demons, three-outers don't spike twice in a row. Forget about the long odds against it — I *know* it's not going to happen. And indeed the nine-six-king flop gives me neither a straight draw nor a flush draw, let alone a sweet deuce. In the end, with an ace on the turn, a ten on the river, it's not even close. I am out.

Now that the Satanic Prince of Noodges has forked me down into the pitch, there's applause. Many zooms. Many clicks. I shake Kaufman's hand, then Hasan's, then T.J.'s. "You played well," T.J. says. And that's something. And now here is Jesus coming around for a hug. "You played great!" he says, bonily squeezing me. Walking away from the table, however, it dawns on me how alive I felt while playing four days in the Big One, and now I feel dead. I mean *dead*. As Thompson and Glazer and Hellmuth and all the other commentators are making clear to the assembled and far-flung poker universe, I've won $247,760 by finishing fifth out of 512. What it feels like is fifth out of six.

Up on the podium, Becky Behnen shakes my hand, pets my arm. "You were wonderful, Jim. And last night! Congratulations!" Shaking my hand in his turn, her son Benny snaps me back to reality. "That four was brutal, man. *Brutal.* You were playing so awesome last night!" Yeah, last night. . . . Tom Elias ushers me a few steps to the left, where the payout booth stands. From his unbashful spiel, I gather that "big winners" have to tip the dealers "between 2 and 8 percent." I have to decide that right now? "We have to take care of our people, Jim. So, I mean, yeah, you do." I decide to tip $7,800, 3.3 percent of my profit and vastly more money than

I'd ever played poker for, or made in one week doing anything. After thanking me, Tom details a Horseshoe security guard to escort me downstairs to the cage. Passing a monitor, I see that Hasan has just been bounced, and I desperately want to keep playing! But I know it's all over when the technician starts removing the sound pack. "If you'd just undo your belt . . ."

At the cashier downstairs, I play hurry up and wait with bucket-toting slot players, then start signing form after form. I slide the tax forms, the tip receipt, and a trayful of five-thousand-dollar brown chips into my lockbox, keeping one of them back to rub against the coins in my pocket.

By the time I get back upstairs, it's down to T.J. and Chris. T.J. has one and a half million, and Chris has about four. It's hard to get close to the action because of all the film and press people. Then I see what the commotion's about: a phalanx of Horseshoe security has just delivered the traditional cardboard box to the table. Benny's pulling out wads of cash and handing them to his mother, who stacks them at T.J.'s end of the baize. Each wad she takes from her son consists of five hundred Ben Franklins subdivided by five yellow and white paper bands marked "$10,000," these in turn held together with rubber bands doubled near the ends of the bills. When Becky has finished there are thirty such five-inch-thick wads stacked in a ramshackle cube three wads high, five across. She lays the gold championship bracelet across the second gray tier, facing T.J., and T.J. can't help staring back. It's the thing he wants most in the world.

I finally find Hasan and ask him what happened. "I had king-queen," he purrs wistfully, shrugging. "Chris had ace-king." Enough said. As we edge two steps closer, Chris makes it $175,000 to go from the button. T.J. calls. When the flop comes K♦K♣6♥, T.J. checks. (In heads-up action, the player on the button bets first before the flop, second on subsequent rounds.) After thinking for over a minute, Chris bets $200,000. When T.J. says, "Call," there is eight hundred grand in the pot. Fourth street arrives a red trey. Check, check. Street five: J♦. No straight draw, no flush draw, but do either of them have a king? T.J. at least represents having one by betting $600,000. Chris takes a while to decide, then calls and turns over a jack and a six, only to watch T.J. turn over K♥10♥. His check on the turn, letting Chris catch his jack for "free," earned him an extra six large and put himself into the lead, with 2.6 million to Chris's 2.5.

"Only in no-limit," says Andy.

A couple hands later, Chris raises $175,000, prompting T.J. to come over the top for another half-million. Chris shows how frightened he is by responding, "All-in." Without a blip of reluctance, T.J. calls. Whoever takes this pot wins the championship.

At Thompson's official request, they show us and the cameras their hole cards: A♥7♥ for T.J., A♠2♠ for Chris. An uproar, then relative silence. From six feet away in his booth, I hear the Discovery director whisper, "Camera 2, give me Jesus." Because Jesus is dead to a deuce or a flurry of spades and we all want to see his reaction. From my vantage point he looks nervous, unhappy, and pale. The flop comes 3♠10♠Q♥. Although still a 3–2 underdog, Chris's four-flush gives him nine extra outs to go with the two other deuces. Both guys have proven they have solid brass balls, but right now all four must feel clammy. When the turn comes K♥, T.J. picks up his own flush draw. But when 10♦ shows up on fifth street, yielding ten-ten-ace-queen-king for another chopped pot, the vibe suggests that maybe they'll play on *forever.* Chris looks tapped out. How many deaths and resurrections can the Son of Man suffer per hour? Even the Texas centurion pretends to wipe sweat from his brow.

The next two small pots go to T.J. when Chris is unable to call even modest $100,000 raises, but on the following hand Chris wins $400,000 with a raise on the turn. The hand after that brings no preflop raises, and when the flop comes K♥3♥8♣, Chris checks again. T.J. bets a mere hundred grand, Chris calls, and we all sense a trap being set. The question is, who's trapping whom? Because when 7♠ hits on the turn, this time it's Chris betting a puny $150,000 and T.J. who's warily calling. Four of clubs on the river, and both of them check. While they stare at each other, Chris flashes what must be a king. T.J. mucks. They've been at it now for four and a half hours — a long time with this much at stake and dozens of lenses and mikes jabbing into your poker space.

Ten minutes later, on Hand 93, T.J. raises to $175,000. When Chris reraises six hundred thou, T.J. moves in like a shot. The pulse in his cheek makes me think that he feels like he's finally got Chris where he wants him. Certainly, if Chris manages to call him, this will be it — unless we get another chopped pot. Chris scratches his beard, shakes his head, exhales. Two minutes pass. I can't speak for T.J., but no one else seems to begrudge all the time he is taking. "Call him, Jesus!" shouts a rowdy fan twenty rows back. T.J.'s eyes narrow as he drags on his umpteenth Salem. He puts his left fist to his mouth, clears his throat. Won't anyone give him a lozenge?

"T.J. likes his hand," Andy whispers to me, "and I think Chris has ace-nine." I remember the matching A-9's Chris and I turned out to be holding last night, how the untranquil mood had been scalpeled by laughter. I watch now as Chris takes off his hat, then his sunglasses — *whoa* — in an instant defanging his aura. The thinning hair above his temples accentuated by the length of the strands, brown eyes a tad bloodshot and sunken, he also looks much more like Jesus.

He calls. As the low-dB buzz from the previous five or six minutes rises to a crescendo, he turns over A♠9♣. T.J. immediately shows him A♦ and . . . Q♣. The crowd gasps and whistles.

"Pretty astonishing call," I tell Andy.

"Chris's?"

"No, yours."

He nods modestly, as though he hasn't been making reads like this the whole tournament, then elbows my arm. "Ace-queen look familiar?"

"Oh, boy . . ."

The flop — 4♥2♥K♣ — keeps T.J. in the lead. When K♥ falls on the turn, Andy groans, "Not again!" Because now any deuce, four, king, or ace will give us another chopped pot. Exuberant Ferguson boosters entreat the poker deities for a nine. Cloutier fans are more numerous, but it isn't clear what they should beg for. Hollering "Let's go, T.J.!" is pretty much all they can do.

Jesus leaps from his seat with his fists in the air and T.J. thrusts his big paw across the table before I see the last card. What else could it be but ". . . a nine!" Bob Thompson ejaculates. No one, especially Bob, seems able to believe it. Chris reaches across the table and clasps T.J.'s hand. "You outplayed me," he says. T.J. shakes his head, disagreeing. That he just got harpooned through the ventricles doesn't register on his vast, craggy features. He's smiling!

Cathy Burns and the Fergusons are all over Chris now. Hugs, kisses, pogo hops, shimmying. Chris still makes his way around the table to where T.J. is standing with his wife, Joy, inside a crush of reporters. While Chris is almost as tall, when the two men embrace their difference in mass is straight out of vaudeville: the burly tight end hugs the sinewy swing dancer, steel-wool ringlets meshing with yard-long chestnut locks. "Are we still friends?" Chris asks.

"Of course. Don't feel bad. You played great." But once they let go of each other, T.J. asks, "You didn't think it would be that tough to beat me, did you?"

"Yes, I did."

I congratulate Chris, then try to tell T.J. how brilliantly he played. "There's a lotta luck in poker," he rumbles, "and if you're gonna play this game you better get used to that."

Needing oxygen and sunlight, I go for a walk down on Fremont, then head south along First Street. Strip joints and flophouses, pawnshops and T-shirt emporia, a few dozen down-market tourists. In Las Vegas, fifth street is Las Vegas Boulevard South, which also is known as the Strip. Family Vegas. We are far, far away from that world. Already the scorching southwest wind has driven some grit through my lips and made my pale forehead feel crisp. I think of my children, my wife. By this time tomorrow, I'll see them.

At the far eastern tip of the Pacific time zone, Las Vegas sunsets come early. Even at five-thirty or so on a May afternoon, even through polarized lenses, there are horizontal shafts making you squint and ricocheting dazzlements that make you shade your eyes, and then there are glares that make you *duck*. And then there are thermal traps where it must reach 130 degrees. And when these are interrupted by gelid blasts from gaping casino doorways, it's a little like wandering along the perimeter of the eighth and ninth circles of Hell — all of this, mind you, while heading a block north toward Paradise.

But the thing is, I maybe could've won the damn thing.

Ranking of Poker Hands

Straight Flush: five consecutive cards of the same suit, such as 8♥9♥10♥J♥Q♥. The highest possible hand is an ace-high straight flush, called a *royal flush*.

Four of a Kind: four cards of the same rank, such as 10♣10♦ 10♠10♥.

Full House: three cards of one rank and two of another, such as three fives and two queens.

Flush: five cards of the same suit, such as 2♦5♦7♦J♦A♦.

Straight: five consecutive cards of mixed suits, such as 5♣6♦7♠ 8♥9♠. (In a straight, an ace can be used as either a high or a low card.)

Three of a Kind: three cards of the same rank, such as 6♦6♣6♥.

Two Pairs: two cards of the same rank and two other cards of another rank, such as Q♦Q♣ and 9♦9♥.

Pair: two cards of the same rank, such as 4♦4♣.

Glossary of Poker Terms

all-in: having all one's chips in the pot

belly draw: a straight that lacks an inside card

Big Slick: ace-king

boss trips: the highest possible three of a kind

button: disc that rotates clockwise around the table to indicate which player is the last to bet

crying call: a call with a hand you think has a small chance of winning

flop: the first three exposed community cards, dealt simultaneously

freeroll: to compete with other people's money

johnnies: jacks

kicker: a side card accompanying a higher card or cards

muck: to discard or fold

rainbow: a flop of three different suits

semi-bluff: to bet with a hand you don't think is the best hand but which has a reasonable chance of improving to the best hand

slow-play: to check or call an opponent's bet with a big hand in order to win more money in later betting rounds

smooth call: a call when a raise is expected

steal: a bet big enough to cause your opponents to fold, especially when your own hand is weak

suck out: to make a lucky draw on fifth street, especially with a hand you should have folded earlier

wheel: a five-high straight, such as A-1-3-4-5.

WILLIAM NACK

Bang for the Bucs

FROM SPORTS ILLUSTRATED

*The perfect ending for a World Series — if you're one
of us less than enamored of the Yankees — B.C.*

Sport as much as steel has cast the image of Pittsburgh to the world.
Pittsburghers have used sport to tell a story about who they are both to
themselves and to others. It's about tough, hard-working, gritty people
who struggle and win and lose and win. The 1960 World Series was
that story.

— *Robert Ruck, lecturer in sports and urban history, University of Pittsburgh*

TOWARD THE END of that autumn afternoon at old Forbes Field,
near the close of a record-breaking World Series that had already
emerged as the weirdest, wildest, most improbable ever played,
Pittsburgh Pirates second baseman William Stanley Mazeroski, the
twenty-four-year-old son of an Ohio coal miner, sensed that he had
been through all this before, felt he'd already lived and seen it.
Sensed it as he stepped off the field and inhaled the moment's bitter, ascending air of gloom. *How did this happen?* he thought. *How is
it they always come back?*

It was 3:30 P.M. on Thursday, October 13, 1960, forty years ago
last week, and the last half of the ninth inning of the Series' seventh game was beginning. The Pirates and the New York Yankees
were locked in a 9–9 tie. Less than thirty minutes earlier Pittsburgh
had scored five runs in the eighth inning, coming from three runs
down to take a 9–7 lead. All the Bucs had needed to win it all, to ex-
orcise those roistering ghosts from the '27 World Series — when
Ruth and Gehrig, Lazzeri and Combs had swept them in their
last go at a world championship — was one more peaceful inning,
three more painless outs. But, as Mazeroski knew, these were the

3M Yankees of Mickey Mantle, Roger Maris, and Moose Skowron, the Yankees who had won eight pennants and six of ten World Series in the 1950s, who had won their last fifteen regular-season games while running their home run total for the year to an American League record 193, three more than their old mark, set in '56. New York had won its three Series games against the Pirates by the scores of 16–3, 10–0, and 12–0, setting a passel of club and individual World Series hitting records. Sure enough, in the ninth, just as Mazeroski had feared, the deathless Yankees had struck again.

After Mantle singled in a run, driving second baseman Bobby Richardson home as he raised his batting average in this Series to .400, he kept New York alive by pulling off the strangest act of baserunning in the Series. With one out and Mantle on first, and third baseman Gil McDougald representing the tying run on third, Yankees leftfielder Yogi Berra pulled a hard, one-hop smash down the line that Pittsburgh first baseman Rocky Nelson snatched deftly. After stepping on the bag to get Berra at first, Nelson moved toward second base to throw out Mantle. But Mantle, instead of racing for second, dove back toward first and crawled like a lizard to the bag, slipping under the surprised first baseman's reach as McDougald scored.

Many saw what Mantle did as dumb. All he had to do, to ensure that McDougald would score and tie the game, was dash for second and force a rundown. Had Nelson tagged out Mantle, the Pirates would have been world champions. So why did Mantle scramble back to first? Nelson says Mantle later told him that he thought Nelson had caught Berra's drive on the fly and that, since he had not tagged up, the only way to save himself and McDougald was to scramble safely back to first.

In any event, after Skowron, the Yankees first baseman, hit a grounder that forced Mantle at second to end the top half of the ninth, the game was tied 9–9. The Yankees had new life. Recalls Richardson, "We thought, *Boy, we got 'em now!*"

Stunned by the turn of events, Mazeroski went down the stairs into the Pittsburgh dugout, sat on the bench, and stared vacantly across the ancient playing field — toward the vines that climbed the outfield fence, past the silent thousands shifting uneasily in their seats, beyond all those damned Yankees grinning as they took the field and waited for pitcher Ralph Terry to finish warming up.

Mazeroski lapsed into a kind of trance, as though peering into his backwoods past, into the days when he was growing up in a little wooden house with no electricity or running water, on a glade known as Skunk Hollow, on the banks of the Ohio River near Rush Run. The sun lit his days, kerosene his nights, and on many summer afternoons he listened to his battery-operated radio tell stories of the distant suffering of his beloved Cleveland Indians. In the dugout, Mazeroski remembers, "all I could think of was how the Yankees used to beat up on Cleveland for years and years, and how the Yankees would come back and how, just now, they'd come back on us with all that hitting. I felt so bad; we all did. I was staring out of the dugout and thinking about this when. . . ."

"Maz, you're up!" he heard a voice call out from down the pine.

So absorbed had he been in memory, Mazeroski hadn't realized he was leading off. He rose from the bench, picked up his helmet and bat, and walked to the batter's box. For weeks preceding the Series, Yankees scouts had tracked the Pirates from city to city, and their report on Pittsburgh had been unambiguous: "They're high fastball hitters. Give them low, breaking stuff all the time."

So Mazeroski, who'd been seeing a steady diet of curves, was expecting another. He was a notoriously dangerous clutch hitter, and all he could think of, as he stood facing Terry, was getting on base, giving the Pirates a chance to end the game before New York had another go in the tenth. He thought, *Just hit the ball someplace. Get on base. Hit the ball hard. Line drive! Line drive!* When Terry fired a fastball high and inside, a surprised Mazeroski took it for a ball, and Yankees catcher Johnny Blanchard stepped forward and hollered to Terry, "Get it down! Get it down! This guy's a high fastball hitter."

Terry peered in at Blanchard. It was 3:36 P.M. Terry wound up and fired his second pitch. It was lower than the first but still up in the zone and looking as fat as a melon to Mazeroski as it whistled toward the plate — a high hummer just where he wanted it. He swung and struck the ball flush, sending it in a rising white arc to left centerfield. Mazeroski was racing toward first base when he saw what everyone else saw, what Pirates Bill Virdon and Bob Skinner saw from the first base dugout, what Skowron saw from first and Richardson from second, what all those millions saw who were watching from the stands and on national TV: Berra, the unmistakable squat figure in left, crabbing back to the 406-foot mark, to the warning track, his back turned to the infield diamond as he faced the wall and looked up, his rounded figure looking like the eight ball he was now behind. "Soon as you saw Yogi's back, his number 8, you knew dang well that ball had a chance," says former Pittsburgh pitcher Vern Law, who won two games in the Series. "A dream come true!"

"I didn't think the ball was going out," Berra recalls. "A lot of people thought I turned around to see how far it would go. I thought it was going to hit the wall. I turned around because I was going to play the carom."

The bespectacled Virdon, along with Skinner and every other Pirate, leaped off the bench the instant Mazeroski swung. "We knew he hit it good," recalls Virdon, "but we didn't know if it was going out. We all looked at leftfield, and we saw that Yogi was not going to catch it, so we started rooting for it to go."

Maz had no idea what he'd wrought. All he knew was that he had hit a fastball solidly and that it had whizzed over short and was climbing for the fence. He felt a rush as he sprinted around first, hoping to stretch the hit into a triple. "I knew Yogi wasn't going to catch it," says Mazeroski. "When he turned, I knew it was over his head, and I thought maybe it was going to be off the wall. I'd hit it hard, but it was 406 feet out there, and the wall was twelve feet high. I was thinking, *If Yogi misplays it coming off the wall, then I could be on third base with no one out, and I can score a hundred ways from third base, and we win!* Then I round first and I hear the fans going crazy."

Helpless, Berra watched the ball sail over his head and clear the wall. "It grazed the vines as it went over the fence," he says.

Galloping toward second base, Mazeroski glanced over short and saw the leftfield umpire, Stan Landes, make the call: "He was holding up his hand and giving it this little circle thing, and I knew it had gone out. From the time I hit second base, I don't think I touched the ground the rest of the way home."

He pulled the helmet off his head, held it high, and screamed to himself, *We beat the Yankees! We beat the Yankees! We beat the Yankees!* Fans raced onto the field and pounded his back as he turned on third and headed for the plate. Pandemonium shook the rust and coal dust from the girders of the fifty-one-year-old ballpark. A man later dug up home plate with a shovel as policemen watched. Mantle sat by his locker and wept. Blanchard sobbed into his hands. A red-eyed Skowron, who had tied a World Series record with twelve hits, joined them in wordless mourning.

All over Pittsburgh, for the next twelve hours, reigned a state of merriment unprecedented in the city's 202-year history. Confetti rained on the just and the unjust alike. Office workers emptied whole file cabinets into the streets, covering the trolley tracks with so much paper that the trolleys stalled. It was bigger than V-E Day, bigger even than V-J Day. So many thousands of revelers descended on the town from outlying cities, from places like Youngstown, Ohio, and Erie, Pennsylvania, that the cops closed off the bridges and tunnels leading into the city. Unable to get home, many commuters slept in hotel lobbies. By midnight, all the downtown bars had run out of glasses — two-fisted drinkers were wandering the streets with them — and to buy a drink you had to bring your own tumbler. Except for the Pittsburgh Crawfords and the Homestead Grays, both of the old Negro leagues, the city had not had a championship team since 1925, when the Pirates beat Walter Johnson and the Washington Senators 9–7 in the seventh game of the World Series. The Steelers, as beloved as they were, had had an undetectable pulse for decades, and the familiar greeting of long-suffering Steelers fans was SOS, for Same Old Steelers.

"It had been a long time," says Robert Ruck, the Pitt historian. "There were two generations in Pittsburgh who had known nothing but defeat."

Never had there been a World Series like this one, and no sooner had the last stragglers left town than press-box wags were calling it the Weird Series. Frederick G. Lieb, the estimable baseball writer for *The Sporting News*, who had seen all but three of the previous fifty-one world championships, said this one was the "wackiest ever." For fifty years, since the 1910 World Series, when a young team of Philadelphia Athletics teed off on a cork-centered baseball, beating the Chicago Cubs in five games, their team batting average of .316 had survived as the highest in Series history — higher than that of any of those vaunted Yankees clubs that followed. Then came 1960. New York, hitting a phenomenal .338, eclipsed the record by twenty-two percentage points and outhit Pittsburgh by eighty-two points.

And lost. The Yankees had thirty-one more hits than the Pirates (ninety-one to sixty), outscored them by more than two to one (fifty-five runs to twenty-seven), had six more home runs (ten to four), twenty-eight more runs batted in (fifty-four to twenty-six), and the three liveliest bats in the Series: Mantle's, Richardson's, and Skowron's.

Richardson, a singles-hitting schnauzer at 5'9", had hit only one home run all season, on April 30, so no one was more surprised than he when, in Game 3 of the Series, he punched a grand slam over the Yankee Stadium fence in left — for four of his six RBIs that day, a single-game Series record. That was far more than pitcher Whitey Ford needed, and he went on to win the game 10–0. By the end of Game 6, in which Richardson had two triples, he had knocked in twelve runs, a World Series record that still stands. Lieb crunched the numbers and quietly asked, "Who ever would have fancied, even in his wildest dream, that a club launching such an offensive could lose a Series?"

As if credulity had not been strained enough, the whole unlikely megillah came to the most dramatic finish possible — no other Series in the Classic's ninety-seven-year history has ended with a homer in the last inning of the seventh game — and only after the lead had changed hands twice. No matter what the Yankees did, no matter how hard and how far they hit the ball, the Pirates were ultimately favored by the baseball gods to prevail. Tilting at windmills had become as much a part of Pittsburgh's drill as shagging flies and watching Ralph Kiner hit boomers in BP, but at the start of the '60 season, after a disappointing fourth-place finish the year before, no one except family and friends had expected the Bucs to be in the chase for the pennant, much less the world title.

Only eight years earlier, in 1952, the Pirates had finished last in the league, with a record of 42–112, and had been proclaimed to be among the worst teams in baseball history. They also came in last in the next three years under general manager Branch Rickey, but by the time the Mahatma was fired in the fall of '55 — the franchise had been hemorrhaging financially for years — he had assembled the core of the '60 team, including pitchers Law, Bob Friend, and Elroy Face; shortstop Dick Groat, an All-America basketball player whom Rickey had signed out of Duke in '52; Mazeroski; and rightfielder Roberto Clemente.

Rickey left his fingerprints all over the franchise. In early '54, at a pre-spring-training camp for young players, Mazeroski was one of seven shortstops doing fielding drills when he took a turn at second base to pivot on the double play. Rickey saw that Mazeroski was a natural second baseman, quick and agile, who could throw without cocking his arm, and told the coaches, "Don't move him. He stays at second."

It was the sea-change moment of Mazeroski's life. He taught himself how to turn the double play, how to catch the ball and release it so quickly that it seemed to enter one end of a bent stovepipe and exit the other. He taught himself not to catch the ball in the pit of his glove and then dig it out to throw — that took too much time — but rather to deflect the ball off the heel of the glove into his throwing hand and, in the same motion, toss it to first.

That spring of '54 was propitious for the Pirates. Rickey told Face that he would need more than a fastball and a curve to stick in the big leagues, even with the last-place Bucs. "You don't have a changeup, and you need an off-speed pitch," Rickey said. At the Pirates' camp in Fort Pierce, Florida, former Yankees reliever Joe Page was trying to come back, and Face saw him throw his storied forkball, for which he fit the ball deep between the first two fingers of his throwing hand and fired with the same speed and motion he used on his other pitches. Today that pitch is known as the split-finger fastball. Thrown well, it looks like a fastball but, at the plate, falls off the world. Rickey's decision to ship Face to Double A New Orleans for a year to work on the off-speed pitch was the turning point in Face's career.

But nothing Rickey ever did for the Pirates quite matched the way they picked the Brooklyn Dodgers' pocket. Rickey, a former Dodgers general manager, knew that Brooklyn was hiding a gifted Puerto Rican outfielder on its Montreal farm team. So he drafted Clemente for Pittsburgh. Clemente was a rookie in 1955 and five years later a .314-hitting All-Star with a Springfield rifle for an arm and racehorse speed.

Those were the players Joe Brown inherited when he took over as Pittsburgh GM in '55. By the 1960 season he had subtracted one catcher and added three more, including lefthanded-hitting Smoky Burgess and righty Hal Smith; acquired a fiery third baseman, Don Hoak; and added the wiry, chain-smoking spot starter Harvey Haddix, a lefty nicknamed the Kitten because as a rookie with the St. Louis Cardinals in '52 he had studied at the paw of aging lefty Harry (the Cat) Brecheen. Brown, who would win two championships in Pittsburgh, in '60 and '71, traded with St. Louis for the sweet-fielding outfielder Virdon in '56, the year after Virdon had been voted National League Rookie of the Year. Brown also added utility outfielder Gino Cimoli — a cheerful butt-slapper in the clubhouse — and dug around the minor leagues in search of missing links.

Because of his zeal, Brown took some ribbing from his colleagues. Before the 1958 draft he asked one of his scouts to name the best lefthanded hitter available. "Rocky Nelson," said the scout, referring to a first baseman with Triple A Toronto, but he warned that Nelson had been up and down and never stuck in the majors. At the draft Brown was sitting in front of his longtime friend Chub Feeney, GM of the San Francisco Giants, and when it was Pittsburgh's turn to pick, Brown said, "The Pirates draft Rocky Nelson from Toronto."

The Adventures of Ozzie and Harriet, the TV show starring the Nelsons and their sons, David and Ricky, was all the buzz in those days, and in a loud voice — to much alpha-male laughter — Feeney intoned, "Don't you mean *Ricky* Nelson?" Brown tells that story in a flat, humorless voice, as though the remark still bites him. "A lot of people thought Rocky was a joke, but he was not," says Brown. "He served us admirably." Indeed, in the most crucial game of 1960, Brown was the man still laughing.

No one knows why such things occur, whether it's the alignment of the planets or the karma of the clubhouse, but every now and then a team begins to play as though it has been touched by magic. Unexpectedly, the 1960 Pirates started to win, and before long they believed they would win every time they played. The city folk started believing the same thing, and they came to games flashing their BEAT 'EM, BUCS signs. All the while the team's tobacco-chawing manager, beagle-faced Danny Murtaugh, thought the world was his spittoon, and he sat there spitting on everybody's shoes. "I started chewin' so I could spit back on his," says Mazeroski.

Before you could say Pie Traynor, the Pirates had won ninety-five games and the pennant, losing only fifty-nine. Groat hit .325 to win the National League batting title. Nelson hit .300 in two hundred at bats. Law won twenty games, and Friend eighteen, while Face forkballed his way to twenty-four saves. Mazeroski led major-league second basemen in putouts (413), assists (449), double plays (127), and fielding average (.989).

By that year, his fourth full season in the major leagues, Mazeroski had asserted himself as the finest second baseman in the game, a nonpareil turner of the double play and a student of the position who had brought his own aesthetic to playing defense. "Nobody ever played second base like he did," says Virdon, "and I've been in it for fifty years. One thing I know for sure: Many second basemen could make the double play if they got good throws. Maz did not have to have a good throw to complete the DP. He worked on it constantly, every day."

Groat would play seven years at short with Maz at second base, and together they would turn hundreds of double plays. Groat came to view his teammate as an artist. "Mazeroski's release on the double play was phenomenal," he says. "Bill *made* himself a great defensive second baseman. And let me tell you something: You and me, we couldn't catch a ball with the glove he used, it was so small. But he had the most marvelous hands in the world."

In fact, says Brown, Mazeroski's hands were so fluid and smooth that no one talked much about his quick, nimble feet, perhaps the most important element of his genius as a fielder. "Danny Murtaugh always said that no one mentioned what great feet Mazeroski had," recalls Brown. "He had that blocky build, but he was so graceful. He made everything he did look easy. So quick with his feet, his body was always standing and facing the right place to make the catch and the throw. Guys would slide into him, into those powerful legs, and they'd just stop and drip off him."

Talented as they were, however, the Pirates would be hard-pressed to beat the Yankees, and they nearly squandered what chances they had in the World Series on September 25, the day they clinched the pennant despite losing to the Braves in Milwaukee. On the Pittsburgh team bus a rowdy gang of players, tearing off one another's shirts, grabbed Law — a nondrinking deacon in the Mormon church — and wrestled him down. At the bottom of the pile, someone grabbed and twisted Law's right foot, trying to pull off his shoe, and sprained it. That was the pitcher's push-off foot, the one that helped generate his power, but he insisted on playing through the Series.

The bookmakers made the Pirates underdogs against New York, but these Yanks were not Ruppert's Rifles, the Ruth-led team of the '20s, nor the Bombers of Gehrig and DiMaggio and King Kong Keller in the late '30s and '40s, nor even the Yankees of the '50s, with Hank Bauer and the young Berra and Mantle and all that pitching. In a paragraph almost eerie in its foresight, *New York Herald-Tribune* columnist Red Smith wrote before the first game of the '60 Series, "Chances are the importance of the manager's role is exaggerated oftener than it is underestimated, but in a series of seven games or fewer it can be the deciding factor. There may not be time to repair the damage caused by a single error in judgment."

Casey Stengel's first error was surely his worst. He picked Art Ditmar (15–9), who had no decisions in World Series play, to start the first game over the vastly more seasoned Ford (12–9), the Chairman of the Board, who had a Series record of 5–4 and was the ace of the Yankees' staff. "Ford was our big pitcher," says Richardson, "and in any big game he would be the one to start. Stengel said that Forbes Field was a small park and Ditmar throws a sinker, and he was saving Whitey for New York — double-talk like that. Stengel was always playing hunches, but that didn't make any sense. I remember Mantle saying, 'How can you not start your best pitcher?' It was a topic among the players."

It was an even bigger topic when Ditmar was lifted in the first after facing only five batters, getting one out and giving up three runs. Pittsburgh went on to win 6–4, with Law getting the victory and Face the save. Mazeroski's Game 7 home run would be so stunning that it would relegate his other decisive swing of the Series to the precincts of half-forgotten trivia: In the fourth inning of Game 1, with one out, Hoak on first and the Pirates leading 3–2, Maz crushed an 0–2 fastball from Jim Coates that flew over the scoreboard in dead left and gave Pittsburgh a 5–2 lead. "I was on cloud nine," Mazeroski says. "A home run in the World Series! I thought it was the greatest thing that had ever happened to me. It relaxed me for the rest of the Series."

New York won the second game 16–3, and all the Pirates could talk about was Mantle's second homer of the day. Struck from the right side of the plate, it was a 450-foot blast that sailed over the iron gate in right centerfield and was still carrying as it left the park. Groat was whirlpooling an injured wrist at the end of the game when Virdon dashed into the clubhouse and blurted to him, "Roomie, you missed the granddaddy of them all! I never in my life saw a ball hit as hard as Mantle just hit it. So help me, it went over the iron gate, and it was still going straight!"

Those first two games set the tempo for the next four. The Yankees won in blowouts, the Pirates in tight games. In Game 3 in New York, Ford pitched a nearly spotless 10–0 shutout, deepening suspicions that Stengel had blundered in Game 1, but Law came back and won Game 4 for the Pirates 3–2, with Face again getting the save. The Series was even, 2–2. Matters only got worse for Stengel. He went with Ditmar over Bill Stafford in Game 5 and came under even greater fire when Ditmar gave up three runs and was chased in the second inning. Stafford pitched five scoreless innings as a middle reliever, but the Pirates won 5–2. Haddix got the victory, and Face threw two and two-thirds hitless innings in relief for his third save.

Face was a carpenter and lumberjack from upstate New York, and like his fellow backwoodsmen Law (an Idahoan who once worked as a deliveryman for a creamery) and Mazeroski, he was seen in blue-collar Pittsburgh as a hardscrabble working stiff. Nothing buoyed his teammates or the home crowds more than the sight of Face coming in from the bullpen, all 5'8" and 155 pounds of him. "He had that swagger," says Maz, "a little guy walking in there with that cockiness. He threw strikes and feared nobody."

All the Pirates had to do was win one more game at Forbes, and they would be world champs. The celebration would have to wait, however. Ford was back in Game 6, and he threw a seven-hit shutout, and New York won 12–0. In the New York clubhouse after that third slaughter of the Series, Berra muttered to Joe Reichler of the AP, "I dunno. This game is getting funnier and funnier. We do everything but punch 'em in the nose, and here we are all tied up. . . . How do you figure that?"

That was the question of the day. From the Pirates side, Red Smith reported, "Immediately on reaching the safety of the clubhouse, Pittsburgh's well-read leader, Danny Murtaugh, thumbed through the rule book and gleefully announced a discovery: 'The series will be decided,' he said, 'on games won, not total runs scored.'"

All of which made the prospect of the seventh game as delicious to contemplate as any in World Series history. Would the Pirates, starting Law, win another squeaker? Or would the Yankees, going with their Game 2 starter, Bullet Bob Turley, end it all with thunder?

The game went neither way. In fact, the old script was rewritten at the outset. By the end of the second inning, it was the Pittsburgh bats that had been heard. In the first, after Skinner, the leftfielder, had walked, the butt of Chub Feeney's little joke, Rocky Nelson, pulled a Turley fastball into the lower rightfield stands to put the Pirates ahead 2–0. In the second, with Hoak on third and Mazeroski on second, Virdon stroked a long single to center, scoring both runners, and the inning ended with the Bucs ahead 4–0.

Just as it looked like a rout by the wrong team, little Bobby Shantz — at 5'6", even shorter than Face — came in to start the third inning for the Yankees. Shantz could tease hitters into madness. Throwing a whole farmers' market of sinking pitches, the lefty had the Pirates hammering balls like stakes into the ground: Over the next five innings Shantz gave up just one base hit, a single to catcher Burgess that would prove to have unforeseeable consequences. Murtaugh lifted Burgess for a pinch runner, Joe Christopher, and brought Hal Smith in to catch in the eighth.

Aside from allowing Skowron's solo homer in the fifth, which made the score 4–1, Law had frozen the Yankees' bats. Unable to push off on his injured foot, he had to draw on his arm as his only source of power. "I'd more or less fall toward the plate and make up the difference with my arm," Law says. "In doing that, I learned later, I tore my rotator cuff."

Murtaugh came to the mound in the sixth, after Law had given up a single to Richardson and had walked shortstop Tony Kubek on a full count. Murtaugh was ready to bring in Face, but Law didn't want to leave the game. "Skip, I feel O.K.," he said. But Murtaugh just shook his head. Hoak came in from third as Law, his head down, stood on the mound waiting.

"Look here, Deacon," said Hoak. "You walk off this mound, you hold your head up! You've done a good job."

Face's fourth Series appearance came at the end of a season in which he had pitched in a National League–leading sixty-eight games, and he was tired and not at his sharpest. After Mantle rolled a single through the box, scoring Richardson, Berra golfed a towering shot down the foul line toward the upper deck in right field. It looked to Berra as if the ball might hook foul. As it flew past the

pole, a three-run homer, Richardson saw the stoical Berra do something he'd never seen him do. "Halfway between home and first, he
was jumping up and down," Richardson recalls. "Boy, was he happy
to hit that ball!"

The Yankees mobbed him. Now they were ahead 5–4, and they
finally had the measure of Elroy Face. When they scored twice
more off Face in the eighth, the Yankees led 7–4 and were looking
like winners yet again.

Then came the most bizarre half-inning of the Series. Cimoli led
off by clipping Shantz for a dinky single to short right. Skowron
and Cimoli had played on the same all-star team when they were
teenagers, and as Cimoli stood on first base, Skowron needled him
about the dinker: "Jeez, Gino, did you eat any breakfast today? Hit
the ball!" The next batter, Virdon, slashed a low grounder toward
the rocky Forbes infield at short. It was heading right at Kubek for
an easy double play, and Virdon shouted, "Oh, s——!" But when
the ball struck the dirt, it rose suddenly like a high-kicking tennis
serve and struck Kubek in the Adam's apple. Kubek fell backward,
holding his throat. Cimoli stopped at second, and time was called.
Stengel ran over to Kubek and tried to break up the crowd gathering around him. "Stand back!" he yelled. "Give him room. He'll be
all right."

Cimoli drifted over. "He started to choke; he was gasping for air,"
he says of Kubek.

Skowron watched the shortstop gag. "He was coughing up
blood," he says.

Richardson heard Kubek gasp, "Get me to the hospital. I can't
breathe." When Kubek was taken off the field, the crowd gave him
a standing O. It was not much consolation to the Yankees. Instead
of two outs and nobody on, the Pirates had two on and nobody out.
Then, after Groat had lined a single to left, scoring Cimoli, Stengel
made another fateful move. With no one out, men on first and second, and New York leading 7–5, the situation called for the batter,
Skinner, to bunt. But Stengel had another hunch, and though
Shantz could field anything — "Bobby was probably the greatest
fielding pitcher in the history of baseball," says Brown — the manager lifted him for Coates.

The Pirates were euphoric. "Bobby Shantz had dazzled us,"
Groat says.

Skinner's sacrifice bunt was fielded cleanly by Clete Boyer, but it

moved Virdon to third, Groat to second. After Nelson flied out to
Maris, with Virdon holding at third, Clemente came to bat with two
outs. What happened next is now a part of 1960 World Series lore.
Clemente hit a slow chopper toward first. Skowron backhanded it
and looked to throw to Coates covering first, but Coates was not
there. It is the Series moment that Richardson remembers best.
"Routine play!" he says. "Any ball to the right side of the infield, the
pitcher covers first."

The inning should have been over, the score still 7–5, Yankees.
Instead, Virdon scored from third, making it 7–6. Groat was on
third and Clemente on first as catcher Hal Smith walked to the
plate. In the stands, Virdon's wife, Shirley, was sitting next to
Smith's wife, also named Shirley, when Coates fired a fastball.
Smith swung and missed. Coates threw a second heater to the same
spot, and Smith launched it on a 420-foot flight over the leftfield
wall. All of Forbes went up in a roar. Shirley Smith threw her camera high into the air, and Shirley Virdon reached out to catch it.

Smith was rounding second before it dawned on him what he
had done. "I looked over, and people were dancing on the dugout," he recalls. "They were dancing in the stands and screaming
and hugging and jumping up and down all over the ballpark. I remember thinking, *Boy, this is something!*"

Groat and Clemente met Smith at the plate, and both yelled to
him above the din, "You won the game! You won the game!"

Pittsburgh's euphoria disappeared, of course, when New York
roared back in the ninth to tie the score. As the Pirates sat in the
dugout, waiting for Maz to hit, a saddened Smith said to Skinner,
"Bob, I guess I wasn't destined to be a hero."

Forty years have come and gone since Mazeroski hit the Home
Run, and it has remained a part of Pittsburgh's mythology, as big
and vivid now as when it happened. It left its imprint on many lives.
Stengel did not survive it as Yankees skipper. Many sportswriters
speculated during the Series that the seventy-year-old Stengel
would retire after the last game, but he wanted to stay after suffering the bitterest loss of his career. At his final press conference, five
days later, he said, "They have paid me off in full and told me my
services are not desired any longer by this club."

Ralph Houk took his place and led the Yankees to two world titles, in '61 and '62. Seeing Mazeroski years later, Houk kidded him,
"If it weren't for you, I might not have got that job."

Some of Maz's former teammates think that, in a perverse way, the Home Run has prevented him from gaining induction into the Hall of Fame. "That's all people remember about him," says Groat.

There is considerably more to remember about Mazeroski as a player. Bill James, the guru of baseball statistics, has developed a numerical system for judging fielders, and his conclusion is unequivocal: "I have no doubt that Mazeroski is the premier defensive second baseman in the history of baseball, and I would list him among the five best defensive players of all time." James puts him in the company of Ozzie Smith, Honus Wagner, and Johnny Bench. Mazeroski was a .260 lifetime hitter, but he had 2,016 hits over seventeen seasons, and no doubt he prevented more runs with his glove than most major leaguers have scored. Like many of his teammates and many fans who saw him play, Mazeroski hopes the Veterans Committee will vote him into the Hall.

Mazeroski is sitting in the living room of his house in Panama City, Florida, which he shares with his wife, Milene, whom he met through Murtaugh and married in 1958. The old second baseman spends his days fishing for striped bass and playing golf. A shy, humble man, protective of his privacy, he is not one for indulging in nostalgia.

Every year since 1985, on the anniversary of the Home Run, several hundred people have congregated on the Pitt campus at the site where Forbes Field stood until 1970 and where a part of the centerfield wall remains. At 1:00 P.M., the time Game 7 began, they start listening to a tape of the game's radio broadcast. At 3:36 P.M., sure enough, the announcer calls the Home Run.

Where the wall in left center used to be, a bronze plaque embedded in a sidewalk marks the spot where the ball sailed out to win the World Series. Mazeroski has never attended the ritual rebroadcast of the game. He has trouble fathoming all the fuss. He shifts in his chair at home. "Forty years ago!" he says. "I never dreamed when it happened that people would still be talking about it forty years later. It has seemed to grow and grow and grow. Amazing, really amazing."

What he appreciates is that he was blessed to live the oldest of youthful dreams. As a boy in Skunk Hollow, he would go down to the highway with an empty bucket, fill it with stones, and trudge back up the hill. He would then spend hours whacking the stones with broken broom handles.

"That is so clear in my mind, throwing those stones up and hitting them," he says. "All summer long. I didn't have anybody to play with. I'd hit it so far for a single, so far for a double, so far for a home run. I was Babe Ruth. Always. You always got in a situation when it was the seventh game of the World Series, everybody's counting on you. Then you hit the home run. I was no different from any other boy doing that."

Just one difference, really. He nods his white-thatched head.

"I got to do it in real life," he says.

Beach Boy

FROM AMERICAN HERITAGE

A bare-chested, saltwater Edison who turned on the
light for surfers — B.C.

I WAS HURRYING DOWN an endless corridor in San Francisco's international airport, in a swirl of shapeless people and with a storm raging around, when I was suddenly brought to a stop.

For lining my route were blown-up photos of bronzed surfers in tints and monochromes, old-fashioned athletes wearing shapely bathing costumes, not the youths of today, snug in their thick rubber wet suits. A sign told me this was a special exhibit celebrating the history of surfing in California. I paused to look and to read, a lone peruser in that airport rush of cell phones and baseball caps.

Of course I found plenty of tributes to Duke Kahanamoku, the famous Hawaiian waterman and reputed father of modern surfing. That was fine. I'd shaken hands with the great old Polynesian during the 1960s, when I was in Honolulu appearing in a rock TV show, and a nicer gentleman you couldn't imagine; he'd even shown us a couple of Watusi steps and said he admired the Beatles.

The problem for me was that there wasn't a picture of George Freeth, his predecessor.

Poor forgotten George! Dead of influenza at thirty-five in 1919, after rescuing yet another victim from the angry Pacific. He who had innovated and innovated but not uttered a word that was ever reported. A perfect physical specimen but only part Hawaiian and therefore lacking the romantic ethnic appeal of Duke Kahanamoku. Yet, long before the Duke, George Freeth had formally introduced surf-riding to Southern California, and from there it had spread around the world. After that he'd shown them water polo, water basketball, and the crawl.

As the very first professional lifeguard, he had devised the torpedo-shaped "rescue can" — a four-foot-long can attached to a cable that can be thrown out to a sinking swimmer. It is still in use. The dives he demonstrated at Redondo Beach were legendary; boys followed him around, copying his walk. Still, he said nothing, hardly smiling. Silent George, always in sportswear, clean as a whistle, master of the agitated water.

I thought of Freeth, of his world of sun and sky, as I hurried down the concertina corridor and into the metal tube of the plane and out into the tin-can car and finally back in my furnace house in Los Angeles. At my basement desk at the Huntington Library I tried to fill in the details of how this man had brought beach culture to America.

The first stop would be Waikiki Beach in the late spring of 1907. Jack London, the famous and excitable all-American author, had just arrived there with his "wife-mate," Charmian. According to London's side of the story, he caught his first sight of surfing while he was lolling in the shade of a date palm one morning on Waikiki. He and Charmian had sailed in on their homemade boat, the *Snark,* after a rough journey from San Francisco. Kicking back in paradise, he was presented with a thrilling vision.

All morning the surf had been thundering and churning and forming battle lines of waves with smoking crests or welters of spume and so on. Now, atop one of these growling rollers, there appeared a sea-god, flying through the spray-filled air until — boomph! — he landed at London's feet, effortlessly picked up an enormous board, and left him gazing at the remnants of breakers falling spent on the sand.

This splendid fellow, decided the writer, was a "member of the kingly species that has mastered matter and the brutes." It occurred to London that he was as good as this blackened creature with the big redwood plank. He, too, would ride the waves.

But he turned out to be hopeless at the surfing game — until a friend, Alexander Hume Ford, gave him some pointers and then, a little later, introduced him to the sea-god himself, a kid named

Freeth. Silently the lad showed the author how to duck under or dive through the killer waves: Remember never to be rigid, never to struggle against the mighty smokers; always relax and yield to nature. This London fully understood and always had. All day long he tested the waves, and they tested him back, with a vengeance. The next morning he was flat on his back with a bad case of sunburn.

Though in pain, London was determined to produce his daily thousand words. He ran way over, well into the thousands, and by lunchtime he had a complete article, straight from his heart. "A Royal Sport" he scribbled at the top. I have held the manuscript in my hand here at the Huntington Library: loose, lined pages that start in ink and go into pencil (did he run out of ink, or did the nib break under his passion?), lots of crossings out, but mainly one continuous stream of words, punctuated with stains (jam? or blood?), until, at the climax, he declares his desire, his determination, to become a "sunburned, skin-peeling Mercury." The *Snark* will not leave Waikiki until he has achieved his aim.

Actually, London sailed off before long. In October the article was published in *A Woman's Home Companion* and, a little later, as a chapter in his book *The Cruise of the Snark*. Thus word was spread about a fabulous new sport.

But Jack London's story, stirring though it be, is not what really happened. Charmian wrote her account in a later book called *Our Hawaii*. This, together with articles by Ford, provides the monochrome necessary to counterbalance London's purple.

Jack and Charmian had met Ford at their dinner table in the Royal Hawaiian Hotel, Honolulu, on the evening of May 29, 1907. The couple were enjoying cocktails and canapés when up strode the young man, who introduced himself. Jack London had heard of him; Ford had a reputation as a travel writer. The Londons learned that he had been born in South Carolina to an old Southern family, had written plays with Mark Twain himself, had been globetrotting in the 1890s, and had a string of articles published by *Harper's* and *McClure's*. He'd arrived in Hawaii only a few weeks before but was already burrowing deep into the local culture and was anxious to revive the almost extinct art of riding down hills of boiling foam.

Suddenly Ford got up and snapped his fingers. "Look here, old chap!" he shouted. "Look here! If you'll let me, I can introduce you to some whacking good material for your stories." He proceeded to invite the couple to join him the next day for a trip to Waikiki. "And you must meet Freeth — he's just your handwriting!"

So the following morning the trio traveled by trolley car to Waikiki. That evening they dined al fresco at the Moana Hotel, amid trees hung with Chinese lanterns, serenaded by guitars and ukuleles. Charmian wished aloud that Jack would dance. . . . But he and Ford were immersed in beach plans for the morrow.

"Wait till you meet Freeth! Never speaks, you know," said Ford. "He's a man of deeds, not words. His walk alone is eloquence in motion." Jack pressed for more. "Well, he's twenty-three and only part Polynesian. His father was an Irish sailor and his mother we're not quite certain about — probably a mulatto. Of course, the family claim to be descended from a local prince, but everybody here is royal, don't you know, ha, ha! . . . Anyway, some noble uncle gave young Freeth a surfboard after the boy had seen an old picture of surfing in his relative's house. By this time the missionaries had well nigh exterminated the sport. Well, the clandestine board was hellishly long — about sixteen feet — and Freeth had the bright idea of chopping it in two so's he could at least pick it up. And then, of course, with the lighter board he was able to do lots more on it — like standing up, as the ancients did.

"There's something spiritual about Freeth that makes him stand out from the rest, like a bright light. He's a paragon of modern youth, yet he resists the mainland imports, and holds to the old pantheism. . . . When he rides the waves he's almost — dare I say it? — a Christ-like figure. No — I've gone too far: he's *pre*-Christian, of course. Sorry I'm overdoing it, Jack. Must be the wine. You chose a good vintage."

The Londons were up early. Within the hour Jack had scribbled his ritual thousand words, while Charmian busied herself about the makeshift kitchen, chopping up raw beefsteak to stir into his mess of eggs. Then they waited — and waited. What kind of time did people keep out here in Hawaii?

Ford appeared at noon to escort the couple to nearby Kuhio Beach, where the local watermen congregated. It was here that Jack actually saw Freeth for the first time. Ford pointed him out, a silhouette way out beyond the reef, one hand resting easily on his hip. "Come," ordered Ford. "He's out where the blue breakers are." Jack put down his notes, eager to be active. (So far he'd written, "Freedom, beauty, wonder! No more celebration of the beast! Beauty conquers all! I must enter the contest!!") But when he dashed off down the beach to join the siren out beyond the reef, Charmian held back, frightened. "Be a boy!" said Ford. He grabbed her hand and led her down to the sea and into the small waves and, eventually, out to where Freeth was still standing. "Tell us your secrets, boy!" shouted Ford.

But Freeth never replied. Perhaps he never heard. All he did was slowly turn and disappear, like a conjurer's trick, into a thundering huge wave.

"They don't know what they've got here," said the author to the promoter on the day of leaving. The *Snark* was ready; further adventures were waiting. "I mean, Ford," he continued as he gave his new friend a hearty farewell handclasp, "that you are in a paradise on earth. Remember that!"

A few months later "A Royal Sport," London's article on surf-riding, appeared, and soon boatloads of tourists began arriving, eager for pleasures of the outdoor flesh. Ford was ready for them: He replaced the lackadaisical local surfer hangout with a proper organization, the Outrigger Canoe & Surfboard Club, complete with its own acre of beachfront, on a twenty-year lease at five dollars a year; he had trails cut in the mountains to facilitate hiking. He boosted Hawaii and surfing in the same breath. He was tireless. And all the time hotels were springing up, and friendly shrubbery was planted, and drinks were iced and towels fresh and always available. By 1911 the waves were getting thick with riders; sometimes a hundred of them could be seen where once had been only Freeth's silhouette.

In 1915, when Jack and Charmian returned to Hawaii for a breather, the Outrigger Club had a long waiting list, and the couple had a hard time getting a hotel room for the night. But where was George Freeth? He had answered the call of the mainland. Shortly after the publication of "A Royal Sport" there arrived in the islands some heavy-suited men who were agents of a business empire. They represented one Henry Huntington, a railroad and real estate magnate of Southern California. They had an offer to make to the twenty-three-year-old surfer: For a certain amount of money, at a certain time and a certain place, would the lad demonstrate his "walking on water"? George was willing and able. The Bronze Mercury was to be a lure.

For Huntington owned — among many other properties — a seaside town called Redondo Beach, which, prior to his purchase, had been a barren spot, good mainly for cattle ranching. Huntington's brother-in-law, himself a canny businessman, had written that the very name Redondo made a capitalist "shy like a horse at an automobile." However, Henry had vision and plans. In 1905 he bought 90 percent of the town; by 1907 he'd built a three-story pavilion, a good restaurant, a large theater. The Hotel Redondo, designed on classic English lines with dreamy spires and tall, wobbly chimneys, its walls covered with gold-framed prints of hunting scenes, had been built earlier. Now he needed customers not only to come out for a holiday by the sea but also to buy up the available real estate. To this end he utilized his famous fleet of electric Red Cars, shipping out as many as a thousand trippers by the day from nearby Los Angeles. "Free Excursions Every Twenty Minutes!" shouted his ads in the *Los Angeles Times*. "Dirt Is Flying! Spikes Are Being Driven!"

George Freeth was imported in time for the summer season of 1908. The Red Cars took visitors a short walking distance from the Hotel Redondo, where, after a full lunch, they could watch an extraordinary exhibition. At 2:00 P.M. and again at 4:00, a young Hawaiian "walked on the waters," came creaming in on a wave, picked up his huge plank, and ambled off with the smallest hand gesture. The announcer said that his board was eight feet long and two feet wide and weighed more than two hundred pounds. Also, Freeth was single and had blue eyes and brown wavy hair. Women of all ages watched him closely.

The dollars that rolled in because of George's surfing eventually found their way to Huntington, way up in his solid, stately home in San Marino, a stultifying town far inland, where the sun beat down mercilessly but where, safe behind thick brick walls, was a growing treasure of great British art. Eventually the grand haul would include a Gutenberg Bible, Shakespeare's Quartos, crates of eighteenth-century British oils and watercolors, and — the crowning glory — Sir Thomas Lawrence's *Pinkie* gazing at Gainsborough's *Blue Boy*.

Came the autumn of 1908 and the crowds melted like sandcastles. But there was still plenty of good work for Freeth. In nearby Venice, a city of canals created by the cigarette baron Abbott Kinney, George set up a volunteer lifesaving crew based on the pier. Who bankrolled him nobody knows. But he got by; his needs were few. By wintertime he and his boys had saved fifty people from drowning. George was always the first to dive in. And what a diver, too! At every incident, it seemed, he was inventing a new dive — triple somersault, double twist with head between knees, cannonball curve (for a laugh) — and always he came home with his victim safe and sound.

On Wednesday, December 16, a terrible storm blew up in Santa Monica Bay. Huge walls of water came crashing in. Eleven Japanese fishermen, unaware of the danger, had set off in skiffs from their beach village near the port of Los Angeles. By noon they were in big trouble. Freeth and his fellow lifesavers, however, were on the pier. "Masses of foamy waves . . . [were] picked up by the gale and flung half a thousand feet into the streets of the little city," said the *Los Angeles Times* the next day. George was "the hero of the hour," as he "dived into a great breaker just before it broke. The other members of the crew thought to see him dashed to death against the bulkhead. But he pierced the wall of water like a gigantic needle. . . . With skill born of long experience, Freeth caught the side of the little boat and . . . board[ed] the craft."

Then, without a pause, he did an amazing thing: He seized the rudder and, standing up straight, he *surfed* the skiff through what the *Times* called "thousand-ton breakers" all the way back to the beach, where Venice residents lined up to shake his hand and "girls crowded around [him] just to pat his tanned shoulders and smile at him."

Huntington's men were reading. The next year, when Redondo opened its magnificent bathhouse, Freeth was hired as the chief swimming instructor. It was a place such as only California could boast: the largest heated indoor saltwater "plunge" in the world, with three pools, 1,350 dressing rooms, Turkish and steam baths, even a trapeze. It could accommodate 2,000 bathers at the same time. Freeth got an office, with a panoramic ocean view. Not only did he give swimming lessons, teaching the newfangled "crawl" and the "trudgeon" (his specialty, a stroke like the crawl but with the head kept above water), but he daily demonstrated the most amazing dives, elaborations on the ones he'd done from the Venice pier, including a two-and-a-half forward somersault with a double twist and a swallow dive from almost fifty feet.

In the 1980s ex-pupils of his, old men now, remembered the magic of those dives. "He was doing a swallow but he looked more like a hawk," said Harold Braude, a retired insurance salesman still living in Redondo Beach. "I see him in slow motion, almost frozen in the moment. I see him as a creature of the air. Yet at other times, when he was teaching us the trudgeon or playing water polo, he seemed permanently attached to the water, like he was part of it."

Freeth started one of the first water polo teams, then formed another for water basketball. He led his teams to national championships. One night, up with one of his teams in San Francisco for a contest, he was seen strumming a ukulele as his young admirer and protégé Duke Kahanamoku executed a hula. The Duke was to win a gold medal for swimming at the 1912 Olympics and two more golds in 1920; Ludy Langer, another Freeth pupil, later won a silver medal. But George Freeth won nothing, because he was ineligible: He had been paid money to swim and dive and surf and stroll. He was a pro, not a gentleman.

He set up the first lifeguard corps at Redondo Beach. He had a cigar-shaped rescue canister (with cable attached) manufactured for use in lifesaving; if the drama was taking place a long way from the plunge, he'd send out his motorcycle-and-sidecar unit, fully armed with can, cable, bandages, and iodine. In between all this, often at sunset, he could be seen creaming in on a wave. Small boys followed him as he walked up the beach, until he disappeared into the gloaming.

Where did he go? Nobody knows. But in 1915 he was engaged as swimming instructor by the Los Angeles Athletic Club. Henry Huntington may have been behind this, for he'd had a big say in the construction of the club's enormous, handsome swimming pool. Frank Garbutt, an L.A. booster and oil magnate, was a mover and shaker of the club, and he loved the newest things: planes and autos and especially movies. He brought Jack London back into George Freeth's vicinity by building a movie studio nearby for the purpose of filming London novels, starting with *The Sea Wolf* in

1913. Lots of sea and violence, but no work for George. Had London dropped him? What had George done — or not done? We'll never know. But the writer was deteriorating. In 1915, during what was to be his last stay in Hawaii, he roared out passages from his recent novel, *Mutiny of the Elsinore,* to a rapt Alexander Hume Ford: The Northern European white man is being crowded out of America, but before he disappears beneath the weight of the Latin, the Slav, and other lesser races, he will go down fighting. "Darn the wheel of the world! Why must it continually turn over? Where is the reverse gear?" cried London. The next year, death claimed him. And Ford stayed in Hawaii to count the tourists and to regret the boosterism of himself and his great friend; the sea was becoming cluttered.

Perhaps Freeth began to feel the pressure of population. At any rate, by 1917 he had moved on down the coast. In San Diego he continued to teach and to set up lifeguarding teams. Surfing became his secondary occupation; he kept saving lives. In April 1919 he was in Oceanside, some distance from his San Diego base, rescuing a bunch of distressed swimmers. He emerged from the operation thoroughly exhausted and came down with a cold that turned into flu. But this was a special kind of flu, the Spanish influenza pandemic that had been raging since 1918 and which was eventually to kill more people than the Great War had. It claimed Freeth on April 7, 1919. Like one of A. E. Housman's "smart lads," he slipped away while still in his glory.

Did he leave papers, to be indexed and stored at an institution such as the Huntington Library in which I now sit and write? No such luck. Nor is there a swimsuit or a movie. But near Redondo Pier stands a bust of George.

George Freeth's real legacy, though, is his vigorous, silent life: the introducing, by glamorous example, of surfing into Southern California, and thence to the world; the saving of sea-threatened lives, which led, without any desk-bound scheming, to the fully equipped lifeguard who still today sits silent, high on a wooden perch, scanning the ocean for trouble.

After Freeth, Southern California beach culture expanded slowly for two decades, even clandestinely in one notable case: The Malibu Ranch, a private and heavily guarded estate, was breached by two adventurous youths who found an Eden of a beach, watered by small, fast, and sexy waves. Word was passed along to a select few. The next year saw the inauguration of the Pacific Coast Surf-riding Championship in Orange County, with Duke Kahanamoku himself giving a demonstration of his skills. In the 1930s hermetic knots of surfers were to be found in such spots as San Onofre, where they had a penchant for grass skirts and ukuleles, and Bluff Cove on the Palos Verdes Estates, where the waves could be monsters.

In the tradition of George Freeth, surfers were looked up to as heroes, for they were always rescuing swimmers and boaters. They were also in terrific shape, because of the weight of their boards and their Spartan diets (dictated by the Depression), fighting fit on the eve of being shipped out to World War II. They had picturesque names: Red Dog, Black Bass, Scobblenoogin, and even Nelly Bly. Soon they'd be merely numbers. Some would be statistics. The pristine beaches of Eden waited.

In the early 1940s it was estimated that there were no more than five hundred surfers in the world (which meant California). Nevertheless, when Leroy Grannis, later a legendary surfing photographer, returned from the war and made his way to Malibu, the beach of his dreams, he was disgusted to find as many as fifteen guys crowding the waves. "That's it!" he announced. "That's the end of paradise!"

First came a revolution in boards. Freeth's muscle-making planks disappeared; instead, thanks to the technological demands of the war, a new breed of manufacturer offered lighter, streamlined products made out of fiberglass and Styrofoam. Perhaps the leading surfboard scientist was Bob Simmons, a Caltech graduate in aero- and hydrodynamics and a bit of an eccentric: He found other people a distraction from his study of the perfect board to suit his withered arm and was known for ordering interlopers away from his Malibu waves with profane fluency. In 1954, at the age of thirty-five, he died in wicked surf near San Diego, not far from where Freeth had rescued his last bathers.

In the 1950s Malibu was the place for what was being called the in-crowd, blond and beautiful and even famous. At the Pit you might find Peter Lawford and his pal Cliff Robertson. Pretty girls in tight sweaters hung out with the boys. One of them, little Kathy Kohner, insinuated herself into the coterie of kookie beach-bum surfers and was eventually accepted as their mascot. She told her father, Frederick, of her adventures in this subculture, and he rattled out a yarn called *Gidget* that sold a lot of books. Cliff Robertson, a real surfer and Malibu regular, played Kahuna in the hit movie of 1959. He lives in a shack and studies existentialism — a supercool dude.

Now the secret was out, and the outsiders — the gremmies — flocked in. *Gidget* spawned all the beach movies starring Frankie Avalon and Annette Funicello, both clearly wave-scared. There were *Dr. Goldfoot and the Bikini Machine* and *Beach Blanket Bingo*. The lone surfer in his simple swimsuit was now jostled by a horde sporting Pendleton shirts, white Levi's, baggies, and woodies, lured by the siren song of the Beach Boys with their chocolate harmonies.

The older original surfers began to feel like outcasts and sometimes like outlaws. Mickey "Da Cat" Dora, who had laughed at Gidget's surfing attempts back in the fifties, was the leader of the naysayers. He had film-star looks and a laid-back way with a surfboard. The way he moved, the way he combed his hair, the way he pouted defined the ultimate in Southern California style. He was the King of the Malibu Pit, and though he wasn't shy about accepting money to show off his prowess in beach movies, he'd vent his anger on the new beach crowd stealing his waves by hazing them out of the ocean with supple use of his board. He hated lifeguards because they wouldn't let him light a fire to wax the board. Indeed, he hated anyone in authority.

In the late sixties Mickey Dora made a visual statement of disgust by dropping his trunks and mooning the crowd (including a national television audience) during a Malibu surfing competition. Later he put his beef into words: "I remember how things were before the subdivisions, the concessions, the *lifeguards* — before exploiters polluted the beaches like they do everything else. . . . The water's already curdling from the football-punchy Valley swingers, surf dopes, magazine and photo hacks. . . . I hope you all become One while stewing in your own juices. For myself, I'm dropping out." This is more than George Freeth said publicly in his entire life. But at least Mickey Dora was as good as his word: After some brushes with the law and a spell in jail, he disappeared. Since then sightings have been reported in France, South Africa, and a college library in Orange County.

Meanwhile, back in the late sixties, beach culture was inducted into a drug culture of surf thugs in Nazi helmets and swinging metal iron crosses and swastikas. In Hawaii, where our story began, the islanders grew impatient with overweening, exploitative haoles (mainlanders), and they came to wage a war ranging from the throwing of angel food cake to gang rape at gunpoint. One leading American surfer, visiting the islands for a big wave contest, kept a loaded shotgun under his hotel bed. Too many people chasing too few waves.

Today, on once-pristine and comradely beaches, I find sand stuck with plastic and glass, rocks covered with graffiti, boom boxes thudding out war chants, and signs posted ordering you not to do this, that, and the other.

And so I return to the image of George Freeth, the complete waterman, a fellow who could not only surf but also swim and dive and spearfish and paddle an outrigger canoe and save lives. I see him at Waikiki, in that early summer of 1907. He is standing on air, out in the blue, beyond the reef, beyond the grasp of Jack and Charmian London and of Alexander Hume Ford. As the sun sets, he evaporates, becomes part of the ocean, part of creation.

"Was he crooking his finger to us? Was he?" wrote Ford to London. "My binoculars are pretty powerful — and I say HE WAS." No reply came from London. Ford wrote again: "If he WAS crooking his finger, then what was he telling us??" Again, no reply.

To me George Freeth is not crooking but beckoning. He is saying that there is somewhere a grand swimming place of endless crystal water and friendly Loreleis, beyond time and beyond present understanding and belief.

KEVIN CONLEY

A Stud's Life

FROM THE NEW YORKER

Father's daze. Nevertheless, some stud has to do it — B.C.

MY FIRST CONTACT with the world's number-one stud at his place of business — that would be Storm Cat, at the stallion complex on W. T. Young's Overbrook Farm, in Lexington, Kentucky — came over the phone. "There's his holler now," Dr. Joe Yocum, the farm vet, said calmly, from his office in the breeding shed, above a noise that sounded like the fury of hell. "He just jumped on her. I'll look out my window here and tell you when he's finished. . . . Yup." The doctor chuckled. "He wouldn't be real popular with the women."

The Kentucky Derby is often called the most exciting two minutes in sports; Storm Cat is probably its most expensive thirty seconds. His stud fee for the 2000 season hit $300,000, nearly double that of his closest rival. It could easily have gone higher. A final pair of contracts offered at auction last November, before the farm shut his book for the season, brought in $415,000 and $430,000, respectively. Based on a conservative estimate of seventy guaranteed-live-foal contracts, Storm Cat will earn $21 million this year. If he played in the NBA, that figure would make him the league's third-highest-paid player. As a stud, no one's even close.

Why would anyone pay that much for Storm Cat's services? Last year, Storm Cat's offspring earned more than $12 million dollars at the track, almost $4 million more than anyone else's. Furthermore, several Storm Cat colts who have recently launched their own stud careers — Storm Boot, Hennessy, Forest Wildcat — have begun siring stakes winners and high-priced yearlings, justifying hefty hikes in their stud fees. In other words, just thirty seconds with Storm Cat gives you a chance of landing your own franchise Thoroughbred.

If he were any other breed — miniature, trotter, quarter horse, Standardbred, Lipizzan, Arabian, American warmblood — Storm Cat could just jump on a padded phantom breeding mount (like a pommel horse, but "natural, mare-like," and equipped with a "side opening and quick release valve") and his half of the bargain could be frozen and shipped Priority Overnight to any mare in the world. But Storm Cat will never suffer this indignity, because the Jockey Club, the official registry of Thoroughbred racing, forbids artificial insemination. Only registered horses can race on the Thoroughbred circuit, and the Jockey Club registers only horses conceived by what is delicately termed "natural cover." Storm Cat's job — and the most profitable sector of a high-stakes industry — is safe.

Success at the track is merely a first step toward such profits. Take Cigar, who won sixteen races in a row and retired to stud in 1997, after earning a record $9.9 million. Not one of the eighty mares booked for his first and only season became pregnant, but his owners were lucky: Italy's Assicurazioni Generali made good on Cigar's $25 million infertility-insurance policy. Far more common than infertility is mediocrity, and no policy covers the champion horse who fails to produce a winner. As Tom Wade, the groom to the 1977 Triple Crown winner, Seattle Slew, said, "Just because a horse wins a million dollars, that don't make him no stud."

For a stallion, the eagerness of a teenager is considered the mark of a professional — breeders call it "great libido." Although Storm Cat's libido is spoken of mostly in economic terms, from time to time something else creeps in: awe, fear, relief. Breeding horses is dangerous — last March, Class Secret, a twelve-year-old son of Secretariat, the 1973 Triple Crown winner, had to be euthanized after a mare he was mounting broke his leg — so dawdling is not appreciated. It's risky for the people involved, too. One stallion manager told me that sildenafil citrate — Viagra — had been tested on horses and rejected, largely because nobody who works in the breeding shed wants to fool around with a rearing half-ton, hormonally enraged animal trying to set a personal endurance record.

With a horse like Storm Cat, however, the worrying doesn't stop at the breeding shed. He's only seventeen years old, comfortably mid-career for a stud. (Mr. Prospector, the sire of this year's Derby winner, Fusaichi Pegasus, was twenty-nine when he died last year.) But even innocent conversations about him — what he likes to eat (bluegrass, oats, and sweet feed), where he sleeps (in a hilltop barn, near his winter paddock), what he does for fun (lies down in a big sandpile and rolls around) — tend to veer into elaborately imagined premonitions of his death and the state-of-the-art precautions taken to guard against it. One of his sandpiles, for example, is bounded by an unusual stretch of solid wood, because somebody worried that he might roll a foreleg under the standard fencing and break a bone as he tried to stand up. And if you want to meet the farm's entire staff in the next forty seconds? Just light a cigarette near Storm Cat's stall.

On a sunny morning in May, halfway through the four-and-a-half-month breeding season, the sire looks vigorous. In his official photographs, Storm Cat can come across as smug and bullnecked and a little thick in the waist, but the camera must add a few pounds, because in person, prancing in his paddock, he has the hauteur and the low body fat of an underwear model. He's a dark bay, but when he moves in the sunlight you can pick up flashes of a honey-gold color that comes from the chestnut horses on his mother's side — Terlingua, Storm Cat's dam (his mother), and his grandsire, Secretariat. He has white spats on his left legs, also from Terlingua, which give him a light-footed, high-stepping look, even when he's just pacing over the grass.

"I like his weight now," Wes Lanter, who manages the ten stallions at Overbrook Farm, says. "Twelve hundred and sixty pounds. I think that's a real good weight for him." Lanter runs the operations in the breeding shed with the nimbleness of a linebacker coach, but everywhere else he moves with hound-dog-like deliberateness. To introduce me to the planet's most valuable piece of horseflesh, for example, he folds his arms and says, "There he is." At first, Storm Cat just rips at the grass, pretending he doesn't see us, but after a while he edges over to the fence to investigate. He has a smoldering dark patch between his eyes with a white diamond on it, and a sharp crescent moon way over near his left nostril, a curious marking that makes him look moody and dangerously attractive. He ducks his head behind a board on the fence and gives me the once-over — more eye contact than his mares usually get — and I raise my hand to the little white line that runs down his muzzle. "Stand back," Lanter says, since stallions bite. "He can fool you." As soon as I touch him, Storm Cat ends the interview and walks away.

Suddenly, he lights out for the end of his paddock. Through a break in the trees, he looks over the creek, past the horses nearer the breeding shed — it's standard practice to place stallions with libidos lower than Storm Cat's closer to the parade of action, a cheap sort of stimulant that cuts down on the time spent waiting for arousal — and roars convincingly. "A mare has arrived," Lanter says. "Not yours, Stormy." Undeterred, Storm Cat paces back and forth beside the fence — he has worn a path there — and roars again. Lanter seems pleased, in a proud and wistful prom-chaperon way. "He's looking for dates," he says.

Storm Cat has 714 children at last count, but he has seen only three: Mountain Cat, who was recently shipped off to Turkey, and two fellow-studs on the roster at Overbrook Farm — Tactical Cat, a pretty gray horse (whose dam was Terre Haute), and Tabasco Cat, the winner of the Preakness and the Belmont in 1994 (whose dam was Barbicue Sauce). They often pass each other on the way to or from the breeding shed and he cuts them every time — no nicker, no friendly whinny. Apart from a few pointed, work-related roars, Storm Cat is laconic, even for a horse. But it's a menacing, eloquent sort of silence: it's on purpose.

Menace, apparently, is a job requirement for stallions. The senior managers at Overbrook, who generally live in picturesque houses tucked into the farm's manicured hills, like to expound upon the equine instinct for violence. They'll tell you how, in the wild, a lone stallion would command a roving harem-cum-nursery of broodmares and foals, until some other horse, probably one of his own sons, decided to bite, kick, and break his legs for it. Add to these instincts a few centuries of breeding specifically for aggressiveness — a trait Storm Cat is prized for and seems to be able to pass on to his foals — and you have the potential for some very volatile relationships.

That's the theory. In practice, Storm Cat — apart from his twice-daily acts of sexual congress with the fastest, wealthiest, and most attractive available partners in the world, seven days a week throughout the breeding season — lives like a monk. He eats mostly grass, sleeps on straw, drinks only water. He has no visits with the other stallions. His one diversion is running away from his groom, which he is doing less of lately, because his current groom is kind but strict. He wears only a leather halter. He does not race, he does not train for racing, he does not even exercise. He has given all that up.

Regularly, en route to the breeding shed, he steps on a scale. If the number seems high, he cuts back on the sweet feed that is his sole indulgence. His weight is monitored minutely. When he dropped a few pounds in February, at the beginning of the breeding season, he was rushed to the Hagyard Davidson and McGee Veterinary Clinic, in Lexington. "It wasn't much — enterocolitis," Doc Yocum said. "With any other horse, we probably wouldn't have bothered." He traced its onset to a few instances when Storm Cat arrived at the breeding shed wringing wet before he even started: "My theory is he was just so worked up to get back at the mares."

Storm Cat's stall — where he goes as infrequently as possible, to get his coat brushed, say, or to sleep during inclement weather — is outwardly unremarkable: a foot and a half of straw in a white-washed cinder-block room with two wooden doors. (Even here, value creates value: Storm Cat's muck is carted off and resold to the Campbell's Soup Company, which uses it as the breeding ground for the mushrooms in its mushroom soup.) But while he sleeps, a box nestled in the ridge of his barn projects an infrared beam that looks for obscurity — smoke. An ultraviolet device picks up flickers of light in the hydrocarbon range — flame. A third mechanism compares ambient temperature against its rate of rise — heat. These three devices monitoring the separate elements of fire are tied into the forty-second alarm system and into a sprinkler system, fed by massive pipes capable of delivering six inches of standing water to the stall in seconds. Fire is a problem because barns are drafty by design and straw is extremely flammable, but Ben Giles, who guides the building projects at the farm, compares Over-brook's safeguards favorably with fire-detection measures in museums. "We don't have the luxury of being able to cut a barn up into small spaces to confine or suppress a fire, because a horse needs air. In that sense, the museums have it a little easier," Giles says. "Plus, their van Goghs are worth a whole lot less than Storm Cat."

It took a long time for people to see that Storm Cat was a lucky horse. As a yearling, he was smallish, longhaired, potbellied, with the kind of turned-out knees that got him booted out of Kentucky's best auction. Twice at the track, he lost races that he should have won, once because he shouldered an inferior horse in the final stretch out of sheer cussedness, and later because his mind wandered when he was too far in front at the Breeders' Cup, a race that would have established him as the leading contender for two-year-old horse of the year. He missed all his Triple Crown races as a three-year-old because he was recovering from knee surgery, and when he tried to come back, late in the year, he trained on dirt that had turned greasy after a hard rain, and was never the same. When he retired from racing, in 1988, people quickly forgot about him. His stud fee dropped from thirty thousand to twenty-five to twenty, and he couldn't fill his book of mares.

Then his first crop of colts and fillies hit the track. Suddenly, people started remembering what a brilliant, blazingly fast runner he'd been, how he took a competitive streak that bordered on the criminal and used it to overcome his natural unsoundness. By the time his second and third crops hit, people knew that Storm Cats could run. They could run at two years old, or three, or four; colts or fillies, they could run long or short, turf or dirt, in Europe, Japan, or America. By 1994, when Tabasco Cat took the last two jewels of the Triple Crown, it was clear that Storm Cat had a calling.

The mares arrive for their appointments by horse van and walk over a gravel loading dock into the receiving barn — a sort of greenroom for mares in estrus. When a mare enters, somebody pushes a button, a window opens, and Cooperstown, an Overbrook teaser stallion, sticks his head in to try his luck, nuzzling her flank and nosing her haunches. If she kicks, he's the one she kicks at, not Storm Cat. ("If they don't make it at the track, they end up being teasers," Doc Yocum says. "So it's a little incentive deal.") In the past twenty years, veterinarians have grown very precise in pinpointing ovulation (an increase in accuracy that has allowed stallions to double their workload — and farms to double their profits — since fewer and fewer mares require follow-up visits), but final verification is still left to the teaser stallion. If there are any doubts about her receptivity after Cooperstown's initial interview, he is forced to try a jump himself — wearing a leather butcher's apron to insure that the dry run goes unconsummated. Usually, though, she's willing, the window shuts for Coop, and the mare is led into a padded chute to be washed for the breeding shed.

Just before Storm Cat's mare is ready, his groom, Filemon Martinez, a quiet man with a Clark Gable mustache, walks the sire of sires across a covered bridge over Hickman Creek to the stallion

barn. From the doorway of the barn, where Storm Cat and Martinez wait like actors in the wings, you can hear the business of
breeding: "Easy, boss," and "Go, buddy," and, if it's a stallion with
problems in the Valentino department, the pacesetting shouts of
"Hyup! Hyup! Hyup!" Most do just fine in the breeding shed, although farm policy seems to be anywhere that works. At least one
stallion, Cape Town, prefers to perform al fresco, on the grass,
with all the usual team in attendance, plus one guy giving helpful
pushes from the rear.

By the time Storm Cat enters the shed, the video camera is rolling (for lawsuits and insurance) and the mare — Rootentootenwooten, in this case — is standing with her head against the wall,
wearing padded booties on both hind feet. Storm Cat neighs or
hollers or roars — whatever it is, it's frightening and long and full
of the inevitable, like the squeal of tires that you know will end in
shattering glass. Then he measures himself and rears while the
team rushes around him. There are two schools of natural cover:
pasture breeding, where horses are let loose in a paddock together,
and hand breeding, where a squad of breeding-shed professionals
choreograph the proceedings for safety and speed. Overbrook prefers the latter, as practically all large-scale breeding operations do,
and their version of it takes at least five people: two to soothe and
distract the mare, one to steady the stallion, a tail man, and the stallion manager. When Storm Cat rears, the tail man lifts up the
mare's tail, and Wes Lanter, wearing a latex glove, pilots Storm Cat
to the place he probably would have found on his own, but not as
quickly.

All the majesty of the act is in the roaring, apparently — count to
fifteen and it's over. Somebody says "Good cover" with a mixture
of appreciation and relief, and Storm Cat, still draped across
Rootentootenwooten's back, fits the curl of his neck to hers and
allows himself a moment of unstallionlike tenderness before he
backs off and puts his feet on the ground again. The stallion manager pulls down a handheld shower nozzle, of the sort you find in
French bathtubs, to wash Storm Cat off. Then the groom leads the
sire away, through the stallion barn, down the hill, and back into
the shadows of the covered bridge. Lanter pulls off his latex glove
and says, "He's what everybody hopes happens to them when they
retire."

GEOFFREY DOUGLAS

The Double Life of Laura Shaw

FROM YANKEE

Her kingdom for a horse — B.C.

She is middle-aged, bucktoothed, and homely, with thick, gold-rimmed glasses and frizzled blond hair she wears in a ponytail. She rarely bothers with makeup. Her clothes are cheap, dowdy, and mostly out of style. It's unlikely she cares. She has no one to dress for: no husband, no boyfriend, no friends. There is only her mother — whom she lives with — and a son by a man she says she never married and hasn't seen in years.

She lives in a rented cottage on the Massachusetts shore and drives to work each morning in an old Dodge pickup to a job in downtown Boston, where she sits all day in a cubicle the size of a toilet stall. She hates it, she says, but needs the money — about $10 an hour after taxes — and has had the job twenty years.

She is timid, awkward with strangers, and is said to walk in a slouch. One acquaintance describes her as "mousy," another as "pathetic," a third as "a loser without a life." No one who knows her, when asked, can say for sure the color of her eyes.

She is rich. A millionaire horsewoman with homes in three states. Some say she's a lottery winner. Or the daughter of a Midwest jeweler. Or a supermarket heiress from old New England money. It's hard to know which story to believe.

But the horses are real. She lives for them: saddlebreds, quarter horses, broodmares — she owns as many as thirty at a time. She bids for them at auctions, then rides them in showrings, in black tie and tuxedo, jodhpurs,

and a high silk hat. She's won ribbons and trophies. She owns champions.
She golfs with owners and trainers. She trains three afternoons weekly in a
practice ring in Massachusetts, while her mother watches in a full-length
mink.

She spends money like water: horses, horse vans, a camper, a Mercedes,
hotel bills, riding lessons, vet bills, trainer fees, airfares to Kentucky, Vir-
ginia, Pennsylvania — wherever there is a show — $3,500 monthly in
boarding fees alone. She gives ponies to children, sponsors shows, donates
trophies, buys her mother anything she wants. It's all she can do to stay
within her income, which averages $400,000 a year.

In the early summer of 1994, Lillian Gilpin, who trains horses on
the south shore of Massachusetts, got a call from another trainer, a
New Hampshire friend named Rob Turner, about a client he had.

"There was this lady, who boarded some horses with him. And
there was this one saddlebred — a three-year-old, his name was
New Trial — that she wanted to show. But the lady couldn't ride,
Rob told me. She couldn't ride worth a damn. He asked if I'd teach
her. I said I'd give it a try." Gilpin is sitting in a small tack room
alongside the barn at Rocking Horse Farm in Plympton, Massachusetts, a stable she owns and runs. She is tall, blond, and small-boned
— like a jockey — compact and leathery, the sort of woman you
could pretty much bet doesn't make her living behind a desk.

"So she shows up here one day — it was the beginning of summer — and says she wants to learn [to ride] by the fall. . . . Well, I
put her up on a horse. And yeah, she could sit him all right, but
that was just about all. Rob had it right. She couldn't ride worth a
damn.

"But she was just so *determined.* So willing. And she had so many
questions — 'Why this?' 'Why that?' 'How do you do this?' 'How do
you do that?' Plus she knew a lot. She read all the magazines, whatever there was to read. If she saw a horse walking down the street,
she could tell you the sire and the dam. She just flat out *loved*
horses. She ate, slept, and breathed horses. No one knew more
about saddlebreds than Laura Shaw."

So they began. Every Tuesday, Thursday, and Saturday afternoon, Laura Shaw would show up for lessons at Lillian Gilpin's
barn. She bought a practice horse, Against All Odds, for $4,500 —
"a skinny, ugly, scarred-up, eight-year-old saddlebred mare," recalls
Gilpin. "But she was obliging. Laura needed that. She was no natu-

ral. She wasn't athletic, she wasn't graceful. She needed an easy horse."

The lessons went on. Through the summer, fall, and winter of 1994, then all of 1995. On the weekends Laura would drive with her mother to Rob Turner's farm in New Hampshire, where she would practice her skills on New Trial — who was gentle and obliging, as saddlebreds go, but still, remembers Gilpin, "too much horse" for Laura to handle in a show.

Over time, the two women grew close, the gritty, plainspeaking trainer with dirt under her fingernails and the shy, fervent horse lover who seemed to have no other life. But it was a closeness, says Gilpin, that had more boundaries than bonds: "I liked her. You couldn't help but like her. But she was different — there was all this stuff that didn't make sense. Here she was, with all that money, all those horses, all those gorgeous [riding] clothes — but she wasn't a bit classy. She looked rough. She had those big buckteeth of hers, she never wore makeup, she wore her hair pulled back like this. . . ."

And there were other things, she says.

"I knew she worked for an insurance company. She never talked about it or anything, but I had her number at work. And anytime I'd call, she'd always answer the same: 'Laura Shaw, Claims.' I thought that was weird. Here was this millionaire horse lady, working in a claims department. Makes you wonder. But I try to never ask questions — not as long as they pay their bills. And she paid."

The year after they met, Laura invited Lillian to a Christmas party at her house, in Marshfield, Massachusetts, on a cul-de-sac off a thickly settled country road.

"I don't know what I expected, but not that. Here was this little cottage [in Marshfield] with these two little bedrooms. *Rented.* This little old rented cottage that was only barely big enough to walk around in. And nobody else. No friends, no neighbors. Just Rob [Turner] and his wife, me and my boyfriend, and Laura and her mom. That was it. And all we talked about, the whole night — just horses, nothing else."

Laura's mother was another matter. Nell Shaw, by all accounts, was a stylish woman — or did her best to be. Small and frail-seeming, she was in her late sixties, with gray hair, stooped shoulders, and a halting, uncertain walk. But she had a presence. She was a talker, a joiner; she liked people. She lived in the moment and was happiest when the moment was hers. She was fond of her evening cocktail. She had a taste for mink.

"A fun person," Rob Turner says of her. "A classy lady, and she liked her alcohol." His wife, Hazel, puts it differently. "She wasn't like Laura. She wore the money well."

Mother and daughter were inseparable. Whether by choice or necessity, it was never quite clear.

"Where one went, the other went," says Lillian Gilpin. "She'd come here with Laura for the lessons and just sit over there and watch. It was all they had, all they did. They'd be in New Hampshire with Rob on the weekends, then here three afternoons a week after Laura got off work. I don't think Nell cared one way or another about the horses, but it seemed like she was happy that Laura was living her dream."

By this time, the winter of 1995–96, according to the records of the American Saddlebred Registry, Laura Shaw owned twenty-five horses, most of them stabled at Rob Turner's barn, and had bought and sold roughly thirty more. In the small, circumscribed world of show-horse owners, she was a medium-to-major player, with one certified champion to her name — Shelby Stonewall, a once-and-future third-place finisher in the three-gaited Grand Championship at Louisville's Kentucky State Fair. Several others had won ribbons at smaller events — the Eastern States Exposition, the Devon Horse Show, the Syracuse International. Virginia's Bonnie Blue — but nearly always, as with Shelby, with Rob Turner at the reins.

Laura wanted her own horse. Her own honors. More than anything else she had ever wanted — and there is no one who knows her who doesn't say the same — she wanted to ride in a big-event showring, on the back of a three-gaited champion, and drink in the cheers of a packed-full arena when the judges named her the best.

It's impossible to know where she came by her dream. She said nothing of its origins to anyone she knew. Even those closest to her in the horse business — Turner, Gilpin, a magazine photographer named Maureen Jenner, and two or three more — knew only that she had been born somewhere in Kentucky, had a grown son by a man she never mentioned, a day job in a Boston insurance firm, and a mother who almost never left her side. And that she was rich. And that to bring up any subject more personal than horses was, as Lillian Gilpin puts it, "to get this big, dead stare."

But maybe — and it is only one theory — maybe it had nothing to do with horses at all: "Laura Shaw is a very sad person," says Bridget Parker, a Kentucky trainer who knows her, knows Rob Turner, and sold her at least one horse. "There's no question she loved the horses. But she loved the attention more. . . . She's the sort of person, well, it could have been anything: dogs, [antique] dolls, just about anything at all. She's a sad, needy person. If someone pays her the attention, makes her feel important — that's all that has ever mattered to her."

When she wasn't working, or taking lessons, or in New Hampshire with her horses (she had rented a small place near Rob Turner's farm), she was coming or going from shows. Kentucky, Virginia, Pennsylvania, Maine, Massachusetts, New York. Sometimes she drove and stayed in a camper; other times she flew and lived in hotels. It's hard to imagine how she managed it. When someone would ask how she balanced her job with travel, she would answer only that she "planned out the year in advance."

Nearly always, her mother was with her. And so was Rob Turner, whose job it was to stable and care for the horses, then to show them in the evening or afternoon events. If it was Kentucky, it might be the state fairgrounds auditorium or Lexington's Big Red Mile: at the smaller shows, there would be tents pitched around showrings, with the judges at long ringside tables and the audience in sun hats, bright jackets, and dresses behind them in the stands. The prize money was a pittance: $50 or $60 for a small-event win, a few thousand for a grand championship — but it was never, even remotely, the point.

A top-level saddlebred horse show is as arcane, as regimented, yet as honestly elegant, as any spectacle in sports. To the first-timer, it would seem foppish, even comic, and utterly beyond understanding: a tentful of overdressed, overserious people sitting around watching horses doing double-jointed things with their legs. To the true saddlebred lover, a three-gaited champion, in seamless transition from walk to trot to canter — head high, left foreleg raised and stretched impossibly, bent downward at the joint as though there were elastic in there, its rider erect and unmoving, in perfect fusion with her mount — is no less sublime than ballet.

Somewhere, somehow, Laura Shaw had come to this vision of things. Perhaps it was the horse magazines she pored over or that she'd been born in Kentucky and was seeking some link to her roots. It's hard to know. But one thing is clear: that perfection on horseback and the world that it opened were, to her thinking, the only truths that held weight.

In March of 1995, after only nine months of lessons, Laura rode New Trial for the first time in a show, the three-gaited Ladies' Class at the Bonnie Blue National in Virginia. Lillian Gilpin hadn't felt she was ready. "She still rode rough, she still wasn't pretty." She'd finished third in a field of six, won $25 and a yellow ribbon. It was a start.

She was easing off on the horse buying: only six horses each in 1995 and 1996. Her focus was the riding now. In November of 1995, she showed New Trial a second time: in the three-gaited Amateur Championship at the Children's Benefit in Pennsylvania. She finished second in a field of five. She was ecstatic. Her next target, she told Rob Turner, would be the three-gaited Ladies' at the Roanoke Valley in January of 1996; and a month after that, her biggest test yet: the United Professional Horsemen's Association Amateur Spring Championship in Massachusetts.

She and Rob Turner had become close. Part of it was business. Most of her horses were stabled at his barn; she accounted for close to half his income, more than $3,000 per month in boarding fees alone. And there was Shelby Stonewall, her champion gelding that Rob just kept riding to wins — twenty-eight first-place finishes in forty-one events, before Shelby would be retired, at fifteen, in the spring of 1997. But it was more than just that.

"She needed a lot of attention," he says. "You could see she was lonely, that she needed companionship, that she had no other life. She'd be here on the weekends with her mother; then we'd do the shows. Then during the week she'd always be calling, sometimes four or five times in a day. It got kind of exhausting. But I knew she was lonely. And she spent a lot of money. And I guess I felt sorry for her."

Rob's wife, Hazel, is blunter: "She acted like Rob was her boyfriend. I think, to herself, she pretended he was."

That December was the Christmas party at the little house in Marshfield, with just the six of them. Nell was in a gay mood — looking forward, she said, to next month's trip to the Roanoke Valley; the people in Virginia were always so friendly, it was such a lovely state. Laura talked with Rob about New Trial and about Town Memories, a five-year-old mare she'd just bought. Her son, Mark, made a brief appearance but was on his way to meet someone and said he couldn't stay. It was an early night.

They shipped New Trial to Virginia a day or two ahead. Laura was nervous. She fretted about the weather, New Trial's grooming, the judges, her clothes. She had picked out her outfit: a dark tan riding coat with a flare in the back, matching jodhpurs, a blue-on-gray tie, and a black derby hat. (It would be an afternoon event. Tuxedo and silk top hat apply only after six.)

Laura was up at dawn the morning of the show — as she was most mornings in those days — in the stall with New Trial and Shelby Stonewall, who likewise would be showing that day. (Shelby would finish first out of five entries, with Rob Turner riding, in the three-gaited open event.) She scarcely left the barns all day. Her mother, who had met some friends the night before, came and went.

She got a smooth ride from New Trial, who was at his best that day. So was Laura. She sat straight and unmoving, kept her eyes fast forward and her hands held high on the reins. "She rode pretty," as Lillian would say. There was applause. Then she waited five minutes, stared hard at the ground as there came the judges' voting, and learned that she had won.

Five weeks later, at the UPHA three-gaited Amateur Championship — her biggest show ever, with ten entries contesting — she won again. Two championship points and $100 in cash. Her first win with a champion, a pinnacle.

That was the high point. There were other shows after that and other wins — though only one more for Laura and New Trial, in November of 1996. But when you look at the record of things after that wonderful, winning winter of 1995–96, it seems as though life, for Laura, began about then to turn sour and sad.

Relations with the Turners were growing more brittle by the week.

"She was just getting too close," says Rob Turner. "Wanting too much. She knew too much about my business and too much about my life."

That's all he'll say, though Hazel Turner adds that "there was lots of fighting, fighting going on, lots of screaming, and a couple of times she threatened to leave." She remembers one incident, at a show in Massachusetts — possibly the UPHA in February, she can't recall for sure — when Laura "threw a tantrum, just threw herself on the ground."

In August of 1996, Laura took her horses and departed Rob Turner's farm — taking all except Shelby Stonewall, whom she left behind as a gift. He was fourteen years old at the time.

"I considered her a friend," says Rob today. "I thought I knew her pretty well. I guess I was wrong about that."

Laura showed New Trial for the final time at the Children's Benefit in November. They won together. She sold him three months after that.

She moved her other horses to Danville, Kentucky, to the farm of an older trainer, Bill Wise, who'd earned most of his reputation a generation before, with a national five-gaited champion named Sure Fire. She bought five saddlebreds under his guidance and showed at least two of them. She began spending more time in Kentucky, where she also took up golf. She and Bill Wise played often together in the dead time during shows.

"Kentucky was the big leagues," says Rob Turner. "I think she got attracted to that. I know her mother did."

Bill Wise won't talk publicly about Laura anymore. It is his wife who answers the phone. "Laura spent a lot of time in our home," she says. "We were very fond of her. I'm sorry, but that's all I have to say."

Then, in the winter of 1997, Nell Shaw was diagnosed with cancer. It spread quickly. She died, at home in Marshfield, in May of 1998. Then came the end.

December 17, 1998, a Thursday. Laura Shaw was in her cubicle at New England Financial, in an old, marble-lobbied building in downtown Boston that its denizens call the "Burial Urn." She had come dressed for the company's Christmas party, which was to take place at the end of that day. She got a call to come to her boss's office. It's likely she knew why.

The FBI was waiting. They showed her the canceled checks: $14,239, $16,630, $25,219, made out to the phony claimants — Jeanne Davidson, James Emory, James Worth. Dozens of them. More than $4 million, they said, embezzled over nearly eleven years.

She had begun in February 1988, with a false claim of $2,493, drawn on an older policy, which was processed manually at the time. It had been easy. Her pace picked up; the checks grew larger: $39,000 by the end of 1988, an average of $400,000 a year in the ten years after that.

No one had noticed. It might have gone on forever. But in December of 1998, she slipped: a paperwork error, a check canceled, then — unbelievably — redeposited. When it bounced — New England Financial checks do not bounce — the FBI was called in.

By that time, her mother was dead, relations with the Turners had ended, New Trial was gone, the stream of checks had slowed, and then the dumbest of dumb mistakes. It's tempting to believe that Laura Shaw just wanted it over, that the deception had grown too heavy to carry, that ten years of two lives in the end just wore her out.

Briefly she denied it. Then she confessed. Those who questioned her reported that she seemed relieved.

"Around the horse industry, I guess I was just — I was — I felt like a human being," she told the sentencing judge in federal courts in Boston last September 9. "I was accepted . . . just an inward feeling of . . . just peace. I mean, there's . . . I guess you have to be a horse person to understand, and it's five o'clock in the morning and you're out there . . .

"I love horses. They were living things. They were my total responsibility. I couldn't just walk away. . . ."

Her lawyer, federal public defender Stephanie A. Jirard, appealed to the judge for a brief sentence. She spoke of a "significantly reduced mental capacity" that was the result of the "alternatively symbiotic and parasitic relationship" between Laura and her mother. She asked for clemency in view of Laura's "exceptional degree of responsibility in confessing to her crime."

Judge William G. Young would have none of it. This was "typical, garden-variety embezzlement," he said, then sentenced her to three and a half years.

"I did it," Laura told an AP reporter before her sentencing last September. "I'll pay the price. The old life is finished now. The horses are all gone." It was, outside of her courtroom statement, the only time she has ever spoken publicly about any aspect of her crime.

Laura Shaw today is an inmate in the Federal Correctional Institute in Danbury, Connecticut. Through her lawyer and later through prison officials, she has declined all requests for interviews and has reportedly asked those who know her to do the same. Most of them have complied; it's not hard to see why. The saddlebred world is small, rarefied, and in general closed to outsiders. Laura, in the eyes of most of them, is an embarrassment — who, in the words of Bridget Parker, "has made a mockery of what we do."

And so her story has holes. Unanswered questions, problems with emphasis, unaccounted-for periods of time. Because one trainer, for instance, was willing to talk and a second was not, the importance of the first may seem outsized. How it was, exactly, will probably never be explained.

Who is the real Laura Shaw? How did she come by her dream? Is her contrition genuine? What is known, beyond what has been told already — however imperfectly — is only this: her house in Marshfield — a weathered Cape with a small, overgrown garden — is still in her name as tenant; her son, Mark, as of last December, was living there alone with an unlisted telephone.

Her horses were signed over to New England Financial, then put up for sale through an auctioneer; most, by now, have been sold. Shelby Stonewall remains with Rob Turner. He is eighteen now; his showing days are done.

The memories and judgments of others are mixed. Lillian Gilpin is happy that Laura "finally learned to ride pretty" and that she "enjoyed ten wonderful years." Rob Turner recalls her now as "a sad, lonely woman who had only horses as friends." Bridget Parker's view is simpler: "A thief is a thief. It's just a matter of what you steal."

It's hard to guess what will become of her. She is forty-eight years old. With time off for good behavior, she'll be a fifty-year-old ex-felon — broke, jobless, and largely alone in the world the day they turn her loose.

"I've been embarrassed," she told the judge at her sentencing. "I've embarrassed my son . . . I have no retirement. I will have some kind of civil judgment against me. I will never be able to work in my profession again. . . ."

Lillian Gilpin, at least, doesn't see it that way:

"She loves the horses. She's good with them, they're all she knows. She'll be shoveling shit somewhere."

DAVE KINDRED

Gate Crasher

FROM GOLF DIGEST

Couldn't keep ol' Charlie off the hallowed grass — B.C.

AT 2:15 P.M. on October 22, 1983, Charlie Harris crashed his truck through a locked gate at Augusta National Golf Club, rumbled to the golf shop, used his .38-caliber revolver to disarm Secret Service agents, took seven people hostage, and demanded to talk to President Ronald Reagan, who was on the golf course that day.

Sounds like a story. So all these years later I'm calling Charlie Harris from an Interstate rest stop. I'm lost. He says, "Where're you calling from?"

I name a stop between Atlanta and Augusta.

"You've done gone too far."

A rich country-speakin' bottom to his voice, he tells me to go west one exit, get off, and drive 10.4 miles. "There's a four-way stop," he says. "Go straight on to my mailbox."

His house is the one with cars making the yard look like a used-car lot.

"And that jacked-up Dodge pickup truck is out front."

Here I am driving lost in Georgia piney woods to see a man who spent five years in prison and was called Smiley because he never smiled and wore a trench coat so he could carry a sawed-off shotgun under it.

Now he's giving directions to what sounds like a redneck's junk-mobile graveyard. If you write stories, you go find stories. This one's worth finding. You could tell that the first time talking to Charlie Harris's daughter.

"Daddy's a different man than in '83," Charlene had said. "The alcohol got him then. He's sober now, and he goes to churches and tells his story. Only good things have happened since."

When Harris mentions "that jacked-up Dodge," I wonder if that's the truck he drove through Augusta's Gate 3, yanking the twenty-foot-wide gate off its hinges, the whole thing teetering on the truck's front end as Harris hightailed it onto Bobby Jones's hallowed grounds, a bottle of tequila clanking on the floorboards.

Driving toward Harris's house, you pass two little wooden Baptist churches on the edge of a ghostly town that, like every ghostly Southern town, has an unpainted general store across from a Confederate monument. Then you come to his mailbox. There's no junkyard. Turns out, Harris has lived twenty-nine years (minus the five) in a ranch-style house where he and his wife, Eleanor, raised four children. It's ten acres of land with everything trimmed up, a swimming pool for the four grandkids, coon dogs yelping sweet music.

Harris comes out all crisp in blue jeans, white T-shirt, and sneakers. Forty-five years old when he crashed the gate, he's now sixty-one. He's a strong man with bright brown eyes, neat mustache, square jaw, dimpled chin, and the thick shoulders of an aging athlete. He was a lineman, linebacker, and fullback for the semipro Augusta Eagles until he was thirty-eight. Football, car wrecks, and bar fights ruptured his spleen, tore up his knees, gave him scars, and broke his nose six times. ("First bar fight? I dunno. I can tell you the worst. It was the night Johnny and I leveled Tomcat's. As we were leavin', si-reens were arrivin'.")

Tilting my head toward the Dodge truck by the patio, I ask, "Is that the truck that did it?"

"Yep, Ol' Blue," Charlie Harris says. "A '74 Dodge. Still runs good."

Bill Clinton has never played at Augusta. His predecessor, George Bush, played the course as Ronald Reagan's vice president and after his own presidency. The only fully committed presidential golfer, Dwight D. Eisenhower, spent so much time at Augusta before, during, and after his White House years that the club provided him a residence and called it the Eisenhower Cabin.

Reagan rarely played golf, and the planned two-day trip to Augusta would be his first time on the course. He visited as the guest of his Secretary of State, George Shultz. Their foursome included Secretary of the Treasury Donald T. Regan and Nicholas F. Baker, a former U.S. senator from New Jersey.

According to White House accounts of this cloudy day late in 1983, the Reagan group was near the sixteenth green when Charlie Harris stood with Ol' Blue outside Gate 3.

There, in the middle of Washington Road, Harris walked to the front of his truck to lock its hubs, reckoning he might need four-wheel drive to bust through that gate and see the president. He knew the president was there, because he'd been told so earlier in the day. When he'd driven past that morning, he and his sister, Harriet, saw peace officers stationed along the fences that keep poor folks from seeing rich folks at play. Harriet recognized a county deputy. "Mitch, who you got in there?"

"The president's here to play golf," Mitch said.

Which meant Secret Service, state troopers, armored limousines, Uzis, and helicopters. An army protected this president. He'd been shot in Washington two years before.

With that manpower/firepower security, the deputy was so impressed that he said, "An ant can't crawl in there."

Charlie Harris heard him.

Harris looked down from Ol' Blue, looking down because Ol' Blue runs on high springs, jacked up to clear logs, creek banks, and other obstacles you might otherwise bump into, such as the fool who once thought to irritate Harris by dead-stopping ahead of him, shooting him the bird, and refusing to move, causing Harris to stomp the accelerator and put the fool and his car sideways in a ditch while Harris explained he was just being helpful: "Seemed he couldn't get her cranked up."

Augusta National was familiar to Harris. Through high school, he worked concessions at the Masters. He also sneaked in to scavenge for balls in a bullfrog pond behind the famous cottages. He used to play golf on hardpan called the Cabbage Patch. One bad day, storming off, he handed his clubs to a boy and never played again.

After that morning conversation with the county deputy, Harris went home. Having a drink, he heard TV say U.S. Steel would lay off thousands of workers because it was losing business to foreign-made steel. He had another drink. Two drinks is all, he wants you to know, because after he did this thing, people who knew him said he must have really been drunk this time. He says not.

This wasn't about Jim Beam. This was about the U.S. of A., and he'll tell you he loves this country to death. He just doesn't trust our government. He believes the government is against anybody who doesn't go along with what he calls the politicians' crookedness.

On this day in 1983, out of work himself for the first time in thirty years, Harris felt bad for all those steelworkers. That's when he remembered what Mitch said about the president.

He thought, "Why don't I just ride up there and see him?"

Charlie Harris wasn't thinking all that well back then.

His father had died shortly before. H. R. Harris had been a Navy man twenty-one years and then an Augusta police detective until age sixty-five. Like brothers, Charlie and H.R. hunted together, drank together, told each other stuff they didn't tell their wives.

His daddy's death left an awful hole, and Harris filled it with drinking. At the same time, his marriage had fallen apart, and so had his job at the paper mill, where he'd worked twenty-three years and been a union steward.

He'll tell you he'd been a terror. Raised rough, was rough. Had the scraggly beard, the Dixie ballcap. Was in trouble, was trouble. These are his words. A ruffian, a hard-knocker, a man who slipped a .38 into the small of his back under his belt because you never knew where you might find yourself.

We're at the Harris kitchen table, where Charlie's wife has made up some sandwiches, tea, and red-velvet cake. Charlie calls Eleanor a sweet-faced angel, because even though they had drifted apart before he did the Augusta thing, she stuck by him through prison and they've been together ever since.

She's a Sunday school teacher at their Methodist church; he's the Sunday school superintendent and lay leader. Their minister, Charles M. Smith, says: "This church means everything to Charlie. If it weren't for him and his family, we'd fold up."

Harris tells this story because — well, he might as well tell it, because it's not going away. Yes, he did the thing at Augusta, and he's not ashamed of one bit of it. He paid for what he did and he found God. Good story. So he's telling it because he wants everybody to know if God can do this miracle for Charlie Harris, He can do it for anybody. "People like me can get transformed, but not by prison life," he says. "It's when the Lord gets you by the ears."

That hadn't happened as of October 22, 1983. "I believed in God, but I didn't live the Ten Commandments. If I'd had God in my heart the way I do now, I'd have not done it. I was weak."

Anyway, Harris busted through the gate and rolled down the driveway toward the clubhouse. There he saw Ronald Reagan. Not at the sixteenth green, as the White House later said.

"I never had any idea of shooting the president. If I'd wanted to kill him, I'd have driven up to him and done it. I just wanted to talk to him. I was protesting our government giving our jobs to foreign people."

Driving through the gate had been worry enough. "They might've had rocket launchers to blow me back to Washington Road." Still alive, a guy better not pull right up to Reagan. That might really get him dead.

He parked Ol' Blue and took out the .38. "It wasn't to hurt anybody, it was just to get where I needed to get."

Gun in hand, he walked a club chauffeur, Roy Sullivan, toward the golf shop. There he let Sullivan go. "I told him, 'If you look behind my seat in the truck, there's a bottle of tequila, and I'd be pleased if you drank it all.'"

In the golf shop, Harris held six people — four club employees and two White House staffers, one of whom he sent to tell the president he wanted to talk. Kris Hardy, a golf shop clerk, saw Harris come in. "He was very agitated and kept saying, 'They don't think I mean business.' I think he was stunned he got that far. You could tell he'd been drinking. He said, 'I've lost my job and I've lost my family and my daddy's gone and I want to talk to the president.'"

Hardy saw the .38 at the chauffeur's back. "Roy's eyes were big as saucers."

Because it got quiet, Hardy's nervous foot-tapping caught Harris's attention. Hardy says Harris asked, "How old are you, anyway?"

Someone whispered to Hardy, then twenty-three, "Tell him you're twelve," and Hardy compromised: "I'm nineteen."

"You're too young to be in here," Harris said. He let him go.

Hardy today is an Augusta real estate appraiser. "Whatever story you're doing," he says, "I hope it doesn't make it sound like 'poor ol' Charlie was just a good ol' boy down on his luck and didn't mean anything by it.' My take is, I've had good days and bad days, but I've never threatened anybody with a gun."

One by one, Harris let hostages leave. He saw helicopters lower black-suited commandos. Sharpshooters set up near the putting green.

Harris says he took from bodyguards "a stack of guns." White House accounts didn't mention that, but would they? If a rowdy good ol' boy packing heat ker-lumphed his pickup truck through your perimeter, the truck's horn playing "Dixie," and drove up within eyeball distance of the president, would you tell the whole Keystone Kops truth? When Charlie chose to knock down Gate 3, after all, there was no guard there.

Jim Armstrong, now as then Augusta's general manager, was a hostage. About all he'll say is, "That's wrong," when asked about accounts that he was the last hostage and escaped. "I honestly was not in there that long."

The escape story likely came from David Spencer, the club's co-professional. An authorized history of Augusta National reported that Harris "held a pistol to Spencer's head, and he threatened to shoot off Spencer's fingers one at a time if the president wasn't brought to see him. . . . Spencer was held at gunpoint for two tense hours. He finally managed to escape during a moment of confusion when some food was sent in for Harris."

Harris calls that account "the biggest lie." Spencer today will not talk about the incident.

Reagan made at least two phone calls to the golf shop. In one call monitored by news media, he said, "This is the president of the United States. This is Ronald Reagan. I understand you want to talk to me. . . . If you are hearing me, won't you tell me what you want?"

Harris thought it was Reagan on tape, a trick. He hung up without speaking and told Secret Service agents, "I'll give you my gun when he shows his face through that door. I've risked my life here. I'm not going to hurt anybody. I just want to talk to the man." Hey, he'd voted for Reagan. And loved his movies. Still does.

By 4:20, two hours in, Harris was done. The president had left in a speeding motorcade that included grim Secret Service agents hanging on an open car, machine guns pointing in every direction. You'd have thought Charlie Harris had been identified as the point man of a massive redneck assault.

"With Reagan gone, I put my gun down and figured I might as well take my punishment," Harris says.

Secret Service agents treated Harris courteously. They did pick up his .38 and say it never would have fired. "Bouncin' at clubs, I'd done hit so many people with that trigger guard, it was bent in," Harris says. "I picked the gun back up and shot through a window, just to show 'em."

That was the day's only gunshot.

Horrific news came seven hours later. A suicide bomber, driving a truck, penetrated the defenses of the U.S. Marine barracks in Beirut, Lebanon, and detonated 12,000 pounds of explosives, killing 241 Marines, soldiers and sailors.

Charlie was off the front pages.

No federal charges were filed against Harris. He spent five years in state prison for false imprisonment. When Georgia's maximum-security prison put the hell-raisin' Harris "in the hole," a solitary-confinement guard brought Harris a small Bible.

"I hadn't been sleepin' and eatin', and I was so full of hatred I didn't care if I made it or not," Harris says. "Finally, I took that little Bible off the shelf and started readin'. More I read, better I slept and ate. My temper started layin', everything started easin' out."

There in the hole, God took him by the ears. "It's hard to be a Christian in jail, but I told the Lord every night, if He just give me my family back and get me out of prison without killin' somebody, I'll do whatever He wants."

After his release in 1987, Harris regularly reported to his Augusta probation officer. Robby Hardaway says: "I never had a minute's trouble with Charlie."

The Secret Service monitored Harris for four years. Now he says an agent calls and asks to visit only if a high-profile government official is in Georgia. Harris works at a chemical plant near Augusta. He long ago quit drinking, cold turkey. He does his church work. He goes hunting and fishing.

We're standing by the truck. He shows me dings in a chrome frame around the right headlight. "That's where we hit the gate."

He puts a hand on Ol' Blue's hood. "Y'know, if trucks could talk, you'd really have a good story."

One more question: "Charlie, you ever been back to Augusta National?"

He says, "They asked me not to." There's a twinkle in his eye. "But you got a ticket?"

GREG CHILD

Fear of Falling

FROM OUTSIDE

Climbing out of hell — B.C.

THE FIRST SHOT hits the cliff at 6:15 A.M. The sun is rising over Central Asia, sending shafts of daylight through the gaps in a ridge-line of craggy summits, brightening the steep, shadowy Kara Su Valley of Kyrgyzstan's Pamir Alai range. Deep in sleep, their two Portaledges dangling one thousand feet off the ground, the four climbers barely react to the thump of lead hitting granite. But when the second report echoes through the gorge, Jason "Singer" Smith bolts upright.

"What the hell was that?" he shouts, donning his helmet instinctively, assuming the rifle crack is the clatter of rockfall.

"We're being shot at, Singer!" Beth Rodden calls out in alarm from the other portaledge.

"That's irrational," Smith replies. "It's probably local hunters."

Then the third bullet hits right between the two platforms. Rock chips fly out of the crater, spraying the climbers.

"That was definitely for us!" Rodden shouts.

The climbers are bunked high on Mount Zhioltaya Stena, a twelve-thousand-foot peak in this rugged former Soviet republic. It is August 12, day two of a planned four-day ascent of the twenty-five-hundred-foot Yellow Wall, and they are making their way up to a sheer headwall, looking forward to sinking their hands into a highway of cracks splitting the face. The quartet represents a re-markable pool of American climbing talent, friends from years on the rock-wall circuit out West. A self-assured twenty-two-year-old Utah native, Smith lives in his van in California. He has made a slew of notable ascents, including a fourteen-day solo of the four-thousand-foot big wall of Mount Thor, near the Arctic Circle on Canada's Baffin Island. His nickname, Singer, is derived from his penchant for stitching up kitschy clothing on an old sewing machine. Lying beside Singer is Texas-raised John Dickey, the team photographer. Bearded, lanky, and at twenty-five the old man of the group, he's a seasoned world traveler and, since he moved to California six years ago, a frequent backcountry climber in the High Sierra. Rodden is a diminutive blond twenty-year-old from Davis, California, with an angelic face that makes her look five years younger. Her appearance belies her toughness, however; she is one of the very few women — and the youngest — to have climbed at the top 5.14 rating of difficulty. Her soft-spoken boyfriend and bunkmate, Tommy Caldwell, twenty-two, is from Colorado. Built like a cross between a pit bull and a greyhound, he has laid claim to what is possibly America's hardest sport route, Kryptonite, a pitch near Rifle, Colorado, rated 5.14d. The group helicoptered into the Kara Su Valley from Bishkek, Kyrgyzstan's capital, two weeks ago, and they've got another good month of climbing to go. After they set up a base camp, Rodden and Caldwell began putting in this new route up the Yellow Wall while Smith and Dickey spent four days trekking down valley in an unsuccessful search for a telephone, to call about a lost duffel. Their journey had taken them past a Kyrgyz army camp and over a fourteen-thousand-foot pass, where they met yak herders who'd never seen foreigners.

The climbers peer over the edges of their portaledges and in the gathering light spot three men on the rubble-strewn slope below. The men wave their hands, gesturing that they should come down. The Americans yell to them to cease fire. Still sitting in their sleeping bags, they stare at each other with stunned expressions. Among them they can cope with any horror the mountains might dish out: avalanche, rockfall, stormy weather; surely this situation can somehow be worked out, too. Hanging here they are sitting ducks, so they start to draw straws to see who'll go down first to meet the guys with the guns.

Dickey steps up to the plate. "I'll go," he volunteers.

They tie their ropes end to end and Dickey clips his rappel device onto the nylon strand. He eases over the edge of the Portaledge and swings into the void, carrying down a Motorola two-way radio. As he departs he blithely suggests he'll offer the gunmen a cigarette, a gambit that the laconic Californian has found useful in the Third World for defusing tense situations.

The climbers can't figure out what the trouble is. The area they are in — a complex of high valleys dubbed the Ak Su region — has been visited every summer for twenty years by scores of Russian, European, and American climbers. Renowned for its huge sheets of tawny granite, the Ak Su has been called the Yosemite of Central Asia. All that is required to climb here is a frontier permit from the government of Kyrgyzstan, which the Americans have.

Dickey spins slowly as he rappels down. Twenty-five long minutes pass before he reaches the slope. Through a two-hundred-millimeter camera lens, Smith watches the handshakes between Dickey and the gunmen, sees them reject the proffered pack of cigarettes. Then Dickey radios up.

"These guys want you to come down. They just, er, well, you better come down. They want to go back to our base camp for, er, breakfast." Smith knows Dickey well enough to glean from his quavering tone that something is seriously wrong.

Smith clips his rappel device to the rope and slides down. On the ground he is confronted by two men — the third has left the scene. They are young; they wear fatigues and sport long black hair and beards. The men are packing Kalashnikov assault rifles, grenades, sidearms, and sheathed knives. Smith nervously shakes hands, and they trade names in a patois of gestures and the odd common word of English, Russian, and local dialect. The gunmen are Abdul, who seems to be the commander, and Obert. Smith sees that one is wearing a black Patagonia Gore-Tex jacket under his camo vest and a high-tech rucksack with a German label. Clearly these items were not mail-ordered; at the very least, the Americans figure, they are in the clutches of bandits. But Dickey also remembers seeing a short news story about Japanese geologists taken hostage here in 1999 by a group called the Islamic Movement of Uzbekistan, and the gunmen appear to fit the bill.

Rodden and Caldwell rappel down, and the gunmen indicate that everyone will head to the climbers' base camp, a mile down valley. Their tone is more matter-of-fact than menacing. They even smile occasionally. Yet there's no doubt who's in control. Half out of optimism, half out of a desire to suppress panic in the rest of the team, Dickey coolly reiterates that the gunmen just want some breakfast.

But when the climbers arrive in base camp they see that their tents, which they had sealed by tying the zippers together, are slit open at the walls. The third gunman — Isuf, or Su for short — is posted in the grassy meadow of camp, his weapon at his hip. He's wearing some of their clothing. A fourth man sits against a rock.

At first the Americans mistake this man for another bandit, until Caldwell and Rodden recognize him as Turat, a young Kyrgyz soldier who was friendly when he checked their permit a few days earlier. He's wearing civilian clothes now, and his face is stern. The Americans sit beside him, and when the gunmen aren't looking, Turat starts gesturing and scratching numbers in the sand. He manages to explain that he is a prisoner — taken off-duty, they judge from his dress. Next he holds up three fingers. Then he sweeps his hand across his throat.

"It wasn't hard to figure the math on this one," Smith tells me later. "There were three guys and one girl. I thought he meant that they'll take what they want from camp and then shoot the men."

"*Nyet, nyet,*" Turat insists when he sees the Americans' stricken faces. But the story he eventually gets across is hardly more encouraging: Yesterday he and three fellow soldiers were captured; the rebels executed his comrades, and they are keeping Turat alive as a guide. Turat points to his bloodstained pants — the blood of his friends.

Then Abdul summons Smith and Dickey to their big, yellow main tent. Inside, he and Obert are raiding the larder. They want to know the contents of each can and packet. A strange game of charades begins: When the rebels hold up a can of chicken meat, the climbers cluck "bok bok bok." When they point to a strip of beef jerky they intone "moo."

What the rebels don't want is anything that smacks of "oink oink." And, as Dickey has learned, they are not into tobacco. Turat warns them in a mix of Russian and English not to offer them vodka, either — the Muslims don't drink.

The rebels order the climbers to stuff four packs with about thirty to fifty pounds each of cans, candles, sleeping bags, and clothing. Then they confiscate their four two-way radios. As he packs, Dickey turns to Singer. A crooked, nervous smile contorts his lips.

"We're hostages," he says flatly.

*

This valley, these mountains, this country: It is all remote, but it was widely believed to be safe. As Lonely Planet's guide to Central Asia encourages, "Most travellers vote Kyrgyzstan the most appealing, accessible, and welcoming of the former Soviet Central Asian republics," touting the incredible peaks of the central Tien Shan and Pamir Alai ranges. Tourism, the book continues, "is one of the few things Kyrgyzstan has to sell to the outside world." Certainly Rodden, Caldwell, Dickey, and Smith had been welcomed warmly here, and their expedition, backed in part by The North Face (which sponsors Smith and Rodden), had not ventured far off the beaten climbing path. In fact, I had climbed here myself in 1995, on an earlier expedition sponsored by The North Face, with Lynn Hill, Alex Lowe, and Conrad Anker. We found a pastoral scene of verdant meadows and a scattered population of seminomadic Kyrgyz — Islamic subsistence farmers who come here in summer, tending yaks and cows. We also found a slew of virgin routes on the stupendous walls of Peak 4810, Peak 3850 (so-called for their heights in meters), and Russian Tower. Two Russian teams and another American group were also there, having helicoptered in from Tashkent, in Uzbekistan, and none of us encountered any hostility.

The next four years were equally calm, and Kyrgyzstan gained a reputation as Asia's hottest mountain playground. As recently as August 1999, the outfitter Mountain Travel–Sobek took trekkers to the same base camp where the climbers were kidnapped. But the frontiers of adventure, those last undiscovered and unspoiled places, are often the frontiers of political instability and civil conflict. They are often unspoiled not only because they are geographically remote, but also because they were historically frozen in place — for more than fifty years in Kyrgyzstan's case — by the geopolitical dictates of the Cold War. And now, as former outposts of the Soviet empire become hot zones of regional tension, they can also become dangerous to travelers. Fearing trouble, Mountain Travel–Sobek canceled its Ak Su trek this summer. And as Lonely Planet Online does warn adventure travelers heading for the boondocks of Kyrgyzstan, "There's a great temptation to hop off the bus in the middle of nowhere and hike into the hills, but this is not recommended if you value your life."

Indeed, Central Asia is a political powder keg — so much so that U.S. State Department officials refuse to even discuss the remote border regions of Kyrgyzstan, Tajikistan, and Uzbekistan on the record. But one official lists a Balkans-style litany of troubles: a five-year civil war that has killed fifty thousand in Tajikistan; a weak Kyrgyzstan army; a repressive Soviet-style Uzbekistan government whose policies inflame the fundamentalist Islamic opposition. The most unstable element in this cauldron is war-torn, Taliban-controlled Afghanistan, now the world's greatest narco-state, churning out forty-six hundred tons of opium last year — even more than the Golden Triangle. Afghanistan is widely believed to be where militant groups like the Islamic Movement of Uzbekistan [IMU] — the climbers' captors — get their training. Funding is handed out in the form of heroin. Rebels sell the drugs through pipelines to China, Russia, and Europe, and use the proceeds to buy arms from Russian, Chechen, and other sources. Much of this contraband is funneled across Central Asia's porous mountain borders, through high valleys like the Ak Su and Kara Su.

The IMU is a twelve-hundred-man "cross-border, multinational fighting force," says Ahmed Rashid, author of the recent book *Taliban: Militant Islam, Oil, and Fundamentalism in Central Asia*. Mostly Uzbeks, the group's ranks include Afghans, Tajiks, Chechens, Pakistanis, emissaries from Saudi terrorist Osama bin Laden, and Filipino revolutionaries. The IMU, its Sunni Muslim membership having been repressed first by the Soviets and now by Uzbekistan's president-for-life, Islom Karimov, seeks to overthrow Karimov, who has detained up to fifty thousand Muslim men from the country's Ferghana Valley. The ultimate goal is to create an independent Islamic state in the valley — one that, like Afghanistan, would adhere to the strictest eye-for-an-eye Sharia religious law. Led by Juma Namangani, an Uzbek warlord, the IMU operates out of the high mountains of Uzbekistan and Tajikistan, which embrace southwestern Kyrgyzstan from north and south. The Ak Su lies between their mountain stronghold and Ferghana, the object of their desire.

On August 23, 1999, IMU guerrillas poured over Tajik passes in the Pamirs into southwestern Kyrgyzstan, attacked Kyrgyz soldiers, and seized four Japanese geologists. The hostages languished in Tajik camps for sixty-four days until their release. The Japanese and Kyrgyzstan governments claim that no ransom was paid, but as sources in the U.S. State Department and the independent Central

Asia Institute confirm, several million dollars may have changed hands.

If ransom was paid, then the climbers who flock to the Ak Su would represent an irresistible cash crop. And since the Japanese incident, the State Department insists, it has posted explicit warnings on its Web site about fighting and kidnapping risks in the area. When Smith, Dickey, Rodden, and Caldwell left the States on July 25, the site displayed a "Public Announcement" dated June 15, 2000, and, as it does for every country, a "Consular Information Sheet." Dated November 17, 1999, Kyrgyzstan's sheet cautioned U.S. citizens "to avoid all travel west and south of the southern provincial capital Osh." But these alerts stopped short of a full-fledged "Travel Warning," which advises Americans to avoid a country completely. The climbers read some, but not all, of this advice, and they interpreted much of it as outdated. They did not contact the U.S. embassy when they landed in Bishkek. Their Kyrgyz travel agent, Ak Sai Tours, made no mention of danger, nor did the helicopter crew that flew them to the Ak Su, nor did the Kyrgyz soldiers who checked their permits.

At around noon on August 12, Abdul orders his five captives to dismantle the base camp. When Turat tugs a long, sturdy aluminum tent stake out of the ground, he feels the pointed end with his finger and catches Smith's eye. It is clear that Turat wants to use the stakes as daggers. Earlier, he furtively signaled that he will try to kill the rebels if he can, and that there are fifteen Kyrgyz soldiers in the valley and seventeen rebels. Fighting is imminent.

Seeing the desperate look on Turat's face, Smith scans the ransacked base camp and decides that the odds are not very good. The three men carrying assault rifles are alert and wary. "No way, Turat," Smith whispers, shaking his head. "No way."

The climbers pack their leftover gear into duffel bags, and the rebels conceal these under pine boughs. Abdul indicates to them that they should carry their passports in their pockets. That's a good sign, Dickey thinks; it means they want us alive. Still, as they prepare to move out, they are terrified; their teeth are chattering. Rodden, as the only woman, is particularly apprehensive, her mind racing, thinking, "What'll these guys do to me?"

As they pack, Abdul comes across a photo of a smiling Beth and Tommy, arm in arm. He points to the young couple, and in sign language asks if they are together. "Yes — married," Dickey says instantly. If the rebels think Rodden is married, he reasons, maybe she'll be safer.

Then the radio squawks — a message from Su's nearby position on the small rise. Abdul orders everyone to scramble under trees, and seconds later the windy roar of a Russian-made Mi8 gunship fills the valley. The climbers watch as the dronelike helicopter flies toward the Yellow Wall and rises until it is level with the deserted portaledge camp. Abdul sees that Rodden is distraught; he shakes his finger at her and smiles, signing, "Don't cry." The chopper hovers long enough to see that the platforms are abandoned and then retreats down the Kara Su Valley, seemingly in the direction of the Kyrgyz army camp, twenty-five miles away, that Smith and Dickey had seen on their trek.

Abdul barks orders, and they quit base camp hastily. It is clear they are going on a long walk — probably, Turat is indicating, all the way to Uzbekistan, fifty miles north. About a mile from base camp they near the confluence of the Kara Su and the Ak Su, at which point the two rivers form the Karavshin. Scouting for soldiers, the rebels creep from one boulder to another along the riverside trail. Suddenly the helicopter makes another sweep and the climbers are ordered into the bushes. Leveling his rifle point-blank at Dickey, Abdul screams that anyone who attracts the attention of the helicopter crew is dead. Again the Mi8 departs.

As they walk, Smith tries to reassure Rodden. "Your concern is no longer Beth," he tells her. "I'm thinking about Beth from now on. All you are thinking about is whatever these men tell you to do. If you see a helicopter I want you to play James Bond and jump headfirst into whatever tree these guys tell you to jump into. This is just a big giant video game and we are gonna turn it off in a couple of hours."

Quaking, Rodden nods.

The group traverses along the slope of a hill separating the Kara Su and the Ak Su Valleys. At this point Obert marches off down valley. At about 1:00 P.M. they stand two hundred yards uphill from a mud-brick farmhouse. Beyond it a footbridge spans the Ak Su as it crashes downstream. Two Kyrgyz soldiers are outside the house, talking to the farmer. The rebels order their prisoners to sneak uphill through the trees; then Abdul urges them to run. When Rodden starts lagging under her pack, Smith grabs it. It is bright orange, a certain target. Twenty minutes later the group crests the hill. Gasping and sweating, they rest. Turat sits among the climbers, with the rebels watching from a few feet away.

"Over there," he signs to his fellow captives, pointing across the river. "Over there they kill me."

Sometime after 3:00 P.M. the shooting starts. The band of guerrillas and prisoners has stumbled downhill, across the bridge, and up the east side of the Ak Su Valley onto a steep, forested slope covered in boulders. The rebels have then split the hostages into two groups and hidden them under sprawling junipers. Another young rebel named Abdullah has joined them and the fighters have taken up positions among the rocks, laying, Dickey figures, an ambush. Everybody waits.

More soldiers are advancing up the hill, shouting to one another, when Abdul gives the order to fire. Within minutes two Kyrgyz soldiers are felled. Adbul's firearm is a cannon, a fast-action AK-74 — more like an M-16 than the other rebels' AK-47s. Rodden, Caldwell, and Turat hunker behind a tree trunk, shielding their faces from the flying shell casings, ricochets, and rock chips. Ten minutes into the firefight Abdul scurries to the boulder and calls Turat's name. Turat is calm, Caldwell notices — "the toughest man I've ever seen," he'll say later — though it is clear the soldier is about to be executed. Caldwell has his arms around Rodden. She is weeping and shaking.

Turat turns to Rodden and, in the mix of words and hand signs with which they have learned to communicate, he tells her, "You, don't cry. I don't cry, and I am the one who will die."

Then he stands and walks toward Abdul, and the two disappear behind a car-size boulder two hundred feet up the hill. The climbers hear two quick reports of a pistol, and then silence.

The battle continues, as Kyrgyz soldiers outflank the rebels. Abdul announces that everyone must move up to the boulder where Turat was taken. Dickey takes the lead, shouldering his pack and sprinting. The Kyrgyz soldiers draw a bead on him. Shots thump around his feet as close as nine inches. He sloughs off his pack and dives toward the boulder. The pack, lying on the ground, is riddled with bullets.

Smith runs to the boulder next; then Rodden. When she arrives, he twists her head away from Turat's corpse. Caldwell arrives last, chased by rifle fire, and wraps himself around Rodden like a shield. Behind the boulder now are the four Americans, Abdul, Su, and Abdullah.

"Abdullah was sitting against Turat's corpse," Smith will later recall. "He picked up Turat's arm and dropped it. Both he and Abdul laughed. Then Abdul kicked Turat's legs aside so he could make room to do his evening prayer. Bullets were raining over his head and he was kneeling, praying."

It is 4:00 P.M. when the first mortar round whistles in, exploding against the front of the boulder. The climbers huddle together in a ball of arms and legs. Heavy rifle fire zeroes in on them. When they look up they see Kyrgyz soldiers in positions one hundred feet from the boulder. The whup-whup-whup of a helicopter, spotting overhead, adds to the noise. Smith is crouched over Turat's legs, wondering if he should pull the body over him and his friends. But the head wound is grotesque.

A third mortar round explodes eighty feet behind them at dusk, and Abdul makes them lighten their loads, ditching the packs and taking just a small sack with a few articles of clothing, credit cards, Turat's sleeping bag, a dozen PowerBars, and a handful of candy. This will be the total rations for six people for the next four days. At nightfall they run uphill, from tree to tree, through random fire. They march roughly four miles, heading north, downstream toward the Karavshin. They climb high on the rugged hillside to outrun the creeping light of the waxing moon, which backlights a skyline of shark-tooth peaks.

August 13, 3:00 A.M. The climbers have been moving for eighteen hours. They shuffle forward like zombies. Abdullah has vanished into the night on another mission, and it is just Abdul and Su. At dawn the rebels stop beside a fast-flowing tributary of the Karavshin and order their hostages to crawl into two small caves.

Singer and Caldwell take one, with Su bedded down, gun in hand, at its mouth. Rodden and Dickey, with Abdul on guard, take the other. At first Dickey cannot believe that Abdul is serious when he motions them into "a small-ass little hole with a mud floor." The cave is eighteen inches tall at its highest point. It is cramped for Rodden, who is five-foot-one, but Dickey, at six feet, can only lie with his knees to his chest. Spooning with Dickey, Rodden cries on and off all day. "Do you think anyone knows where we are?" she asks. "They're not gonna kill us, are they?" Dickey is as terrified as she. In the early afternoon, sun-warmed glacial melt swells the river, and the stream pours into the cave. Wallowing in four inches of ice water, in thermal undershirts, Dickey and Rodden shiver for seventeen hours.

They emerge as the moon creeps over the opposite ridge. The food in their stomachs is long gone, replaced by lonely cramps; their captors are as hungry as they are. The rebels intend to cross the river, but fording it is out of the question — the rapids are Class IV. So Abdul and Su try to maneuver a log over the foaming torrent. They push the log halfway across; then it jams.

Suddenly Smith kicks off his shoes and wades into the waist-deep water. The current nearly overpowers him and the rebels call for him to return, shouting and gesturing, "danger, danger." Smith ignores them. He muscles the log toward the opposite bank, crouches atop a slick boulder, and steadies the log. Shouting above the roar, he motions for everyone to cross. Dickey goes first.

"What the hell was with that?" he asks.

"We gotta get out of here," Smith says.

Watching the rebels bungle the river crossing, Smith and the others realize that there are a lot of things they can do to help themselves. As Smith will put it later. "One: They should think we were 100 percent behind their cause. Two: We should show them we were tough as nails because for all we knew they might eliminate the weak; somebody twists an ankle, they would kill them. Three: It would help if we were super-cool and helpful to them, because that would lead to . . . Four: They could trust us."

And indeed, as Abdul balances across the wobbling log, he pauses at the final hop onto the boulder. Smith extends his hand and — to his astonishment — Abdul hands over his rifle. Smith passes the weapon to Dickey, then grips Abdul's hand. There is only one moment to react: Smith must kick the log out from under Abdul and send him into the rapids, and Dickey must flip the safety on the automatic and drop Su. If the idea works they are free; if not, Su will kill them. But the moment passes and Abdul reaches the bank.

The guerrilla smiles and praises Smith's courage. "You soljah?" he asks.

Half a PowerBar per day, brown, silty river water to drink, and cold, torturously confined bivouacs take their toll on the hostages as they spend the nights of August 14, 15, and 16 marching around cliffs and steep rubble on the east flank of the Karavshin Valley. On the third night they only get four hundred yards before Smith collapses. Rodden sees that he's exhausted, so she takes out their last candy bar, a Three Musketeers — how fitting, she thinks — breaks it into small chunks, and pushes it into his mouth.

They pass no huts, no farmers. None live this far up the steep hillsides, and afraid of both the soldiers and the rebels, the locals give each faction a wide berth. Surreal moments abound. The whole valley, in fact, has turned nightmarish. On August 14 the hostages may have noticed the faint sound of a gun battle far down the Karavshin Valley. Rebel snipers had thirty Kyrgyz soldiers pinned in a crossfire in a narrow canyon. None survived. Later the Americans will pass that way and find blood-spattered rocks and a bullet-riddled field jacket. During the next two weeks the conflict will escalate all along the Kyrgyzstan-Tajikistan border. Firefights will claim up to forty-eight Kyrgyz soldiers, twelve antirebel Uzbek soldiers, and seventy-five rebels. More foreigners will be kidnapped. Elsewhere in the region, Russian border guards stationed near the Afghanistan-Tajikistan border will clash with rebels, and a passenger on a train leaving Tashkent bound for Kyrgyzstan will be arrested carrying twenty kilos of explosives.

But for all the climbers know, they are alone. Surely, they think, the Kyrgyz army knows they've been taken: Helicopters are ever-present, and one afternoon, as Rodden and Dickey lie hidden beside Abdul at the second bivouac, two soldiers walk to within a yard of them. Rodden's blond hair is visible through the pine boughs. The men say something in Kyrgyz and leave. But nobody moves: Abdul carries a grenade fixed to his belt; if someone makes a move he pulls the pin and everyone dies.

Killing has become the main topic at Smith and Caldwell's bivouac. Bashing in the rebels' heads with rocks, stealing their handguns, pushing them off cliffs, using choke holds and sharp sticks, punching them in the larynx, and strangling them with bootlaces are all discussed. Smith talks; Caldwell listens, quietly taking it in.

"How do you know all this stuff?" Caldwell asks.

"I hung out with thugs at school. I read *The Anarchist Cookbook,*" comes the glib reply. Then Smith pauses and thinks about what is happening to his mind.

"Tommy, when I woke up today I realized I had lost all compassion for these men. I don't hate them. But I'm ready to do whatever it takes to get out of here."

Caldwell nods.

That day Smith begins working on winning Su's trust. When helicopters appear he nudges him awake and helps to camouflage their hiding places with more brush. On the move, he stops to lend his captor a hand on short cliffs, patting him on the back and telling him he's a "good alpinista," much to Su's amusement.

Su clearly defers to Abdul, who looks ten years older than his claimed age of twenty-six. (The climbers doubt he's even called Abdul, in fact, as the other rebels carefully avoid addressing him by name.) But, Smith will say later, "At first Su scared me the most. He had a really blank look on his face. But soon I was doing things like showing him my passport, comparing ages and birth places with him. He told me he was nineteen and came from Tashkent."

By the night of August 16, day five, the group descends the hillside back to the Karavshin. To their amazement they start walking upstream, toward their Kara Su base camp. During the five-mile march the rebels shift into battle mode and fan out in front. The Americans consider running, but they know that in their weak condition — they are now out of food — they won't get far before they are mowed down. Yet the rebels are getting lax.

They cross the bridge near the battleground and enter the Kara Su Valley. Abdul gives the order to bivouac — in another set of coffinlike holes in the riverbank — and signals that he'll go ahead and kill some soldiers to get some food. Before he leaves he pulls Dickey's boots off his feet and tries them on. They are too large so he tosses them back.

"You fucker," Dickey sneers.

Then Abdul makes Smith hand over his insulated coat, leaving him in a T-shirt, angry and freezing. But what catches Smith off guard is Abdul's parting message — a mix of words and gestures that clearly means, "Su will protect you." As if he were now one of them.

Before a storm, climbers always sense tension. The changing weather charges the atmosphere with a last-chance sort of feeling. On August 17, the sixth day of captivity, clouds fill the sky. The temperature is near freezing, the air damp. Something's brewing. Before dawn Abdul returned with two stinking, greasy forty-pound sacks. One contains salty yak butter, the other balls of congealed yogurt — Abdul and Su, as desperate and starving as their charges, start in on the provisions, most likely taken from a farmer. The Americans each force down one or two of the rancid balls. In his bivvy cave Smith sits on the suitcase-size slab of butter, insulation against the cold rocks. For the first time in a long time, Caldwell prays.

At dusk they get under way again. Abdul explains that they must climb the rugged west side of the Kara Su Valley to a plateau three thousand feet above. There they will rendezvous, waiting several days if necessary, with Abdullah and Obert — who the Americans think must be dead, judging from their radio silence these last two days and several distant bursts of fire. Eventually they will be taken north, to Uzbekistan, the hostages are told.

Then Abdul turns away, signing that he will catch up after he heads up to the Americans' base camp, where the stashed duffels hold fresh radio batteries. It is 10:00 P.M. From where they stand, at the foot of a perilously steep climb that they'll have to tackle without ropes, it is an hour to base camp, an hour back. Su is now their only guard; the hostages will have most of the night alone with him. As they begin to climb the succession of slabby cliffs and steep grassy slopes, Dickey turns to his companions and says, "We gotta whack this guy, tonight."

Stifled by rain clouds, the now full moon rounds the mountainside and bleeds onto the group as it reaches a point two thousand feet above the river. The Americans and their guard climb a moderately difficult rib, a series of 5.2 pitches, flanked by glacier-carved cliffs. Smith and Dickey shadow Su the whole way, openly talking about finding a place to push him off. But they are each burdened with the heavy bags of butter and yogurt balls, and Smith has Turat's sleeping bag draped clumsily around his shoulders, like a shawl.

"We had all been talking about killing someone for days," Caldwell will remember, clearly uncomfortable with the memory, "but Beth had said to me she just didn't think I could emotionally handle it. So I was staying out of it."

"Alpinista!" Su orders Smith to the front. He waves his hand at the cliff as if to ask, "Which way?"

Smith heads up the sixty-degree face, pointing out the handholds to Su, urging him on like a guided client. Su slings his AK-47 over his shoulder and scrambles up. A shove here would be fatal, and Smith steps into position to body-slam Su off the ledge. But the rebel skirts around him, oblivious, and starts up another step of rock.

"O.K., this is it," Dickey says in a trembling voice. He hands Smith the sack of yogurt balls and climbs into position, just below Su.

"Come on, do it, John," comes a collective murmur out of the night. But Su moves beyond Dickey's reach. It is now midnight. They are near the top of the last cliff. Somebody has to do something.

Caldwell is thinking his friends might not do it. And he starts worrying about how they would survive a storm up here, worrying about Beth, wondering what will happen to them all in Uzbekistan. He turns to Beth and asks, "Do you want me to do it?" She doesn't say anything. Then he starts moving toward Su.

Fueled by a wave of adrenaline, Caldwell scrambles across the ledge and up the cliff. He reaches up, grabs the rifle slung over Su's back, and pulls. A faint breath of surprise, a sound like *whaaa*, escapes Su's lips. He is falling.

The rebel arcs through the circle of the moon, pedaling air. The climbers see him hit a ledge thirty feet down with a crack. Then Su rolls off into the darkness, over the fifteen-hundred-foot cliff to the river below.

Caldwell is screaming. Clambering up the cliff in seconds, he curls up in a ball and begins gasping, "Holy shit, I just killed a guy."

Rodden reaches him and embraces him. "How can you love me now?" Caldwell sobs. "After I did this?"

"You just saved my life, Tommy," she answers. "I couldn't love you more."

Then Dickey is shouting, "Let's go, let's go!" But Caldwell, the one least likely to have acted on their talk of killing Su, is beside himself.

"Tommy, listen to me," Smith shouts into his face. "We did nothing wrong. We just saved our lives. When we get home we'll say we all did it, O.K.? But right now we have to get the fuck out of here. Go!"

They take off at a frantic pace, moving diagonally downhill, occasionally pausing to console Caldwell and catch their breath. Then the sound of rocks sliding behind them stops their hearts and they run again, stumbling over scree until, at 1:15 in the morning, they reach the Karavshin.

Beside the river is a well-worn trail that Smith and Dickey recognize from their trek; from here it is eighteen miles to the Kyrgyz army camp. They are nearly hallucinating from fatigue, yet they keep stumbling forward. A herd of cows, moonlit in their path, frightens them: They mistake them for rebels. The climbers hug the shadows, running from tree to tree.

Hours later, they cross a footbridge near a bend in the river; now they are just a mile and a half from the army camp and a few hundred yards from a forward outpost. They're on the home stretch. But suddenly three men — rebels — materialize out of the forest, one of them just fifteen feet behind them. One shouts something, then the muzzle flash and crack of AK-47s fills the night. Yellow tracers fly past their heads.

Dickey dives behind a bush. Caldwell and Rodden hide behind a rock. Smith starts running, dodging bullets, but alone and in front he suddenly feels naked, and he turns and runs back to the others. The four collide and then run together toward the outpost. It occurs to Caldwell that rebels might be manning that, too, but there is no turning back. Then shots from the front streak over their heads. Shots in front, shots behind. They are in no-man's-land. A figure stands in the doorway of a nearby hut, aiming a rifle at them. Army or rebels? They can't tell. They dive into the dark hut anyway.

Smith is first over the threshold. "*Americanski! Americanski!*" he shouts, holding his hands high.

All they see are gun barrels. Heaving with fear the four sprawl facedown on the dirt floor. Hands frisk them. Then one of the dark figures detects that Rodden is a woman.

"Oh, madame!" the man says, surprised. He removes his hands from her and steps back apologetically.

"We almost made it," shouts Rodden, confused, thinking Abdul will step forward any moment.

"We did make it, Beth!" Smith cries.

Minutes later Kyrgyz soldiers are thrusting cans of sardines and canteens of water into their hands. The soldiers have turned back the rebels. It is 4:00 A.M. on August 18. The climbers have escaped.

*

If their ordeal took place in a mountainous black hole, the four Americans now step into a whirlwind. A hurried hike with soldiers through the blood-soaked canyon gets them to a helicopter that whisks them to the town of Batken. That morning, the U.S. embassy learns for the first time that Americans have been kidnapped. Dressed in ill-fitting Kyrgyz army fatigues — their clothes are in tatters and they have lost all their gear — the climbers appear on Kyrgyzstan's state-run TV. They are hailed as heroes. They board the private jet of President Askar Akayev. They fly to Bishkek, where they are met by U.S. embassy officials and they make their first calls home. While in Bishkek they learn they weren't the only climbers taken hostage: Six Germans, three Russians, two Uzbeks, and a Ukrainian either escaped or were rescued in military operations on August 16. By September 5, Minister Councillor Nurdek Jeenbaez of the Kyrgyz embassy in Washington, D.C., claims that the rebels have been pushed out of the area by his country's forces. Abdul, Obert, and Abdullah have most likely died fighting or faded back into the mountain passes of the Pamir. No one can say if Su's body has been found.

By August 25, all four climbers are home. When they hit the San Francisco tarmac, they slip back into their lives — or try. Caldwell and Rodden are reunited with their close-knit families, and Tommy is soon back up on the Colorado cliffs with his main ropemate, his father, Mike. Dickey and his girlfriend head to the Burning Man Festival in the Nevada desert. Smith returns to his Chevy van and to his job at The North Face, where he runs the A5 division, which makes high-end climbing accoutrements. And in press conferences, morning TV shows, and interviews, the four friends hedge around discussion of the death of Su. We all pushed him, they insist. That's the pact they had made; they would stick together.

Then one night Caldwell phones me from the Roddens' house in Davis. He has been reticent all along, reluctant to talk. This time, though, he sounds sure of himself. "This is the deal," he says. He takes a deep breath. "I was the one who pushed Su. It was something I wasn't prepared to do, so when I did it I was pretty shaken up. Jason and John said that we would say we all did it. That helped me a lot. I'm still coming to terms with it."

Smith is coming to terms with the experience in a different way. "When we reached the army camp," he tells me as we drive in his van to the Oakland airport in late August, "I said to everyone that if there was a week in my life I would want to relive, then this would be it. To experience every human emotion in such a short time, under those intense, life-threatening circumstances. I would gladly go back."

I have heard war veterans say such things. And I have said the same, in private, about peaks that took friends' lives and that I felt sure had been about to take mine. But veterans of combat and survivors of high-mountain accidents carry a burden that takes time to understand.

In the long run, Beth Rodden may be speaking for all four climbers when she admits to me, three weeks after their return to America, that she has begun having nightmares. "I see Abdul," she says. "I see weird concoctions of battles. My friends are in them, and I'm always running from something."

Postscript

In a remarkable twist of fate, while the issue of *Outside* magazine that ran this story was being printed it was discovered that the rebel Su had survived his fall and was a prisoner of the Kyrgyz military. In March 2001, I traveled to Kyrgyzstan with the former hostages Jason Smith and John Dickey, and in a prison cell we interviewed Su (whose real name turned out to be Rafshan Sharipov), who was awaiting trial on charges of terrorism. For all parties, it was an emotional encounter.

MICHAEL DILEO

Deer Prudence

FROM TEXAS MONTHLY

Michael got his gun — B.C.

WHEN MY FATHER-IN-LAW handed me the rifle that first time, I
nearly dropped it, caught off guard by its heft. This was not entirely
surprising, since I had never shot a gun in my life. Growing up in
the suburbs outside New York City, having a heart murmur that
kept me out of the Vietnam War, and spending my post-college
years at a commune in the Northern California woods where hunting was banned and animal spirits were worshiped — all these kept
me a gun virgin well into midlife.

"Just try to hit the drum first," Radcliffe told me, pointing at a
blue oil barrel he'd set out across a field at his South Texas ranch.

I raised the bolt-action .270 and looked for the drum in the
sights. "Back your eye away from the scope," Radcliffe advised with
a chuckle. "Otherwise you'll get a shiner when the gun recoils,
and people will think I've been beating you. That's called 'getting
scoped.'"

We made an odd couple, my father-in-law and I: He, a true
Texan, rancher, oilman, expert hunter, Harvard law grad, World
War II vet; I, a Yankee, writer, ex-hippie, pacifist, ecology freak. Still
fit and trim then at eighty, as he is today at ninety, with gray eyes
and a rancher's thin-lipped smile, he was dressed in his typical off-
work wear: a tan hunting shirt, khaki slacks, and a beat-up round-
brimmed fishing hat. I had on my trademark and most un-hunterly
black T-shirt and blue jeans. "By the way, you need to get yourself
some hunting clothes," he told me with apparent disdain. "The
deer are going to see you coming a mile away."

*

For the first several years of my marriage to his daughter, I'd sniffed at Radcliffe's overtures to introduce me to the pleasures of deer hunting. "Maybe with a video camera," I told him once, and he rolled his eyes at my sixties-influenced opinions. In fact, one year I did go out stalking with his VHS camera, an early-eighties model the size of a Gatling gun, and took some terribly indistinct footage of what seemed to be either a big buck or Big Foot.

Then, out of the blue, I gave in. Was it pure curiosity? A desire to please? In truth, I had begun to feel guilty for not taking Radcliffe up on his offer. For here was a man with so much knowledge of the outdoors, the earth, of life itself to pass on. It wasn't his fault that two of his daughters had brought home Yankee writers instead of, more appropriately, flinty-eyed real Texans, the kind who own camouflage Suburbans and learned to shoot before they could crawl.

It had taken me a while to figure out how important deer hunting was in this family, in this whole part of the state, for that matter. Before Tracy and I were married, she'd informed me that Christmas would often be spent with her family in Laredo. *No problema,* I figured. Eat those sugary crispy *buñuelos* for breakfast, shop across the river in lieu of enduring mall madness, carol in Spanish. *Feliz Navidad.* Not being a hunter herself — she'd shot a buck when she was ten years old but was so disheartened by the experience that she never tried again — Tracy neglected to mention the deer thing.

Christmas in South Texas, it turns out, is more about whitetails than reindeer. Deer hunting is a big deal all over Texas — last season some 420,000 whitetails were killed in the state — but in the brush country "buck fever" is truly a sickness. My wife's mother, normally a paragon of social graces, will abandon any family gathering to pursue the eighteen-pointer she's been tracking. All over Laredo people leave work early to head for their deer leases and blinds. The first question at Christmas parties isn't, "What'd Santa bring you?" It's, "Huntin' much?" Or, more typically, "Seen anything?"

One year there was word of considerable poaching on various ranches in the area, so state game wardens helped set up a sting operation. A faux trophy buck with a monstrous set of antlers was created, set in a field on private property, partly concealed in brush, then attached to a system of ropes and pulleys so that it could be moved or pulled down if it was shot at. Sure enough, on the second day, a young fellow stopped his truck, slipped through the fence, and fired. Down went the buck. As the man ran headlong toward his prey, he was apprehended by a game warden. "Okay, okay, you got me," he said breathlessly, "but just let me see my deer."

I took a couple of deep breaths and tried to hold the crosshairs steady, but they kept flopping around uncontrollably. Then Radcliffe demonstrated how to use the gun strap as a brace. Much better. The blue target was relatively calm in the scope.

"Squeeze the trigger. Don't pull," Radcliffe said.

I squeezed. Nothing happened. Perhaps I was taking the squeeze thing too literally, I thought. I squeezed again and sneaked in the slightest suggestion of pull. Something big happened. Lulled by the thousand harmless TV gunfights I'd watched, I was shocked by the power, the kick, the crack of the real thing. Guns stop time. Guns change the world. One moment there is silence, the next there is a break in the space-time continuum, a hole in the universe. Or at least, I hoped, in one blue fifty-five-gallon barrel.

Radcliffe looked through his binoculars. "Dead center!" he cried. "Now try for one of the cans."

Feeling incomparably pleased with myself and inexplicably confident, I aimed the gun at one of the three beer cans Radcliffe had set on top of the barrel but found I couldn't hold steady on such a small target. Patiently, my father-in-law showed me how to shoot from a seated position, a kind of violent lotus pose, with the arm supporting the barrel resting on one knee. As if by magic, the crosshairs were tranquilized. This time, though, I succumbed too much to the temptation to pull the trigger and missed badly.

"Way high," Radcliffe reported. "Just squeeze it."

When the crosshairs settled again, I breathed once and fired. The can flew off the barrel as if blown by a mysterious wind. A clean kill. We drove straight to the convenience store, where I bought my hunting license.

School, however, was not yet out. "Shooting at a still target from close range isn't that hard," Radcliffe told me. "But there's a lot more to hunting. You need to learn gun safety, how to find deer, and how to pick the right one to shoot."

That night I watched a couple of videos. One, called *Fighting*

Whitetails, was a bit of soft-core hunting porn featuring some amazing racks — of antlers, that is. The other one taught how to estimate a deer's age, no mean feat given that there's no cocktail-party conversation to go on, and you can't check their teeth until it's too late. The idea, of course, is to shoot older deer, ones that are going to die within a year or so anyway. The greatest crime would be to wipe out some Gen-X dude with splendid horns on the verge of developing into a truly wondrous beast and thus prevent him from spreading his excellent genes throughout the local populace. The video gave me a feel for judging age, how to look for a certain thickness in the neck, an overall burliness, a heaviness of horn.

Radcliffe offered to drive me around in his truck, but I declined, supremely sophomoric in my purist stance. No truck-hunting for me, and no using the glorified shooting gallery of a corn feeder either. (Even deer blinds struck me as cheating, although I have come to appreciate them in subsequent years and have been known to head out on a misty morning with the *New York Times* and a mug of coffee for a few hours of soul soothing disguised as hunting.) If I was going to be a hunter, I would be a real one: a quiet, reverent stalker. I would get my deer the old-fashioned way. I would earn it.

Then Tracy announced that she wanted to come along. This surprised me, since she'd said her hunting career had ended with the trauma of her tenth year. Back then, her mother had gone to get Radcliffe to clean the deer Tracy had shot, leaving her alone. When they returned, they found their daughter overcome by the magnitude of her deed. She composed an animal-rights haiku titled "The Shot" and swore off hunting forever.

"It will be something we can do together," she said. An imaginary Greek chorus of "real men" groaned in the background. "Besides," she added with a coy smile, "I know some tricks for finding deer." We would set out the next morning, with Radcliffe's blessing.

There are two kinds of winter days in the brush country: Gulf-breeze sweet and cold-front nasty, with not much in between. This happened to be one of the former: a gentle zephyr whispering like the vermouth in a dry martini, a sense of almost amniotic warmth, as a friend once described, "the ambient temperature of the human nap."

The place we chose for our first hunt was a hollow beneath a long ridge that runs toward Mines Road, a once-deserted stretch of highway that now carries heavy truck traffic between the new Colombia bridge and the interstate. This was a decade ago, before NAFTA transformed Laredo into an eighteen-wheeling boomtown, so it was quiet. Only the occasional sound of a hunter's truck broke the silence.

Still stubbornly attired in T-shirt and jeans, I quickly became comfortable with the feel of the rifle on my shoulder, appreciating its weight and solidity. As we wandered in the dreamy morning light through the landscape of velvet and thorn — prickly pear, mesquite, retama, and huisache — I marveled at the peculiar beauty of the countryside. When I first came here from California, the brush country seemed awfully barren and bleak, but over time I've learned to see the subtle charms of a place where nearly every plant has a sticker or thorn, a protective mechanism of some kind. The soft, warm air in midwinter can have a hallucinatory quality. Once, my wife and I fell asleep watching birds by a ranch stock tank on a day just like this and were startled awake by a family of javelinas snuffling at our boots.

The brush country is well known as one of the best deer-hunting areas in the country. The bucks are big — they make Hill Country deer look like a Shetland subspecies — and plentiful. We soon spotted several does, then a couple of bucks, a six-pointer and an eight-pointer, but they were young. It was easy to tell, from their light horns and air of casual naiveté. After an hour or so of walking, we stopped on the crest of a small hill, with a good view of the hollow and the surrounding countryside. Tracy chose that moment to reveal her secret weapon: two pairs of deer antlers, gray and weathered with age.

"Don't tell me you're going to pretend to be a deer," I said.

"No, silly," she replied. "I'm going to rattle you up a buck."

During the rut, or mating season, Tracy informed me, male deer, hyped up on hormones and musk, are attracted to the sound of deer horns clashing. They assume that the ruckus indicates two other males fighting over the affections of some particularly nubile female. Best of all, the most prized examples of masculinity are those likely to be drawn to the bar fight.

"That is ridiculous," I said. "I'm not that gullible."

"Just shut up and watch," she said. "My father taught me how to do this when I was little."

So my wife set to whacking these deer horns together, first one hard clash that rang out over the hills like a rifle's report, then all manner of clacking and rubbing, a percussive mating song. I maintained my skepticism; the whole idea of rattling horns seemed patently absurd. At the same time, I was lulled by the sweetness of the day, the scent of crushed sage in the air, and drifted into a reverie.

I was seated under a couple of small mesquites in my gun-bracing lotus position, looking south, the low morning sun on my face, thinking about nothing much at all, when I snapped to attention for no apparent reason. All I can remember is that I had a sense, inexplicable by rational means, that something was about to happen. Nearby, an old jeep trail ran down the hill we were on and up over another slope. From behind that second hill a set of horns appeared. A big buck with a wide rack, clearly a mature deer, heavy in the chest, was running full tilt toward the rattling sound, until he reached the top of the hill and stopped dead in his tracks, about seventy-five yards away. I peered at him through my binoculars: He appeared huge, elephantine. My heart began pounding. My hands started shaking. I felt sick from the gravity of the moment.

Slipping the gun's safety off, I hesitated for a few seconds, wondering if I really had it in me to attempt to end this animal's life. There wasn't time to think, though; a deer of that size and maturity would not stick around for long. What ended my internal debate was desire: I wanted those horns. More than anything else about the experience, this craving for antlers remains unexplainable to me. It came from deep within, a part of my nature that lay undiscovered for more than four decades. As the crosshairs fixed on the animal's broad chest, I squeezed.

Now I know what it means when someone says, "He went down like he was shot." The buck fell, no, flew backward with tremendous force. His hooves were the last things I saw before his body disappeared behind the hill. "Oh!" my wife cried out, which told me that she hadn't really believed I would pull the trigger, and certainly not hit something if I did. We ran up the hill together, and even though I felt sure the deer would be there, I had heard enough stories about deer getting up from being shot and running off into the brush that the sight of his large body came as a shock. He was just there, fallen between a couple of cacti.

He was not quite as big as he'd seemed but still a fully mature deer, six and a half or older (because deer are born in the spring, they're always half a year past their birthday during hunting season). Nor were his horns as ample as I'd thought: Most of the tines were rather short, although the rack was indeed wide, with eleven points, the smallest just long enough to hold my wedding ring, a good field test for official status.

He was dead yet still in the process of dying, his eyes turning opaque, going from lambent brown to cataract blue as I stared at him. I reached down and felt his warmth and his bristly fur. A series of strange thoughts ran through my head. I was elated, surprised at myself, and yet chastened somehow by the irrevocability of it all. I recalled the 1978 Vietnam War film *The Deer Hunter,* in which Robert De Niro's character expounded on the connection between hunting and manhood and war. This was not my rite of passage to manhood; that happened long ago and through other, more complicated contests. But I did feel somehow as if, for better or worse, I'd at last become a Texan.

"Did my father show you how to clean a deer?" Tracy asked. Her voice was oddly high-pitched. She was excited, too, or upset. I couldn't tell which.

"No," I said, "thank God."

"Well, we have to. We're going to eat this deer. He's not going to waste. Should I?"

She drew out a hunting knife three times the size of the puny Swiss Army blade I carried and, with a cool efficiency, slit the deer up the middle, from his testicles to his chest, where the bullet hole was. Although Tracy grew up on this ranch, she'd left it long ago for Yankee art schools and had always seemed to me far more bohemian than border girl. From that moment on, though, my estimation of her nature and the way her South Texas background still lives within her was forever changed.

Afterward, we shared a moment of silence, giving thanks to the Great Spirit for the chain of plenitude that brings life to the world. I went to get the jeep, we loaded our deer onto it, and headed back to the house. I could hardly wait to see the look in Radcliffe's eyes.

TOURÉ

Kurt Is My Co-Pilot

FROM ROLLING STONE

Step on it! It's in the high-test blood — B.C.

DALE EARNHARDT JR. IS PRETTY GOOD at telling a story. He's telling one now about the thing that changed his life.

"Up until I was fourteen or fifteen, I was real short, and I was kind of an Opie," Junior begins. He's twenty-five now. "I wore Wranglers and cowboy hats and fished and raced around on boats and listened to country music. Then one day changed it all." He's telling this while standing behind the bar in the nightclub he built in the basement of his Mooresville, North Carolina, home. The basement club is dimly lit with purple neon and has tall black stools, mirrored walls, a cooler large enough for eleven cases of Bud, and a framed poster of Kurt Cobain.

"I was a junior in high school, and I went to a buddy's house, and this song came on MTV," he says. "We was gittin' ready to go do some shit, and he's like, 'Man, dude, this song is kickass! Let's just sit here and listen to it 'fore we leave.' And I sit down, and, man, when it was over with I was just fuckin' blown away. It was 'Teen Spirit,' by Nirvana. It fit my emotions. I was tired of listenin' to my parents, I was tired of livin' at home, I didn't know what I was gonna do, I didn't have any direction. The fact that Kurt Cobain could sit there and scream into that mike like that give you a sense of relief. And the guitar riffs, and the way Dave Grohl played the drums? It was awesome." Dale was, that moment, pulled from the good-ol'-boy path and rebaptized by rock & roll.

He went out and bought Nirvana's *Nevermind*. "I couldn't really get anybody else to dig Nirvana like I dug it," he remembers, "and I never heard nobody else listenin' to it in the high school parking lot. When I was listenin' to Nirvana, I felt like I was doin' somethin' wrong. But I didn't care. I'd just sit there and turn it up."

Nirvana led to Pearl Jam, which led to Smash Mouth, Tupac, Third Eye Blind, JT Money, Moby, Mystikal, Matthew Good Band, Busta Rhymes, and Primus. ("That was my first moshing experience. That was awesome.") According to Carlos Santana, "Sound immediately rearranges the molecular structure of the listener." Junior is a prime case study.

"When I was twelve or thirteen, Dad's races came on the country station," Junior says. Dad is Dale Earnhardt Sr., widely considered to be one of the three best drivers in the history of stock-car racing. "And I 'member sittin' there playin' with Matchbox cars on the floor. I had the perfect little bedroom with the perfect toys and the perfect friend up the road who always played every day I wanted to play and played all day till I couldn't play anymore, and I thought everybody fished, everybody listened to country, and everybody lived in a cool house on a lake, and it was sunny all the time.

"Then I got my driver's license and I was able to buy music and listen to it on my own, and you hear the words and you think, 'Man, I never thought about that.' I never really was rebellious against my parents. I never really thought the government was fucked up. I never really paid much attention to the schools suckin'. Up until I was sixteen, I thought every cop up and down the road was just happy and glee, and now you hear these songs and you're like, 'Is that the case? Is that what's goin' on?' You don't learn from anywhere else."

Junior followed Dad into big-time stock-car racing, and now, in a sport filled with good ol' boys, he's known as the rock & roll driver. That's him in the red number 8 Budweiser Chevrolet Monte Carlo in the NASCAR Winston Cup Series, facing off against heavyweights like Jeff Gordon, Dale Jarrett, Tony Stewart, and Dale Sr. In seven starts since February, Junior is ranked first among rookies and eighteenth overall. On April 2nd, he won his first big race, the DirecTV 500. He has now won more than $600,000 this season, but the numbers don't show that Junior is also a fan favorite. People see in him a kid from the MTV generation invading one of America's most stubborn subcultures. A kid like you, maybe, who on Monday, Tuesday, and Wednesday does little or nothing — fixes up the house, plays paint ball and Sega NFL2K with the guys, surfs the Net, hangs with best friend T-Dawg (his mom still calls him Terrell), and watches videos on MTV, BET, and MuchMusic, a Canadian channel. A kid who gets to the racetrack and thinks, "Can't wait to get home so I can fuck off some more."

(Apparently, fuckin' off actually helps him on race days. "The thing about drivin' race cars is mental," he says. "How long can you concentrate? How long can you focus? And if you don't focus good and you cain't be in deep thought for a long time, then you're not gonna be very good at it. The things I do every day prepare me for that. When you're on the computer playin' a game or on the PlayStation whippin' your buddy's ass in Knockout Kings, you gotta be on top of it.")

When not fuckin' off, Junior is raisin' hell, as in gettin' in one of his cars and peelin' the tires, every gear wide-ass open (read: goin' real fast). He's got a Corvette he won that he almost never drives. He's got a Chevy Impala with a global-positioning system, a VCR, and TV screens in the front and back. He's got a hulking red four-door Chevy pickup truck with a monster stereo system, and, if you lift the back seats, on top of where the bass amps are hidden, there is this skull-and-crossbones design that Skippy from Freeman's Car Stereo etched in there without Junior even askin', and the darn thing lights up when you push a button on a keypad, but no one knows that, 'cause Junior ain't one to show off. And then there's the breathtaker: a mint-condition midnight-blue 1969 Camaro with an exposed grille on the hood and an oversize finger-thin steering wheel and a gearshift shaped like a bridge and a top-of-the-line Alpine stereo. Junior bought this piece of art for a mere $12,000.

Junior eases into the piece of art and floats down the road to get some pizza from Pie in the Sky. "When I got this," he says, "I took it out and thought, 'This thing has no fire.'" He added a new transmission, a new aluminum-head Corvette engine, and a 2,500-rpm stall converter that allows you to shift and keeps the piece of art from changing gears until it reaches 2,500 rpm. Now the thing runs pretty awesome.

"It's real stiff and hard and doesn't have the handlin' package like a new car," Junior says, cruising at a leisurely forty miles an hour on the thin, desolate Carolina road. "So you gotta really know what you're doin', have your hands on the wheel at all times and stuff." The piece of art is loud, the engine rumbles and gurgles and practically drowns out the stereo, but the ride is cool, and he turns *Dr. Dre 2001* up way loud and it still sounds crisp. "I like Dr. Dre," Junior says. "He's got a good attitude. I saw him on that VH1 deal, that *Behind the Music*, and that really give you an idea of who he was. I mean, he enjoys success. I mean, that's kinda the way I've tried to be. There's a lot of money comin' in, and there's a lot of talk about how good the future is gonna be and how much is gonna happen, and I'm excited about it, but I don't wanna be molded or changed. I wanna be able to go back to $16,000 a year and be O.K. I wanna be able to still realize the value of a dollar bill. And I think that's what Dr. Dre's done. He's still maintained his coolness and not turned into a big jerk."

Junior pulls back on the shifter and says, "Check this out." The engine seems to constrict slowly, tightening like a coil, roaring and snarling as if it is angry at us, and then, after three slow seconds of build, the engine growling louder all the time, it reaches 2,500 rpm and there's a loud *pop!* like a gun, and we slingshot off, leaping in a millisecond from forty miles per hour to eighty — like light speed in the *Millennium Falcon* or something — and suddenly we're flying down the backstretch, zipping past cows and tractors and horses and go-carts as the malevolent funk of Dr. Dre booms out the window: *Nowadays, everybodywannatalk, liketheygot sumpintosay, but nuttincomesout whentheymovetheirlips, justabunchagibberish, andmotherfuckersack liketheyforgotaboutDre. . . .* It sounds so alien in this Waltons-ish country town, like music from another planet. And Junior is cool with both.

Vegas two days later, a Friday, is cloudless blue sky, heavy wind, a lot of sun. Out at the Motor Speedway, it's qualifying day for Sunday's race, the CarsDirect.Com 400. The fifty-five guys vying for the forty-three spots in the race go out one at a time, tearing around the track as fast as they can. Today's top twenty-five finishers are guaranteed spots in the race, their starting positions based on their qualifying speeds.

The hours before qualifying are for practice. Crews work on their cars, send the driver out for a lap or two around the track so he can judge what adjustments are needed, and then tinker some more. Junior has spent years working on cars, so he's really good at feeling what they're doing and at communicating to his crew what will make the car go faster. After laps, the guys — Favio, B, Brendan, Keith, Jeff, and Tony Jr. — jump all over the car, soldering, clipping, pouring, cramming like in the minutes before a final exam, wrenching, wiping, welding, tweaking the $250,000 beast, $50,000 engine, and $6,000 transmission, turning the engine into "a time bomb," as Steve Crisp, Junior's manager, calls it. "All loose and sloppy and about to all fall to hell."

Whereas Sunday is about being consistently fast for four straight hours, qualifying is one lap of brute strength and balls-out sheer speed — so the qualifying engine isn't made to last. For example, to improve the aerodynamics, they tape over the car's every hole and crack. But this makes the engine very hot — hence, a time bomb. Another example: Just before Junior gets in the car, there'll be a little portable heater linked up to the oil tank to get the oil up around two hundred degrees. "The hotter the oil, the thinner it is and the faster you can go," Crisp says. "It's like runnin' with Vaseline 'tween your cheeks. If you're lubed up, you can really haul ass."

At 11:00 A.M., after four practice laps, Junior is the eighth-fastest qualifier. At a quarter past noon, after fifteen laps, he has fallen to sixteenth place, but he isn't worried. The tires haven't been changed all morning, and at high speeds tires wear down very fast, making them crown, which means your contact with the ground lessens and you can't grab the track — try to turn at 140 miles an hour on crowned tires and you'll think you're on ice. At one o'clock, the crew finally throws on stickers (new tires), and Junior beats around the big oval like there's a killer on his tail, finishing practice with the day's fastest lap, faster than the next guy by more than three-tenths of a second, a monster lead in this business.

When at last it's time for the qualifying lap, Favio and the guys wheel the Chevy out to the track. Soon after, Junior joins them. As he walks down pit road, the Allman Brothers' "Midnight Rider" is booming on the track's loudspeakers, and twenty thousand fans are in the stands cheering, and Junior, with his impeccable military-school posture, the red and black race suit snug on his long, slender body, the blazing sun gleaning off the silver on his racing shoes, the black wraparound shades and the stubble and the chiseled chin and the movie-star cheekbones, shit, Junior looks like got-damn Steve McQueen.

He slides into the doorless beast, straps on his crimson skull-and-crossbones helmet, pulls on his black gloves and goggles, then screws on the steering wheel, which sits about a foot and a half from his face, so close that he can't slide in or out of the beast without unscrewing it, so close so that he can drive using his forearm muscles instead of his back and shoulder muscles. There is only one seat (roll bars are where the passenger seat would be), and that seat is form-fitted to Junior's body like shrink-to-fit jeans. There are gauges for water, oil, and fuel, and a tachometer to register rpms, but no speedometer, because it doesn't matter how fast you're going, just that you're going faster than everyone else. There is a thin rearview mirror about two feet wide, and a clear tube Junior can suck on to get water, and on Sunday there will also be a black tube stuck down into his suit to blow cool air, because the car's interior gets up around 100 degrees, and sometimes, during the summer, 130. One more thing: All the teams paste decals of headlights and brake lights onto their cars to heighten the illusion that they're driving the same sort of car that Bob has out in the driveway.

Ironically, stock-car racing is the most popular form of racing in America because it seems to be the most pedestrian. Back in the sixties, guys bought regular Chevelles or Dodge Chargers, yanked out the passenger seats, threw in some roll bars, and went racing. Nowadays the cars are constructed by the race teams themselves — I actually saw someone bending and molding a big piece of sheet metal into a door — and they're nothing like any car you can buy from Chevy. But Junior's "Chevy" shows up on TV, shaped like the car Bob owns, with headlights and brake lights — which doesn't even make sense, because why would a race car need headlights? They drive during the day! — and Bob says to himself, "Hey, that car's just like mine," or, even better, "Hey, that's like the Chevy down at the dealership. Think I'll go get me one." You think Bob doesn't think like that? One of the oldest sayings in racing is: Win on Sunday, sell on Monday.

Early this morning, all the drivers pulled numbers to determine the order of qualifying. Junior drew a two. When his turn comes, he flicks the lever to start the engine, and the beast cackles loudly, then begins to ripple and roar as if it were a lion growling through clenched teeth, or a gigantic, demented bowl of Rice Krispies snap-crackle-popping in a fury. A NASCAR official drops his arm, and

Junior steps on the gas and flies off like a low-slung comet, sounding like the humming of a six-foot-long hornet an inch from your ear, and when the lap is over and the speed is flashed on the board — 172.216 mph, a new track record — the crowd thunders. He has bested the old record — correction, demolished it — by more than two miles an hour.

He parks, and his team runs over to celebrate. "When ya drove into the corner," says a breathless Favio, "ya went all the way wide open! We didn't think you was gonna lift! The whole pit road just sit and looked at ya, amazed!" (Translation: "It seemed as though you took that first corner without braking — an impossibility! We thought you'd never get off the gas! You the man, baby!")

Junior jumps out of the car, ecstatic. "It doesn't matter if we git the pole [position]," he says, beaming like a kid getting good presents at Christmas. "That was awesome!"

But when ESPN and local TV rush over to get a comment, he mutes his excitement: "The car handled real good. I don't know if it'll stand up as far as the pole goes, but it'll be up there somewhere toward the front. My expectations at the first of the week were to come in here and make the top twenty-five, and that hasn't changed."

After the cameras disappear, Junior says, "I don't wanna sit here and go, 'Whoo-hoo!' and then get beat, and have everyone go, 'What an asshole.'"

And sure enough, his track record lasts about six minutes. Ricky Rudd tops him by three-tenths of a second.

Junior looks down the track and sees his father walking onto pit road for his qualifying run. "There's Dad," he says. "Let's go talk to him. A hundred bucks says my daddy give me shit for gittin' beat. He don't say, 'Nice goin'.' He'll say, 'Why'd you get beat?'"

Junior jogs down the track and catches his old man. Before Junior can say a word, Dad ribs him in a barbed but loving tone, "What happened? Why ain't ya first? What'd ya do wrong?"

"I don't know," Junior says with a laugh. Photographers snap wildly behind them.

"What should I do?" Dad says as another car flies by. "What were ya doin'?"

Junior says, "Run deep, brake hard, turn left." It was about the most smartass thing he could say without being rude.

"Run deep, brake hard?" Dad laughs. Terry Labonte, another top driver, is walking by. Dad grabs Labonte's arm and says, "Listen to him," then turns back to Junior. "How ya get 'round there, now?"

"Run deep, brake hard, turn left."

The veterans laugh. "He don't even know how he did it!" Dad says. There is a pause. Then Dad pats Junior on the shoulder, silently saying, "Good job."

A little later, Junior is back in his trailer, watching other cars qualify on ESPN2. No one beats Ricky Rudd, and only one other driver, Scott Pruett, beats Junior. At the press conference for the top three qualifiers, a reporter asks about Junior's relationship with his father.

"Well," Junior says, "durin' practice and qualifyin' it was 'Dad, car owner.'" Junior actually races for Dale Earnhardt Inc., in a car owned by Dad, although the car Dad races doesn't actually belong to him, because he's still loyal to Richard Childress, the man who put him in a race car long before he could buy one himself. "He's all, 'How's it goin? We need to get faster. We need to do this, we need to do that,'" Junior says. "Then when the race starts, it's diff'rent. Last week at Rockingham, we were goin' into Turn Three. I was on the inside of Jeff Gordon and got loose [lost control] goin' into the corner, and I slammed into him. About a straightaway and a half later, Dad went by shakin' his finger out the window at me. I guess that was where the father was goin', 'You'd better watch it. You'd better straighten up.'"

After the press conference, Junior is asked, If you were leading on the last lap and Dad was right behind you, would Dad use one of his legendary tricks to spin you out and take the checkered flag for himself? Junior doesn't pause: "He would do what it took to win."

In the 1940s, in North Carolina, South Carolina, Georgia, Tennessee, and Virginia, there were some good ol' boys fresh from the war with a little money, a little training in how to service military planes and jeeps, and a talent for brewing moonshine. They made their outlaw liquor in hidden stills in the woods and got it to the dance halls, speakeasys, and bootleggers in cars big enough to carry a hundred gallons of the stuff — maybe seven hundred pounds — and still fast enough to outrun the cops: Ford or Pontiac sedans with killer engines and real stiff suspensions — liquor cars. Racing's first superstar, Junior Johnson, was a moonshiner. He could always outrun the cops, until they got radios.

Sometimes some good ol' boys would get together and brag about who had the fastest liquor car, and if the braggin' got too loud, they'd pick a Sunday, head out to some deserted field, plow out an oval, and race. Thus was born American stock-car racing, now the country's most popular spectator sport — bigger than football or baseball or basketball, bigger even than professional wrestling. On any of thirty-six weekends a year, as many as 150,000 people or more show up to watch NASCAR at the tracks, and many millions more watch on TV. "In the South," says Crisp, a natural comedian, "ya see stock cars everywhere — from the time you're a little kid to the time you're put in the grave, you're gonna be around a stock-car track. Hell, ya can't sling a dead cat 'thout hittin' a shop."

In the late forties, the National Association for Stock Car Auto Racing was founded. It presided over a sport where the track and the stands and everything in between were filled with good ol' boys. Crisp describes the average fan: "He hunts, his dad taught him to hunt, and his dad taught him to hunt. He drinks Jack Daniel's and Maker's Mark. He listens to Hank Williams. He loves his huntin' dog and his pickup truck, and he married his high school sweetheart, and he lives in the town he grew up in, or a stone's throw away. He puts God first and then his family, then his truck."

Dale Earnhardt Jr. has a pickup truck, loves dogs, and maintains a certain down-homeness about him, but Junior ain't no good ol' boy. For example, he hates to hunt. He's got a story about that, too: "My dad's always been a deer hunter. He loves that shit. He took me a coupla times. I went out there and sat in a tree stand all freakin' day. And it's great to sit there and think about shit and reflect back on what's been happenin' with ya, but, really, it's just a waste of a day. Just pissin' it away.

"After a while, a deer walked out there, and I shot the hell out of it. You shoot him right in the chest, and it's s'posed to go right into his heart. When I saw it, I thought, 'Dad's gonna like this.' And then I'm like, 'Man, *I* don't like it.' The only excitement I got out of it was seein' him bein' excited, but I didn't enjoy sittin' there all day, and I didn't enjoy havin' to drag it over to the truck and pickin' it up and throwin' it in there and then sit there watchin' him skin it and gut it — and that pissed away all night, so there went a day and a night! So the next time I went in a deer stand, I'm like, 'I ain't shootin' shit, 'cause I got shit to do tonight.' So then I'm like, 'What am I doin' up here?' I got down and never went back."

Stock-car racing is still dominated by good ol' boys, though Junior is part of a class of new blood, some of whom aren't from the South — Matt Kenseth from Wisconsin, Tony Stewart from Indiana — and some Southerners who aren't good ol' boys, a titanic shift in the cultural direction of NASCAR. Imagine the NBA beginning to be dominated by white guys.

"There's a lot of drivers within this age group that are diff'rent," Junior says. "It's just the way things are goin', and NASCAR's not immune to it. Even the image is something more modern. Just look at the TV coverage. Ten years ago, when they'd go to break, it'd be some fiddle banjo-pickin' music. And now it's this jammin' rock music. Somebody somewhere said, 'Hey, let's change it.'"

But things change slowly. It's not easy to refuse all the cultural stimuli around you in favor of another drummer's beat. Sure, Junior hates to hunt, but there, mounted on the wall of his living room, are the head and neck of a deer.

On Friday night, the Speedway is quiet and empty, and around ten Junior heads out for a walk around the track and another story. "I'd just started drivin' my late-model car," he says. The late-model series is the lowest rung of organized stock-car racing. "We had this shitbox of a car, and we was racin' at this track with all the big dawgs." The Speedway's rock-concert bright lights are on. The only sound, besides our feet on the concrete, is the muffled snarl of dirt-track racing half a mile away.

"My crew chief was an old-timer everyone knew, named Gary Hargett, and he ordered a brand-new car for me from Rick Townsend, the most popular car builder. And we were so excited. So we git to the track, and Gary's like, 'Man, we ordered that car, when you think you're gonna git on it?' Rick's like, 'Well, we're behind. It's gonna be a couple months 'fore we even start on it. You guys should get it midway through the season.' And then he says, 'By the way, where's your driver at?' And I was standing a little ways away, and Gary's like, 'He's over there.' And Rick says, 'Boy don't look like much. Looks like he barely know how to get out of the rain.'

"So we started the race 'bout midpack and beat our way up through there, and two laps to go I came up on Rick's house car runnin' second. And I drilled him straight in the ass, man! Right in the fuckin' ass, and turned him sideways and went past him and finished second in the race. They don't do that here, but that's how we do back home. After the race, Rick come up to Gary and said, 'That was pretty awesome. We'll start on your shit Monday.' And Rick's been a good friend ever since. But I always remembered what Rick said, and everywhere I go, when I walk into a room with people I don't know, I assume they look at me and say, 'He don't look like much.' That's kept me real humble and small-time."

Junior was born in Concord, North Carolina, an hour's drive from his house in Mooresville. His parents separated when he was two or three, and he and his older sister, Kelly, were raised by his mother in a small mill house until Junior, at six, awoke to a fire in the kitchen. Everyone ran out, the house burned down, and nothing was ever the same. Mom handed over custody of her kids to Dale Sr. and moved to Norfolk, Virginia. "She didn't have the means to git us another house or take care of us," Junior says, "so she said, 'Man, your dad's doin' good, and he can put ya in school, so this is the best thing for ya.' I was just like, 'Are my toys here?'" She still lives in Norfolk and works as a loader for UPS. Junior has seen her once or twice a year since he was six, but she calls often. "She puts forth a lot of effort in our relationship," he says, and talks happily of her plan to retire and move back to the Charlotte area within the next year. "She's awesome."

When Junior arrived in his dad's custody, racing was a very small sport. "The tracks they raced at were shit holes," Junior says. "If you got fifty thousand fans there, you were lucky." Dad was away a lot of the time, so Junior was raised by his stepmom, Teresa. "When he and Kelly were growin' up," Dale Sr. says, "I was workin' and racin' and goin' all the time."

"We'd go upstairs and sit down on the couch," Junior says, "and he'd be sittin' there watchin' TV in the recliner, and you ask him a question and he wouldn't hear you. You rarely even get a response. He was so in his racin' thing, you could hardly sometimes have a conversation with him, 'cause his mind was on what he was thinkin' about." It's been suggested by people who know them that Junior became a driver to get his father's attention. Both deny it. But there seems to be a kernel of truth to it.

Dad grew up at the track, watching his father, Ralph, a champion stock-car driver in the fifties. Dale drove his black number 3 Chevy to a record-tying seven Winston Cup season championships. Called the Man In Black and the Intimidator, he's the consummate winner with a questionable reputation, like the Bill Laimbeer Detroit "Bad Boy" Pistons or the Lyle Alzado Oakland Raiders. But winning wins company, so he's also one of the most revered drivers in the history of the sport.

He took his winnings to Mooresville and built a giant palace of a racing shrine, perhaps the greatest ever constructed by NASCAR money, lovingly called the Garage Mahal. There are security guards in cowboy boots and red button-down shirts that say DALE EARNHARDT INC., surrounded by corporate offices for DEI's 160 employees, all of Dad's trophies, old winning cars preserved for public view, and big glass display cases for the tuxedos he wore to the Winston Cup banquets during his championship seasons and the gowns worn by his wife and the cute pink polka-dot toddler's dress sported by their daughter Taylor and pictures of Ralph Earnhardt and all the commercials Dad and Junior have made and a gift shop with all sorts of souvenirs — spoons, toy bears, pins, watches, shirts, robes, beer steins, shot glasses, tiny model cars (all of which earned Junior around $2 million last year), and, this just in, a Dale Earnhardt Monopoly set. The game pieces include a car, a checkered flag, and a helmet. Earnhardt's face is on the money. He's the first individual to have a Monopoly set made around him. The shop's best-selling item, the clerks say, is a decal you can affix to your car to give the impression you bought it at the old man's dealership.

As all of this was being built, Junior was at Mitchell Community College in Statesville, North Carolina, getting a degree in automotives, and then at his father's dealership working as a grease monkey for $180 a week. "I got to where I could do an oil change in eight minutes," he says. "I was really proud of that."

Then one Saturday night in Myrtle Beach, South Carolina, he raced his late-model car: "It was $1,000 to win and 100 to 150 fans, but it didn't matter. It was kickass, man! It was like buildin' a freakin' remote-control car and goin' to where everybody else went to play with it. I learned everything — how to save your tires, pace yourself, not wreck your car, communicate with your team, motivate 'em to work — you got volunteer guys, and you gotta be able to get 'em to work or they're gonna go to the track and drink up the sodas. And that's just people skills."

In time, he moved up to the Busch Series — which is like the supercharged minors to the Winston Cup's majors — was season champ in '98 and '99, and graduated to the Winston Cup. "But growin' up as a kid, I didn't try to drive race cars, so I know inside that it's not a live-or-die thing. I'm a little more three-dimensional than, 'Oh, drivin's kickass.' Drivin' is fun, but that's not the ultimate high. Right now, I'd rather be home. I'd much more enjoy kickin' it on my couch."

At ten o'clock Sunday morning, Junior is in his trailer with Crisp and his trailer driver, Shane, eating Corn Pops, listening to Pink Floyd's *The Wall*, arguing about racing movies. The race is just over an hour away, and there is about as much tension in the air as there is in your house before you drive to the 7-Eleven for milk.

"*The Last American Hero* is real redneck-y," Crisp says of the film many consider the best ever made on racing.

"But it's the only racin' movie that's about racin'," Junior says. "I didn't like *Le Mans*," he said of the Steve McQueen classic. "They were just raisin' hell and racin' cars. There's no dialogue. It's just racin' and sittin'. It didn't have a plot."

"*Heart Like a Wheel* is uncool," Shane says of the Bonnie Bedelia film, "'cause they had it like she's gittin' her ass beat by her boyfriend."

"What about *Days of Thunder?*" someone asks about the Tom Cruise movie. All at once everyone says, "Sucked!"

"*Grand Prix* kicks ass," Crisp says.

"Here's *Le Mans*," Junior says. "A bunch of people sittin' aroun' for five minutes. Then, all of a sudden, snap, they're racin', then, snap, they're all sittin' around. No dialogue whatsoever. It's like someone actually followed the guy around, filmin' him."

"Yeah," Shane says. "It was realistic."

"Yeah, it was real," Junior says, "but it didn't have a plot and shit like *Grand Prix*. Who was the guy in *Grand Prix?*"

"James Garner," everyone says.

"I like that guy," Junior says.

"The girl liked him in *Grand Prix*," Shane says.

"'Member? And her husband got in a wreck and she turned out

to be a bee-itch!" Crisp says as though he were Snoop Dogg. The room crumbles in hysterics. "She was a big *beeee-itch!* A biznitch!"

There is no pre-race ritual, no discussion of strategy, no prayer, no psyching. It seems strange. Junior is moments away from the event that defined his week, and, more, is about to spend four hours risking his life, and he seems largely unconcerned. You don't do anything special before you go out to race?

Junior looks puzzled, as if the idea of doing something special had never occurred to him.

"I think ya do a lot of soul-searching," Shane says. "I don't think you notice it, but you usually walk around in a daze."

"One thing I do," Junior says, "is, when I walk out the trailer door, I don't wait up for people."

"His mind is already there," Shane says.

"I go at my pace. Real fast."

"Almost to the point where if ya didn't know him, you'd think he was rude," Crisp says.

"It would wear me out to psych myself up all mornin'," Junior says. "I pray to God before the race. I don't pray to win. I say, 'When it's over, can I go the next five days till the next race with a content, satisfied attitude so I can live comfortably and not be all down on myself on a bad finish all week? 'Cause if I finish bad, I'm depressed as hell for the next week."

That's it? C'mon! You could die today!

With childlike innocence, Junior says, "Ya think?"

Everyone laughs.

"Nah, man. It's safe as hell in there. All that paddin' in there, how I'm buckled in there, all the bars and things? Dude, man, that car is bulletproof."

But no one is shooting at you. Seriously, man, this is worse than boxing. You must know that.

"Yeah, sometimes guys get cocked just right. That's the way it is. There's things in there your head can hit, and if it hits it just right you could be permanently injured. But guys normally walk away."

Suddenly he turns to Crisp. "You know what I wanna do? When they do driver introductions? I wanna say somethin' into the mike like, 'I gotta say hi to my friend Chester McGroovy. Get well soon!'"

Then Junior says, "Last week we were drivin' up to the racetrack, and there were all these people campin' outside, thousands of people, and I'm like, 'That's what the fuck I'd like to be doin'.' That's fun! Just raisin' hell at the racetrack with your buddies, drinkin' beer, campin' out, watchin' the race. No pressure, man. I mean, you don't get no money, but, shit, you're havin' a good time. It'd be fun. And I'll never get to do that."

He pauses. "When I turn seventy, that's what I'm gonna do. Go campin' and park outside the track and sit there and drink beer and just raise hell and aggravate all the fuckin' rednecks with all this rock & roll music."

Pumping Irony

FROM GQ

The Blond Bomber muscles into a return engagement — B.C.

"THIS GUY — *this guy*," said Lou Ferrigno as he unwrapped his 6′5″ assemblage of muscle tissue and ropelike veins to reveal a middle-aged man of more plausible dimensions blushing beneath, "was my hero." The *Incredible Hulk* star grinned, and continued, "No foolin'. Two guys inspired me to get into bodybuilding: Arnold and this guy."

This guy wore a thin-lipped smile as he studied the office carpet of Weider Publications, the muscle-mag empire that had made both men stars in an earlier day. Ferrigno then said. "Hey, Dave, I'm goin' boar hunting this weekend. You do any hunting?"

Looking up then, his eyes squinting apologetically, Dave Draper said, "No. I can't hunt animals. I feel sorry for them."

Ferrigno seemed surprised at first. He blinked, smiled incredulously, and reared back as if to say *Who the hell is THIS guy?* Then he regarded Dave Draper afresh — and as others have done, reminded himself that only one of his two inspirations had been the Terminator, while the other had nearly been terminated. Now Dave had returned from the dead, emerging as a force in the bodybuilding industry that he had helped popularize three decades earlier. But this was not a comeback, technically speaking, as Dave Draper didn't want to go back to where he'd once been. Besides, *I'll be back* was the other guy's line.

This guy? This guy was the anti-Arnold.

Here is the stake some of us had in Dave Draper, way back when:

Before O.J. and Heidi Fleiss, Reagan and Eisner, the Eagles

and Warren Beatty, the Watts riots and Charlie Manson — before all the weirdness and schlock and hard-charging verities — there once was a Southern California that could make a runt from the hinterlands go deranged with American dreams. To see the promised land for myself, I needed only to buy a comic book or a true-crime or muscle magazine and thumb through the ads. And there, on a page devoted to bodybuilding products, would be California personified by the guy they called the Blond Bomber, posing dramatically alongside the waves of the Pacific in his cocktail napkin of a swimsuit — a sun god at ease in his western paradise, flanked by a host of bikini-clad sun goddesses who clung to his uncanny rack of muscles as if all hope and glory were encased within.

The image required no embellishment. It was complete and universally understood. From the snowbound netherworld of Graz, Austria, a dark-browed teenager with the impossible last name of Schwarzenegger contemplated that very same tableau and, as he told me, "not only wanted to look like Dave Draper but to live like him — to live in Southern California with all those great-looking women on the beach and to be on TV shows and in film like him. If it wasn't for him, I might not have had the determination to train hard and move to America." He did so in 1968, and immediately the Blond Bomber and the Austrian Oak were viewed in tandem. Arnold trained with Dave at the original Gold's Gym in Santa Monica, admiring the ridges of Dave's serratus anterior while mimicking his improvisational approach to workouts. They competed and toured the world together, twinned by the gawks of mere mortals.

Meanwhile, back in suburban St. Louis, I stared at the advertisements and wondered what kind of joke God was playing on me. *This* Draper was the 1965 Mr. America and the 1966 Mr. Universe — "The World's Strongest Youth," as the muscle mags had it. This Draper had been on Johnny Carson and was Sharon Tate's boyfriend in a Hollywood movie. Simply to behold him was to know the bountifulness of his life and to be taunted by the feebleness of mine. Throughout the mid-'60s, the kids at school would ask if he and I were related and barely get the question out before shrieking with laughter. I was convinced Dave Draper was a real asshole, but he had my attention. And in particular, that metaphorically potent image of the radiant, straw-haired Hercules with the modest smile and the day's catch of beach bunnies slung across his deltoids took up long-term residence in my preteen imagination.

Soon the family basement was cluttered with barbells, hand flexors, and other mail-order gadgetry. I drank protein milk shakes and performed sit-ups. I squeezed lemon juice onto my hair and languished in the sun while dreaming the Dave Draper dream. Then one day, we moved back to Texas, where it was too damn hot to lie out. The weights stayed in their boxes somewhere in the back of the new garage. The money I'd once spent on comics now went toward rock 'n' roll records. It was 1970, and I'd turned my back on Dave Draper — unaware that the twenty-eight-year-old Blond Bomber had turned his back as well, vanishing from Venice Beach, from the bodybuilding competitions, and from the magazines and comic books, effectively cast out by bodybuilding magnate Joe Weider in favor of someone who would take Weider's sport to the next level, someone who hungered for superstardom and who would delight in bullying, instead of shying away from, the competition. Someone named *Ah-nuld.*

Now Dave Draper was back in my sights. He had returned from an alcoholic abyss to boast two Santa Cruz–area gyms, advice columns in national fitness magazines, and an energetic Web site that had set the obsessive weight-lifting community into a clamor: *The Blond Bomber's back!* To be pronounced a bodybuilding guru at a time when the once lumpen practice has swelled into a billion-dollar colossus is to never again worry about the fate of our Social Security system. Dave's timing looked all too perfect. And thus I could not help but conjure up a new image to supplant the old — that of a slick-talking, information-age, Central Coast boomer-cynic only too willing to hype his fool's-goldenness for as long as his follicles held out. That's whom I'd encounter. And, as the family name was at stake here, I would flay him in print for it.

So I showed up in Santa Cruz, whereupon Dave Draper hid from me.

"I think he's nervous about seeing you," said the attractive young woman at the reception desk of Dave Draper's World Gym. She winced a smile. "Can I fix you a protein smoothie while you wait?"

He was two hours late to his morning workout, which was commonplace for some Drapers, but not for Dave. When at last he strode in, head down, he muttered something about a previous engagement, "something that couldn't be helped." It was obvious he did not want to work out in my presence. He shuffled around his gym in sweats, looking down at the weights, then sidelong at me. I crouched behind an exercycle, peering out from behind my notepad, and before long I was pissed off. I was here to write about the improbable resurrection of a bodybuilding legend, but at the moment I felt more like an Audubon geek stalking a bronze-cheeked wood thrush. By the time Dave Draper at last commenced his ab crunches, dark fantasies consumed me. What would it be like to kick Mr. America's ass?

"I want to tell you everything, even though I'm a nervous wreck," he said over lunch that day while consuming his usual orgy of protein. "These people who write me nowadays or come up to me in gyms — they say, 'Dave, man, I *idolized* you! I'd see you on the beach with all those girls — you're why I moved to L.A.!' And I feel this responsibility to them. Not just to give them good training advice but also not to disappoint them. But all that California stuff. . . ."

Dave put down his fork and made sure I was listening before he said it: "I've never surfed before in my life."

Then, as if regretting the effect this revelation might have on me, he added, "Though I do love the ocean."

At the age of fifty-eight, and in the most narcissistic substratum of our youth-obsessed culture, Dave Draper has been granted a second act, one that is real. It was the first act that was phony.

He was born not in California, but in Secaucus, New Jersey. Frank Zane, the thinking man's bodybuilder, told me, "In every bodybuilder's background, there are issues with our father" — and this is famously so with Schwarzenegger and Lou Ferrigno and their domineering cop dads. But though Dave's salesman-and-laypreacher father was preoccupied with spreading the Word, the boy turned to weight lifting for that most basic of reasons: to feel big. "I was always fascinated with guys I'd seen around town with muscles," he said. "I just thought they represented strength, ability, and respect — things I sought, somehow or other. I started school at four, graduated at sixteen. That's part of it, like in team sports: 'He's the only guy left; you've gotta take him.' The least equipped guy in the class."

As his parents had taught him the virtues of humility, Dave kept his muscles well swaddled, and so only in the gym where he trained did anyone know how big he was becoming. He began to buy his barbells in Union City, at the Weider Barbell Company, and one day the boss checked out the Secaucus kid whom the shipping clerks were working out with in the warehouse. This young man, Weider would later tell me, "looked like the kid next door, and people could identify with him." In 1962 he gave Dave a job in the shipping department, then offered to employ him at Weider's new distributorship in Santa Monica, where Dave could train with the greats of Muscle Beach and one day become a champion himself.

When I asked Weider, thirty-eight years later, if he really believed that a champion was what Dave Draper wanted to be, the body-building publisher *pshaw*ed me, saying, "He had the fire in the belly, don't kid yourself. He wouldn't have gotten the kind of body he did without hard work." But for Dave, the hard work, the process, was more than enough. "I developed this relationship with the weights," he said, "and I was satisfied being alone with them." Now, however, he would have to learn how to compete — how to pose and strut his stuff onstage. One of the most celebrated body-builders at the time, Bill Pearl, took the twenty-year-old newcomer under his wing. "I'd say, 'Dave, you're not posing right,'" recalled Pearl, "and he'd actually hit himself in the head and say how stupid he was. The guy liked to train. But he didn't enjoy the limelight."

The limelight found him anyway. Within a year of his arrival in L.A., golden-haired Dave became the designated cover boy for Weider's *Mr. America* and *Muscle Builder* magazines, not to mention the choice model for his product advertisements. Thus did Dave Draper find himself on the beach, surfboard in hand, windblown and chick flanked. As current bodybuilding powerhouse Shawn Ray observed, "Joe sold that dream with Draper on Santa Monica Beach, which was why you rarely saw Dave photographed alone. You always saw him with a girl." But Dave was married — had been since the age of nineteen, to a sixteen-year-old New Jersey girl with a bun in the oven — and besides, the most frequent female model holding hands with or nuzzling Dave was none other than Betty Weider, the publisher's curvaceous wife.

*

In 1965, as foretold by Weider's magazines ("Look out, Mr. America and Mr. Universe . . . here he comes!"), the "Weider-trained" — as the magazines called him — Dave Draper won the Weider-sponsored Mr. America contest. In 1966 he won Mr. Universe. Dave's body was now a shredded 235-pound testament to fevered training. He'd become an exemplar of the classic three-quarter-back pose (those flaring lats!), as well as the overhead-biceps shot (pecs and delts, ten-*hut!*); all across America and beyond, the pimply-faced masses were standing on their tiptoes in front of the bathroom mirror, emulating the man Joe Weider had dubbed the Blond Bomber.

Though Hollywood was decades away from viewing a muscle as something not akin to a tumor, Dave Draper garnered screen opportunities never before afforded a bodybuilder: host of a year's worth of TV Movies of the Week, guest roles in episodes of *The Beverly Hillbillies* and *The Monkees,* and an eccentric turn as Sharon Tate's heartthrob in the zany Tony Curtis–Claudia Cardinale vehicle *Don't Make Waves.*

Which, to Dave, was great. He could've quit right there. He *wanted* to quit right there. He hated cattle calls; he hated competing, period, and gave the trophies away as fast as he won them. (Except for the Mr. Universe trophy, which his wife, Penny, hurled at him during a domestic set-to.) What Dave loved was the gym and the sweaty, honest, individualized missions undertaken there. When the pressure built for Dave to enter the 1967 Mr. Olympia contest — the previous winner, Larry Scott, had dropped out, telling some he knew he couldn't beat Draper — he descended into a funk and his training habits faltered. "What the hell's the matter with the guy?" Joe Weider would say. "He's got a chance to be something!"

Dave hated the pressure from Weider, who kept demanding more of him, when all Dave wanted was what he'd already been promised. Though, according to Dave, the original deal included a salary, car, housing, and royalties for the use of his image, Dave received only one hundred dollars a week in exchange for working full-time in Weider's office, selling and inventorying products. ("We made less than the guys working at JC Penney's around the corner," recalled one of Dave's coworkers.) For supplemental income, Dave took up woodworking, in which his muscles would actually be of some use to humanity. He also took up vodka and PCP, or angel dust. His training for the '67 Mr. Olympia contest was half-

assed. Upon entering, he took one look at top contender Sergio
Oliva's pyrotechnic musculature, knew he'd screwed up, and with-
drew after the prejudging. Though Oliva won, he was a black Cu-
ban with a radical physique, so Dave Draper remained Joe Weider's
cover boy for a while longer. But the writing was on the wall: Dave
was only keeping the throne warm for a newer, hungrier prince.

"He shook my hand the day I arrived and said, 'Welcome to America,'" said Arnold Schwarzenegger. "I'd seen this guy in the magazines on the beach with all the girls, and he ended up being quite
the opposite. Dave was an extremely sensitive man. He gave me
such a warm feeling — a feeling in my heart I'd never felt before: *I
really am welcome here.* Weider welcomed me, too. But he'd fallen in
love with me because I filled this vision of a Germanic machine de-
stroying and conquering. I became a kind of exterminator for him.

"But with Dave, it was all on a human level. He helped me lease
my first car. And got me a PO box, a phone number, silverware,
dishes, posters for the wall. And when I made my first money, I saw
Dave's woodwork and I thought it would be such a pleasure to have
this man I admired so much make me a bed. And he made this *powerful* bed, six hundred pounds — so big, he had to take it apart to
get it into my room. And he did it one day, and I came home, and
there was incense burning in my apartment and all these candles lit
and this bed so big that I could only walk into the bedroom sideways against the wall. I still have that bed. I'd never get rid of it."

The extraordinary thing was that Arnold had arrived literally
at Dave's expense. In 1968 Weider imported him from Munich,
along with two of Arnold's friends to keep him company, putting
the three of them up in an apartment, giving them a car, and paying Arnold two hundred dollars a week for the use of his image.
The new kid in town did not have to sell barbells or vitamin packets
at the distributorship. He did not have to do much of anything, except train. As a prominent bodybuilder told me, "Arnold got everything Dave hadn't gotten." And in the meantime, Dave's weekly
one-hundred-dollar checks came to an end.

"Joe is a star builder," Arnold told me. "If you let him, he will create you and turn you into something very special. Dave didn't have
that killer instinct. I will go until the end, until everyone drops. I
will use the personality; I will give the speech to the judges — I will

do everything necessary to be a winner. But Dave wasn't really that interested in being in front of five thousand people and saying, 'Look at my naked body. Isn't that great?' Why did he train in dark dungeons in the early morning with all those shirts on, never showing his body and not running around the beach like the photographs showed? That wasn't Dave's reality. That was Joe's reality."

No one could fault Weider for his investment in Schwarzenegger, whose genetic gifts were boosted by a furious work ethic and who would dominate the Mr. Olympia arena from 1970 through 1975 before leaving for the movies. Said Weider, "Arnold was able to express what bodybuilding was." And when Hollywood instructed him to lose the last name, the muscles, and the Austrian accent, Arnold's reply was, *You'll be back.* He feared nothing — not competition, not pain, not failure, and certainly not Joe Weider.

Dave, in the meantime, had become the picture of alienation. He grew his hair out and took up woodworking full-time, though even that would become too high-pressure. "He could've made a fortune in furniture," said his older brother, Don. "He had a two-year backlog. But he no longer enjoyed making it, because people would call and say, 'Dave, when's this going to be done?' and it wasn't fun anymore." He worked out at dawn and was out of the gym by nine. The few who would see him there would notice, as Frank Zane did, that "he was already loaded and totally out of it." Dave had given new meaning to his moniker. The Blond Bomber was drinking two fifths of vodka a day, and on the rare occasion that he would attend a bodybuilding exhibition, "he'd be so shit-faced he couldn't find his butt with both hands, and I'd have to collect his money from the promoters," said Bill Pearl.

He'd nearly blown up his house in Marina Del Rey trying to manufacture PCP. As a crowning ignominy, when director George Butler visited Dave's home in 1974 to persuade him to participate in Butler's forthcoming bodybuilding documentary, *Pumping Iron*, he found a fit and handsome Dave Draper — but one who couldn't talk. "My jawbone was paralyzed from doing drugs," Dave said. The filming proceeded without him.

In 1972 Dave had sued Joe Weider for fraud. His case was strong, despite the fact that Arnold showed up in court as a defense witness. (Asked about Weider's reputation among bodybuilders, Arnold testified, "It is not too good.") Weider telephoned Dave and offered to settle, a move that would liberate Dave's image from Weider's control. Dave agreed just as the jury was returning with its verdict. The settlement awarded Dave $17,500, enough to cover attorneys' fees and other trial-related costs. After the deal was struck, the judge requested the jury's verdict for the record. It had found in favor of the plaintiff and had intended to award Dave Draper compensatory and punitive damages totaling $892,350. The money would stay with Weider.

Dave sent each juror a handcrafted cheese board anyway.

In 1984 Dave Draper requested a meeting with Arnold Schwarzenegger.

The two convened at the residence of gym owner Joe Gold in Los Angeles. Dave showed up on a bicycle he had borrowed from the friend he'd been staying with nearby. He was now forty-two, divorced, and noticeably weak from having been hospitalized for congestive heart failure and eczema, both brought on by alcohol, which he had given up. Dave wanted to ask Arnold if he thought a book written by Dave about his experiences might be publishable — and if so, would Arnold be willing to write the prologue?

The multimillionaire actor, author, and businessman told his old gym partner that a book about Dave's rise, fall, and recovery would be inspirational to many. And, yes, he'd be happy to pen a prologue.

Dave said thanks and prepared to go. Arnold stopped him. "Dave," he said, and held him with a stare. "Is that really all you wanted to ask me? That's all you needed?"

"That's all," said Dave.

Something else caught Arnold's attention. "And that's what you came here on?" he asked. "That bike?"

"Yeah," said Dave.

Arnold shook his head. "O.K., Dave," he said, and drove off in his luxury car.

It would be fully fifteen years before Dave got around to writing that book. But a few years after their encounter, when the first Dave Draper's World Gym was built in Santa Cruz, Arnold flew in for the grand opening and stayed in the packed house for several hours, signing autographs and posing for pictures. At one point, Arnold gave a speech. He wanted everyone to know how important Dave

Draper had been to him and to the world of bodybuilding, and how proud of Dave he was. The gesture was humbling to Dave.

In 1998, just after Arnold underwent surgery to correct a congenital heart defect, Dave and his new wife, Laree, happened to be visiting L.A. and thought to drop off a get-well card at Arnold's office. It turned out that Arnold was there, and for fifteen minutes or so, they chatted about his health, which was surprisingly robust. Upon returning to Santa Cruz, Dave wrote a few upbeat sentences in his newsletter to gym members about Arnold's splendid recovery. Some two months later, Dave launched his Web site and added the Schwarzenegger tidbit to the array of advice columns, bodybuilding lore, and archival photographs.

A stern, legalistic letter from Arnold followed. Their conversation had been private. The information he'd imparted had been given to Dave Draper, not to DaveDraper.com. As Schwarzenegger explained to me, "Look, I know Dave well enough to know he'd never do harm to anyone. But since the days when we used to hang out, so many things have changed, and I have to be very careful about what's said. He could've written something wrong about my medical situation, and then the insurance company would've come after me and I would've been screwed."

But the letter stung anyway — serving, however unintentionally, as a reminder of the one's station versus the other's. Dave removed the column from the Web site — along with, at Arnold's request, the photos of the two together, which had not been posted with Arnold's permission. "I wrote a pretty good letter back," Dave said, "not trying just to be submissive. Saying it's good for both of us; it's good for the people; it's good for everyone. . . ."

There is the stubbornly prideful side of Dave Draper, and then there is the side that seems forever apologetic about having somehow let all of us down. It never mattered a damn to him that he didn't burn with ambition, or nail all the babes who flocked around him on the beach, or date Sharon Tate in real life, or make more movies, or win more competitions, or amass a fortune, or at least cut into Joe Weider's fortune, or surf. But that guy on the covers and in the ads seemed to promise such things about Dave. Who's the misfit, the image or the man? It's hardly a metaphysical question, but it will weigh on him just a little, for as long as he thinks it's weighing on anyone else.

He can bear it, because the name Dave Draper also signifies one hell of a bodybuilder, which he was and is, and today that means more than it ever did. "If it ever came down to a popularity contest," said Schwarzenegger, "Dave would win. Everywhere I travel — Russia, Germany, Japan, Mexico — the name that comes up most frequently is Dave Draper. He is loved so much and has so much to offer to so many young kids, because he just wanted to have a great body. He didn't want to be onstage and destroy and conquer like me."

His bodybuilding manual and confessional, *Brother Iron Sister Steel*, will be published this month. He'll hawk the book, sell his Bomber Blend protein-supplement powder, run his gyms, and pen his columns for *Muscle & Fitness* without having to answer to Joe Weider. Dave has come to discover a humanity-affirming truth, which is that credibility is marketable. In the gym and in writing, Dave preaches a retro ideology of high protein and daily, disciplined, dopeless workouts — which, in fact, was how the Secaucus introvert first drew Weider's attention, decades before the bodybuilding world went wild-eyed and freaky framed with growth hormones.

"It's chemical warfare out there," Shawn Ray, the perennial Mr. Olympia contender and self-made franchise, explained to me over lunch at a Santa Monica bodybuilder's haunt one afternoon. "A drug-driven, freaky industry. Everybody's doing *something*. The question is how far you're willing to push the envelope. When you look at my physique, you don't see me playing with fire, pushing it too far."

The short, egregiously hard-bodied African-American went on about the sorry state of his sport — biased judges, zero camaraderie among the athletes — but in the end, he could hardly complain. "You reap what you sow," he stated in his smooth, learned voice. "I just bought a $650,000 house. I've had every car in the world, from a Lamberghini to a Ferrari Testarossa, Corvette, Porsche, four or five Mercedes. I've had the material things." He ticked off the means: prize money, Weider endorsement contracts, video sales, posters, Shawn Ray weight-lifting gloves and hats, guest appearances, seminars. "It has everything to do with being marketable," he said.

In that sense, things had changed and yet remained the same. "I'm a bodybuilding historian," he told me. "In order to see the future, you've gotta see the past. As a kid, I used to train in Orange County, where they had all the old bodybuilding magazines. And I'd see Dave Draper on the covers. See, I always wanted to go to Hollywood. And he *was* Hollywood. Dave Draper was always on the beach, lying in the sand, always with two or three girls around him. It just seemed like he came out here, trained, and then hung out on the beach all day. . . . And man, I'm like, I wanna be that guy!"

Arnold. Lou. Shawn. Me. We all wanted to be like Dave. Now it's Dave's turn to be like Dave.

PETE KOTZ

Tough Guy

FROM CLEVELAND SCENE

It's an in-your-face living — B.C.

THE TOUGH GUY CIRCLES forebodingly in the grainy, homemade videotape. He suddenly lurches forward, throwing a wild series of punches before tumbling to the ice. The next moment, he is seen stripped of his jersey and shoulder pads, swapping mean, arching fists with a player from Rochester. In the next fight, he is clutching a man, holding tight, unwilling to do that for which he is paid: hit people.

Steel pins had just been removed from his broken hand, he explains apologetically. One must be prudent with one's professional tools.

The Tough Guy possesses many such tapes, sent from fans across the North American Snow Belt. This one consists of twenty-odd minutes of bare-knuckles fighting, awkwardly edited from minor-league cablecasts, the color heavy with luminescent pinks and greens.

The Tough Guy doesn't sit while he watches. He is large, muscled well beyond nature's boundaries, giving him a stiff look as he leans against the wall of his cluttered Independence hotel room. Until this moment, he has been relentlessly gracious, spinning stories with the laugh of a little boy. But now he is clearly disappointed. This is not his best work.

After all, the Tough Guy was the most prolific fighter in professional hockey last season, recording fifty-three bouts. A mortal enforcer might drop the gloves every three or four games. But when one calculates in suspensions — "I usually get four or five a year," he says, smiling — the Tough Guy fought nearly every game.

Unfortunately, this is a greatest hits tape from three seasons before, when he was a mere lad of twenty-two, a novice in the art.

"Now, if I was fighting that guy, I could get in uppercuts," he says as a bout from Kitchener, Ontario, crosses the screen.

The next moment he laughs at a close-up of himself. "My nose used to be straight before a guy made it unstraight for me."

Then there is footage from Hershey, Pennsylvania. The tape shows little more than a pile of arms and legs and torsos, striped shirts attempting to unravel the mess. When the Tough Guy is eventually pulled away, his prey remains on the ice, splayed in the ungainly form of the unconscious. Seconds later there are gloves, sticks, and fists everywhere.

This provides the Tough Guy with a teachable moment. "The guy was stupid," he says of the unconscious man. "I beat him. I had him down. But he was still saying he's gonna kill me. I *had* to hit him."

Such is the Tough Guy Code. For those who fight on skates for a living, these are the unwritten laws, and they have served Garrett Burnett well. He is, after all, the last man who should be playing professional hockey.

Since he embarked on his road to the pros in 1994, Burnett has been discarded by teams from Saskatchewan to Jacksonville. He's been called a goon, a bully, a no-skill bum. In a game where twenty goals a season is the benchmark of a good scorer, Burnett has but twelve — over six years. In fact, so many coaches have given up on him — six in one season alone — that he struggles to remember them all.

Still, through a childlike exuberance and a sheer love for propelling big fists into other people's heads, Burnett has managed to slowly, painfully climb his way up in this game. He may well be the most loved and hated man in all of minor-league hockey.

And now he has come to fight for the Cleveland Lumberjacks.

To understand hockey, one must first understand the Far North. Though it doesn't share the same beat-the-wife/shoot-the-brother-in-law traditions of the rural South, it is a curiously violent place nonetheless. Fighting is a cultural staple of this land, a means to administer justice, to settle grievances, to relieve the overstocking of testosterone, its greatest natural resource. It's also cheap and accessible entertainment for those isolated by snow and subzero temperatures. To fight, or talk of fights past, is among life's great pleasures.

"There's a lot of outdoors kind of people," says Burnett, who was raised outside of Vancouver. "They work long hours in the mines or in the forest. People work all week out in the bush, and they come in on Saturday, and they drink like all hell. And if they can't get a woman, they get a fight."

Hockey is the sport and official religion of this land. Fighting, quite naturally, has always been a part of it.

The game's loftiest perch, the National Hockey League, was conceived in 1917. The *Toronto Star* tells of a battle that season between Bad Joe Hall and Alf Skinner. After fighting on the ice — a bout that entailed a good bit of stick swinging — the players were hauled away for disorderly conduct. Festivities continued in the paddy wagon, where five policemen were needed to yank the men apart. Hockey has maintained its brawling ethic ever since.

While fisticuffs in most sports call for automatic ejection — and handsome suspensions — the NHL did not crack down until 1922, when it decided to rebuke combatants with a five-minute penalty — the equivalent of a parental time-out. NHL officials weren't about to vanquish such a closely held tradition.

Besides, fighting was viewed as a safety valve, a way of releasing tension when play became too furious.

It also served as a secondary justice system, according to Stan Fischler, a commentator for Fox Sports Net New York and author of such scholarly texts as *Ultimate Bad Boys: Hockey's Greatest Fighters*. "Hockey was a frontier game. It was basically played in the pioneering areas of western Canada, in the prairie. If somebody got hurt, and the referee didn't call a penalty, they took matters into their own hands."

Of course, everyone fought, from the smallest players to the biggest stars. To do otherwise was to flirt with cowardice.

But something changed in the early 1960s. The Montreal Canadiens, the Yankees of hockey, thought others were taking liberties with their stars. So they hired John Ferguson, considered to be the original designated fighter. Such men were called policemen.

If others got too rough with the more skilled Flying Frenchmen, it was Ferguson's job to exact justice.

By 1967, the game had changed again. The NHL expanded, and the increasing number of jobs corresponded with a decreasing level of talent. Though men of Ferguson's ilk were actually talented players, a new breed of fighter emerged, one whose résumé began and ended with his ability to punch people. He was known as The Goon.

Hockey was embarking on its Roving White Street Gangs on Ice period. There were bench-clearing brawls, bands of players chasing fans into the stands. Magazines of the trade were filled with photos of men with long hair and bushy Fu Manchus, blood streaking down their faces.

The Philadelphia Flyers' Andre "Moose" Dupont best described the times. After a game in which Dupont used his stick to create an eight-stitch cut in an opponent's face, he said contentedly, "That was a lot of fun. We don't go to jail, we beat up their chicken forwards, we score ten goals, and we win. And now the Moose drinks beer."

The bedlam would continue well into the '80s, until hockey — finally concerned about its reputation for bloodlust — began to enact more severe penalties. One-on-one fisticuffs between willing combatants would remain kosher. But to clearly instigate a fight or to be the third man in on someone else's fray would be no more.

It was a business move. The NHL hadn't had a national TV contract in years. Outside its native lands of Canada, the Rust Belt, and the Northeast, the sport was viewed as an oddity, something akin to the World Wrestling Federation on ice. It's one thing to sell the occasional bare-knuckles fight; it's quite another to market a series of miniature riots.

The league hired a new commissioner, a marketing geek pirated away from the National Basketball Association. It launched teams in places like San Jose, Dallas, Miami, and Nashville. And the fighter, who had since seen his title changed to the more romantic calling of "enforcer," was becoming an afterthought.

By the late 1990s, hockey was a shadow of its former violent self. Teams that once employed three full-time fighters were now hiring just one. Some even went without. The number of fights was falling dramatically. In fact, the NHL hadn't witnessed a decent bench-clearing brawl since 1987. Many believed the enforcer would be extinct in a matter of years.

Garrett Burnett has the misfortune of being born twenty years too late. He is decidedly old-school, a player whose own father describes his son's brand of hockey as "extreme."

Kevin Neibauer, a columnist for *Just Hockey*, recalls seeing Burnett when he joined the Philadelphia Phantoms three years ago. "His first game here . . . Burnett had three shifts and three fights."

But the most telling assessment comes from last season's stats, when Burnett played for the Kentucky Thoroughblades of the American Hockey League. The numbers: 3 goals, 3 assists, 506 penalty minutes — despite missing 24 games. To put this in perspective, Denny Lambert led the NHL with 219 minutes. When Lumberjacks Director of Media Relations Tom Caudill first examined Burnett's numbers, "I thought it was a misprint," he says.

Bryan Kurzman owns Drop the Gloves, a Newton, Massachusetts, company "specializing in game-used enforcer jerseys and equipment," the fight fan's version of a collectibles shop. His is a doctoral knowledge of all matters pugilistic.

"Cleveland has never seen a pure enforcer like Garrett," says Kurzman. "A guy like Garrett, he just eats, sleeps, and breathes fighting and hockey. He just loves the art of hand-to-hand combat. He understands the role and what it takes to get the job done. He doesn't have any qualms with it."

On a sunny September afternoon, Burnett sits in a Euclid Avenue eatery, talking about that job. For a professional fighter, his face is relatively damage-free. Sure, there's the bent nose and a small cut across the bridge, the hint of a scar above his eye. But he is a handsome man, with a chiseled, angular face and gelled black hair. When he smiles, which is often, he looks like a model for some rugged brand of cologne. When he doesn't, fierce eyes and the requisite goatee make him look to be sired by a third cousin of Mephistopheles.

An inquisitor asks if he enjoys fighting. He launches into a long monologue on the role of the enforcer, known to players as simply The Tough Guy. He solemnly recites the official job description: to protect his teammates; to look out for the talented, the small, those too important to waste away in the penalty box.

But the inquisitor presses on. Does he enjoy fighting?

Burnett pauses for a moment, trying to maintain the Earnest Athlete Doing an Interview Routine, then breaks out a sheepish smile.

"Yeah, I guess I do. I really do."

Genes are what brought him to this day. Burnett's sister was a three-time British Columbia wrestling champ. And Dad — let's just say Burnett the elder could knuckle in his own right.

Bob Burnett played senior amateur in Vancouver and admits to fighting "quite a bit. It went hand in hand with being big in those days. I guess it's just something I handed down to him."

Such things are important heirlooms in Canada, where hockey is invariably described in hallowed terms. A sample day from Garrett's youth: "You go to school, talk about hockey all day at school, then get home, get your stick, play street hockey — like in *Wayne's World* — then eat supper, go to your hockey game, then get home, and it's late, so you watch hockey with your parents.

"It's like a religion."

Actually, it's a theology bordering on fanaticism. Take the case of an Oakville, Ontario, league. Officials suspected some of the town's best talent was playing in another Metro Toronto league, despite residency requirements. So Oakville hired private investigators to stalk the players. The offenders' ages: nine to thirteen.

By the time top prospects reach sixteen and seventeen in Canada, they are drafted away by elite junior leagues and sent to live in distant cities with new families.

Burnett was never subjected to such attention. He was not a skill player, the euphemism for quick feet, soft hands, a cunning shot. Nor had he discovered the joys of fighting. He recalls his first bout as a seventeen-year-old trying to earn a spot in the British Columbia Hockey League. He was in preseason camp when he noticed a bigger, older kid pushing others around.

"I had never fought before. I don't know what happened. My gloves just kind of fell off the first time I was on the ice, and the next thing I know I'm on top of him."

Young Burnett had found his gift in life. But the road to becoming a tough guy is indeed the road less traveled — and for good reason. He would later try out for the Saskatchewan Hockey League. A preseason game proved instructive when he took on a tough guy three years his senior. "He probably hit me eight to ten times before I got going. I realized it was going to be a tougher job to be a losing fighter than a winning fighter."

His mother, Vicci, agrees. During those early days, she had difficulty watching her little boy play. "When he was fighting, I would pick the program up and start reading, so I didn't have to watch."

Still, Burnett was good enough neither at hockey nor fighting to make a name for himself out West. "A lot of teams would say, 'You don't have the foot speed; the skills are not there,'" he says.

So at age nineteen, elderly by Canadian junior league standards, he offered to pay his own way to a tryout with the Sault Ste. Marie Greyhounds. For a northern boy, the Ontario Hockey League is a princely station. It is the NHL's best finishing school, chock-full of high draft picks and gems awaiting polish. Burnett was a decided longshot to make the team. Yet he would see his defining moment the first shift of preseason camp.

On that day, he took the Greyhounds' number-one draft pick hard into the boards, knocking him to the ice. The player came up swinging. With one punch, Burnett crushed the bridge of his nose. "He couldn't breathe for two months."

The fighter had landed a spot on the roster.

But the Ontario League proved an alien land. Burnett was eager to learn the craft of the tough guy — a bit too eager. In the Western League, he says, "it's so intense that they won't let teams warm up at the same time. They're old-school. In the OHL, they let you warm up together. I was getting in fights all the time during warmups."

By December, he would be traded to the Kitchener Rangers, where, incidentally, he was invited to stay with the family of the number-one pick whose nose he crushed. Such are the live-and-let-live ways of the North.

Kitchener, however, would not go particularly well either. He recalls his first home game with the Rangers. A tough guy from Sarnia was beating a Ranger not known for fisticuffs. In between punches, the tough guy would raise his finger in the "We're Number One" salute, before unloading again. Burnett emerged to avenge the slight on the next face-off. It turned into an all-out brawl. "My coach was pounding on their coach. It was funny."

Not so funny was that Burnett had become a marked man. "I ran into a lot of problems with suspensions. I was looked at as a one-dimensional player that came out of the West." After the season, he was traded once again, this time to Portland.

Burnett saw no use playing further in the junior leagues. He was, in many respects, the one-dimensional player others thought him to be. He readily admits that fighting was the only thing keeping him in the game. So he did what any player who's short of options would do. He turned pro.

"He just decided if he was going to be knocking heads, he would knock heads with the men," says father Bob.

He tried out for the Binghamton Rangers of the AHL, hockey's equivalent to AAA baseball. He was cut in camp.

He signed on with the Utica Blizzard of the Colonial League, a landfill for has-beens and never-will-bes. The pay was three hundred dollars a week, the play uninspired, and the owner, who bought the team with his wife's money, decided to coach as well, though he had never actually played hockey. Burnett asked for his release after fifteen games.

He fired up his 1980 sedan and headed to Oklahoma City. Three games, cut. Then Tulsa. Six games, cut.

Bob Burnett recalls these as trying times for his son. "The phone bills were fairly extensive there for a while."

By all accounts, the Burnetts are a close family. It may seem corny, even contrived, but Garrett speaks earnestly — constantly — about the support he receives from Mom and Dad. By this time, however, their son had already been dropped from four teams, and the season wasn't yet over. Even mother Vicci, who speaks with the warmth of a saint, was second-guessing that support. "I've always told him that good things happen to good people, but sometimes I was really questioning what I was telling him."

Garrett listened nonetheless. He heard of a coach in Hampton Roads named John Brophy. The former minor leaguer was said to like tough guys, said to be someone "who would carve out your eye and not think anything of it," says Burnett. For a fighter down on his luck, Brophy looked like the Second Coming.

So Burnett once again packed up and headed for Nashville, where Hampton Roads was playing. When he went to mooch a free ticket at the Nashville office, the team invited him to join the pregame skate. He was hired on the spot. But this, too, would not last. Two weeks, cut.

"I was halfway across America," recalls Burnett. "I don't know where I am. I want to come home. People were just telling me I wasn't a good enough player. But my parents kept telling me not to listen to them, kept pushing me to knock on doors."

So he would knock on the door of the Jacksonville Lizard Kings. The team had nailed one of the last playoff spots, and the coach wanted toughness. He promised extra instruction if Burnett worked extra hard. When the season concluded, however, Burnett received a pink slip — his sixth of the year.

He was claimed by Peoria the next season. Cut.

So he signed with Knoxville in what proved to be his best season. He picked up 5 goals, 11 assists, 321 penalty minutes. More important, Burnett got his confidence back.

The turning point came when Roanoke arrived in town. A former Knoxville player, regarded as the team bully for hazing younger guys, was now skating for Roanoke. He had terrorized Knoxville during the preseason.

"Everybody had fear of this guy," says Burnett. "They were saying we should just leave this guy alone."

By the second period, Knoxville was down 3–1, and the Roanoke badass was skating toward him. Burnett offered up the international tough guy mating call: "Hey, you wanna go?"

"It almost seemed like the first time I ever fought. I just kept throwing and throwing. I hit him maybe twenty, twenty-five times, just hammering the shit out of him." Knoxville ended up winning 5–3.

It was a moment of clarity. Burnett discovered his role in the ecosystem — that with a few well-placed punches, he could purge the fear of an entire team, give bravery to those who had none.

Perhaps miraculously, he would stay with Knoxville the whole season. But life in Tennessee was not to last.

Burnett worried about becoming a franchise player. In the context of minor-league hockey, the designation is not as exalted as it sounds. They are usually aging scorers, notorious fighters, kept by the same team year after year to provide a marketing identity, with no chance of moving up. The East Coast Hockey League, the infamously brutal venue where Knoxville played, owns a good share of these men. The pay is low and the perks are few, but it beats the hell out of getting a real job.

Burnett never saw it this way. "I thought they just wanted me there to bring in fans," he says. Besides, NHL scouts did not ply the land of okra and grits. Their work was done north. So he requested a trade.

In the meantime, he landed tryouts in other leagues. Las Vegas: Cut. Utah: Cut. Syracuse: Cut.

But in Johnstown, Pennsylvania, a man named Nick Fotiu liked what he saw. He spent fourteen years in the NHL, a legendary tough guy. Now coach of the Johnstown Chiefs, Fotiu understood the import of tough guys. He traded for Burnett, and the player would serve his mentor well. In just 34 games, Burnett had 1 goal, 1 assist, and 331 penalty minutes.

The numbers, specifically the last one, were good enough to land a tryout with the Philadelphia Phantoms by midyear. He was supposed to stay ten days; he ended up staying the season and made a name for himself in the process.

"He put the fear in other clubs," says Fotiu. "Other clubs didn't want him playing, because they knew they would get hit."

Most tough guys pick their spots, maintaining a large, looming presence on the outskirts of the game, waiting for the roughness to start. Burnett, by contrast, was an impatient madman. If there was no trouble to be had, he would create it himself. It was not uncommon to see him throwing punches moments into his first shift. And if that fight ended in a draw, he would seek the man out a second, a third time, until the matter was settled.

"What you have to understand about Burnett is he wants to go every night, and he won't wait for you to fight him," says fellow tough guy and former teammate Adam Nittel. "He knows before the game that he's going to go out there and tear somebody's head off. His model is to instill fear before the puck's dropped. He comes right out straight and says, 'You wanna go?' And if they don't want to, he won't leave their side by more than five feet the whole game. He has everybody else hearing footsteps out there."

Cleveland teammate Chris Armstrong puts it more succinctly: "Sometimes it's like he's almost out of control, like he's almost certifiable."

Such aggression got him noticed. After the season, he was signed by the NHL's San Jose Sharks.

It is one thing to make the NHL as a conventional player. It is another to do it as a tough guy. The interview process requires kicking the living shit out of other candidates, who just happen to be your teammates.

Prior to his first camp in San Jose, Burnett had spent the past few years making $400 a week. The prize for winning a new job in the Silicon Valley: $300,000 annually. In that first year, he fought six times in the initial scrimmage, only to be sent down to minor-league Kentucky, where the pay was $50,000. He would eventually be injured and play but thirty-one games.

Last year, he returned to San Jose, fighting Nittel every chance he got. Yet the Sharks already had a resident tough guy. Burnett was sent down once more.

It wasn't necessarily a bad move, for the Burnett legend would reach full bloom in Lexington, Kentucky. He fought fifty-three times — the NHL record is a mere thirty-nine — and racked up so many penalties that fans in one section kept a running tally on a homemade sign, the way fans in St. Louis chart Mark McGwire's home runs. He was the consummate showman, blowing kisses to the crowd, appearing for the team in WWF-style TV commercials. He had long autograph lines, was a prime ambassador to the community. Here was a man who knew how to play a crowd.

"After he got kicked out of a game, he would return to watch the rest of the game with almost nothing on," says Thoroughblades' booster club member Keith Coleman. "He would return with just a Speedo on or something, making sure his big chest showed. The women just loved him."

Whether one is a goon or not depends upon which jersey one is wearing. The routine that played so well in Lexington sank in opposing arenas. Internet forums for other AHL teams are filled with references to Burnett as a "knuckle-dragger," "Mr. Neanderthal," and "Hit 'Em From Behind Burnett." They catalog a long list of muggings, cheap shots, and untoward behavior.

On a fan site for the Cincinnati Mighty Ducks, Kentucky's archrival, an article describes the tough guy as "a gutless goon." But the story's last line is the most telling: "We won't miss his antics, but most fans agree that we won't forget him either."

Indeed, Burnett had become the most loved and hated man in the American Hockey League.

Apparently the Thoroughblades, like the parent club in San

Jose, were not as impressed. When his contract expired last spring, he wasn't resigned.

About to enter the NHL were two new teams in Columbus and Minnesota. Expansion franchises are Job Service programs for players like Burnett, who huddle at the fringes of hockey's top league. They are places of opportunity, rebirth. And they tend to be keen on employing tough guys. New teams are inherently bad. Fights distract fans from noticing this.

After last season, Burnett told his agent, "'Just tell me when you have a place for me to go.' I just wanted a chance."

That chance would be granted by the Cleveland Lumberjacks, Minnesota's top affiliate.

Burnett is sitting in an Independence restaurant, one of those pre-fab joints decorated in rough lumber to simulate character. He is eating his customary dish of meat, gravy, and potatoes when he remarks out of the blue, "I just feel good today. I don't know why. I just feel really good." He is known to bubble like this.

One might expect a tough guy, especially one of Burnett's pedigree, to be the brooding, surly sort. Some are. One of the baddest men he ever fought would later land in jail. Kurzman has a tape of another actually stealing a foe's necklace during a fight, then showing off the bounty to teammates.

But most are regarded as the pleasant men of hockey, as agreeable off the ice as they are mean on. Burnett, of course, is the extreme. His is a yes, ma'am/no, ma'am politeness. He recounts his battles with laughter and shy smiles. "He's basically a big kid," says *Just Hockey* columnist Neibauer. There is no talk of himself in third person, no threadbare ego easily snipped by a pointed question. In fact, nearly everyone who knows him stresses his essential goodness.

There's the story of a young brother and sister in Kentucky. Unlucky genes forced them to have their feet amputated. Burnett visited them at the hospital and brought them to a game as his guest. "It gave him so much pleasure to see them there," says mother Vicci.

Then there's the tale of the eight-year-old boy who had a heart attack and lapsed into a coma. When he came to, the first thing he said was, "How are the boys doing? Is Burnie still suspended?" His mother called the Thoroughblades, and Burnett soon arrived with sticks, memorabilia, tickets to the game, and an invitation to the locker room.

Carol Williams, an editor at two hockey periodicals, tells of another eight-year-old in Philly, this one battling leukemia. "Josh took a liking to Garrett, and Garrett took a liking to Josh. Whenever Garrett's in town, he makes it his business to find Josh. I asked Garrett one night where he got his courage from, and he said, 'You want to meet somebody who's brave?' and he took me to meet Josh. Garrett's just that type of person. He's so human. He's just constantly reaching out."

No doubt Burnett is genuine. His sparkle and missing-in-action vanity tell you so. But there is also a calculation evident. Everyone in hockey is basically a tough guy, from coaches to general managers. Unlike in other sports, they suffer neither prima donnas nor punks easily. Burnett understands it's in his best interest to be a model of decorum off the ice. After all, there are other tough guys where he came from.

Talk to him away from the game, and only his hands betray what he does for a living. They are huge, meaty things, with so much scar tissue they light up under nightclub neon. Each hard knob, each bent knuckle has a fight attached to it.

It is the principal hazard of being a tough guy. "My hands are a mess," says Eric Boulton, a Burnett nemesis who plays for the Buffalo Sabres. "I have a couple ligaments torn off the bones in the fingers of one hand."

Then he adds, with requisite tough-guy understatement: "Nothing big. I can still fight."

"You look at guys, and their skin splits open, and it becomes infected," says Mike Brophy, a writer for *The Hockey News*. "[Detroit's Joey] Kocur had the worst I've ever seen. They looked like a road map: stitches and scabs and scars. It was really gross. It hurt to look at his hands."

It is one reason so few players want the job. To be called on to fight nightly, to go home with cut fists, headaches, to look in the mirror and see scar tissue where a face once was, to wake up in the morning unable to bend fingers, pick up children, hold the car keys — no, this is not a job others seek.

There is also the fear. Says Lumberjacks center Brett McLean:

"I'd have a hard time sleeping at night, knowing some of the guys I'd have to square off with the next night."

And for good reason. With tough guys increasingly trained in boxing and martial arts, according to Burnett, "I wouldn't be surprised if somebody gets killed someday."

"Bare-knuckle boxing was outlawed when?" asks Steve Dryden. "And we still have sanctioned, bare-fisted bouts? It's hard to believe we're having this discussion in the year 2000."

Dryden is editor-in-chief of *The Hockey News*, regarded as "The Bible of Hockey." He is among the most prominent critics of fighting, at times known as a "conscientious objector," at other times referred to with the less flattering label of "Greenpeace puke."

To fight or not to fight; this debate has clung to hockey for years. Dryden is among the few close to the sport in vocal opposition. Most hand-wringing comes from outside. Conduct a newspaper search with the phrase "hockey fighting" and it produces mounds of commentary on the game's blood thirst and absence of civility.

Compounding the problem is a brutal past year for the sport. Tough guy Marty McSorley was recently convicted in a Vancouver court for using his stick to deliver a two-handed knockout blow to another player's head. In Illinois, an amateur player was checked into the boards after a game, leaving him paralyzed. And in Massachusetts, one parent, upset that the coach of his son's team was letting play get too rough, showed his displeasure by beating the coach to death.

This is what is known as an image problem.

Hockey officials have always skirted the issue, offering denunciations of illegal play, yet never moving toward an outright ban of fighting. "The owners don't want to attack this issue, because they know a lot of people just come to the games because of the fights," says Larry Wigge, who's covered hockey for *The Sporting News* since 1969.

Tough guys respond with a shrug. They remain among the most popular players, the subject of memorabilia stores, Web sites like "Knuckles, Blood & Ice." Canadian broadcaster Don Cherry's fight tapes have sold over a million copies.

Rob Skrlac, resident tough guy for the Albany River Rats, sums it up best: "Nobody ever gets up to get a cup of coffee when a fight's going on. But when I'm watching two Europeans run up and down the ice, I might get thirsty."

Still, these are ominous times for the fighter. Rules changes have withered his ability to exact revenge. Moreover, coaches are less tolerant of tough guys taking reckless penalties. When the playoffs come around, today's enforcers are usually found in the press box; they don't even dress. The man who throws fists and does little else is soon to be extinct.

"The fighter who can't skate and can't play is a dinosaur," says Sean Brousseau, Burnett's agent. Which is why he delivered his client to Cleveland. Here awaits the chance to prove once and for all that Garrett Burnett is not a goon.

On a recent Wednesday night at Gund Arena, a sparse crowd seems to barely outnumber the ushers and concessionaires. Pity, because the Lumberjacks are a fine-looking team. Theirs is a roster filled with speedsters and jitterbug forwards. Most played in the NHL or are legitimate prospects. Only two remain from last year's team, the rest descending upon Cleveland in hopes of seizing a precious new expansion job with the parent club in St. Paul.

Aside from one brief shift in the first period, Burnett will be restricted to shouting encouragement from the bench. The Lumberjacks blow a 4–2 lead, eventually losing 5–4. This is the season's third game; Burnett didn't dress for the first, didn't play a shift in the second.

The post-game locker room finds coach Todd McLellan in a distracted yet courteous mood. He speaks of Burnett as a role player, of his need to improve — just as many coaches have spoken before him. But McLellan also invokes the phrase "hard worker," words forever linked to Burnett, and he seems sincere when saying the tough guy's time will come as the season wears.

On this night, Burnett is unusually terse. He responds to questions with quick, monosyllabic sentences. There are no laughs, no little boy's grin, no sign of the big kid who has slugged his way across America, maintaining good cheer while others said he wasn't good enough.

But later this evening, back at his Independence hotel room, he will likely remember the mantra he so often recites. "It doesn't matter if it takes me till I'm thirty-five years old. I'll never stop trying."

It is a long-money play to bet on Garrett Burnett. The numbers, the trends of the game, those swift, diminutive teammates who skate while he yells from the bench, all are barriers before him. Yet the tough guy cares little whether you believe in him or not. He will happily wait his turn in Cleveland. After all, it is a town with the attributes a fighter seeks.

"I really like this place, because it has a Jumbotron screen," he says. "You can see your punches in slow motion while you're in the penalty box."

Toughest Miler Ever

FROM THE TORRANCE DAILY BREEZE

Survivor *is just a bland TV show to the real thing,*
named Zamperini — B.C.

LOUIS ZAMPERINI IS SITTING in a cafe in Hollywood, not far
from his home in the hills, and orders the day's luncheon special:
meatloaf.

Apologetically, the comely waitress informs him they are out of
gravy for his meatloaf and mashed potatoes, expecting him to order something else. As though no gravy would matter to a man who
once had no water for seven days, and no food — other than two
small sharks, a few fish, and a couple of birds he managed to catch
while floating nearly two thousand miles in the South Pacific — for
forty-seven days.

No gravy? That reminds Zamperini of a story. But then everything reminds "Louie" of a story. This one is about the boat trip to
the 1936 Olympic Games in Germany and the recipe for winning a
medal that a U.S. Olympic coach gave him:

"No pork, no gravy, and no women."

Louie's smile tells you that he followed two-thirds of the advice.

He didn't win an Olympic medal in Berlin, placing eighth as the
top American in the five-thousand-meters, but it wasn't because of
pork, gravy, or women. Rather, because of youth. Louie was only
nineteen years old, freshly graduated from Torrance High School.

Surely at age twenty-three or twenty-seven he would have won a
medal in the 1940 and/or 1944 Olympics had World War II not
canceled both Games.

"In '40 and '44, I would have been at my running peak," Zamperini confirms matter-of-factly, not a trace of braggadocio in

his voice. "Those would have been my Olympics. I'd have brought home a medal.

"Or two."

And that he didn't?

"It doesn't bother me," Zamperini, now eighty-three, replies. His eyes remain as blue as the summer sky, but oh what darkness they have witnessed. "Not after what I'd gone through."

Hell is what he went through.

And lived to tell about it.

Devil at My Heels he titled his autobiography, to give you an idea.

On May 27, 1943, United States Air Force Captain Louis Zamperini was a bombardier on a B-24 Liberator flying a secret experimental mission when it was shot down south of Hawaii. Eight of the eleven men aboard were killed in the crash.

Zamperini and another crewmate — the third crash survivor died in the life raft — drifted nearly two thousand miles in the South Pacific, living in terror twenty-four/seven of enemy attacks while fighting hunger, fighting thirst, even fighting sharks.

"Two big sharks tried to jump in the raft and take us out," Zamperini retells.

That wasn't the worst of it, though.

"We went seven days without water — that was brutal," he adds, ironically taking a sip of ice tea before continuing.

"We managed to catch some fish, a couple of birds, two small sharks — even took their livers out for nourishment."

On the fifth day of the seventh week, the two survivors were picked up by a Japanese patrol boat. The 5'9" Zamperini, who had weighed 160 pounds when *The Green Hornet* crashed, was now down to 67 pounds, and about 37 were his heart.

When the famous Olympian refused to make propaganda broadcasts for the Japanese, he was imprisoned. Ask him about the slave labor camp and Zamperini responds politely, "Those are stories for another time."

This time being lunch time, he merely offers an answer that won't ruin your meal or his; an answer that you can read here over breakfast: "It was daily torture, beatings, starvation. It was hell."

Hell for two and a half years.

Initially listed as "Missing in Action," Louis Zamperini was declared officially dead by the War Department in 1944.

"Lou Zamperini, Olympian and War Hero Killed in Action" read one newspaper headline.

New York's Madison Square Garden held "The Zamperini Memorial Mile."

Zamperini Field at Torrance Airport was christened.

One problem — Louie was not dead. He was living in hell.

Louis Zamperini remembers the hell that was his very first track race — 660 yards — as a freshman at Torrance High in 1917.

"It was too much pain. I said, 'Never again,'" he retells. "I thought that was the worst pain I could imagine."

He thought wrong.

He never imagined war, never imagined forty-seven days in a raft adrift at sea, never imagined two and a half years as a prisoner of war in Camp 4-B in Naoetsu.

And, even in his worst nightmares, never imagined "The Bird." That was the nickname the POWs gave Japanese Army Sergeant Matsuhiro Watanabe, the devil incarnate in this hell.

The Bird preyed on Zamperini, using a thick leather belt with a steel buckle to beat him bloody. In one mean streak, he belted Louie into unconsciousness fourteen days in a row.

A devout Catholic, Zamperini's faith was tested supremely. But, like his iron will, it was never broken.

"Faith is more important than courage," he allows.

We often make sports out to be more important than they are. And yet in Louie Zamperini's case, you cannot overestimate the importance.

"Absolutely, my athletic background saved my life," Zamperini opines. "Track and field competition sharpens your skills. I kept thinking about my athletic training when I was competing against the elements, against the enemy, against hunger and thirst.

"In athletics, you learn to find ways to increase your effort. In athletics you don't quit — EVER.

"I'm certain I wouldn't have survived if I hadn't been an athlete."

He survived hell, Louis Zamperini did, but this hero — an authentic hero, mind you, not one created by Nike — was never the same athlete after Camp 4-B.

"My body never recovered," he shares. "My body was beaten."

His body weighed just eighty pounds at war's end, sixty-seven pounds below his running weight. The Olympic Games resumed in 1948 without Louie. He never won the Olympic medal — or two — he thought he would. But he was a mettle winner. He had already proved himself to be the toughest miler who ever lived.

The Toughest Miler Who Ever Lived will be the honorary starter for today's seventh annual Keep L.A. Running 5K and 10K races at Dockweiler Beach in Playa del Rey. The event is expected to raise $100,000 for various charities.

It is not just a one-time good deed. Louie Zamperini has been working with youth since 1952, taking them running and camping and skiing, and most importantly, taking them under his guidance.

To this day he gives a couple of speeches a week at schools, churches, and clubs, reaching out to as many as three thousand youngsters and teens a month.

The sixty-plus-year-old scrapbook, its leather cover cracked and spine long ago broken, shows the wear of passing decades much more than does the man who was the boy featured inside.

Louie Zamperini, who turned eighty-three in January, turns the tattered pages chronicling his athletic life. Here he is in Torrance High where he set a national schoolboy record. There he is in Berlin for the 1936 Olympics where he represented America proudly. Here he is at USC where he was twice the national champion at the distance of one mile.

The scrapbook is about the size of a large couch cushion, and just as thick, with yellowed newspaper clippings from the defunct *Torrance Herald* and *New York Times* and more. But the amazing thing is that this glorious memorabilia very nearly could have been a police rap sheet instead.

"I was a juvenile delinquent," Zamperini says, confessing to belonging to a gang, to stealing pies and food and, this being the Depression and Prohibition, even breaking into bootleggers' homes to steal their illegal hooch.

"At fifteen years of age, it was touch and go," he continues. "My parents were really worried. My dad, my [older] brother Pete, the principal, and the police chief all got together and decided track was the thing to straighten me out."

This was a strange choice, because other than fleeing from the law, young Louie had shown no aptitude for running.

"At picnic races, the girls beat me," Louie shares, laughing at the distant memory. "I hated running. 'Boy,' I thought, 'this is not for me.'"

His first track meet didn't change his thinking.

"I came in dead last in the 660 behind a sickly guy and a fat guy. The pain and exhaustion. The smoking, the chewing tobacco, the booze — I was a mess.

"Running? 'Never again!' I said."

Never came just a week later. Coerced into competing in a dual meet as the only 660 runner from Torrance High, Louie again found himself in last place.

"I didn't care," he retells, "until I heard the fans cheering, 'Go Lou-EE! Go Lou-EE!' When I heard them cheering my name, I ran my guts out and barely passed one guy."

The moment mattered.

It matters still.

"That's the race I remember most fondly, even more than the Olympic race in Berlin, more than the NCAA titles," Louie says, the memory warming him like the summer sun.

More fondly than the Olympics?

"Yes, truthfully," he rejoins. "You have to understand, that race changed my life. I was shocked to realize people knew my name. That was the start. You never forget your first anything, and that was my first taste of recognition."

Cue the *Rocky* theme music.

"Instantly, I became a running fanatic," Louie points out, proudly. "I wouldn't eat pie or ice cream. I even started eating vegetables."

And he ran. Everywhere. He ran four miles to the beach. And four miles back. He ran in the mountains, sometimes while hunting rabbit (so his mom could cook rabbit cacciatore) and deer, running up the steep slopes with a rifle slung over his shoulder.

His unique training methods worked. Soon he won a race. And another. Once without direction, he now had one forward, fast.

As a sophomore in 1933, Louie set a course record (9:57) in a two-mile cross-country race, winning varsity by *a quarter-mile*. He didn't lose a race (cross-country or track) for the next three years!

En route of the amazing streak, as a junior, Louie broke the national high school record in the mile (4:21). If the time on a cinder track doesn't overly impress you, this will: his mark stood for a full twenty years.

Impressive, too, was being invited to the 1936 U.S. Olympic Trials at the tender age of nineteen.

Unfortunately, the trials were across the country in New York.

Fortunately, Louie's father worked for the Southern Pacific Railroad and got one free pass each year good to any destination. Torrance (pop. 2,500) merchants donated a suitcase and new clothes to the local hero and even some money for food and lodging.

Skipping the mile — "Glenn Cunningham and a few others ran around 4:10, so I thought I had no chance" — Louie entered the five-thousand-meters instead. Smart move. "The Iron Man," as one newspaper headline referred to the thickly muscled Zamperini, tied for first to make the Olympic team.

He was not so wise during the long — and luxurious — boat trip across the Pond.

"My big mistake was eating all the good food until I was too heavy to run," explains Zamperini, who roomed with the great Jesse Owens. "I put on about ten to twelve pounds. I ate myself out of a medal."

Still, he might have turned in the greatest eighth-place showing (in a field of forty-one runners) in Olympic history.

"My brother had always told me, 'Isn't one minute of pain worth a lifetime of glory?'" Louie shares.

He got his glory thanks to a final minute of pain.

Actually, only fifty-six seconds of pain, that being how quickly Louie ran the final lap. Running his guts out like he had in that high school race when he finally beat a runner, Louie gained fifty meters on the winner and passed so many runners that Adolf Hitler was so impressed he asked for the Italian kid from America to be brought up to his box to shake his hand.

After the Olympics, Zamperini took his racing spikes to USC.

With no mountains to climb while chasing after rabbit and deer, Louie would scale the fence at the Los Angeles Coliseum and run up and down the stairs "until my legs went numb."

It worked.

He became a two-time NCAA champion in the mile (1938–39), the first mile champ ever from the West Coast. His mile mark of 4:08 stood as the national collegiate record for fifteen years, but it almost was a mark for the ages.

"I didn't even push it," Zamperini allows. "I was so mad at myself afterwards. I could have run four-flat."

Four minutes flat? In 1939? A full fifteen years before Roger Banister would make history by breaking the four-minute barrier?

"Yes. I know I could have run four-flat that day," Zamperini insists.

Even if he had, that feat wouldn't have been half as remarkable as what he did do: survive forty-seven days adrift at sea in a raft; surviving seven straight days without water; surviving on a couple of birds and little sharks and courage; and then surviving daily torture in a Japanese slave labor camp for two and a half years.

His older brother Pete miscalculated. Louie's lifetime of glory came at a considerably steeper price than one minute of pain.

"Age has a way of catching up to you," says the man who never saw anyone catch up to him from behind on the track.

Actually, he seems to be outrunning Father Time, too.

Sure, the thick, dark, curly hair on the dashing young man seen on page after page in the oversized scrapbook has thinned and turned white. But watch Louie Zamperini, princely in posture still, nimbly climb up a flight of stairs to his second-floor office at the First Presbyterian Church of Hollywood and you can almost picture him, even in his eighty-third summer, chasing deer up a coastal mountainside with a rifle slung over his back.

Louie closes the book of memories and then shares a memory from the pages of his mind: "Gregory Peck once sent over a bottle of champagne to my table with a note: 'Race you around the block.'

"We didn't, of course."

In his day, Louie Zamperini was the fastest around the block, but the most amazing thing is not the national prep mile record he set that stood for two decades or his collegiate mile mark that stood for fifteen years, nor the glory of competing in the Olympics or even surviving forty-seven days lost at sea and two and a half years more in hell.

No, the most amazing thing of all is this: "I forgave The Bird," Louie Zamperini, sitting in a Hollywood cafe, tells you, and he means it.

In fact, he tried to set up a meeting with Watanabe — who had avoided prosecution as a war criminal by hiding out in the remote mountains near Nagano until the statute of limitations ran out — during the 1998 Nagano Winter Olympics. Alas, the extended olive branch was crushed under the heels of Watanabe's family members.

The hell of Camp 4-B was a lifetime ago.

Lunch on a heavenly July afternoon is now.

No gravy?

No matter.

The Toughest Miler Who Ever Lived smiles at the young waitress and orders the meatloaf anyway.

VAHE GREGORIAN

Olympics Dream Ends in Agony

FROM THE ST. LOUIS POST-DISPATCH

To Sammy, silver seems like zinc — B.C.

SYDNEY, AUSTRALIA — In panic and despair, Sammie Henson yanked down his red USA Wrestling singlet top as he bounded off the wrestling platform. His heart felt like it was going to stop.

Then he sprinted and began screaming as he slalomed through a maze of blue temporary barriers, past astonished onlookers, and burst into a hallway. Seeing an opening, he just had an urge.

Legs still churning, he cut left beneath the stands in Sydney Exhibition Hall 1, and his scream changed to a chilling, primal moan that evoked the picture of an animal with its leg caught in a steel trap.

On the other side of the stands, his wife, Stephanie, knew he was screaming somewhere. "I was only surprised I couldn't hear it."

As mortified security personnel, volunteers, coaches, and media followed, he came to a wall and abruptly turned right, the only way he could go.

Then he could run no more, and he fell to the ground, where for minutes he lay on his back, kicking, arms flailing, wailing. He didn't know where he was when assistant coach John Smith and others pulled him up and took him to a restricted area.

Down the hall stood his father, Bob, who sipped a cup of coffee and waited, tears behind his glasses, nitroglycerin pills still in the pouch around his neck.

"I don't know what's going to happen to him now," he said.

Twenty-one years, Sammie Henson had waited for, pointed to, fantasized about this day, this moment.

Think about what you want more than anything, the one thing that would give you peace.

For him, it was an Olympic gold medal — and, of course, the match to earn it. He was eight years old, in family friend Roger Hodapp's boat on Lake St. Louis, when he first blurted it out.

"I will be the Olympic champion," he said, and Hodapp and the others chuckled and teased him.

Through the years, he never stopped saying it. Or believing it.

Not as he won three state wrestling championships at Francis Howell High, where he was coached by Hodapp and Jud Hoffman.

Not when he drank too much, fell into trouble, and was kicked off the wrestling team at Mizzou.

Not when he won two NCAA titles at Clemson before vindicating himself by returning to Missouri to finish his degree.

Not when, over and over, his relentless brother Chuck would call him at 4:00 A.M. to wake him up, to tell him that his competitors already were training.

Not when he decided that to be a champion he must first work harder than anyone in the world, then set about trying to do just that every day.

Not when he won the 1998 World Championship in Iran, where he defeated Namig Abdullayev of Azerbaijan, and the enchanted Iranians threw flowers and roared, "U-S-A, U-S-A."

And certainly not since June, when he qualified for his first Olympics and began introducing himself as "Sammie Henson, Olympic champ."

"Do You Believe in Me?"

On the day of his life, Saturday, Sammie Henson awoke at 9:30 A.M. to the sound of Stephanie knocking on his door at the Pacific International Suites, blocks away from the Exhibition Hall. She had stayed at another hotel Friday, ostensibly to go gather her things since they had arrived at different times here.

On Friday night, he had taken his pre-bed bubble bath *knowing* he would win the gold medal less than twenty-four hours later.

What person he would have to wrestle for it was immaterial, though it turned out to be Abdullayev.

They went to breakfast, and he had scrambled eggs, a pancake-like dish, and orange juice before doing a light workout. On competition days, he is quieter than normal but not distant.

Another bubble bath and a nap, and it was 3:00 P.M. Time to leave. As they parted, he asked, "Do you believe in me?" She said, "I do. You're the best in the world; I know you're going to do it."

On the way to the arena, past the oblivious crowds of revelers and fans, he saw nothing and no one. He prayed, kept praying, and went through a checklist.

The Match

Just after 5:15 P.M., Henson, wearing red, raced out of the holding room up onto the mat to be introduced for the 119-pound free-style championship alongside Abdullayev, in blue.

Henson fidgeted, twitched, and swayed, waited, waited, waited, crossed himself, put up his arms to allow the referee to check his person and his uniform . . .

Suddenly, they touched hands and began.

Only sixteen seconds passed, and Abdullayev had Henson's leg and took him down to make it 1–0. Only forty-five seconds into the match, Abdullayev turned Henson to make it 3–0.

The young Henson would have been frazzled now, but at twenty-nine, he knew he only needed one point, then another, not all at once. They cuffed, swatted, twisted, and turned, and it was 3–1 after Abdullayev was cautioned for an illegal reach.

After Abdullayev was told to let go of Henson's singlet, Henson earned a point for a takedown to make it 3–2 before the break between three-minute periods.

Loud chants of "U-S-A, U-S-A" enveloped the arena, and only twenty-one seconds into the second period Henson tied it by taking down Abdullayev again. This was his time.

But a minute later, after having his singlet clutched again, Henson lost patience and left his comfort zone to try to make something happen. Abdullayev remained ready to exploit Henson's aggression, and he earned a takedown to go ahead 4–3.

The final 1:28 ticked away tediously — and to the outrage of U.S. coaches Bruce Burnett and John Smith at matside and to Stephanie and Bob Henson in the stands. The referee, Smith would say later, let Abdullayev stall, and let him "fishhook" Henson's mouth, and let him use Henson's singlet to steer him.

"It's not that he would have won the match," Smith would say later. "It should have just been called right."

Time Runs Out

The instant time ran out, Henson became disoriented. He went to shake Abdullayev's hand, but he backed away as Abdullayev's coach jumped on and kissed him.

As Burnett ran toward the judge, pulling at his shirt, Henson fell over backward and began to cry.

He shook Abdullayev's hand, because Abdullayev was a virtuous competitor. He avoided the referee to the extent he could. And then he ran.

The Aftermath

The media surrounded Bob Henson, who could think of nothing but the officiating. It would have been O.K. for Sammie to lose, but like this?

"Of course, I'm a losing parent," he said. "What am I going to say?"

For nearly two hours, neither Bob nor Stephanie could find or get access to Sammie. They saw him only when he trudged out to the platform for the medal ceremony, when his zombie-like demeanor changed only to contort into the very face of pain. He shuddered and cried for all to see on the big screen.

He wept as he received his silver medal, the medal he would throw down when nobody could see him after he wandered off the platform back into the holding area, the medal a coach had to pick up for him.

While they waited to see him, Bob considered calling his wife, Shubert, to tell her what happened. Instead, he asked Chuck to make the call. Sammie will be O.K., Bob Henson said, but he might need some time to adjust.

Stephanie tried to figure out where Sammie was and couldn't sit still. She wondered if she could ever watch wrestling again.

Eric Akin, the longtime rival whom Henson beat to make the Olympic team, offered consolation to Bob and Stephanie. Sammie, he says, had been instrumental in his life, taught him to be a better person and how to dig deep into his own heart.

Down the hall, John Smith said he would protest the match — except it's against the rules to protest a medal match. He avoided talking about the condition Henson was in when he helped scrape him up and instead said, "This is the gold medal match. These guys train a lifetime for this."

As for what he told Henson: "It's hard to say anything right now — you *don't* say anything. And you try to make sure he doesn't rip down the world."

Finally, Henson emerged, still in his warm-up outfit, towel over his head, and he was safe in the arms of Stephanie.

He had intended to go to a news conference, but instead they walked out the door arm in arm. Bob Henson followed, and they walked out into the busy mall area before sitting on a brick wall. And talking.

Twenty minutes later, they walked away. Down the street, a reporter approached. Henson turned to shake hands, and then he burst into tears once more. It's O.K. to call later, he said.

Five hours after the match, Stephanie wearily answered the phone in their room. Henson still was in his uniform, still seeing only the match when he closes his eyes.

He laughed a few times, though, and he talked about going for a walk, then maybe taking a bubble bath. He even said he felt relief the match was over.

"I guess what doesn't kill you makes you stronger, but," he said, "I don't know."

CHARLES M. YOUNG

Losing: An American Tradition

FROM MEN'S JOURNAL

Somebody's got to lose. Don't we all know the feeling? — B.C.

JUST NORTH of the north end zone of Blackshear Stadium at Prairie View A&M University in Texas is an unmarked grave.

"We buried last season," said Greg Johnson, the Prairie View Panthers' coach, during a break in football practice. "In March, just before the start of spring practice, we had them write down everything they didn't like about the past — being 0–9 last season, the record losing streak. We used the example of Superman, this guy that nobody could stop unless you got him near some green kryptonite. We asked them, 'Well, what's your green kryptonite? What is it that keeps you from doing what you need to do in the classroom and on the football field? Is it a female? Is it your friends? Is it a drug? Is it alcohol? Lack of dedication? Not enough time in the weight room? You got a nagging injury that you didn't rehab?' Whatever they wanted to bury, they wrote it down on a piece of paper. And the last thing we did, we looked at the HBO tape. The segment that Bryant Gumbel did on us for *Real Sports,* where they laughed at us and ridiculed us as the worst team in the country — 'How does it feel to be 0–75 since 1989?' or whatever it was at that point. I said, 'That's the last we'll ever see of that tape,' and I put it in a big plastic trash bag with the paper. We took it to a hole I had dug near the gate, and we threw it in. All the players and all the coaches walked by. Some of them kicked dirt on it, some of them spit on it. Some of them probably thought I was crazy. I said, 'This is the last time we're going to talk about last year. This is the last time we're going to talk about the losing streak. The past is dead, and anything that's dead ought to be buried. It's history. It's gone.'"

That took place in September 1998, when Prairie View's NCAA-record losing streak stood at 0–77. Now skip ahead to the postgame interviews of the January 9, 1999, AFC playoff game, in which the Denver Broncos beat the Miami Dolphins 38–3. Shannon Sharpe, the Broncos' tight end, called Miami's Dan Marino a "loser." Universally, this was viewed as a mortal insult, far beyond the bounds of acceptable trash talk.

"I cringed when I read that," said Mike Shanahan, the Broncos' coach. "I was really disappointed. Dan Marino's no loser."

So Sharpe, much humbled (and probably at Shanahan's insistence), groveled after the next Denver practice: "In no way, shape, or form is Dan Marino a loser. Dan, if I offended you or your family, your wife, your kids, your mother or father, your brothers or sisters, I apologize. I stand before you and sincerely apologize. I would never disrespect you as a person."

Which is odd. Football, along with every other major sport, is constructed to create losers. On any given game day, half the teams win, and half the teams lose. By the end of the playoffs, exactly one team can be called a winner, while thirty other teams are, literally, losers. So given that 96.7 percent of the players in the NFL can't help but be losers, why should calling somebody a loser be considered such an egregious violation of propriety that the guy who won must debase himself in public for pointing out that the guy who lost, lost?

Consider *Patton,* winner of the 1971 Academy Award for Best Picture and a favorite of coaches, team owners, and politicians ever since. It opens with George C. Scott standing in front of a screen-size American flag in the role of General George S. Patton, giving a pep talk to his troops. Using sports imagery to describe war (mirroring the sportswriters who use war imagery to describe sports), Patton delivers a succinct sociology lesson: "Americans love a winner, and will not tolerate a loser. Americans play to win all the time. I wouldn't give a hoot in hell for a man who lost and laughed. That's why Americans have never lost, and will never lose a war — because the very thought of losing is hateful to Americans."

Which is a view of most Americans that's shared by most Americans. Certain women of my acquaintance refer to men who score low on the Multiphasic Boyfriend Potentiality Scale as losers. *Cosmopolitan* has run articles on how to identify and dump losers before they have a chance to inseminate the unwary.

In *Jerry Maguire,* Tom Cruise suffers his worst humiliation when he spots his former girlfriend dating a rival agent at a *Monday Night Football* game. She makes an L with her fingers and mouths, "Loser."

In *American Beauty,* Kevin Spacey announces during his midlife crisis: "Both my wife and daughter think I'm this gigantic loser."

In *Gods and Monsters,* Lolita Davidovich, playing a bartender, dismisses the possibility of sex with her sometime lover, played by Brendan Fraser: "From now on, you're just another loser on the other side of the bar."

In *200 Cigarettes,* set in the ostensibly alternative subculture of Manhattan's Lower East Side, Martha Plimpton works herself into a state of despair considering the idea that no one will come to her New Year's Eve party. Then, considering an even worse possibility, she weeps: "All the losers will be here!"

At the real-life sentencing last February of Austin Offen for bashing a man over the head with a metal bar outside a Long Island night club, Assistant District Attorney Stephen O'Brien said that Offen was "vicious and brutal. He's a coward and a loser." Offen, displaying no shame over having crippled a man for life, screamed back: "I am not a loser!"

In his book *Turbo Capitalism: Winners and Losers in the Global Economy,* Edward Luttwak equates losing with poverty and observes that Americans believe that "failure is the result not of misfortune or injustice, but of divine disfavor."

I could list a hundred more examples, but you get the point.

Shannon Sharpe, in using the word *loser,* implied that Dan Marino was: unworthy of sex or love or friendship or progeny, socially clueless, stupid, parasitical, pathetic, poverty-stricken, cowardly, violent, felonious, bereft of all forms of status, beneath all consideration, hated by himself, hated by all good Americans, hated by God. And Dan Marino is one of the best quarterbacks ever to play football.

I was standing on the sideline during a Prairie View Panthers practice one scorching afternoon when a large boy on his way to class stopped to watch for a moment. Someone pointed him out to

Coach Johnson and suggested that the boy be recruited for the team. "No, he was out last year, and he quit," said Johnson. "He has female tendencies. He looks like Tarzan and plays like Jane."

Johnson didn't say that *to* the boy, but suddenly my unconscious was barfing up all kinds of post-traumatic stress disorder from my own athletic experience. The next day in his office, I asked Johnson about football as an initiation rite in which aspiring Tarzans get all the Jane beaten out of them.

"That's just an old coach saying," he said. "If I had my druthers, I'd cut a kid open and look at his heart. You never can tell just what tempo it's beating at until you put them in the heat of battle. Football is a test of manhood, a test of who has the biggest *cojones*. Win, lose, or draw, all my guys got great big *cojones*, 'cause they fight when they know the odds are against them."

Johnson's coaching record has ranged from 0–11 as an assistant at Tennessee Tech to winning a couple of championships as a head coach at Oklahoma's Langston University. Feeling the need to migrate out of his "comfort zone," he came to Prairie View for the '97 season, becoming the fourth coach during the losing streak.

Back on the sideline, Anthony Carr, a sophomore cornerback from Houston, told me: "All these people put the streak in your mind. We say that's the past, but when everybody reminds you, it's hard to forget."

One of the lamest clichés in football, I said, was that it's so hard to repeat as champion because the other teams get so fired up to play you. In my experience, they got a lot more fired up to pulverize someone they knew they could pulverize — the incentive being that if you lose to the last-place team, you're worse than the worst.

"Yeah, nobody wants to lose to us. The other team is going to catch it. We've been called the laughing stock of the nation. That hurts. And it will hurt somebody to lose to the laughing stock of the nation."

Josh Barnes, a 165-pound junior quarterback returning from knee surgery, said he had chosen Prairie View to "make history" by breaking the losing streak. "My freshman year was tough. Southern beat us 63–0, Jackson State beat us 76–20. It hurt me. I hate losing. The cynicism was terrible. We heard it from everybody: 'Yawl suck!' If you have any pride, it's hard to take."

"A lot of people say losing builds character. I got enough character for several lifetimes," said Michael Porter, a running back who graduated in 1997. At Jefferson Davis High School in Houston, he lost every game for three years, and at Prairie View, he lost every game for four years. He is now coaching football at his old high school. "It's hard to keep kids on the team when it's losing. It's hard to keep fans in the stands. But I just loved the game. I loved the spotlight. I didn't love losing. You never get used to that. Never. Ever."

So how did he keep going when he was getting crushed 60–0 in the fourth quarter?

"You got to have a nut check. Either I'm going to get whipped like a girl, or I'm going to come out like a man and get on with it. You may be winning on the scoreboard, but I'm going to whip your ass on the next play. It's war, man. That what it is — and it's not for everybody. This is no girlie sport."

When I was losing football games in college, it seemed like the worst thing you could call somebody was a pussy.

"Oh yeah. You don't want to be called a pussy on the field. I remember the times they'd be calling us the Prairie View Pussy Cats, and maybe some names even worse than that. It was a bad situation, having your organization ridiculed all the time. And you really hated it when it happened on campus. But it's all about manhood. Football forces you to be mature, to be disciplined, everything a man should be."

Later, I asked Coach Johnson if there was anything to learn from losing.

"You learn what's wrong, and then you do the opposite. These kids will win even if they lose, because they're going to get their degree. Football helps keep them focused. Every kid wants discipline and structure and a chance to be special. When the world is telling them, 'You're not gonna be nothin',' football gives them a chance to prove themselves."

But maybe most people don't want to find out how good they are. If you give something a complete effort and fail, it would be logical to conclude that you are a loser. An incomplete effort offers the appeal of an excuse.

"Yeah, that's the real loser concept," said Johnson. "That's something you say on the porch with your wino buddies: 'Yeah, if I hadn't beat up that girl when I was sixteen, I'd still be playing foot-

ball. If I hadn't taken that first drink or that first hit of marijuana,
I'd be a star.' That's a penitentiary story."

The literal truth is, I may not be the worst college football player of
all time. I've claimed that occasionally in the course of conversation, but I may be only the worst college football player of 1972. I
was definitely the worst player on the Macalester College Scots of
St. Paul, Minnesota, and we lost all of our games that season by an
aggregate score of 312–46. The team went on to win one game in
each of the following two seasons (after I graduated), then set the
NCAA record with fifty straight losses. So, strictly speaking, the losing streak wasn't my fault. I do think I made a huge contribution to
the atmosphere of despair and futility that led to the losing streak. I
think that as Prairie View was to the '90s, Macalester was to the
'70s. But in the final analysis, I think that over two decades at both
schools, some athlete may have failed more than I did.

I may therefore merely be one of the worst, a weaker distinction
that makes me even more pathetic than whoever it is who can make
the case for sole possession of the superlative — if someone wants
to make that case. No one, though, can question my credentials for
at least a display in the Hall of Failure. In my junior year, on a team
with barely enough players for one string, I was the only guy on
third string. The coach wouldn't put me in the game even when
the other team was winning by six touchdowns. In my senior year,
we got a new head coach who had a terrifying policy: "If you practice, you play." And I did play in every game on the kickoff team, often getting a few additional minutes at strong safety after the game
was hopelessly lost. The opposing third-string quarterback would
throw a couple of touchdowns over my head just so I could feel as
mortified as the rest of the team.

I got injured once. I came in too high to tackle a halfback and he
drove his helmet into the left side of my chest. When I took off my
shoulder pads in the locker room later, I was surprised to discover
that I had a hemorrhaged pectoralis major muscle, which looked
like a large, purple, female breast. To this day, when I am in the
company of big American men and they compare their unstable
knees, necrotic hips, herniated disks, cracked vertebrae, tilted atlas
bones, arthritic shoulders, and twisted fingers, I can't make my
wounded tit, as it was called back then, work even as a joke. No
matter how I phrase it, they exchange "that guy's pathetic" looks.

If your football injury made you look like Marilyn Manson, it definitely won't get you into the club of manly heterosexuals.

As many manly writers and equally manly psychologists have asserted, manhood is something you supposedly win. Females are simply born to womanhood. Males must wrest their manhood from some other male in a trial-by-fire ritual, the hottest of which in America is football.

I failed. I'm a loser.

Losing puts you in the center of a vast vacuum, where you are shunned by your own teammates, scorned by spectators, avoided by your friends. It's a lot like smelling bad. Nobody wants to talk about it in your presence.

Losing is hard to write about, too. Writing was why I went out for football, because the football players I knew had the best stories. I played two seasons. In my junior year, we won just one game, and the coach played me a total of sixty-three seconds over ten games. The losing wasn't quite mine, since I wasn't playing much, and the psychological distance made it possible to write a lot, mostly about stuff other than the actual games, because I didn't want to hurt the feelings of anyone on the team.

In my senior year, though, the shame became mine. Playing every game as a strong safety, I was supposed to line up about seven yards deep over the tight end. I could never figure out who the tight end was. The enemy huddle would break, and all I could see was this undifferentiated mass of enemy uniforms. "Strong left!" I would yell, which was part of my job. Our middle linebacker would turn around and hiss, "Strong right, you fucking idiot!"

In a chronic state of embarrassment, I wrote very little. The one long article I wrote was mostly about a Ping-Pong game I played with a sexually ambiguous linebacker named Wally. (If I won, I got to spend the night with his girlfriend; if he won, he got to spend the night with me.) I beat Wally, and suddenly the words began to flow in the brief absence of humiliating defeat, in the brief presence of a different sport, one in which we could make a farce out of the cult of achieved masculinity. Not that I could articulate that insight at the time, but that's what we were doing. Farce is the only refuge for losers.

A couple weeks after I left PVU, the Panthers won a football game, 14–12, against Langston University, ending the losing streak at eighty. The campus erupted in a victory celebration that was typical of the orgiastic outpourings that people all over the world feel entitled to after an important win. I was happy for them. I felt bad for Langston, having to carry the stigma of losing to the losers of all time.

There being virtually no literature of losing, I became obsessed with reading books about winning, some by coaches and some by self-help gurus. All of them advised me to forget about losing. If you want to join the winners, they said, don't dwell on your past humiliations. Then I thought of George Santayana's dictum: "Those who forget the past are condemned to repeat it." So if I remembered losing, I'd be a loser. And if I forgot losing, I'd be a loser. Finally, I remembered a dictum of my own: "Anybody who quotes George Santayana about repeating the past will soon be repeating even worse clichés."

That Christmas, my local Barnes & Noble installed a new section called "Lessons from the Winners." Publishers put out staggering numbers of books with "win" in the title (as they do with *Zen and Any Stupid Thing*), and they make money because there's a bottomless market of losers who want to be winners. Almost all of these books are incoherent lists of aphorisms and advice on how to behave like a CEO ("Memorize the keypad on your cell phone so you dial and drive without taking your eyes off the road"). Most of these books are written by men who have made vast fortunes polluting the groundwater and screwing people who work for a living, and these men want to air out their opinions, chiefly that they aren't admired enough for polluting the groundwater and screwing people who work for a living. I thought of the ultimate winner, Howard Hughes, who was once the richest man in the world, who had several presidents catering to his every whim, who stored his feces in jars. I got more and more depressed.

Maybe I was just hypnotized by my own history of failure, character defects, and left-wing politics. Maybe what I needed was a pep talk. Maybe what I needed was Ray Pelletier, a motivational speaker who has made a lot of money raising morale for large corporations and athletic teams. Pelletier, a member of the National Speakers Association Hall of Fame, wrote a book, *Permission to Win*, that Coach Johnson had recommended to me. Basically an exhortation to feel like a winner no matter how disastrous your circumstances happen to be, the book deals with losing as a problem of individual psychology. I asked Pelletier if he thought that the emphasis American culture places on competition was creating vast numbers of people who, on the basis of having lost, quite logically think of themselves as losers.

"I don't think you have to think of yourself as a loser," he said. "I think competition causes you to reach down inside and challenges you to be at your very best. The key is not to beat yourself. If you're better than I am and you're more prepared to play that day, you deserve to win. I have no problem with that. Every time I give a presentation, I want it to be better than the last one. I want to be sure I'm winning in everything that I do."

Yeah, but wasn't there a difference between excellence and winning?

"No, that's why I say that if I get beat by a team that's more talented, I don't have a problem with that."

When one guy won, was he not inflicting defeat on the other guy?

"No. I'll give you an example. The first time I worked with a female team before a big game, I was getting them all riled up and playing on their emotions, telling them how they deserved this win and how they worked really hard. A rah-rah, goose-pimple kind of speech. Just before we went on the court, the point guard said, 'Can I ask a question? Haven't the girls in the other locker room worked really hard, too? Don't they deserve to win, too?'"

Pelletier then veered off into a discussion of how the game teaches you about life, of how his talks are really for fifteen years down the line when your wife leaves you, or the IRS calls for an audit, or you can't pay your mortgage. I asked him how he replied to the point guard in the locker room.

"I said, 'Absolutely the other team deserves to win, too. What we have to do is find out if we can play together tonight as a team.' See, that's the biggest challenge facing corporate America today. We talk about teamwork but we don't understand the concept of team. Most of us have never been coached in anything. We've been taught, but not coached. There's a big difference. Great coaches challenge you to play at your best. The key is, you're in the game, trying to better yourself."

But Bill Parcells, the former coach of the Jets, is famous for saying that you are what the standings say you are . . .

"Winning is playing at your best. Do you know the number-one

reason why an athlete plays his sport? Recognition. Once you understand that, everything else becomes easy. Lou Holtz says that
win means 'What's Important Now.'"

That's just standard practice in books about winning, I told him.
They redefine the word to include all human behavior with a good
connotation. In *The Psychology of Winning,* Dr. Denis Waitley writes
that winning is "unconditional love." Winning could hardly be a
more conditional form of love. You are loved if you win, and
scorned if you lose.

"I don't believe that."

If athletes play for recognition, don't they want to be recognized
as winners? And if you've lost, won't you be recognized as a loser?

"I don't think they're labeled that way."

By the press? By the fans?

"To me, unconditional love is an aspect of winning. The problem is that you and I have not been trained to think positively. In
one of my corporate seminars, I ask people to write down all the advantages there are to being negative. I want them to think about it
seriously. It's an exercise that can take fifteen or twenty minutes,
and then they have the 'Aha!' There is no advantage to negative
thinking. None. And yet the biggest problem we face in America is
low self-esteem."

Low self-esteem has its uses, though. Whenever you see a couple of
male animals on a PBS nature special duking it out for the privilege
of having sex with some female of the species, one of the males is
going to dominate and the other male is either going to die or get
low self-esteem and crawl off making obsequious gestures to the
winner. The evolutionary value is obvious: Fight to the death and
your genes die with you; admit you're a loser and you may recover
to fight again or find another strategy for passing on your genes
through some less selective female. Species in which one alpha
male gets to have sex with most of the females — elephant seals are
a good example — need a lot of low self-esteem among the beta
males for social stability.

With 1 percent of the population possessing more wealth than
the bottom 95 percent, the American economy operates a lot like a
bunch of elephant seals on a rock in the ocean. And it simply must
mass-produce low self-esteem in order to maintain social stability
amidst such colossal unfairness.

According to the World Health Organization, mood disorders are the number-one cause worldwide of people's normal activities being impaired. In the United States alone, the WHO estimates, depression costs $53 billion a year in worker absenteeism and lost productivity. While that's a hell of a market for Ray Pelletier and the National Speakers Association, which has more than three thousand people giving pep talks to demoralized companies and sports teams, doled-out enthusiasm is a palliative, not a curative. In fact, demoralization is a familiar management tool; the trick is creating just enough. Too much and you have work paralysis, mass depression, and suicide. Too little and you have a revolution. Ever hear a boss brag that he doesn't *have* ulcers, he *gives* them? He's making sure his employees are demoralized enough to stay in their place.

Consider the book *Shame and Pride,* by Dr. Donald L. Nathanson, a psychiatrist and the executive director of the Silvan S. Tomkins Institute in Philadelphia. Starting in the mid-1940s, Dr. Tomkins watched babies for thousands of hours and made a convincing case that humans are born preprogrammed with nine "affects" — potential states of emotion that can be triggered by a stimulus or memory. These affects are: interest-excitement, enjoyment-joy, surprise-startle, fear-terror, distress-anguish, anger-rage, dissmell (*dissmell* is similar to *distaste,* but related to the sense of smell), disgust, and shame-humiliation. These affects "amplify" an outside stimulus or memory to give you an increase in brain activity that eventually becomes full-blown emotion.

Until recent years, shame was the "ignored emotion" in psychology. But a few people, Nathanson most prominently, built on Tomkins and discovered the key to . . . well, not quite everything, but an awful lot. According to Tomkins and Nathanson, shame erupts whenever "desire outruns fulfillment." An impediment arises to the two positive affects (interest-excitement and enjoyment-joy), and suddenly your eyes drop, your head and body slump, your face turns red, and your brain is confused to the point of paralysis. This is observable in babies and in adults. This is also observable in the NFL, exquisitely so after the regular season, when the coaches of the teams that don't make the playoffs are ritually humiliated at press conferences. A variation on the theme, often seen in losing coaches who manage to keep their jobs for another season, is the compensatory jutting chin and the disdainful stare, both directed at the press and usually accompanied by promises to examine every aspect of the organization and by pronouncements about "recommitment to winning." Players in this state of shame often attack journalists verbally, and sometimes physically. Sportswriters, who in general demand that losing competitors exhibit lots of shame for dramatic purposes and who reinforce the savage lie that losers aren't man enough to win, keep the system in place even as they complain about it.

So I called up Nathanson and asked if he had any thoughts about why athletes get so upset when they are called pussies.

"One of the major tasks of childhood is the formation of gender identity, the shift from saying, 'I'm a kid,' to saying, 'I'm a boy,' or 'I'm a girl,'" he replied. "I don't think anyone gets over the shame we have of not being adequately identified by the right gender. We see a lot of that worry in adults, in the drive for perfection of the body through plastic surgery and steroids. People don't just wish to be someone else anymore, they buy it. Men also face the problem of 'Am I masculine enough?' In Blake Edwards's remarkable movie *Victor/Victoria*, Alex Karras says something to the effect that a lot of men go into football because they want to undo any worry that they're not adequately masculine. Men are concerned that they'll be called not just female, but female genitalia. I don't think any of this is trivial, because of the risk of violence when someone is shamed in public. Sports are an analog of what goes on in everyday life, and it's amazing what people get away with on the so-called field of honor."

Sports events are often described as a morality play, I said, but there's nothing moral about it. Sports decide who will participate in power and who will be humiliated.

"That's understandable when you recognize that our sense of place in society is maintained by shame. Keeping people in their place is maintaining them at certain levels of shaming interaction at which they can be controlled. This issue of winning and losing, it throws us. It defines our identity, doesn't it?"

Calling someone a loser is probably the worst insult in the United States today.

"If you're calling someone that, the person must live in a perpetual state of shame. The only way he can live with himself is to have massive denial, disavowal of his real identity. He has to make his way in the world somehow, and he can't walk around constantly thinking of himself as a loser. Yet if someone in our eyes is a loser and he refuses to admit it, this is narcissism. He has an identity that can't be sustained by consensual validation."

Is there some value in competition, in creating all these losers?

"When you're young and you're learning and it's just a bunch of guys playing a game, that's not shame. That's just figuring out that Billy is faster than Johnny. When parents and schools and bureaucracies start getting involved and demanding wins, then it gets pathological."

Playing for the Chicago Bears, the Philadelphia Eagles, and the Dallas Cowboys from 1961 to 1972, Mike Ditka was All-Pro five times as a tight end, won an NFL championship with the Bears in 1963, won Super Bowl VI with the Cowboys, and was elected to the Hall of Fame. As the coach of the Bears from 1982 to 1992, he won Super Bowl XX with an 18–1 team generally acknowledged as one of the greatest ever and was named Coach of the Year twice. As the coach of the New Orleans Saints for the past three seasons, he had a 15–33 record and is now most vividly remembered for flipping off the fans and grabbing his crotch during and after an especially inept defeat. (He was fined $20,000.) I asked him if he thinks that football fans are inherently interested in the game, or in the hallucination of power they get when their team wins?

"They relate to the winning. Well, you can't say they aren't interested in the game. They watch the game. But the excitement comes from winning."

When football players snap at journalists in the locker room after a loss . . .

"That's only human nature. They probably snap at their wives when they get home, too. Are you saying, Does losing bother people? Sure it does. It's no different from a guy at IBM who loses a sale to a competitor. You just don't like to lose. Most people want to be associated with winning. When you work your butt off and don't get the results you want, you might be a little short-tempered as a coach. That's only life. But that's no different than any other segment of life. Football parallels society, period."

I've noticed that the worst thing you can call somebody in the United States is a loser.

"No. The word *quitter* is the worst thing you can call somebody. Lemme ask you something: If two teams play all year, and they reach the Super Bowl, the one that loses is a loser? Come on.

"I don't like the term. . . . It's not fair. I think as long as you compete and you do your best, if the other team is better, I don't think you really lose. I think you lose when you quit trying."

The problem with declaring a quitter to be a lower form of dirt than a loser is that you're still stigmatizing almost everybody. Studies indicate that up to 90 percent of children drop out of organized competitive sports by the age of fifteen. Extrapolating from my own experience, I would guess that they don't enjoy feeling like losers so that the jocks can feel like winners. Since they associate intense physical activity with feeling rotten, they grow up having problems with obesity and depression, both of which have become epidemic in the United States.

As Mike Ditka would say, it's not fair. But I think there's a way out. And I think that Alfie Kohn has seen it. Kohn, an educational philosopher, has helped inspire the opposition to standardized tests, an especially pernicious form of competition. His first book, *No Contest: The Case Against Competition,* cites study after study demonstrating that competition hinders work, play, learning, and creativity in people of all ages. (In fact, there is almost no evidence to the contrary in the social sciences.) The book is wonderfully validating for anyone who ever had doubts about the ostensible fun of gym class and spelling bees. I told Kohn that in my experience, people get unhinged when you question the value of making other people fail.

"Absolutely. It calls into question America's state religion, which is practiced not only on the playing field but in the classroom and the workplace, and even in the family. The considerable body of evidence demonstrating that this is self-defeating makes very little impression on people who are psychologically invested in a desperate way in the idea of winning. The real alternative to being number one is not being number two, but being able to dispense with these pathological ratings altogether. If people accepted the research on the destructiveness of competition, you wouldn't see all these books teaching how to compete more effectively. I hear from a lot of teachers and parents whose kids fall apart after losing in spelling bees and awards assemblies, and they feel dreadful about it. The adults start to think, *Hmm, maybe competition isn't such a good thing, at least for those kids.* It took me years to see that the same harms were being visited upon the winners. The kids who win are being taught that they are good only to the extent that they continue to beat other people. They're being taught that other people are obstacles to their own success, which destroys a sense of community as effectively as when we teach losers that lesson. And finally, the winners are being taught that the point of what they are doing is to win, which leads to diminished achievement and interest in what they are doing. What's true for kids is also true for adults. It's not a problem peculiar to those who lose. We're all losers in the race to win."

I'm very blessed that way. I didn't have the perspective to spell it out like Alfie Kohn, but I've known I was a total loser since my first college football practice. I've admitted it here publicly, and I am free. You, you're probably holding on to some putrefying little shred of self-esteem, denying that you're a loser in a country inhabited by Bill Gates and 260 million losers. You're still hoping to beat your friend at racquetball and make him feel as bad as you do when you lose, still looking to flatten some rival with just the right factoid in an argument, still craving the sports car in the commercial that accurately announces, "There's no such thing as a gracious winner." Give up, I say. Join me. Losers of the world, unite! You have nothing to lose but your shame.

GENE COLLIER

The Ex-Sportswriter

FROM THE COLUMBIA JOURNALISM REVIEW

A farewell to strong arms — B.C.

IT WAS IN the Steelers locker room, a Wednesday as I recall, and I was doing my famous milling act. Milling about, shuffling wordlessly along rows of lockers at the approximate pace of a drunk at a wedding, pulling my notepad out of my pocket, uncapping my pen, putting my notepad back in my pocket, capping my pen, waiting for some twenty-something from the top one percent for gross motor skills to answer some questions for me.

Some tragically measurable part of my life had been spent in exactly this pantomime, waiting for athletes to get showered, get dressed, get treatment, get ice, get heat, get taped, get whirlpooled, get out of a meeting, or just get familiar with the common courtesy of making themselves available to someone who needed to talk to them.

It is an undignified situation for a writer at any age, but with midlife busting in on you like an unblocked linebacker, the notion nailed me that day that this was, indeed, enough. It was quarterback Kordell Stewart I was waiting for, a fine young man and a willing if dull interview when he got around to it, but that wasn't what I was thinking. I was thinking: "How stupid is this? I don't want to wait for this guy. This guy doesn't want me to wait for him. I know what he's going to say. He knows what I'm going to ask. The readers know what I'm going to write. And I know what they're going to say if they read it."

I left without talking to him and walked out of Three Rivers Stadium feeling as bad as Hal Bodley looked that day in San Francisco seventeen years ago. I was sitting next to him in the press box of

Candlestick Park. We were baseball writers together then, covering the Philadelphia Phillies. Bodley, now the senior baseball writer at *USA Hooray*, had finished maybe his 140th game story of the season a couple of minutes before me, and I looked at his computer screen as he attached some notes to the end of his copy. He had called his notes "Extra Points."

I said, "Hal, that's football."

"I know," he said. "I'm tired of baseball."

But this was worse, definitely. I was tired of baseball, tired of football, real tired of basketball, excruciatingly tired of hockey, contemptuous of boxing, downright hateful of golf and tennis, and immensely uninterested in auto racing, horse racing, dog racing, cat chasing, and anything else they might have on ESPN. I hated sports, and I hated writing about them, and as I was aware from reading the professional journals, those were not the two main things people are looking for in a forty-four-year-old sports columnist.

That was two years ago, and though the *Pittsburgh Post-Gazette* has graciously seen to it that I can play at something else, I can still see sports journalism in the cracked rear-view, looking pretty much the same as the day I left. Sports journalism in America, whether in its traditional forms or as it warps through cyberspace in mutated fractals of itself, remains the culture's virtually omnipotent Department of Hero Maintenance and Disposal, hourly separating the worthy from the flawed, polishing and immortalizing the best, degrading for entertainment's sake the worst.

Sports journalism biblicizes Michael Jordan, imprints his perfectly crafted image onto timeless collector's edition videos or leather-bound books, while simultaneously building databases on the anecdotal idiocies of Dennis Rodman or the pathologies of Pete Rose and Lawrence Taylor, then sells it all to a sports-addled public eager for violence or competitive validation or some definitive moral scorecard.

Not to be critical.

The joke (I'd have used "irony" but it's more a joke) is this: an actual living hero is ten times as likely to walk down your street, sit next to you on a bus, or hold the door for you at the library, than to appear on your television between the never varying pre-game yammer and the post-game lament about who "stepped up" and who just "didn't want it bad enough."

I've been prodded to think hard about these kinds of things in the last couple of years, my first back on earth after twenty-two in the galaxy of sports stars. I'm asked about it all the time, sometimes by people who can't believe I could walk away from the sports columnist's gig. For me, the main factor was a sense of outrage at the impenetrable sense of entitlement among the athletes. This is not often their fault. Indeed, most of them are unaware of it. But a culture that rewards athletic prowess from the time boys and girls are able to walk has, by the time an athlete comes to a station that attracts media coverage, produced a creature that expects its strengths will be celebrated and even embellished while its weaknesses will be tolerated, and that the culture exists merely to extend privileges and ignore flaring evidence of arrested development.

In the early '80s, a colleague of mine took a job in the front office of a major-league baseball team. Before very long, he'd advanced to a position in which he helped prepare arbitration cases against players who were not eligible to become free agents, but were upset with the team's salary offer.

My colleague loved baseball, as did I. We'd have long talks about the players we idolized as kids and we marveled at their skill and at the skills of modern players as well. But he came to tell me, after a few years of sitting in on arbitration hearings, "If you could be there and hear what they want, and see what they think of themselves, you would never, ever, go to another game."

With America's blessing, athletes raised their expectations in terms of remuneration and respect. They have somehow been put in a position to demand respect without giving any. But a larger issue to me is the way the media have simultaneously lowered the standards for hero status. When Jordan re-retired, the sports media became a hurricane of idolatry that devastated all established perspective. Jordan was the plain and simple best basketball player ever, but journalism's attempt to solidify that notion for history was so overwrought it was embarrassing, even sickening.

We heard how Jordan was a "singular athlete" who "transcended the game" and had taken his place in the American sports pantheon with the likes of Muhammad Ali, Jackie Robinson, and Babe Ruth. Get a grip.

Ali cast himself as lightning rod for an overheated '60s culture poised to torture him for it, and gave up his title rather than his religious beliefs. Robinson's courage is perhaps unprecedented in sports, and he inspired and corresponded with repressed blacks from California to Capetown. Ruth, for all his misbehavior, embodied a bigger-better-farther spirit in an America coming to terms with its own roiling greatness in the '20s.

And Jordan, he what? Went strong to the rack? With perhaps more worldwide recognition and influence than the other three had among them, Jordan talked to Tweety Bird on the phone. For money.

It's no wonder that I find myself telling people that I've met more interesting people in the past two years than in all my years on Planet Sports.

I met a blind man who does nothing but talk to troubled and terminally ill children on the telephone. I met a Holocaust survivor who'd been hidden by a nun in a Lithuanian basement. I met some women who spend their days gathering surplus medical supplies to send to countries where people simply die for want of things that we throw away. I saw a father stand on the pulpit of a Pittsburgh church in front of two hundred crying high school students and give the eulogy for their classmate, his son, who'd crashed during a flying lesson two days before.

He quoted his son: "Live for your dreams; reach for the sky, and I'll see you there." And he did that without even a quiver in his voice and without an ounce of self-consciousness or self-pity. Now *that's* heroic. I saw the ball go through Buckner's legs in New York. I saw that piece of Holyfield's ear hit the canvas in Las Vegas. I saw Rose break Cobb's record in Cincinnati. I saw Montana win a Super Bowl in Miami with two minutes of gifted, nonchalant, high-wire brilliance that you could almost weep over. But all that while, there was an immutable sense that it was all highly inconsequential, that I was looking for heroes in all the wrong places. Turned out that was true.

JIM HARRISON

Starting Over

FROM MEN'S JOURNAL

*Catching fish is better than not catching them because
"you can't fry a reverie"* — B.C.

ON THE SURFACE fishing is a primitive activity. I mean in the an-
thropological sense that fishing is included in the hunting and
gathering activities of our remote ancestors. It is all about filling
the tummy.

In a decidedly comic sense it is hard to stay on the surface. Especially in the past two decades, a legion of men (and some women)
have been writing about fishing. It's as if since fish spend their
entire lives underwater we try to join them by going even deeper.
Except in the rarest cases (for instance, Thomas McGuane's *The
Longest Silence*) we utterly fail, because it's as hard to write well
about fishing as it is about anything else. Shocking as it might
seem, we know even less about fish than we do about women. We
even talk about the Zen of fishing with a captious banality. As a
twenty-five-year student of Zen I must tell you that fishing is fishing
and Zen is Zen. The confusion here is that any activity that requires
skill and during which we also manage to keep our mouths shut
seems to acquire a touch of the sacred.

Some of us feel particularly good about essentially Pleistocene
activities. If I walk a full hour through the woods to a beaver pond
and catch a two-pound brook trout on a No. 16 yellow-bellied female Adams I feel very good. The important thing isn't the tech-
nique or the equipment but the totality of the experience, of which
they are a very small part. There are the hundred varieties of trees
and shrubs you pass through, the dozen different wildflowers, the
glacial moraines, the stratocumulus clouds, the four warblers and

the brown thrasher, the heron you flushed, the loon near the lake where you parked the car, the Virginia rail you mistook for a cattail, the thumping of your heart when you hook a fish, the very cold beer when you return to the car just before dark, even the onion in the baked-bean sandwich you packed along. But above all it is the mystery of the water itself, in the consciousness, not in the skill or the expensive equipment.

Nothing is quite so inexplicably dreary as watching a relatively rich guy who has spent a lot of money on a trip to the Florida Keys or to a big western river like the Yellowstone and can't make the throw. You wonder why he bothered or if he assumed his enthusiasm would somehow allow him to overcome the twenty-knot wind, the moving skiff or McKenzie driftboat. Fly-casting is most often a sport without second chances, and, like wing shooting, it requires the study of prescribed motion and the spirit of repetition. And if you can't afford a guide or, better yet, don't want one, your ultimate chore is understanding habitat. Both fish and birds hang out in their restaurants, but there are no signs out front.

So over a period of fifteen years you spent near a month a year on the flats of the Florida Keys fishing for permit and tarpon; your brain relentlessly mapping and remapping the area topographically to figure out where the fish will be, given specific conditions of date, weather, tide, water temperature. Even then you don't have it figured. Why is a school of two hundred tarpon coming in Hawk Channel under the absolutely wrong conditions?

And then one day you don't want to go fishing. You want to go to an art museum or a bookstore. How many times have you gotten up at 6:00 A.M. to meet the right tide after only getting to bed at 3:00 A.M. and not necessarily alone? There's nothing like a windless ninety-two-degree day on the flats to tell you exactly how you behaved the night before. The sweat dripping into your eyes and down your nose smells like whiskey and other not necessarily commendable substances.

And, of course, you forgot that you were simply fishing, and that when you had taken it to a magnum level it was still just fishing, despite the fact that you were fly-casting to a 150-pound tarpon, which you can't really extrapolate by trying to imagine a 150-pound rainbow or steelhead. And this is not including stray shots at Pacific sails, striped marlin, and blue and black marlin off Ecuador and Costa Rica, where you had the suspicion that your body parts might detach. You had become not all that different from the humorless and somewhat doltish moguls who Leared into Key West for a few days of flats headhunting, as if their real quarry were just another form of arbitrage.

So you burned out, and the burnout on magnum fishing also slipped the soul out of the day-to-day fishing in the Upper Peninsula that was a pleasant balm when you weren't running your dogs to get ready for bird season. Burnout is endemic to our culture, whether in a job or in sport. I think it's actually traceable to brain physiology, if I understand Gerald Edelman's "neural Darwinism" properly, which I probably don't. Your responses become etiolated, atrophied, plain frazzled, and in this case you have quite simply fried your fishing neurons, except for the two weeks a year on the Yellowstone River near Livingston, Montana, floating in a McKenzie boat, which was more a retreat from your work life than anything else, and trotting with tadpoles in Kashmir would probably also do the same thing, except your grandsons were in Livingston.

In July I launch my new Poke Boat, a splendid and slender craft that weighs about thirty pounds and is perfectly suited to hauling into remote, uninhabited lakes in the U.P. You can paddle it like a kayak or install a rowing contraption, which I did — or, rather, a friend did for me, as turning doorknobs stresses the limits of my mechanical abilities. I weigh either 130 or 230. I'm forgetful these days, but it's probably the latter, which makes getting in and out of the boat a trifle awkward. A beastly process in fact.

But it's a crisp virgin boat, and I feel younger than springtime as I fairly slice across a river estuary leading to Lake Superior, the body of water that not incidentally sank the seven-hundred-foot freighter *Edmund Fitzgerald* about seventy miles from here.

The first wave wrenches my bow sideways. The second, third, and fourth waves fill my virgin boat to the gunwales. How can this be? I'm nearly tits high in water and why didn't I leave my wallet in the car like I intended? Luckily my next stop, the Dunes Saloon, will accept wet money.

There's inflatable flotation in the bow and stern of the Poke Boat, so I manage to crawl it to a sandbar. At least I drown a swarm of noxious black flies that were biting my legs. I wish mightily an old couple weren't watching me from shore. As a lifelong leftist I have always considered dignity to be faux-Republican indifference, but then everyone wants to look nifty. With a violent surge of energy and upper-body strength, I turn myself turtle on the sandbar, doubtless looking like a giant beetle from shore.

At the Dunes Saloon an especially intelligent Finn says, "You're wet," followed by a French-Canadian drunk who says the same thing. What's extraordinary about the experience is that I do the same thing the next day. The only excuse, unacceptable anywhere in the world, is that I was working on a novella about a closed head injury and was living in a parallel universe where one doesn't learn from experience.

Luckily I moved inland in the following weeks and had a marvelous time drifting among herons and loons and one lake with at least 77,000 white waterlilies. It was August and the fishing was poor, though one day on my first cast with a streamer I caught a pike the size of a Havana corona, a truly beautiful little fish that nearly covered the length of my hand. Her (it had to be female) sharp, prickly teeth gave my finger a bite when I was about to slip her back in the water. With the gout of blood emerging from my finger, there was a momentary and primitive urge to squeeze her guts out, but then I am a sportsman. If the pike had been a male, I might have done so.

During all my benighted years as a dry-fly purist I occasionally did some slumming, partly because I was in my thirties and the molecular movement of hormones made any stupid thing possible. If you trek far out on the ice and spend an entire day in a fish shanty with a friend staring down through a large hole in hopes of spearing a pike, you are demonstrating that it's hard to find amusement in the Great North in January. You forgot the sandwiches but you and the friend remembered two bottles of Boone's Farm Apple Wine and two bottles of Ripple made from indeterminable fruit, plus a half-dozen joints of Colombian buds. Due to this not-very-exotic mixture the day is still memorable.

When a pike finally made a pass on our dangling sucker decoy, I think we said in unison, "Wow, a pike," and forgot to hurl the spear. We wobbled toward the shore in a blinding snowstorm, our compass the church bells in our small village.

Of course drugs and fishing don't mix. It's fun to mouth truisms that have become inanities. The tendency of boomers to tell older folks to "stay active," as Melvin Maddocks points out, infers the opposite, "stay inactive." It was certainly difficult to concentrate or cast well on LSD, but it made the rattling of gill plates on a jumping tarpon a fascinating sound indeed. And, once, in an altered state Jimmy Buffett revved his engine to the max when it was tilted up. I sat there in a questionable daze as the propeller fired out toward the Gulf Stream, glimmering in the blue distance. Mostly on acid you couldn't fish well because you became obsessive about the improbable profusion of life at the bottom of the shallow flats. A passing crustacean became as monstrous as it is to lesser creatures, which might have included yourself.

Recently, a few days before heading to Montana for my annual fishing vacation, I decided to go north pretending I was an enervated businessman who had been strained through a corporate sheet and was desperate for a day of fishing. Parenthetically, I was only halfway to my cabin before I realized that except for my journal and poetry, I had never written for free, and a dense Martian might actually think I was a businessman. Many writers are as hopelessly venal as day traders. This is all the more reason to go fishing, which is a singular way to "get out of your mind" to where you might very well belong.

A friend of mine in the U.P., Mike Ballard, had consented to act as a guide. We've been fishing together for twenty years and often have assumed different names to dispel the ironies involved in adults at sport. Mike is a consummate woodsman and occasionally refers to himself as "Uncas," the James Fenimore Cooper hero. In recognition of my own true character I am just plain Brown Dog. This is all plaintively idiotic but to have fun the inner and the outer child must become the same, which is harder than it sounds. For extended periods of my life I have condemned fishing to death by playing the mature adult, an illusion most of us live and die with.

It was one of those pratfall days. We boated five miles up the estuarine arm of a large lake, the fishing so slow we went ashore and walked a high ridge, which was delightfully wild. The sour note was that from the ridge we could see a huge, black rolling squall line approaching from the west, and by the time we made it back to the boat Uncas said, "Even our balls are wet." So were the sandwiches (capicola, provolone, mortadella), but the two bottles of Côtes du Rhône were secure. We stood under a tree and drank them both, making our way to the landing in a stiff wind and temperatures that had dropped from seventy degrees down to forty.

It's dreary to keep hearing that it doesn't matter if you're catching anything, it's the experience that counts. Well, of course the experience counts and we spiritually thrive in this intimate contact with Earth, but it's a whole lot better to catch fish than not to catch fish. You can't fry a reverie, and I like to fry fish in a cabin in the same manner as my grandfathers, my father, and my uncles did before me. I have supposed that at times you penetrate a set of feelings known intimately to your even more remote ancestors.

Probably 99 percent of the fish I've caught in my adult life were released. I don't say "released unharmed," as a creature's struggle for life is indubitably harmful to it. We should avoid a mandarin feeling of virtue over this matter. It's a simple case that a variety of torture is better than murder for the survival of the species. The old wisdom is that the predator husbands its prey. "Catch and release" is sensible, which shouldn't be confused with virtuous. "I beat the shit out of you but I didn't kill you" is not clearly understood by the fish. This is a blood sport, and if you want a politically correct afterglow you should return to golf. Eating some wild trout now and then will serve to remind you that they are not toys put in the river for the exercise of your expensive equipment.

When you try to start over, you are forced to remember that enthusiasms that have become obsessions burn out rather easily. You think of the talented adolescent tennis and baseball players who withdraw when pushed too hard by neurotic parents. I was pushing myself in my twenties when I, as a dry-fly neurotic on a Guggenheim grant, fished ninety days in a row. Such obsessive-compulsive behavior is supposedly a mental defect, but then I also wrote the title novella of my collection *Legends of the Fall* in nine days, which I view as worth the madness. It can be caused by backpressure in the sense that I had been teaching for two years on Long Island and was longing for my beloved northern-Michigan trout streams, thus the ninety-day binge. In the case of "Legends," I had brooded about the story for too long and had to write quickly or lose it.

Of course, certain fishing behavior is indefensibly stupid. Years of fishing permit and tarpon for thirty days back to back out of Key West naturally sours one, especially when augmented by bad behavior. You need only to check into a hotel when a convention is in progress. Having had my cabin in the U.P. for twenty years, I've been able to study hundreds of groups of men who have come north to hunt and fish. I've had the additional advantage of spending time studying anthropology. There is whooping, shouting, jumping, slugging, and countless manly trips to the toilet to relieve the mighty freight of beer. One could imagine Jane Goodall off in the corner making her primate notes.

This is all an extension of the mythologies of outdoor sport that begin in childhood, when the little brain fairly yelps, "Twelve-point buck! Ten-foot wingspan! Ten-pound brown!" Woods and water might very well be infested with "lunkers" of every variety. Within this spirit of conquest and food gathering I have watched a fishing friend dance with a 350-pound woman so tall he barely nibbled at her chin while trying to kiss her. Early man and later man had become one under the feral pressure of a hunting and fishing trip.

As a language buff I've been curious how quickly speech can delaminate in the face of excitement. Years back, well off the northern coast of Costa Rica with my friend Guy de la Valdéne and the renowned artist and fishing fop Russell Chatham, we managed one afternoon, using a rubber squid and a casting rod, to tease up a black marlin of about six hundred pounds and a blue marlin that certainly approached one thousand. First of all, it is alarming to look closely into a blue marlin's softball-sized eye maybe twenty or so feet away, and when Guy flopped out the fly, the fish sipped it into the corner of its mouth. The ratio would be similar to a very large man eating a very small brisling sardine.

Once hooked (it must have felt like a pinprick), the immense fish did the beginning of a barrel roll, its entire length emerging as it pitched backward away from the boat. And to me the audio was as memorable as the visual; bleak screams, cries, yelps, keening, with each sound swallowed soon after it began.

An hour or so later we nearly had a repeat with the black marlin, but I was doing the teasing and lost the rubber squid to the fish before I managed to get him into casting range for Russell. It took a lot of yelling for me to console myself, but then finally I accepted the fact that we were fishing for the reasonably sized striped marlin, and the encounter with the two monsters, though lunar, was a doomed effort, a case of outdoor hubris similar to trying to take a Cape buffalo with a BB gun.

I have long since admitted that my vaunted maturity is in actuality the aging process. More than a decade ago, in a state of financial panic (fifty years old and no savings whatsoever), I began to work way too hard to allow for spending a lot of time at a sane activity like fishing. Saving money is even less fun than watching corn grow. My sporting life was reduced to a scant month, with two weeks of Montana fishing and a couple weeks of Michigan grouse- and woodcock-hunting. I don't count my afternoon quail-hunting near our winter "casita" in Arizona, which mostly consisted of walking the dog. If your hunting is spliced between a double work shift you're never quite "there" in the field.

Sad to say this thoroughly nasty bourgeois work ethic, taken to my usual manic lengths, quite literally burned down the house of my fishing life. Years passed, and I began to envision my epitaph as "He got his work done," something that fatuous. I think it was the novelist Tom Robbins who said that he doubted that success was an adequate response to life. Saving money, though pragmatically laudable, gets you in the garden-variety trap of trying to figure how much is enough. A straight answer is unavailable during a period in history when greed is not only defensible but generally considered a virtue. When overcome by greed, the fisherman tends to limit himself to headhunting, a kind of showy trophy search on the far corners of the earth. When living correctly and relatively free from greed, I did not differentiate between my humble beaver-pond brook-trout fishing and the stalking of large tarpon.

On one of my Poke Boat voyages I paddled into a ten-acre mat of white waterlilies to protect my ass from gathering waves. As a life-long claustrophobe, to me an uninhabited lake is the ultimate relief from this phobia that cannot clearly be understood. I have, however, considered the idea that I might be somewhat less evolved than others are. After a severe childhood injury I quite literally ran to the woods, which has proved to be my only viable solution. When in Paris or New York, the Seine, the Hudson, and the East River present me with immediate relief from my phobia, as do the

Bois de Boulogne, the Luxembourg gardens, and Central Park. Even as a wacky young beatnik in New York City in the late '50s I'd have to head up to the Botanical Garden in the Bronx.

Nearly all fishing takes place in a habitat that is likely to make you unable to think of anything but the sport at hand. In late August at my cabin I was brooding about my recent financial collapse and drove out to the gorge of a nearby river, basically a sand-choked mediocre river but nonetheless prepossessing. I sat down on a very high bank with a miniature fly rod and glassed a stretch with my monocular. (The only real advantages to being blind in one eye are that I was 4F during Vietnam and I don't have to carry cumbersome binoculars.) Under the shade of an overhanging cedar tree was a succession of decent brook-trout rises. I reflected on the gasping it would take to get out of the gorge, also the number of small grasshoppers in the area, which must be what the trout were feeding on. I had only a small packet of flies with me and a single, small Joe's Hopper from Montana. I made the long slide down the sandy bank on my butt, regathered myself, and took my first throw, only to hook a root halfway up the bank on my first backcast. I didn't yell, "Gadzooks!" I climbed up to the root by pulling myself hand over hand on other roots. I detached the fly and managed to catch the smallest of the rising trout, scaring the others away. Now soaked with sweat, I took off my clothes and wallowed in an eddy. I paddled over an exchange, a blurred glance with several trout that seemed curious rather than frightened. Even the predictably gasping trip back up the bank was pleasurable indeed compared to important meetings in offices high above cities that I have experienced. As Thoreau said, "While I sit here listening to the waves which ripple and break on this shore, I am absolved from all obligation to the past."

Every few years I've taken to the idea of worms or minnows as bait or plugs for casting for pike and bass. The mood usually doesn't last and probably emerges from my modest egalitarianism, also an occasional sense of repulsion from being in the company of fresh- or saltwater fly fishermen when they are especially full of themselves, all fey and flouncing and arcane, somewhat like country clubbers peering with distaste over the fence at the ghetto bait types in the distance. However, I have sense enough to blush at my occasional proletarian masquerades at my income level. I still can't bear to "dress up" like the fishermen I see who, with an addition of one more gadget, appear likely to either drown or sink through the earth's crust from the weight of their equipment, or better yet, the outfits — the costumes, as it were — designed for a terrestrial moonwalk or perhaps ridding an airliner of Ebola virus.

Of course, this is probably only an extension of my own childhood lust for first-rate equipment after I had judged those fifty-cent, fifteen-foot-long cane poles inappropriate to my future as a great angler. For a number of years, all of my earnings from hoeing and picking potato bugs went to rods, reels, plugs, and flies.

I suspect that I'm a fly fisherman for aesthetic reasons, adding the somewhat suspicious quotient of degree of difficulty. My father fished for trout using only a fly rod, whether with streamers or bait, and so I suppose it was all inevitable. He was a well-read agriculturist and fished incessantly, taking me along on every occasion after I was blinded in one eye at seven. We were rather poor, but he was giving me the woods and the water to console me after a bad deal. Right after World War II, he and my battle-weary (South Pacific) uncles built a cabin on a lake where we lived in the summer, with several trout streams in easy reach. I imagine millions of men are still fishing because they did so as children and it is unthinkable not to continue. And it is still a consolation in a not-quite-comprehensible world.

This quality of intensity in one's personal history can be unbearably poignant. After my father died in an accident along with my sister, I gave his fishing equipment — including a large, immaculately arranged tackle box — to a Mexican migrant kid named Roberto who lived with his family on the farm we rented. Roberto was about twelve and fished a lot in Texas when he wasn't working. There were at least a hundred plugs, antiques now, but I'm sure they were put to good use.

In George Anderson's fly shop in Livingston, you never hear fish referred to as "old fangface" or "waterwolves," euphemisms for northern pike up in Michigan. This shop is as discreet as Armani's in New York. When I annually pick up my license, I ask an old acquaintance named Brant how the fishing has been, and he usually says, "So-so," having doubtless answered the question 100,000 times. He can't really say, "As good as your capabilities," which would be accurate.

A few years ago the Yellowstone River suffered serious flooding, but it has begun to recover. I simply love to float it in a McKenzie boat and have booked an expert guide, Dan Lahren, for the past decade. In that I have fished there nearly every year since 1968, I scarcely need a guide, but then it's a great deal more comfortable than stumbling over slippery rocks, and since I'm committed to the fee, I fish six hours every day. Ultimately the cost is nominal compared to evening meals in New York and Paris, where there's little fishing, though striped bass have been reappearing around New York and I've long promised myself the absolute inanity of fly-casting the Seine right in the middle of Paris, particularly the stretch near the Musée d'Orsay. Lest you question my sanity, I should add that I don't value sanity very highly. Besides, we all know that every creature is confronted moment by moment by the question of what to do next, and casting a woolly worm out into the turgid waters of the Seine seems a splendid option.

I fish a total of about seventy miles of the Yellowstone, selecting a piece each day, keeping in mind the specific pleasures of scenery, habitat, the hydrologic shape of the water, the memories each stretch evokes. Tom McGuane moved to the area in 1968, and his friends followed, including Russell Chatham and Richard Brautigan, and in recent years I've fished a number of times with Peter Matthiessen. This year the fishing was mediocre, though I was distinctly more conscious, mostly because I've pulled back from the screenwriting business but partly because I fished a lot in the summer in my attempt to jump-start an old obsession. I had no forty-fish days, as I've had in the past, and no fish over three pounds, but each day was an unremitting delight. During slow periods I'm always reminded of McGuane's essay, the title work in *The Longest Silence*, on how angling is often filled with a pleasant torpor interrupted by truly wild excitement. My friend and guide Lahren likes to remind me of the time I pulled a dry fly away from a giant brown trout, thinking for truly inscrutable reasons that it was an otter trying to steal my fly. Its dense, massive arc seemed too large for a trout. This fall the most noteworthy day brought a squall that turned the river into a long tidal riptide, and when we left the river even the irrigation ditches had whitecaps.

*

It's now October 22, and there's a gale on Lake Superior, with the marine forecast predicting waves from eighteen to twenty-four feet. Perhaps I should get my beloved Poke Boat out of the shed, but first I'll knock off fifty pounds for ease of maneuvering. As a backup, a friend is building me a classic Chesapeake skiff. Also, I'm planning to go to Mexico to catch a roosterfish on a fly, a rare lacuna in my experience.

I won't say I've reached the location of that improbably banal word "closure." You don't start fishing a lot in the same place you left for the same reason you can't restart or renew a marriage back to a state of innocent, blissful passion. It's quite a different person baiting the hook or, better yet, tying on the fly. It is, however, fine indeed to know that if you've lost something very good in your life it's still possible to go looking for it.

BETH KEPHART

Playing for Keeps

FROM PHILADELPHIA MAGAZINE

Hopes and fears of a soccer mom — B.C.

THE WIND HAD COME UP out of nowhere; it felt like the sea at
our backs. Tucked into our caps and hoods, we stood intractably
against it, our arms knotted across our chests, our eyes in a liquid
burn, our feet just this side of the thin white line. The kids were like
leaves that had been blown out on the field — their red and green
nylon shirts tugging them, it seemed, in so many directions. The
ball floated and skittered like a molecule, and then it fell down,
hard, to earth, to be punished by so many muddy cleats. There was
wind and ball and twenty-two rippling shirts, a referee whose whistle's blows were muted. Anything at all could have happened, anything, and that day it really did.

The red team was our team, the Cosmos; they had not been winning much. The littlest kid was our ten-year-old son, still learning
soccer, playing for keeps. The community was the kind of community that is formed when perfect little strangers don identical syn-
thetic shirts, and their parents, every Saturday, do a ragged sideline
dance. *Come on, Cosmos,* we were screaming, stamping our feet. *Take
it down the side!* Exhorting. *Center it.* Pleading. *Come on and shoot! Cosmos, shoot! Ahh.* Despair. *Next time.* Hope. *Next time, guys. Nice try.* The
wind blowing our voices back over our own hunched shoulders,
the kids way far out there, on their own. "Jeremy's in as striker," I
told my husband what he already knew. Bill nodded, quietly. A gust
came up, and so we blew inconsequentially on our hands.

Bob was our man that day, filling in for Coach Said. He was tense
around the eyes the way he gets, and he was proficient with his
clipboard, making his share of coachly notes. "Jeremy's striker," I

pointed out when the wind blew Bob my way. "Yes, he is," Bob said. "That's where I put him." And then Bob was blown down the line even farther, entreating the kids to clear the ball from the Cosmos box, which they somehow miraculously did. Sigh of relief. It was still zero-zero, nil-nil. The Cosmos had more than a chance.

Jeremy was strong, he was focused; his jaw was set. He was staying in his zone, taking some passes and sending others off, his intentions good, his black hair sheening, his eyes two catalytic burners. Striker, I was thinking. *Striker.* Like Ronaldo, Yorke, Owen, Shearer, Bierhoff. Like Pelé, for goodness sake. Just like Pelé. I was getting flashbacks to Jeremy's first game, two years ago. To a time when all we wanted, because it was all he wanted, was for him to get out there and put his foot on the ball. For him to have a uniform, a team, the sense that he belonged, hands held out to high-five his, oranges to snack on between halves. I was flashing back to those who said that it couldn't be done — said that his feet wouldn't co-operate, that he was too gentle, that he'd started too late — and I was also in the present, studying the field, hailing the Cosmos, our bright hopes in red. It was still zero-zero, ten minutes in. "We've got a chance," I said to Bill, and the wind blew his head up and down.

I want to get this right, but it's impossible, see? The air was harsh and cold, so many daggers. The ball kept skittering, sailing, disappearing, returning, smashing the earth at every angle. Collin was looping it like a rope above the green team's head. The other Collin, the Cosmos star, was gracefully weaving. Dillon was punching the ball with his sturdy right boot, and Peter wasn't letting anyone past. "Jeremy's right in there," I said to my husband. "Yes, he is," my husband said. His eyes were leaking.

And the ball was going up and down, and there were geese screaming goose thoughts from the heavens above, and we parents were doing a jig on the sidelines because, like I've mentioned, it was cold. "There's no score," I told Coach Bob, and he nodded his agreement, checked his clipboard, scratched his jaw, yelled out his counsel. It was one of the best games the Cosmos had had all season long, and now they were on the offensive, keeping the ball at the opposite end of the field, where the green team, the Piranhas, were backing up toward their keeper. Jeremy by then had had so many touches on the ball that I — and this is glory — had lost count. Brandon was pumping his elbows and flying, and Brendan was arcing his throw-ins downfield, and the two blond Dans were marking their men, their eyes narrowed into determined slits, their untied shoelaces flopping and zinging.

Some juice you didn't even know existed starts to flow when your child's the show and you're the witness. Every bit of whatever personal worry you brought to the game that day gets trampled and banished, eradicated. It's as if the wind blasts the minutiae free, so that all that matters is your child and his team, the guys in red with a one-and-something record, playing out their hearts against the greens. Every block, cutback, pass, dribble, every modest header, is a triumph, an achievement, a strike against the lousy odds of this complicated world. Our kids transcend us from the moment they are born. They live their own dreams. They play soccer.

Lord, the wind was strong that day, a roiling, heady surf. Lord, it was cold; my throat was hoarse. The game was already twenty minutes along, and still there was no score; it was a deadlock, an all-out battle. The Cosmos were playing their Bob-given positions, and Jeremy was out there as striker — up near the goal, in open space, waiting and wanting that molecule to fall.

It came from Kevin. It sprang high from Kevin's boot toward the gaggle of geese and then loped noiselessly down. Bounce. Bounce. It was in the box for sure, but a green defender trapped it, swung his foot back, tried to clear it, and nevertheless, our son was there — stopping and turning and placing that muddied ball into the farthest left snip of the net.

It was hard to see it all from where I was standing. Hard to know what to look at, how to hold it, how to freeze it for all time. The ball was in the net, in the tangle of strings, and the Piranhas looked disheartened, and Jeremy had turned and he was running. Head down, shoulders forward, a single index finger raised high to the sky, to the geese who'd gone delirious, to anybody anywhere who had ever doubted our only child's brave desire. Jeremy stole one glance at us before the Cosmos swarmed to him, before all those palms hit his own palm raw and the referee was yelling the score.

I have never done a single thing with my whole life that stands as grand as Jeremy's first real soccer goal. I never will. I have never hugged my husband any harder, never seen the man I married beam like that: all incandescent light. "I can retire now," I heard Bill saying. "Oh God," I heard myself. "Oh God, oh God." And

Coach Bob had lost the tenseness near his eyes, and he was laughing, simply laughing, saying he knew our boy'd come through. "You're the best," I was screaming to Jeremy. "The very best!" But the wind just rifled my feeble words back, and Jeremy didn't need them, because he knew. He was lined up now where he was supposed to be, and the whistle blew, and the game got started again.

The rest of the hour, then, was about the big D, about protecting that iffy one-point lead. It was about Ben in the cage, oh mighty Ben — tall as a Grecian pillar, indentured to a soft buzz cut, protected around the eyes by plastic goggles. Ben, the giant in the Cosmos net, his goalie shirt stretched tight across the shoulders. He had never played as well as he was playing that day, and now the pressure was on, and Big Ben knew it. Big Ben kept putting his big hand down, snuffing out the balls that were coming at him now, kicking them way downfield, and not to the center. The Piranhas weren't giving up; there was no way they would lose to the Cosmos. They kept coming back, they kept coming back again, they dominated the second half: gutsy, offensive. But Big Ben was there to shut them out, and Patrick and Peter, and Brennan and Brandon, and the Collins and the Dans, and Dillon and Kevin and Jeremy, all of them in their red flapping shirts, holding on and holding tough, protecting Jeremy's goal, while Bob made coachly notes upon his clipboard and the rest of us parents screamed and prayed.

What do you say about a day like that one, about perfect strangers who become best friends, if only for an hour? About a group of kids who pull it all together, never stop trusting one another, form a wall against a bruised and bruising ball? About a team in red that holds its lonely lead until the whistle finally brings the game to closure? About being there when your kid scores a goal in a game few thought he'd ever play?

What do you say? What do you say when your heart is so much bigger than this page and your blessings so great that you can't count them? How do you tell your only child that you're higher than the geese and rarer than the sky, when language itself won't cooperate? "Jeremy and Ben," the kids were saying, chanting, hailing the team's biggest player and its smallest, the two who had sprung from the margins to the center of the world. "Jeremy and Ben. We won the game, guys. We won. The Cosmos did it." And then the ragtag Cosmos kids were lining up for final ceremonies, bidding the green shirts goodbye. They were pulling Jeremy and Ben, the morning's heroes, to the front of the pack.

"Jeremy," I asked in the Jeep going home, when the hubbub was already trickling through to memory. "What happened out there? And how did it feel? And did you know that this day would be yours?"

"I was where I was supposed to be, Mom," is all my windblown kid had to say. "Tucking the ball into the back of the net."

"It was awesome," I said. "Just amazing. Just awesome. Dad and me — we're not going to ever forget it."

"Yeah," Jeremy said. "Well. And did you see Ben, how he played? How he didn't let a single goal go past him?"

"We saw that," I said. "Jeremy, the whole team played great."

"Yes, they did," Jeremy said. "A whole team effort."

"So how should we celebrate?" I wanted to know. "Tell me anything you want, and I'll go get it."

"Carrot cake would be nice," Jeremy said after a while. "Carrot cake, Cornish hen, some chips, some Coke for lunch."

RICK REILLY

The Biggest Play
of His Life

FROM SPORTS ILLUSTRATED

As Sports Illustrated'*s cleanup hitter, Reilly invariably
lights up his page with a telling farewell shot —* B.C.

ONE OF the captains of the high school football team had something big he wanted to tell the other players. "I was so anxious,"
remembers middle linebacker Corey Johnson, a senior at Masconomet High in Topsfield, Massachusetts, "I thought I was going to
vomit."

He took a hard gulp. "I want to let all of you guys know something about me." He tried not to let his voice quake. "I'm coming
out as an openly gay student here."

His teammates' eyes and mouths went wide as soup plates. "I
hope this won't change anything," Corey quickly went on. "I didn't
come on to you last year in the locker room, and I won't this year. I
didn't touch you last year in the locker room, and I won't this year."

Awkward silence.

"Besides, who says you guys are good enough anyway?"

And you know what happened? They laughed! But that's not the
best part. The best part is what happened next. Nothing.

Corey's teammates had no problem with his sexual orientation.
His coach had no problem with it. His mom and dad and his sister
had no problem with it. His teachers, his counselor — nobody —
had a problem with it.

O.K., somebody scrawled FOOTBALL FAG on a door at school.
True, one cementhead parent asked coach Jim Pugh to have the

team take a new vote on the captaincy, but Pugh told him to stuff it. And, yeah, one week the opposing team's captain kept hollering, "Get the fag!" but his coach finally benched him (and Masconomet fricasseed that team 25–0).

No opponent refused to play against Corey. No opposing coach said, "Boys, the Lord wants you to go out and crush that heathen!" Nobody held up a sign at a Masconomet game that read WHICH SIDE ARE YOU ON, COREY? Nope. Corey Johnson, guard-line-backer, wrestler, lacrosse player, just went out and played his senior football season, same as ever. Masconomet did well (7–4 for the season, 25–8 with Corey, a two-way starter for three years). Now Corey is getting on with his life, hopeful as ever. He'll graduate with his class next month, think about playing small-college football, and become a gay activist, a journey that began on Sunday at the Millennium March on Washington for Equality.

Can't wait for Corey to be on a gay parade float when some beer-bellied yahoo hollers, "Hey, girls! Shoe sale next corner!" The football captain might turn the poor schmo into a smudge mark.

Corey can take the hits now, but hiding the truth about himself was so depressing in his sophomore and junior years that he let his grades drop, skipped practice, and even skipped school. When an adult friend started ripping homosexuals at a Super Bowl party in January 1998, Corey couldn't decide whether to punch him or cry. He knew he had to do something.

First, he told a guidance counselor he was gay and then a few teachers. They all supported him. A year later he told his parents. Fine. Then his best friend, Sean. Uh-oh. Big problem. Sean started crying. Corey asked him what was wrong. "I'm sorry you couldn't share this with me before," Sean said. They're still best friends.

Since coming out, Corey says, he has heard from "hundreds" on the Internet, including athletes who wish they had the guts to come out, too. "But," says Corey, "they always say, 'At my school? No way. It'd be impossible.'"

At Masconomet, a public school with an enrollment of thirteen hundred, Corey is the football captain who had even more moral courage than physical. He's admired by his teammates. In fact, nothing much changed between them, except on bus rides home after wins, when the whole team sang *YMCA* together. Well, it isn't *Hunker Down, You Hairy Bulldogs*, but it works.

Maybe we're actually getting somewhere in the U.S. A young man who leads young men comes out as gay, and it makes such a ruckus you can still hear the crickets chirp. In fact, last month the Boston Gay, Lesbian, and Straight Education Network handed its Visionary Award not just to Corey, but also to his teammates. Can you imagine that? A high school football team getting an award for *tolerance?*

When I was growing up, my best friend was a hilarious kid I'll call Danny. Along about high school, he stopped coming around. Then, in college, he showed up in the Gay Club photo in the yearbook. After that, Danny didn't take my calls.

It's a lousy feeling. I guess I'm not the kind of person he could've shared that with.

Biographical Notes

Notable Sports Writing of 2000

Biographical Notes

H. G. BISSINGER has won the Pulitzer Prize, the Livingstone Award, and the National Headliner Award for his reporting. He is the author of the sports classic *Friday Night Lights,* and *A Prayer for the City.* He lives in Philadelphia and is a contributing editor at *Vanity Fair.*

WILL BLYTHE is the literary editor of *Men's Journal.* His fiction and non-fiction have appeared in *Best American Short Stories, The New Yorker, Esquire,* the *New York Times Book Review, Outside, Mirabella,* and *Epoch.* He lives in New York.

GREG CHILDS is the author of the climbing memoir *Postcards from the Ledge.*

After covering sports for twenty-two years for the *Philadelphia Press, Pittsburgh Press,* and *Pittsburgh Post-Gazette,* GENE COLLIER is now a features columnist for the *Post-Gazette.*

KEVIN CONLEY edits the arts section for "Goings on About Town" for *The New Yorker. Stud,* his book on the breeding industry, is coming out in May 2002 from Bloomsbury Press.

MICHAEL DiLEO is a frequent contributor to *Texas Monthly.*

GEOFFREY DOUGLAS is the author of *Dead Opposite: The Lives and Loss of Two American Boys.*

ROBERT DRAPER is writer-at-large for *GQ* and author of the novel *Hadrian's Walls.*

Tom Friend is a senior writer for *ESPN: The Magazine.*

Vahe Gregorian is a graduate of the University of Pennsylvania and the University of Missouri. He has worked since 1988 at the *St. Louis Post-Dispatch*, where he covers national college football and basketball, the Olympics, and other projects. He has collaborated on two books, including *High Hopes* with former Northwestern University football coach Gary Barnett.

Jim Harrison is the author of three novellas, nine collections of poetry, and seven novels, including his latest, *The Road Home.*

Beth Kephart writes essays, travel stories, and journalism for a dozen magazines nationwide. She is the author of *A Slant of Sun: One Child's Courage,* a 1998 National Book Award finalist, and *Into the Tangle of Friendship.* Her new book, about marriage and remembrance on a coffee farm in El Salvador, is due out in the spring of 2002. Kephart has received grants from the National Endowment for the Arts, the Leeway Foundation, and the Pennsylvania Council on the Arts, among other organizations, and she has had the great, enduring thrill of learning soccer and all its majestic possibilities from her only child, Jeremy.

Dave Kindred is a winner of the Associated Press Sports Editors' Red Smith Award for lifetime excellence in sports journalism. His first job, at the *Lincoln* (Illinois) *Daily Courier,* paid thirty-two dollars a week. Every Friday afternoon the city editor delivered to him a stack of thirty-two crisp, finely cut dollar bills, which felt so new that Kindred believed they were printed in the newspaper's composing room. He's still not sure they weren't. Kindred and his wife, Cheryl, live in Virginia, where they are owned by five dogs.

Pete Kotz is the author of *Dr. Verne's Northern White Trash Etiquette.* Originally from Minnesota, he now resides in Lakewood, Ohio, and serves as editor of *Cleveland Scene.*

Michael Leahy has been a staff writer for the *Washington Post* since 1999. Formerly, he was a magazine writer in Los Angeles and a feature writer and columnist for the *Arkansas Democrat-Gazette.* His work has appeared in *Sports Illustrated, Playboy,* and *George.* In 2001 his story on the life of a paroled murderer received the Best of Show Award from the Maryland-D.C. Press Association.

Bucky McMahon grew up on the east coast of Florida, where he surfed and dove and learned to love the sea. He lives outside Tallahassee, still in striking distance for catching hurricane swells, with his wife, Heather Montanye, and four dogs. He is a contributing editor for *Esquire* magazine.

JAMES MCMANUS's book on Ted Binion's murder and the 2000 World Series of Poker, called *Positively Fifth Street,* will be published next year. His writing has appeared in *Harper's Magazine,* the *New York Times, Paris Review, Atlantic Monthly,* and twice in *The Best American Poetry* anthologies. For *Going to the Sun,* his most recent novel, he received the Carl Sandburg Prize, the Society of Midland Authors Award, and a Bellagio Residency from the Rockefeller Foundation. His novel *Chin Music* has just been reissued as an e-book. He teaches at the School of the Art Institute of Chicago.

DOUG MOST grew up in Barrington, Rhode Island, and spent ten years as a news reporter and freelance sportswriter in South Carolina and New Jersey before joining *Boston* magazine as a senior editor. His work has appeared in *Sports Illustrated,* the *New York Times Magazine,* the *Washington Post,* and *New Jersey Monthly.* He is the author of the true-crime book *Always in Our Hearts: The Story of Amy Grossberg, Brian Peterson, and the Baby They Didn't Want.*

WILLIAM NACK is a senior writer for *Sports Illustrated.* This is his fifth appearance in *The Best American Sports Writing.*

DAVID OWEN is a staff writer for *The New Yorker* and author of *The Making of the Masters* and *My Usual Game: Adventures in Golf.*

CHARLES P. PIERCE is writer-at-large for *Esquire.* His most recent book is his collection of writing on sports, *Sports Guy.*

Sports Illustrated's RICK REILLY's most recent book is a collection of his columns, *The Life of Reilly.*

STEPHEN RODRICK is a contributing editor at *Men's Journal.* His work has appeared in the *New York Times Magazine, GQ,* and *George.* His story about the Knob Creek, Kentucky, machine-gun festival, "Blown Away," appeared in *The Best American Sports Writing 2000.* He lives in Nahant, Massachusetts.

TOURÉ is a contributing editor at *Rolling Stone.* His work has been featured in *The New Yorker,* the *New York Times Magazine, Playboy, Callaloo,* the *Village Voice,* and *The Best American Essays of 1999.* He studied at Columbia University's graduate school of creative writing and lives in Fort Greene, Brooklyn. His short-story collection *Life in Soul City* will be published by Little, Brown and Company in June 2002. A novel called *I'm Too Fly Not to Fly* arrives in 2003. He is also the number-one tennis player in the fiction-writing world.

IAN WHITCOMB is a self-described "writer of pop history, a reviver of older styles, a neo–Tin Pan Alleyman." He has produced many albums and published fifteen books, including *After the Ball: Pop Music from Rag to Rock* and *Rock Odyssey: A Chronicle of the Sixties*.

WOODY WOODBURN is a sports columnist for the *Daily Breeze* in Torrance, California, and the author of *The Pirate Collection*, which features his columns. He has won numerous writing awards, including, in 2001, first place for column writing from the Associated Press News Executive Council and first place for best columnist in the Best of the West contest.

CHARLES M. YOUNG grew up in Wisconsin. He has been writing for a living since 1975 and is grateful to win an award for losing.

Notable Sports Writing of 2000

SELECTED BY GLENN STOUT

THE B·E·ST AMERICAN SERIES ™

THE BEST AMERICAN SHORT STORIES 2001
Barbara Kingsolver, guest editor · Katrina Kenison, series editor

0-395-92689-0 CL $27.50 / 0-395-92688-2 PA $13.00
0-618-07404-X CASS $25.00 / 0-618-15564-3 CD $35.00

THE BEST AMERICAN TRAVEL WRITING 2001
Paul Theroux, guest editor · Jason Wilson, series editor

0-618-11877-2 CL $27.50 / 0-618-11878-0 PA $13.00
0-618-15567-8 CASS $25.00 / 0-618-15568-6 CD $35.00

THE BEST AMERICAN MYSTERY STORIES 2001
Lawrence Block, guest editor · Otto Penzler, series editor

0-618-12492-6 CL $27.50 / 0-618-12491-8 PA $13.00
0-618-15565-1 CASS $25.00 / 0-618-15566-X CD $35.00

THE BEST AMERICAN ESSAYS 2001
Kathleen Norris, guest editor · Robert Atwan, series editor

0-618-15358-6 CL $27.50 / 0-618-04931-2 PA $13.00

THE BEST AMERICAN SPORTS WRITING 2001
Bud Collins, guest editor · Glenn Stout, series editor

0-618-08625-0 CL $27.50 / 0-618-08626-9 PA $13.00

THE BEST AMERICAN SCIENCE AND NATURE WRITING 2001
Edward O. Wilson, guest editor · Burkhard Bilger, series editor

0-618-08296-4 CL $27.50 / 0-618-15359-4 PA $13.00

THE BEST AMERICAN RECIPES 2001–2002
Fran McCullough, series editor · Foreword by Marcus Samuelsson

0-618-12810-7 CL $26.00

HOUGHTON MIFFLIN COMPANY / www.houghtonmifflinbooks.com